Advanced IBM PC Graphics
State of the Art

Michael I. Hyman

Brady Communications Company, Inc., New York, NY 10020
A Simon&Schuster Publishing Company

Advanced IBM PC Graphics

Copyright © 1985 by Michael I. Hyman

All rights reserved. No part of this publication may be reproduced or transmitted in any form or by any means, electronic or mechanical, including photocopying and recording, or by any information storage and retrieval system, without permission in wirting from the publisher. For information, address Brady Communications Company, Inc., 1230 Avenue of the Americas, New York, NY 10020.

Library of Congress Cataloging in Publication Data

Hyman, Michael I., 1965–
  Bibliography: p.
  Includes index.
  1. IBM Personal Computer—Programming. 2. Computer graphics. I. Title.
QA76.8.I2594H96   1985   001.64′43   84-28535

ISBN 0-89303-476-2

Printed in the United States of America

85 86 87 88 89 90 91 92 93 94 95   1 2 3 4 5 6 7 8 9 10

Acquisitions Editor: Gisele Asher
Production Editor/Text Design: Patricia King Macht
Copy Editor: Deborah Corson
Art Director: Don Sellers
Assistant Art Director: Bernard Vervin
Cover Design: Robert W. Blair
Manufacturing Director: John A. Komsa

Printing: RR Donnelley & Sons, Harrisonburg, VA
Typesetter: University Graphics, Inc., Atlantic Highlands, NJ
Typefaces: Avant Garde (display); Meridian (text); Logic Monospace (computer printout and related material)

Contents

Introduction   vii

Chapter 1: Preparing for Graphics   1
    1.1: The Graphics Screens   1
    1.2: Using the Graphics Screens   2

Chapter 2: Two-Dimensional Line Graphics   9
    2.1: Data Structure   10
    2.2: Setting Up a Point-Line Data Base   26
    2.3: Drawing the Shape   29
    2.4: Translation   35
    2.5: Scaling   39
    2.6: Object Speed   42
    2.7: Color   44
    2.8: Graphics Definition Language   46

Chapter 3: Three-Dimensional Line Graphics   55
    3.1: Data Structure   55
    3.2: Translation   60
    3.3: Perspective   62
    3.4: Scaling   67
    3.5: Rotation   68
    3.6: Matrices   78
    3.7: Matrices Revisited   85
    3.8: Keyboard Interaction   90
    3.9: Rotation Complications   95
    3.10: Reflection   96
    3.11: Shearing   99
    3.12: A Step Back—Matrices for Two-Dimensional Graphics   100
    3.13: Rotation in the Graphics Definition Language   102
    3.14: Variable Perspective   103
    3.15: Clipping   107
    3.16: Special BASIC 2.0 Commands   117

Chapter 4: Assembly Language Line Graphics — 123
    4.1: Setting the Graphics Modes — 124
    4.2: Plotting Points — 127
    4.3: Clearing the Screen — 136
    4.4: Drawing Lines — 137
    4.5: Putting Together a Three-Dimensional Line Graphics Package — 142
    4.6: Reading Commands From the Keyboard — 143
    4.7: Getting the Movement Values — 145
    4.8: Getting the Trig Values — 147
    4.9: Loading the Transformation Matrix — 150
    4.10: Transforming the Points — 152
    4.11: Accounting for Perspective and Dot Width and Converting to Screen Coordinates — 156
    4.12: Drawing the Lines — 157
    4.13: Clipping — 159
    4.14: The Final Touches — 160

Chapter 5: True Three-Dimensional Graphics — 163
    5.1: A Brief Introduction to How We Perceive Depth — 163
    5.2: Making True Three-Dimensional Images — 165
    5.3: More on Colored Filtering — 169
    5.4: True Three-Dimensional Images From BASIC—The Colored Filter Approach — 170
    5.5: Adding True Three Dimensions to our Assembly Language Program — 179
    5.6: Printing Three-Dimensional Images — 184
    5.7: Using a Polarizer Filtering System — 188

Chapter 6: Multiple and Structured Objects — 193
    6.1: Multiple Objects — 193
    6.2: Multiple Objects in Assembly Language — 197
    6.3: Structured Objects — 199
    6.4: Storing and Retrieving Objects From Disk — 199

Chapter 7: Advanced Graphics Techniques — 201
    7.1: Preventing Flicker — 201
    7.2: Saving and Loading the Graphics Screen — 203
    7.3: Programming the Color Graphics Controller — 209

Chapter 8: Block Graphics — 223
    8.1: Converting Objects to Block Data — 223
    8.2: Block Graphics from BASIC — 226
    8.3: Experimenting with PUT — 234
    8.4: Animation — 236

8.5:	Multiple Objects	237
8.6:	Manipulating Objects	238
8.7:	Rotating a Dot Matrix	238
8.8:	Scaling the Shape	242
8.9:	Masking	245
8.10:	Increasing Animation Speed	250
8.11:	Block Graphics from Assembly Language	251

Chapter 9: A Graphics Editor — 261

9.1:	The Foundation	262
9.2:	Freehand Sketching—The Pencil	264
9.3:	Choosing the Color	269
9.4:	Changing the Palette	270
9.5:	Changing the Background Color	270
9.6:	Clearing the Screen	271
9.7:	Line Drawing	272
9.8:	Drawing Rectangles	275
9.9:	LINE's Style Option	277
9.10:	Circles and Ellipses	279
9.11:	Painting	284
9.12:	Calligraphy Pen	292
9.13:	Air Brush	294
9.14:	Cut and Paste	301
9.15:	Displaying a Menu of Available Commands	306
9.16:	Suggestions on Additional Features	309

Chapter 10: Graphics on the Text Screens — 311

10.1:	The Text Screen Memory Map	311
10.2:	Setting the Mode	313
10.3:	Clearing the Screen	316
10.4:	Line Graphics	316
10.5:	Block Graphics	318
10.6:	Multiple Pages	321
10.7:	Nonstandard Text Modes	322
10.8:	Text Graphics With the Monochrome Adapter	323

Appendix A: Math/Computer Terms — 325

Appendix B: Using the Optional Diskette — 331

Bibliography — 337

Index — 338

About the Author — 342

Limits of Liability and Disclaimer of Warranty

The author(s) and publisher of this book have used their best efforts in preparing this book and the programs contained in it. These efforts include the development, research, and testing of the theories and programs to determine their effectiveness. The author(s) and publisher make no warranty of any kind, expressed or implied, with regard to these programs or the documentation contained in this book. The author(s) and publisher shall not be liable in any event for incidental or consequential damages in connection with, or arising out of, the furnishing, performance, or use of these programs.

Note to Authors

Have you written a book related to personal computers? Do you have an idea for developing such a project? If so, we would like to hear from you. Brady produces a complete range of books for the personal computer market. We invite you to write to Chris Williams, senior editor, Simon & Schuster, general reference group, 1230 Avenue of the Americas, New York, NY 10020.

Registered Trademarks

Here is a list of products and owners mentioned in this book:
IBM PC, IBM Monochrome Board, IBM Color Graphics Controller, IBM-DOS, IBM Macro Assembler, PC-DOS are products of International Business Machines Corporation.
Epson printers are products distributed by Epson America.

Introduction

When writing graphics programs, I have always had to develop routines—line drawing, three-dimensional perspective, simultaneous rotation, etc.—on my own. I had looked and looked for good computer graphics books, but there were none to my liking. They were either too simple—covering only the most elementary topics—and usually just in BASIC, or they were written by mathematicians for computer scientists and only covered arcane topics applicable to mega-dollar machines.

This book is different. It covers a wide range of topics, from line graphics and block graphics to sketching. It progresses from the most simple to the very complex, and from easy-to-use BASIC to efficient Assembly Language. It is a book with which you can grow. As a beginner, you'll discover the world of computer graphics step-by-step. And when you're ready to move on to more complex topics, the material is here.

Chapter 1 gives the fundamentals for using the IBM PC's graphics.

Chapter 2 discusses two-dimensional graphics, including creating data for line shapes; drawing two-dimensional figures; translating, scaling, and animating these shapes; and drawing with the graphics definition language.

Chapter 3 details three-dimensional graphics, building upon the techniques of Chapter 2. Topics include perspective, rotation, matrices, keyboard interaction, reflection, shearing, variable perspective and clipping.

Chapter 4 delves into Assembly Language graphics programming. Starting with such basic techniques as setting the modes, screen clearing, and line drawing, Chapter 4 progresses to developing a complete three-dimensional graphics system that operates at lightning speed.

Chapter 5 covers everything necessary to create true three-dimensional graphics, including an overview of eye physiology, stereoscopic perspective, colored and polarized filtering systems, and printing three-dimensional images. Programs are developed in both BASIC and Assembly Language.

Chapter 6 wraps up line graphics by discussing advanced data structures for objects.

Chapter 7 discusses advanced graphics techniques such as preventing flicker, efficient saving and loading of graphics screens, and directly programming the IBM color graphics adapter.

Chapter 8 deals with block graphics, the type used by most video games. It includes such topics as converting objects to block data, displaying and animating block figures from BASIC and Assembly Language, rotating, scaling and masking.

Chapter 9 shows how to create a graphics editor—a user interactive sketching program. Topics include interaction, creating pencils and pens, drawing lines, boxes, circles, and ellipses, painting areas, air brushing, cutting and pasting, and creating help menus.

Chapter 10 discusses line and block graphics on text and monochrome screens. In conjunction with Chapter 7, it also covers alternate graphics modes, such as 100-by-160 resolution sixteen color graphics.

USING THIS BOOK

If you are a beginner you should start with the chapters oriented around BASIC—Chapters 1, 2, 3, 5, 6, 8, and 9. When you come across parts you don't understand (for example, Chapter 8 may be a little difficult), skip them, or just try out the programs. Then, when you are more comfortable with graphics programming, return to any areas that gave you difficulty.

If you are an intermediate user, consider reading the Assembly Language sections as well as the BASIC sections. Also, read Chapter 7.

If you are an advanced user, you may wish to skim the BASIC sections and concentrate more on Assembly Language programming and advanced techniques. Important are Chapters 4, 5, 6, 7, 8, and 10.

In general, though, the best approach is to read the entire book. When you come to a section you don't understand, don't worry—just skim it and try out the programs. When you feel you are ready, go back and reread. If you are not interested in Assembly Language (or BASIC for that matter), that is fine. You may wish to read the Assembly Language chapters to understand the techniques. But if not, skip them. You can always come back to them later.

THE OPTIONAL DISKETTE

This book can be supplemented by an optional diskette. I recommend it to all, but especially to the absolute beginner, the novice Assembly Language programmer, BASIC programmers wishing to take advantage of Assembly Language programs, and anyone who doesn't enjoy typing in program listings. Besides all of the programs used in this book, the disk also includes a demo program, Machine Language programs needed for BASIC, an assembled true three-dimensional line graphics program, and a matrix module editor. Instructions for using this disk appear within boxes throughout the text.

If you did not purchase the book/diskette package but wish to purchase the diskette, use the enclosed insert.

EQUIPMENT NEEDED

IBM PC (or equivalent)
DOS disk

Most chapters also require:

IBM Color/Graphics Controller (or compatible board)
Color Monitor

The color monitor can be either a televison, composite, or red-green-blue (RGB) monitor. RGB monitors are preferred because they give crisp, distinct pictures and take full advantage of the IBM's resolution. One section discusses composite monitor techniques.

Several chapters use the IBM Macro Assembler.

1

Preparing for Graphics

This chapter shows how to prepare the computer for displaying pictures.

1.1: THE GRAPHICS SCREENS

We draw computer pictures on *graphics screens,* areas of memory telling what dots to display on the computer monitor. We describe graphics screens by *resolution* and by the *number of colors* they can display.

Resolution tells the number of rows and columns of dots appearing on the screen. Horizontal resolution is stated first; vertical resolution is stated second. For example, 640-by-200 resolution means that there are 640 dots per row, 200 rows per screen—a total of 128,000 dots.

The *number of colors* tells the number of possible colors in which each dot can be drawn. A screen where each dot can be red, blue, or black is a three-color screen.

The IBM PC has four display screens—the *high-resolution graphics* screen, the *medium-resolution graphics* screen, the *40-column text* screen, and the *80-column text* screen. The high-resolution graphics screen has 640-by-200 resolution. Each dot can be either black or white. The medium-resolution screen has 320-by-200 resolution with four colors. The text screens have 40- or 80-by-25 resolution in sixteen colors. We'll almost always use the graphics screens. In Chapters 7 and 10 we will look at the text screens.

1.2: USING THE GRAPHICS SCREENS

We are now ready to experiment with the graphics screens. We'll use BASIC, so place the DOS disk in drive A, and type:

basica

Now we'll learn four BASIC commands: **SCREEN**, **COLOR**, **CLS**, and **KEY OFF**. When we introduce the format of commands, the command itself will be in upper case bold. Values (or variables) to supply will be in lower case bold, and optional entries will be enclosed within square brackets.

SCREEN

Let's begin. To select graphics screens we use the command **SCREEN**. Its format is:

SCREEN n

where **n** is 1 for the medium-resolution screen and 2 for the high-resolution screen. **SCREEN 0** returns to the text screen.

Let's try it out. Type:

SCREEN 1

Then:

SCREEN 2

And finally:

SCREEN 0

So far, the only differences among the text and two graphics screens are that the medium-resolution graphics screen uses big letters and neither graphics screen has a blinking cursor.

Color

In the medium-resolution screen, we can select the *background color* and the *palette*. We do this with **COLOR**:

COLOR [background color] [,palette]

background color is a number between 0 and 15 (see Figure 1.1). This number tells which color to use as a background for the whole screen. Let's start by setting a blue background:

COLOR TABLE

0 BLACK	8 GRAY
1 BLUE	9 INTENSE BLUE
2 GREEN	10 INTENSE GREEN
3 CYAN	11 INTENSE CYAN
4 RED	12 INTENSE RED
5 PURPLE	13 INTENSE PURPLE
6 BROWN	14 YELLOW
7 WHITE	15 INTENSE WHITE

Figure 1.1
Sixteen background colors.

SCREEN 1
COLOR 1

Now let's make this intense blue:

COLOR 9

Next, red:

COLOR 4

You may wish to try all sixteen background colors.
   The IBM's colors are a mix of red, green and blue. Combined, these three give the eight basic colors (2^3). Each of these colors can also be displayed with a higher intensity, resulting in colors 8 through 15 (Figure 1.2).

4 Preparing for Graphics

```
              COLOR COMPOSITION
             ┌─────────────────────────────────────┐
             │  0                                  │
             │  1 BLUE                             │
             │  2 GREEN                            │
             │  3 BLUE + GREEN                     │
             │  4 RED                              │
             │  5 BLUE + RED                       │
             │  6 GREEN + RED                      │
             │  7 BLUE + GREEN + RED               │
             │  8 INTENSITY                        │
             │  9 BLUE + INTENSITY                 │
             │ 10 GREEN + INTENSITY                │
             │ 11 BLUE + GREEN + INTENSITY         │
             │ 12 RED + INTENSITY                  │
             │ 13 BLUE + RED + INTENSITY           │
             │ 14 GREEN + RED + INTENSITY          │
             │ 15 BLUE + GREEN + RED + INTENSITY   │
             └─────────────────────────────────────┘
```

Figure 1.2
All sixteen colors are a combination of red, blue, and green. Colors 8 through 15 have the same composition as colors 0 through 7, but are intense.

In medium resolution, the dots we plot on the screen can be one of four colors, depending upon the *palette* chosen:

Color	Palette 0	Palette 1
0	background	background
1	green	cyan
2	red	magenta
3	brown	white

When **palette** is set to an even number, palette 0 is used. Otherwise, palette 1 is used. The colors in palette 1 are the same as palette 0, but with blue added.

We will experiment with the palette in a moment.

CLS and KEY OFF

Before we draw pictures, we need a way to clear the screen of text or old pictures cluttering it. We do this with **CLS**. Let's try it:

CLS

Everything but the bottom line—the line telling what the function keys do—is cleared. To get rid of this line, we type:

KEY OFF

(To get the function key display back, we type **KEY ON**.)

Our First Graphics Program

To test these four commands and as an introduction to the beauty of IBM PC graphics, we'll use the following program: (Don't worry about the **PSET** and **LINE** commands and all the math; we'll learn about them later.)

```
10 PI = 3.14 / 180
20 KEY OFF
30 CLS
40 FOR BOX = 1 TO 180 STEP 5
50    PSET (160 + BOX/2.5 * (COS(BOX*PI) + SIN(BOX*PI)),
      100 - BOX/2.5 * (-SIN(BOX*PI) + COS(BOX*PI)))
60    LINE - (160 + BOX/2.5 * (-COS(BOX*PI) +
      SIN(BOX*PI)), 100- BOX/2.5 * (SIN(BOX*PI) +
      COS(BOX*PI))), BOX MOD 3 + 1
70    LINE - (160 - BOX/2.5 * (COS(BOX*PI) +
      SIN(BOX*PI)), 100 + BOX/2.5 * (-SIN(BOX*PI) +
      COS(BOX*PI))), BOX MOD 3 + 1
80    LINE - (160 + BOX/2.5 * (COS(BOX*PI) -
      SIN(BOX*PI)), 100 + BOX/2.5 * (SIN(BOX*PI) +
      COS(BOX*PI))), BOX MOD 3 + 1
90    LINE - (160 + BOX/2.5 * (COS(BOX*PI) +
      SIN(BOX*PI)), 100 - BOX/2.5 * (-SIN(BOX*PI) +
      COS(BOX*PI))), BOX MOD 3 + 1
100 NEXT
110 END
```

6 Preparing for Graphics

> Put the program disk in drive A. Then, type:
> **LOAD "CHAPTER1\2**
> The program will now be in memory. (You may want to verify this by typing:
>
> **LIST)**

Let's start by running this program using the high-resolution screen:

SCREEN 2
RUN

A pretty pattern will appear on the screen. All the lines are white or black. (The black lines can only be seen when they draw over white ones.) Note the horizontal width of the picture.

If you have **Syntax error**s or the program only draws a few dots, type **LIST** and compare to the listing in the book. Make corrections to your program. You may wish to refer to Chapter 2 of the *BASIC Manual*.

Now, we'll run the program in medium resolution:

SCREEN 1
RUN

Note the three colors used (plus the fourth background color). Also notice how the figure's size has changed.

Now, let's change the background color. Type:

COLOR 1

And let's change the palette:

COLOR ,0

Note that if we don't enter a background color, the background color is not changed.

Let's look at the palette 0 colors with a black background:

COLOR 0

You may want to rerun the program. Before going on to the next chapter, type **NEW**.

A SUMMARY

Now we've finished our introduction to IBM PC graphics. We have:

- learned about the two graphics screens
- seen how to prepare for graphics
- run our first graphics program

We are now ready to approach the exciting world of line graphics.

2

Two-Dimensional Line Graphics

The first style of graphics to learn is *line graphics* - an easy to learn and very versatile style in which objects are composed of points and lines (Figure 2.1).

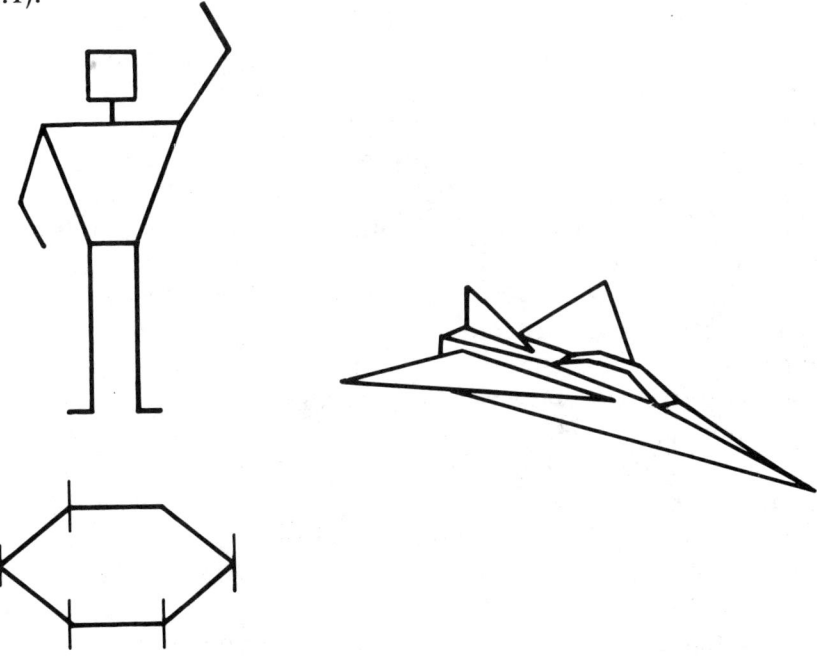

Figure 2.1

Sample line figures: a stick man, a jet, and a glucose molecule.

10 Two-Dimensional Line Graphics

We'll start with the simplest type: two-dimensional line graphics. In two-dimensional line graphics, objects (for example squares and stick men) have only height and width. This chapter will show how to describe two-dimensional line drawings in a form the computer can understand and then how to display and animate them.

PROGRAMS IN THIS CHAPTER

Many sections in this chapter contain small programs. Most are meant to combine to form one long program—a program growing in complexity. You may wish to save the programs from each section separately as ASCII files (that is, **SAVE "file name",A**) and **MERGE** them into the main program. Or, you can just make a "grand total" program as you go along and save it when necessary.

2.1: DATA STRUCTURE

Before we draw an object on the computer, we need to figure out a way for the computer to understand what an object is. We need a way to represent an object as data for the computer. For two-dimensional line graphics we only need a way to represent lines. This representation is most easily done by using the *Cartesian coordinate system*.

The Cartesian coordinate system presents a way to represent points; a line is simply the connection between two points. In the Cartesian system the "world" (that is, the area we are interested in drawing) is broken into a grid, just as a street map is. This grid has two axes: the x axis, which runs horizontally; and the y axis, which runs vertically. These axes serve as number lines. Where they intersect is called the *origin*, designated by the ordered pair (0,0). A Cartesian grid is shown in Figure 2.2.

Every point is represented by two coordinates—the x coordinate, and the y coordinate—each being the distance from the origin along the respective axes. For example, the point 3 units to the right of the origin and 4 units above it is written as the ordered pair (3,4). The point 2 units to the right of the origin and 2 units below it is (2,−2). The x coordinate is always written first; the y is written second. Figure 2.3 shows the points (3,4) and (2,−2) on a Cartesian grid.

As mentioned before, a line is the connection between two points. So, to represent a line we only need to tell the computer its end points. Figure 2.4 shows a line. Note that its end points are darkened. One has coordinates (3,4); the other has coordinates (2,−2). Let's call (3,4) point 1 and

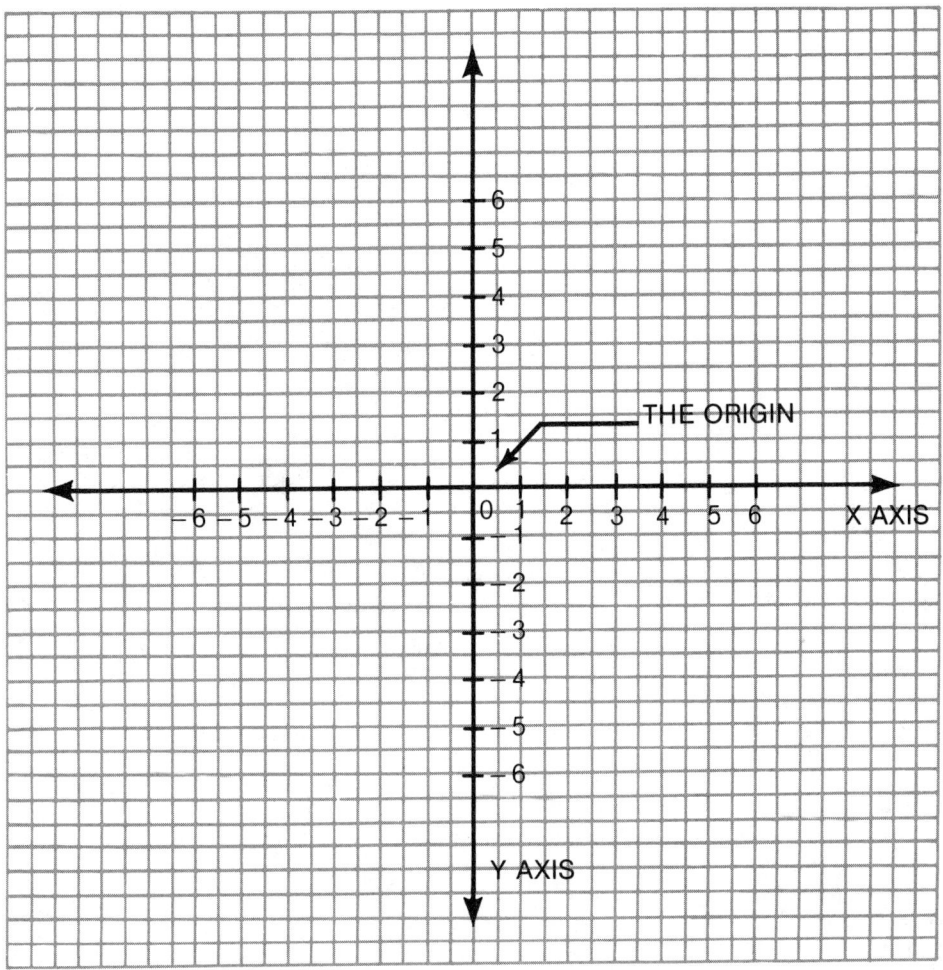

Figure 2.2
The Cartesian coordinate system.

(2,−2) point 2. To draw this line we tell the computer to connect point 1 to point 2. (Or, we could tell the computer to connect point 2 to point 1. It doesn't matter.) This is simple to do, as we will see in Section 2.3.

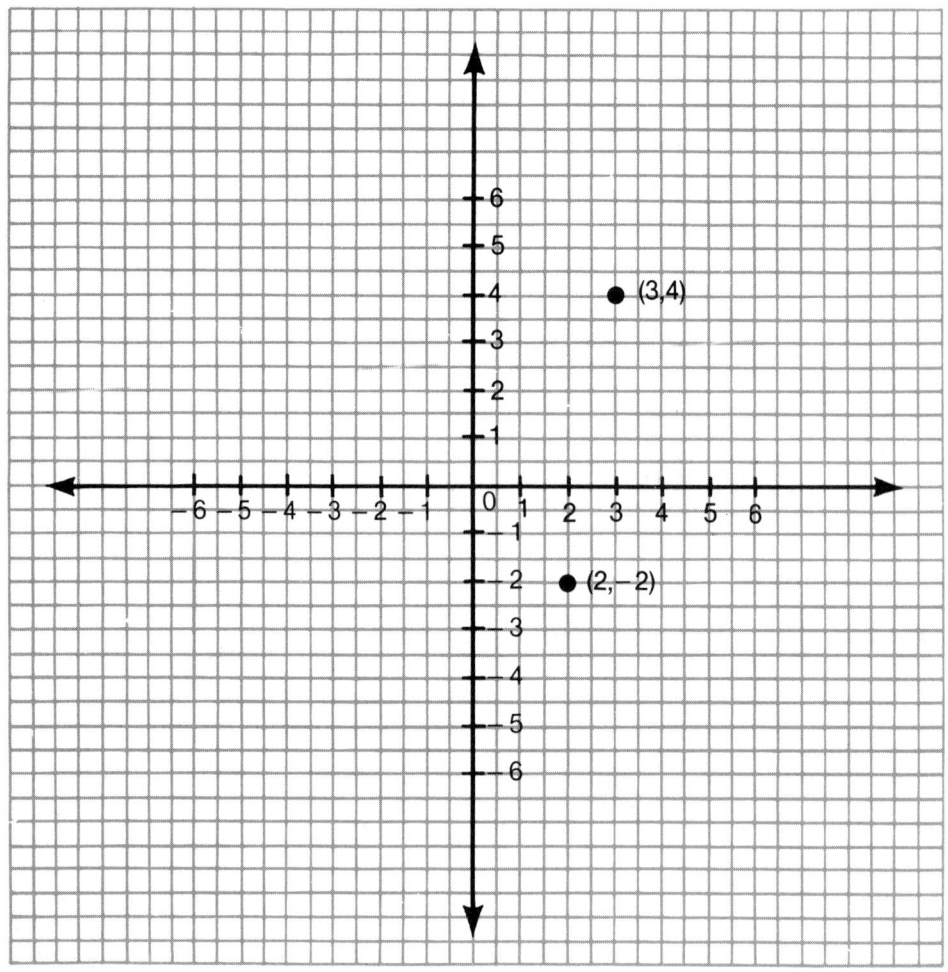

Figure 2.3
The points (3,4) and (2,−2).

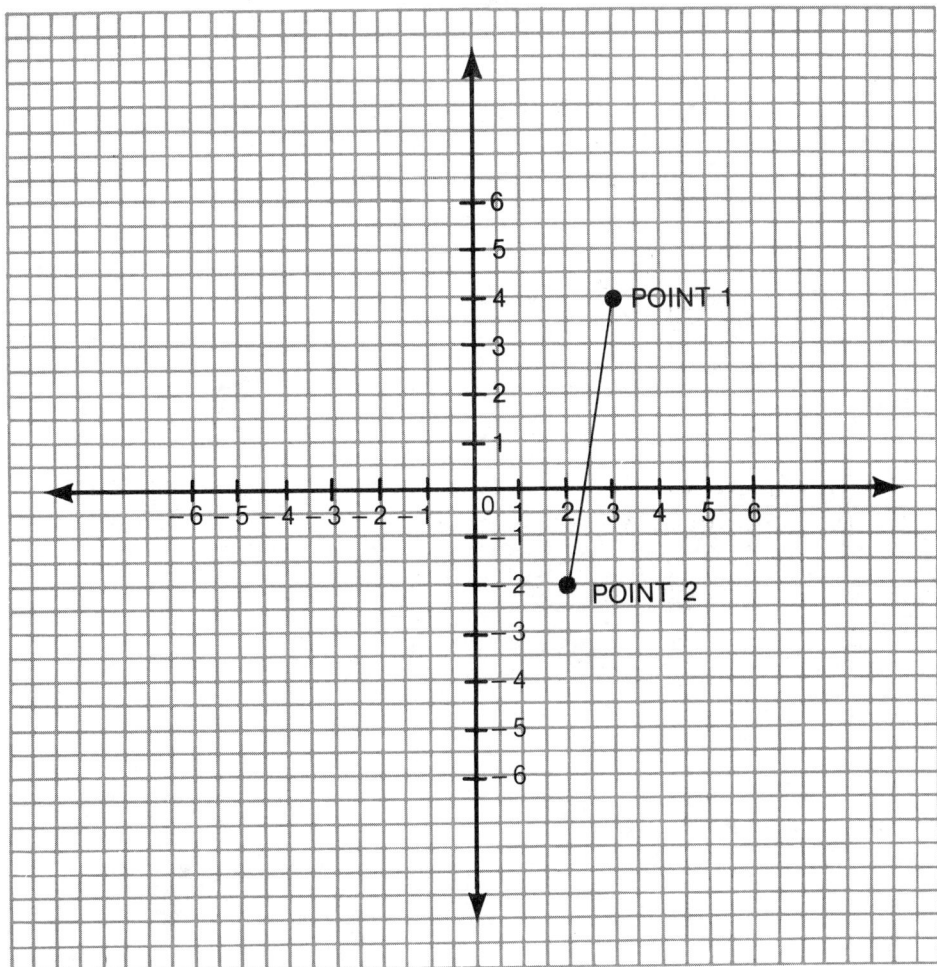

Figure 2.4
A line.

Converting Objects to Data

Now we need a way to convert an object into data the computer can understand. We know it is easy to tell the computer how to draw lines. So we will break down figures into sets of lines and then feed data describing the lines into the computer. As we represent objects by sets of lines, and lines by pairs of points, we will call this process creating *point-line data*.

Let's start with an easy example. Figure 2.5 shows an outline of a space shuttle. First, draw the object on a Cartesian coordinate system. One of the best ways to do this is to draw it on graph paper (Figure 2.6). Now, figure out the coordinates of each end point (Figure 2.7).

14   Two-Dimensional Line Graphics

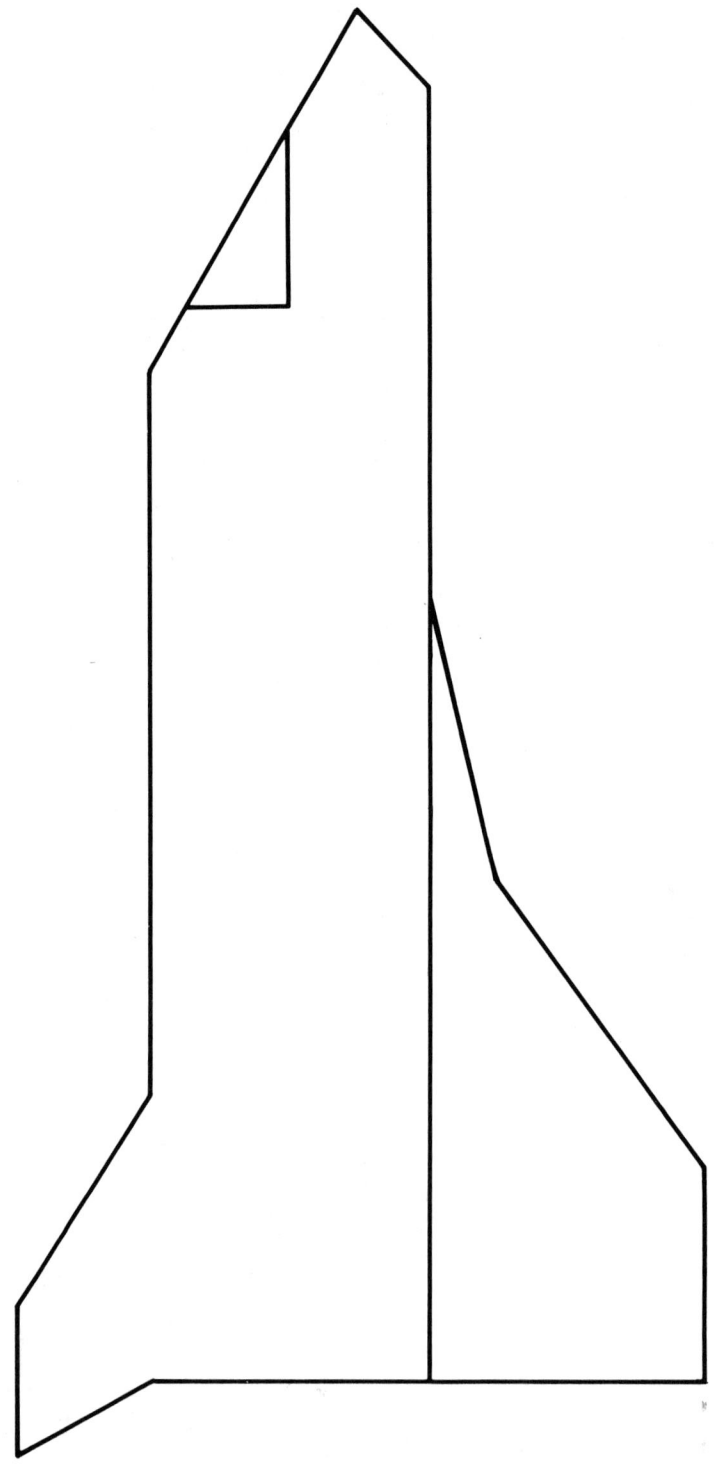

Figure 2.5
An outline of the space shuttle.

Two-Dimensional Line Graphics   15

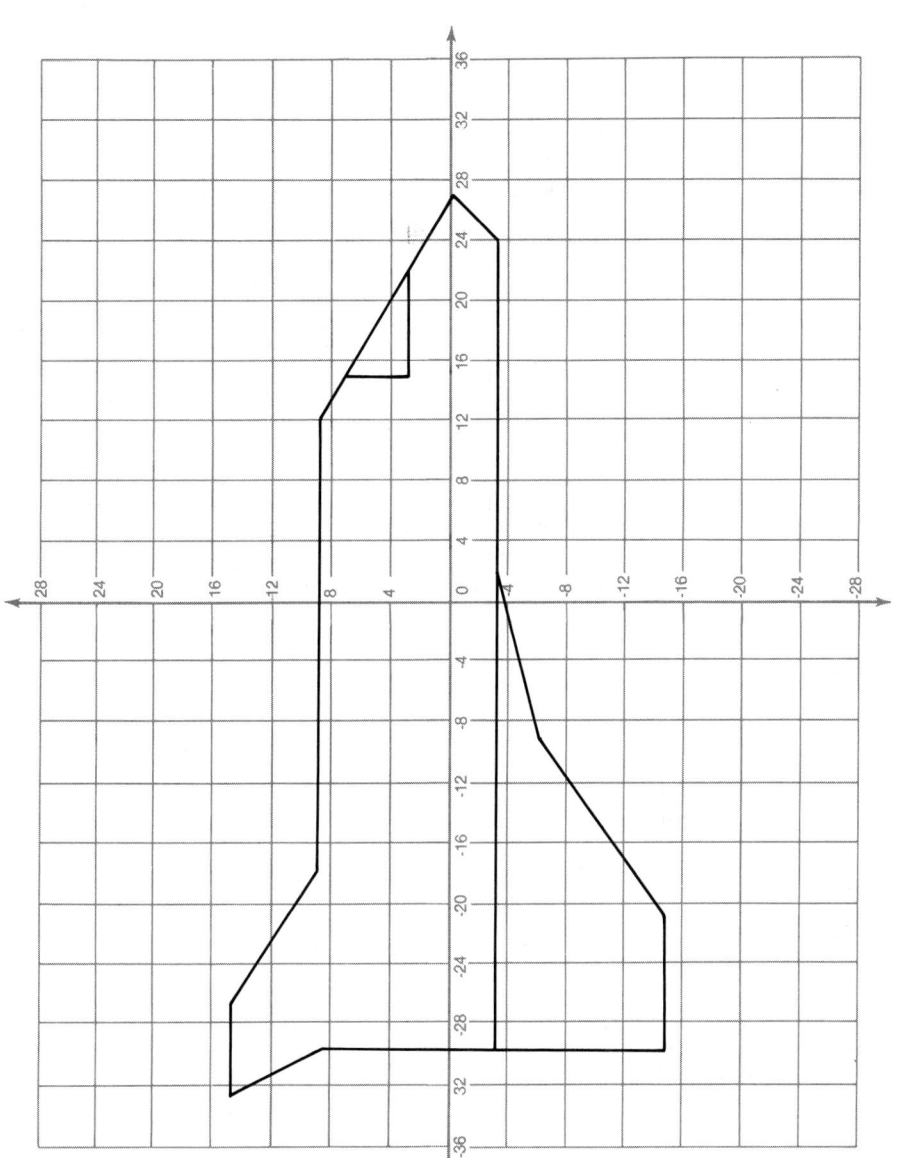

Figure 2.6
Draw the shuttle on graph paper.

16 Two-Dimensional Line Graphics

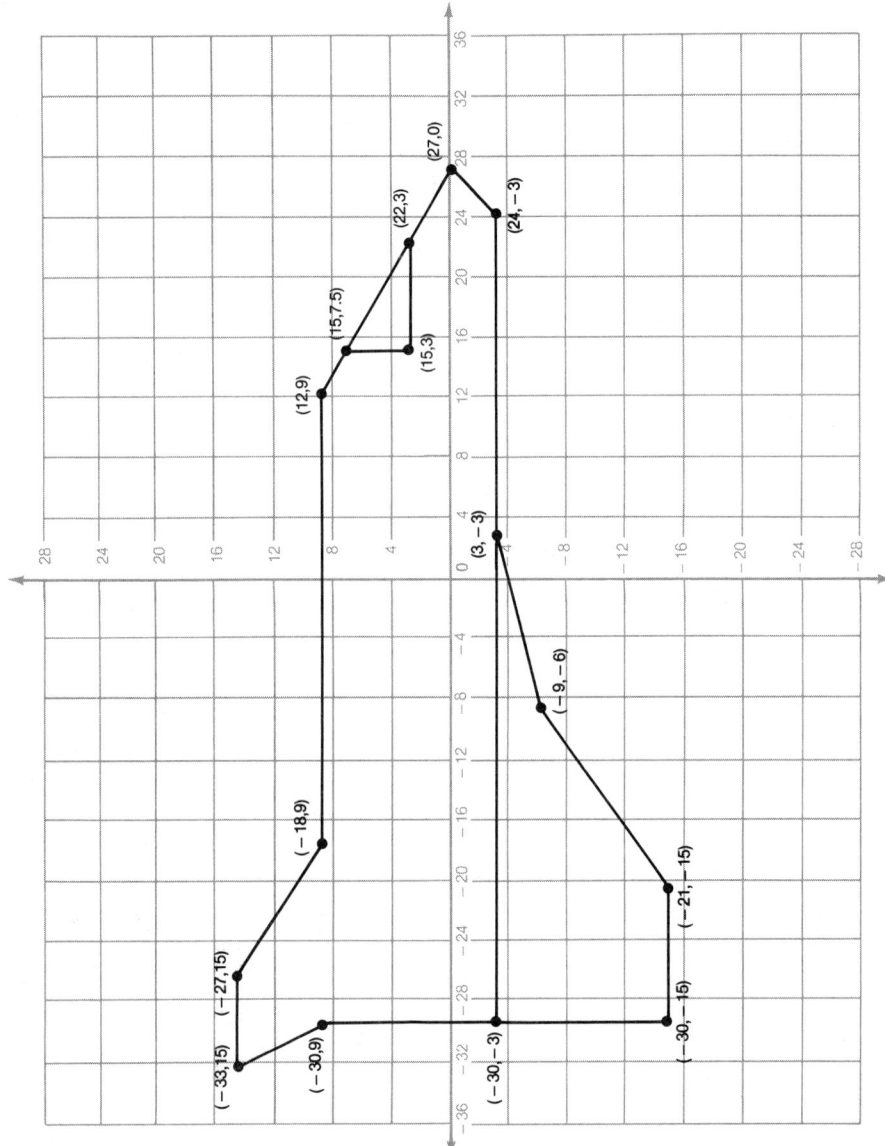

Figure 2.7
Determine the coordinates of the end points.

Next, number all points. Pick any point to start with, and call it 1. Then, move along, labeling 2, 3, 4, etc. until all the points are labeled. For clarity, it is better for end points of a given line to be consecutively numbered (Figure 2.8).

Now label each line on the figure. Number the line starting with point 1 as line 1. If several lines stem from point 1, just select any as line 1. The order in which lines are numbered is for clarity. What is most important is that each line gets labeled. Figure 2.9 shows the shuttle so labeled.

Now, make a table of the points and their coordinates and of the lines and their end points (Figure 2.10). Such a table is easily understood by the computer. In fact, in Section 2.2 we will see how to store it, and in Section 2.3 we will see how to draw it. But first, let's examine some of the difficulties of converting objects to point-line data. (Beginners may want to skip to the summary.)

Converting Curves to Lines

In Figure 2.6 a space shuttle is drawn on a Cartesian coordinate system. It is already drawn as a set of lines. This rendering makes it easy to set up a point-line data base. If we have a more complex shape—one not already made up of lines, such as an actual picture of the space shuttle—the process is more difficult. The first thing to do is to draw the object on a coordinate system. In Figure 2.11 a picture of a space shuttle has been placed over a grid. Note the curves and details in Figure 2.11 not present in Figure 2.6.

Now, we convert this figure to a set of lines. We need to decide how detailed to be. For example, should we keep windows, engines, lettering and wheels? Or are we only interested in the broad outline? Decide which aspects are most important and how large details should be to keep. Also, think how curved you want the resulting picture to be. The more lines used to approximate a curve, the more curved it will appear to be. While a more detailed picture may be more curved, look prettier, and be more informative, it will take more time to display and consume more memory.

Suppose we want a very simple rendition of the shuttle. We will use as few details as possible. Put an outline around these details (Figure 2.12). Now, draw over this outline using as few lines as necessary (Figure 2.13).

18 Two-Dimensional Line Graphics

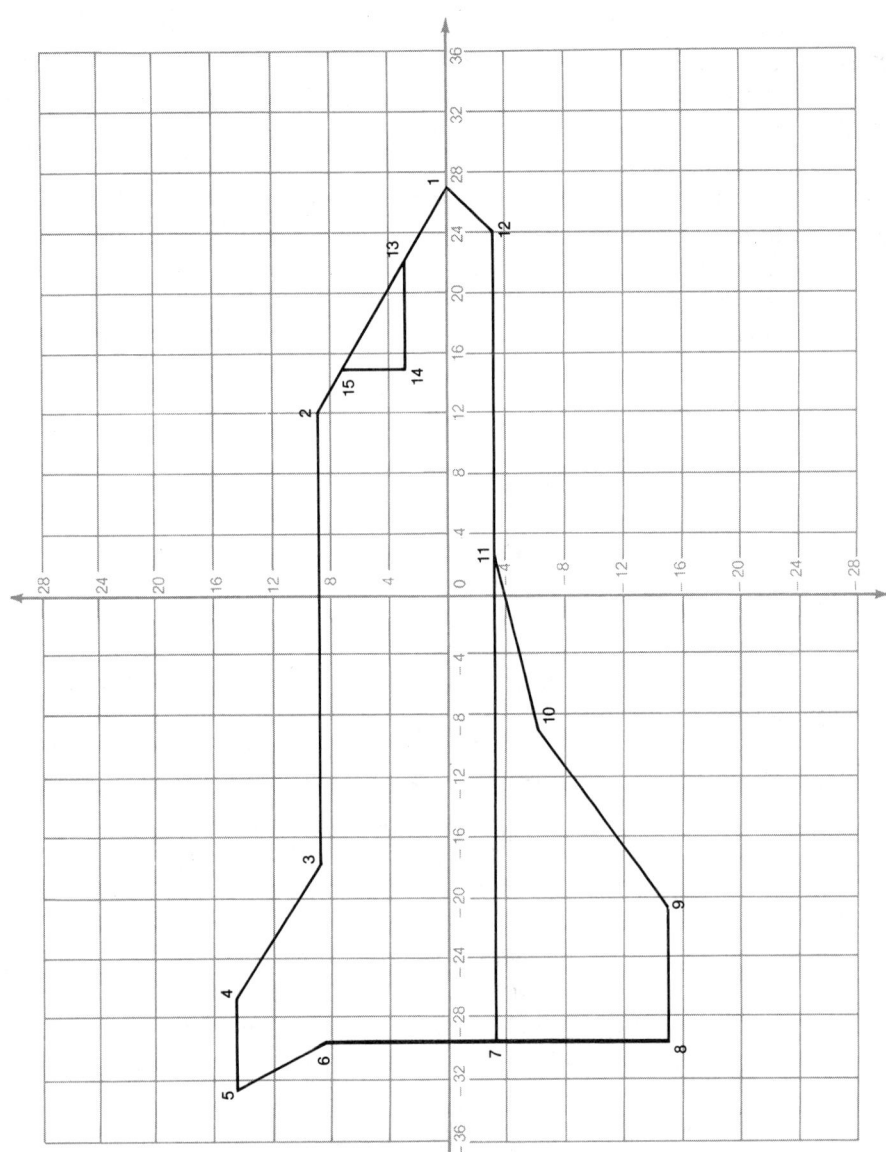

Figure 2.8
Number the points.

Two-Dimensional Line Graphics 19

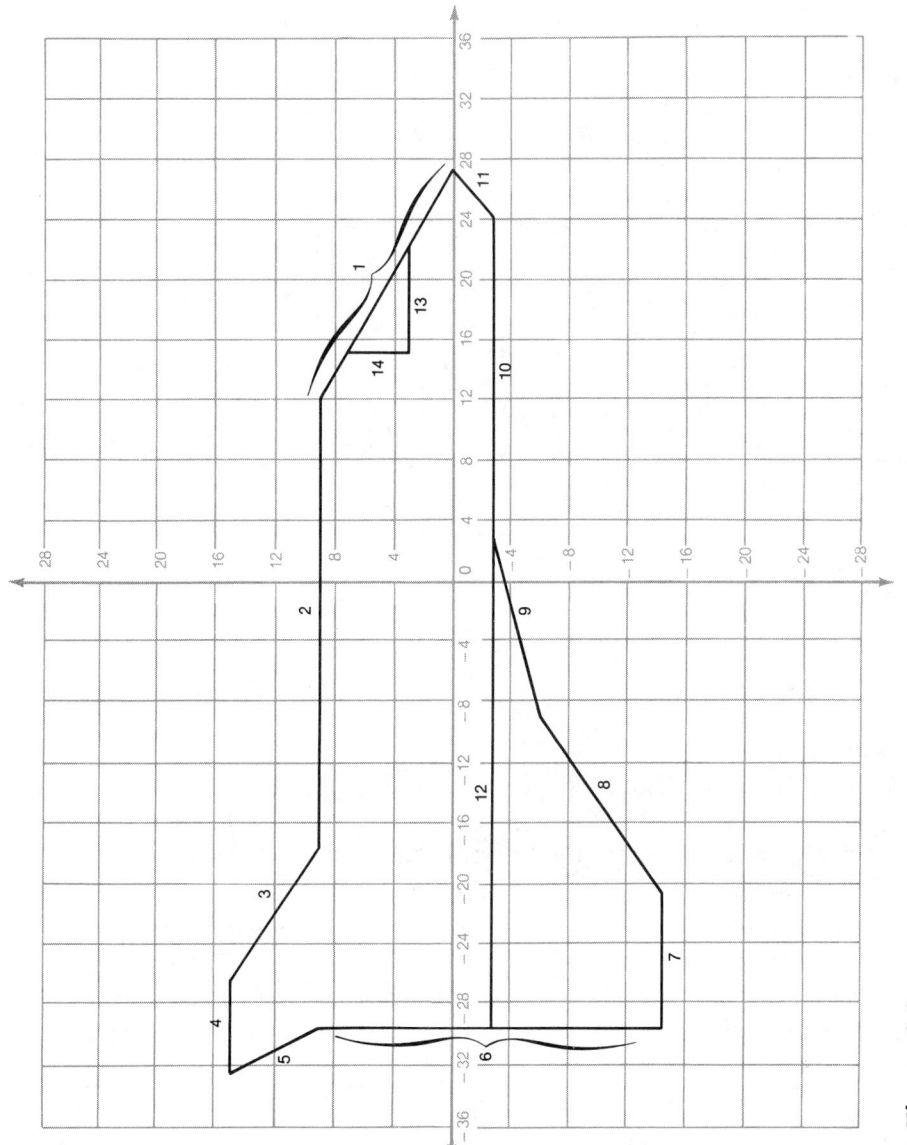

Figure 2.9
Number the lines.

20 Two-Dimensional Line Graphics

POINT	COORDINATES
1	(27,0)
2	(12,9)
3	(−18,9)
4	(−27,15)
5	(−33,15)
6	(−30,9)
7	(−30,−3)
8	(−30,−15)
9	(−21,−15)
10	(−9,−6)
11	(3,−3)
12	(24,−3)
13	(22,3)
14	(15,3)
15	(15,7.5)

LINE	END POINTS
1	1,2
2	2,3
3	3,4
4	4,5
5	5,6
6	6,8
7	8,9
8	9,10
9	10,11
10	11,12
11	12,1
12	7,11
13	13,14
14	14,15

Figure 2.10
Make a table of the coordinates of the points and of the end points of the lines.

If we want more detail, we use more lines. Figure 2.14 shows a close-up of a section of the space shuttle. Figure 2.14a is a very rough depiction of this part; Figure 2.14b is more like the original—more complex—and Figure 2.14c is very curved. The more detailed the line drawing, the more memory needed to store the object, and the longer it takes to draw the object. Looking at the increased number of points and lines makes this seem pretty intuitive. With experience you will get an idea of how detailed to make the drawing.

One final thing to keep in mind is that the screen is limited in resolution. Sometimes a very detailed object will come out looking the same as a simpler one. Yet limiting detail because of resolution can sometimes backfire. Later we will see that after scaling or because of perspective, parts of an object may be enlarged on the screen. Then, details (or their lack) will show up that didn't before.

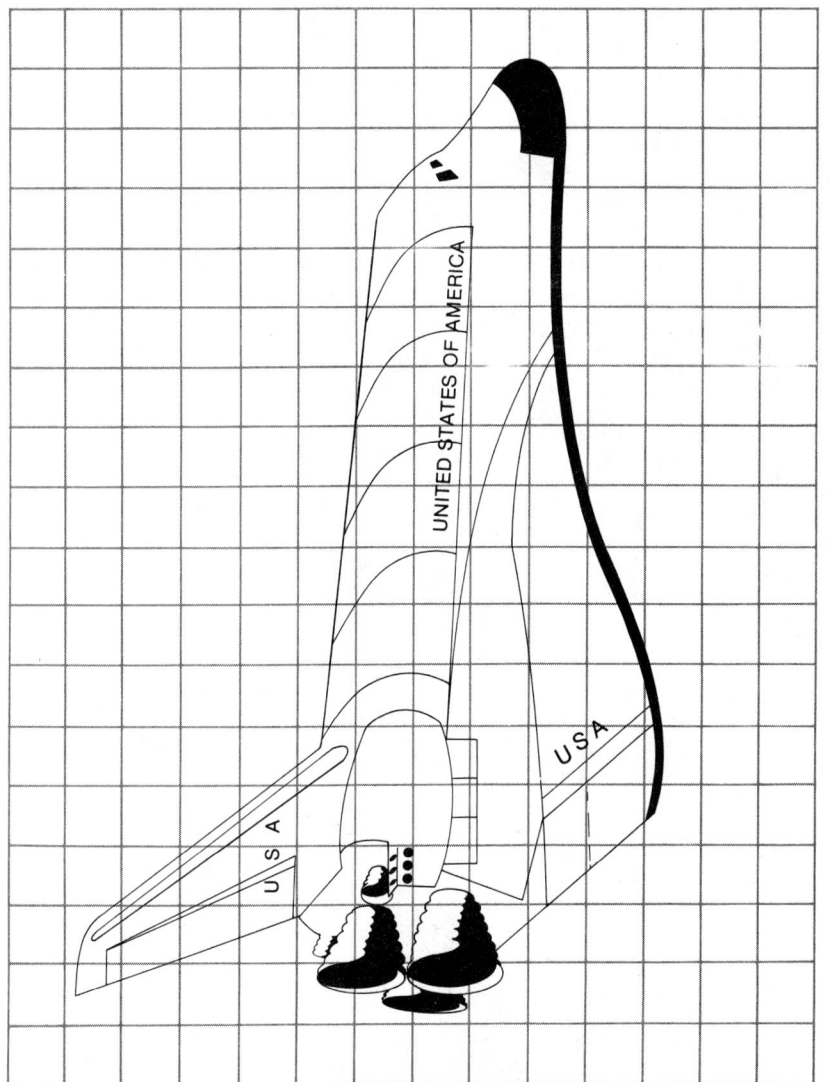

Figure 2.11
A picture of the space shuttle placed on a graph grid.

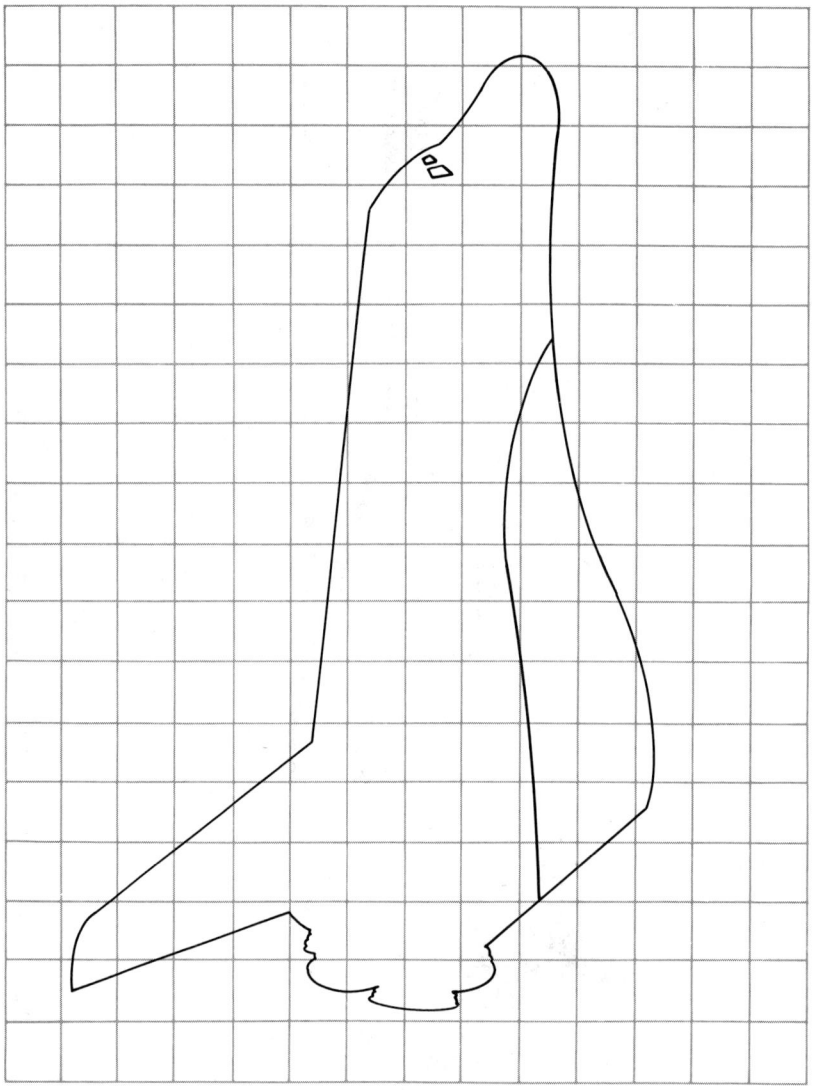

Figure 2.12
Outline details.

Two-Dimensional Line Graphics 23

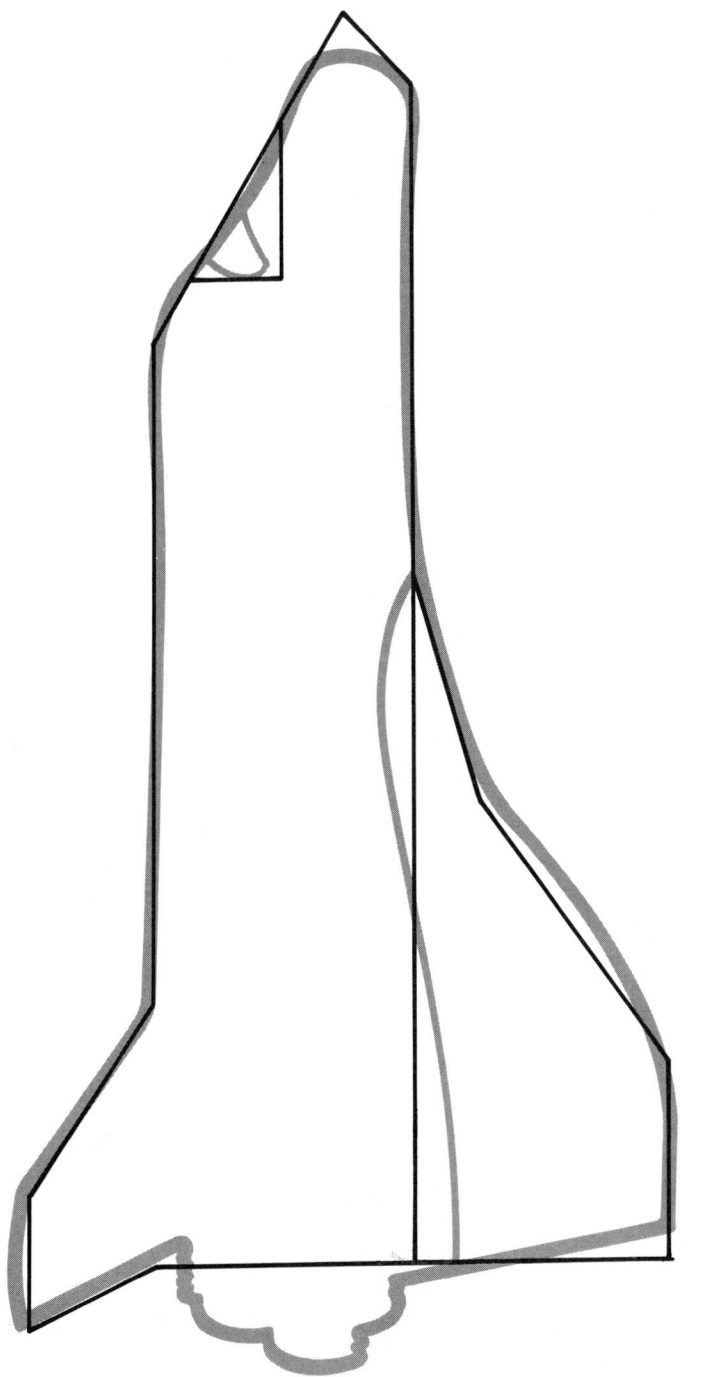

Figure 2.13
Draw over the outline of details, using as few lines as possible.

24 Two-Dimensional Line Graphics

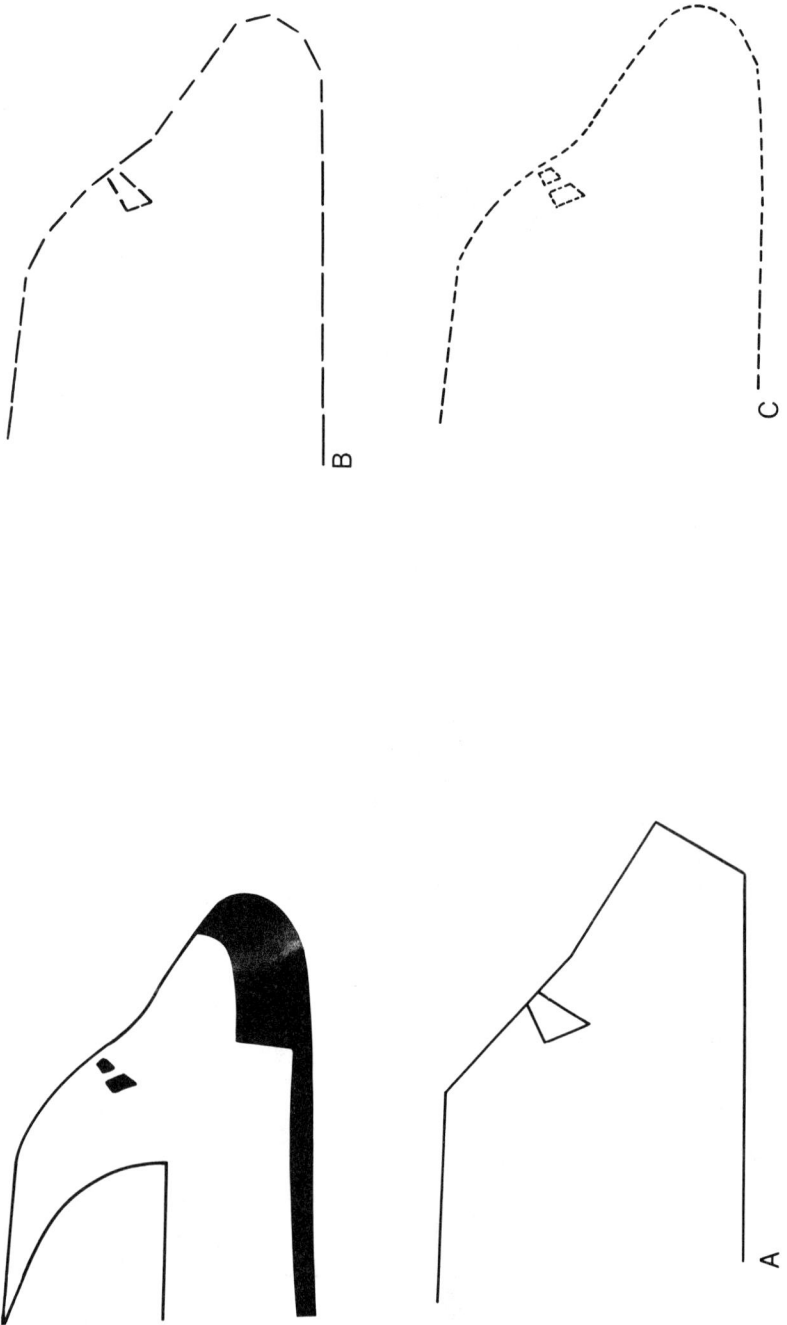

Figure 2.14
A close up of the shuttle. Part a is a rough delineation, part b is more refined, and part c is very curved.

Choosing the Center

One further complication in converting an object to point-line data is choosing the center. This means deciding where to place the object on the Cartesian coordinate system. Figure 2.15 shows three possible placings of the shuttle. Each will result in different coordinates for the points. In general it is best for the center of the object to be at the origin. Of course, it is not always easy to decide what to call the center of the object. Imagine rocking the object back and forth. Choose the pivot point to be the center.

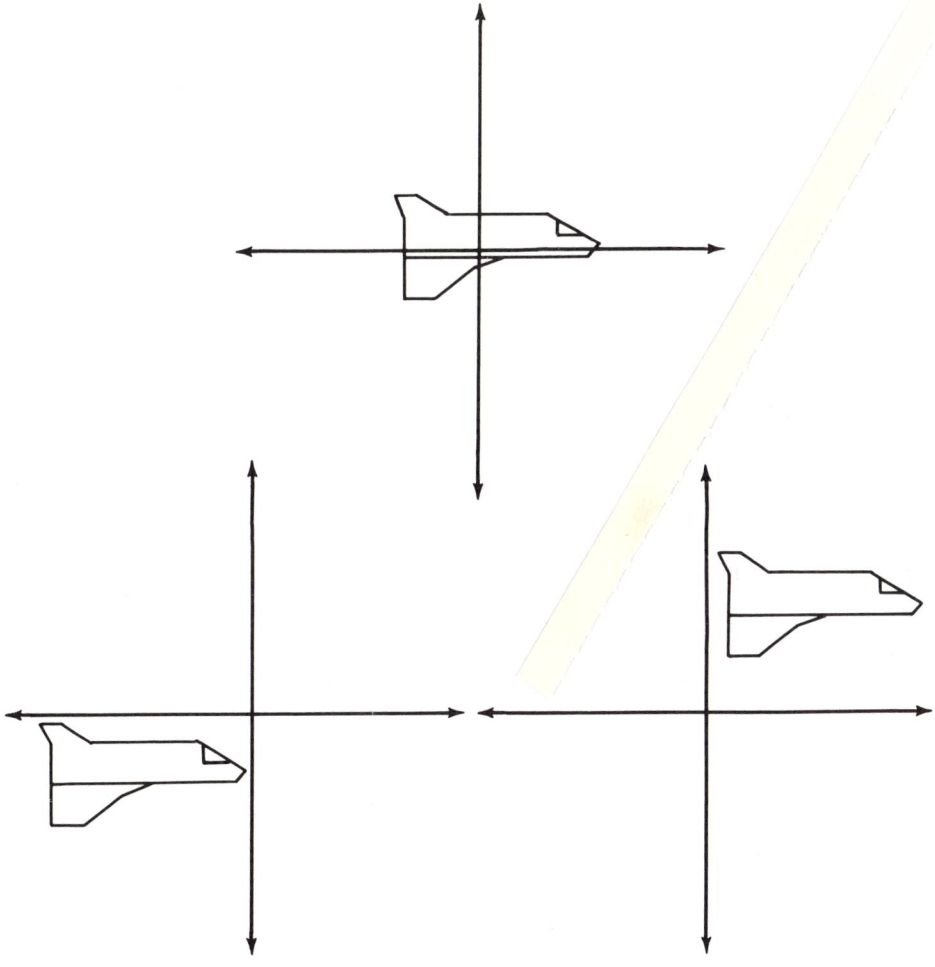

Figure 2.15
Three possible placings of the shuttle. Note how each results in different coordinates for all the end points.

In physics, this point is called the *center of gravity*. When we discuss rotation later, the reason for choosing this point as center will become clear. When we learn how to scale, we will also see the importance of the center's location.

There is another consideration, however. In some cases it is more convenient to place a point other than the center at the origin. For example, suppose we are making a lunar lander program. Let's say we want to draw the ship on the ground, at height = 0. If we place the bottom of the ship on (0,0) when we compute its coordinates, then to have the ship drawn on the ground, we only need to place the ship at height 0.

A SUMMARY

You should now be able to convert any object into a two-dimensional line figure. To summarize the technique:

1. Draw the object on a Cartesian coordinate system. Choose the center carefully.
2. Choose the important features of the object. Delineate them.
3. Label all the points.
4. Label all the lines.
5. Make a table of the coordinates of the points and the end points of the lines.

2.2: SETTING UP A POINT-LINE DATA BASE

Once we have broken an object down into a table of points and lines, it is very easy to convert it to a form the computer can recognize. All we need to do is to use two arrays: one for storing the points and one for storing the lines. (If you are unfamiliar with arrays, refer to Appendix A.) We will feed the data from Figure 2.10 directly into these arrays. To be able to use the array data later, we also need to know the number of points and lines. We will store these in simple variables.

The program below does this:

```
5   'Set up arrays
6   '
10  OPTION BASE 1
20  DIM POINTS(2,100), LINES(2,100)
```

Two-Dimensional Line Graphics

```
100 '
101 'Constants
102 '
110 XCOORD = 1 : YCOORD = 2 'constants used for POINTS
    matrix
120 FROM = 1 : TO. = 2     'constants used for LINES
    matrix

297 '
298 ' Read points and lines
299 '
300 READ NUMBEROFPOINTS, NUMBEROFLINES
310 FOR POINTNUM = 1 TO NUMBEROFPOINTS 'read point data
320    READ POINTS(XCOORD,POINTNUM), POINTS(YCOORD,
       POINTNUM)
330 NEXT
340 FOR LINENUM = 1 TO NUMBEROFLINES   'read line data
350    READ LINES(FROM,LINENUM), LINES(TO.,LINENUM)
360 NEXT
900 END

20000 '
20001 'Data for shape
20002 '
20010 'Space Shuttle
20020 DATA 15, 14
20030 DATA    27, 0,    12, 9,    -18, 9,   -27, 15,
      -33, 15,   -30, 9,   -30, -3,   -30, -15,
      -21, -15,   -9, -6,   3, -3,    24, -3,   22, 3,
      15, 3,    15, 7.5
20040 DATA   1, 2,    2, 3,    3, 4,    4, 5,    5, 6,
      6, 8,    8, 9,    9, 10,   10, 11,   11, 12,
      12, 1,   7, 11,   13, 14,   14, 15
```

The program disk is organized in the same fashion as the book. Each chapter has its own disk section—its own directory; the programs for each chapter are located in that directory.

Let's examine this. Type:

FILES

You will see the names of the demo programs, plus 10 chapter names. Each of the chapter names is followed by <**DIR**>, indicating that it is a directory. When you want to load programs for a

28 Two-Dimensional Line Graphics

particular chapter, you need to be in that chapter's directory. You do this with **CHDIR**.

Let's get into the directory for Chapter 2. Type:

CHDIR "CHAPTER2

Now type:

FILES

You will see a list of all the programs for Chapter 2. If you were to type:

LOAD "2

You would load the file **2.BAS** from the directory **CHAPTER2**. (This file is known as **\CHAPTER2\2.BAS**.)

It's very important to be in the directory for Chapter 2 when you want to load a Chapter 2 program. So, if you come back to a section in Chapter 2 after a break or after another chapter, be sure to get into the **CHAPTER2** directory. You can always do this by:

CHDIR "
CHDIR "CHAPTER2

One further caution: the program disk doesn't have enough room to save files. So when you want to save a program, use a different disk. If this disk is not placed in the same drive as the program disk, there is no problem. But if it is you will need to return to the **CHAPTER2** directory after replacing the program disk:

CHDIR "CHAPTER2

To load the program for this section, type:

LOAD "2

The **OPTION BASE 1** statement in line **10** is of interest. Normally, the first entry in an array is indexed with a zero. This line changes it to a one. That is, the x coordinate of the first point will be **POINTS(1,1)** instead of

POINTS(0,0). This makes it simpler to follow the program. Also, note that in lines **120** and **130** we set up the variables **XCOORD**, **YCOORD**, **FROM**, and **TO.** as constants, used in reading the arrays. This, again, is for program readability. Make sure that you include the period on the end of **TO.**, because **TO** (without the period) is a reserved word.

The program is very simple in operation. First, it reads the number of points and the number of lines. It then goes through loops to read the point data into the **POINTS** array and the line data into the **LINES** array. This data is read from the data statements starting at line **20020**. Line **20030** contains all the numbers from the table of coordinates for the space shuttle. The first number is the x coordinate of the first point, the second is the y coordinate, the third is the x coordinate of the second point, and so on. Likewise, line **20040** contains the numbers from the table of end points of the lines. The first number is the first point of the first line, the second is the second point of the first line, the third is the first point of the second line, and so on.

Reading the data from **DATA** statements is just one way to get the point-line data. Another is to have the user enter the data each time the program is run. This method gives a lot of flexibility, but can be very annoying (especially when the program crashes, and all the data has to be reentered). A better way is to have a *point-line data editor* that saves the data in disk files. These files would then be read or **MERGE**d by the graphics program. Such an editor would have the ability to display, modify and delete the points and lines and to retrieve and save data files to disk.

One final note about the above program: you may have noticed that its line numbers are strange. Throughout this and the next few chapters we will tack on more and more sections to the program, thus, evolving it into a full-fledged graphics system.

Save this program as **2DLG**, for two-dimensional line graphics:

SAVE "2DLG

Before reading the next section, enter:

NEW

2.3: DRAWING THE SHAPE

Now that we can describe shapes in a fashion the computer can understand we can display them. To do this we will use the **LINE** command. Its format is:

LINE $[(x_1,y_1)] - (x_2,y_2)$

(x_1,y_1) and (x_2,y_2) are the coordinates of the points to connect. If (x_1,y_1) isn't specified, a line is drawn from the last point plotted to (x_2,y_2).

Let's become familiar with the **LINE** command. Type in the following short program:

```
10 OPTION BASE 1
20 XCOORD = 1 : YCOORD = 2
30 KEY OFF
40 SCREEN 2
50 INPUT "Starting Point "; POINTS(XCOORD,1),
   POINTS(YCOORD,1)
60 INPUT "Ending Point "; POINTS(XCOORD,2),
   POINTS(YCOORD,2)
70 CLS
80 LINE (POINTS(XCOORD,1),POINTS(YCOORD,1)) -
   (POINTS(XCOORD,2),POINTS(YCOORD,2))
90 FOR A = 1 TO 800 :   NEXT 'Allow time to look at
   screen
100 END
```

LOAD "3P1

Now run it several times and enter a variety of end points. I suggest drawing the following lines:

1. (20,10) to (300,10)   —A horizontal line
2. (20,10) to (20,100)   —A vertical line
3. (20,10) to (300,100)   —A diagonal line
4. (−10,−10) to (700,220)   —A line that goes off the screen
5. (0,0) to (0,0)   —The origin

The last two lines are of particular interest. Line 4 goes off the screen, in both the upper left and lower right sides. As we will later see, this is a problem any line-drawing routine has to cope with. This line will look different in BASIC 1.1 and BASIC 2.0. BASIC 2.0 is more advanced; when the line goes off the screen it is clipped. In other words, the portions that would appear off of the screen do not show. In BASIC 1.1, however, the line is wrapped around. When it goes off one side of the screen, it comes back on the other. (You will figure out why this happens when you read Chapter 4.) Wrap around can be a bit annoying. It can cause confusing, cluttered pictures. Therefore, if you are using BASIC 1.1, you may want to include a clipping routine in your programs. This will be discussed in Section 3.15.

Line 5 is really a point, not a line. Perhaps you didn't even see it. If not, run the program again and look closely at the upper left corner of the screen for a dot. You may ask, if (0,0) is the origin of the Cartesian coordinate system, and the origin is supposed to be in the center, what is (0,0) doing in the upper left corner? The answer is simple: the coordinates of the screen are not in the Cartesian coordinate system. They are in the *screen coordinate system* (Figure 2.16). Because it is so much easier to work with the Cartesian coordinate system, we will do all of our manipulations in the Cartesian system and then convert to the screen coordinate system just before drawing. In Section 3.16 we will learn a BASIC 2.0 command that makes this conversion unnecessary.

The formula to convert from the Cartesian to screen system is quite simple. Add half the maximum x value to the x coordinate, and subtract the y coordinate from half the maximum y value. That is:

$$(x,y)_{Screen} = (x_{Cartesian} + maxxres/2, maxyres/2 - y_{Cartesian})$$

For high-resolution graphics, **maxxres** = 640, and **maxyres** = 200. For medium resolution, **maxxres** = 320, and **maxyres** = 200.

Let's plug in (0,0) to see where this places the origin. In high resolution, (0,0) maps to (320,100)—just about the center of the screen. You can see that (0,0) also maps to the center of the medium-resolution screen.

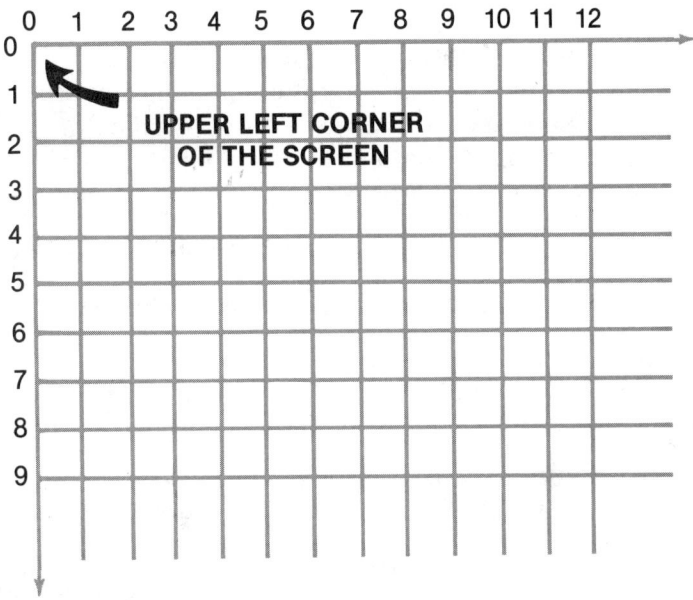

Figure 2.16
The screen coordinate system.

The STEP Option

Normally (x_1,y_1) and (x_2,y_2) are the coordinates of the points to plot. But if they are proceeded by the command **STEP**, they indicate by how much to move from the last point drawn. For example, to draw a line going 20 units down from and 10 units to the right of the center of the screen, try:

LINE (320,100) — STEP (10,20)

This is the same as:

LINE (320,100) — (330,120)

The **STEP** values can be negative.

Putting It Together—The Shuttle

Now let's write a program to draw the shuttle we entered before. To do this, we will make some additions to the program from Section 2.2, **2DLG**. Type:

LOAD "2DLG

We will add one more step here: instead of just reading in the points and modifying them directly, we will copy the points into another array and do all of our modifications on this array. This will make things easier later when we will be doing many complicated manipulations of the points. The following copies **POINTS** into **NEWPOINTS**:

```
20 DIM POINTS(2,100), NEWPOINTS(2,100), LINES(2,100)

530    GOSUB 1010     'load points for changing

1000 '
1001 'move POINTS to NEWPOINTS to compute new point
     locations
1002 '
1010 FOR POINTNUM = 1 TO NUMBEROFPOINTS
1020    NEWPOINTS(XCOORD,POINTNUM) = POINTS(XCOORD,
        POINTNUM)
1030    NEWPOINTS(YCOORD,POINTNUM) = POINTS(YCOORD,
        POINTNUM)
1040 NEXT
1100 RETURN
```

Now we want to convert the points in **NEWPOINTS** from Cartesian to screen coordinates. We will do this by calling another subroutine:

```
140  MAXXRES = 640 : MAXYRES = 200
710
720     GOSUB 8010          'convert to screen coordinate
                             system

8000 '
8001 'Convert to screen coordinate system
8002 '
8010 FOR POINTNUM = 1 TO NUMBEROFPOINTS
8020    NEWPOINTS(XCOORD,POINTNUM) =
           NEWPOINTS(XCOORD,POINTNUM) + MAXXRES/2
8030    NEWPOINTS(YCOORD,POINTNUM) = MAXYRES/2 -
           NEWPOINTS(YCOORD, POINTNUM)
8040 NEXT
8100 RETURN
```

The only thing we have left to do now is to make a routine that draws the lines. It needs to go through every line in the shape and feed the end points of the line into the **LINE** command. This procedure involves a lot of indexing. It looks complicated on paper, but it really is rather simple. Add the following lines:

```
740  GOSUB 9010           'draw the shape

9000 '
9001 'Draws the lines
9002 '
9010 FOR LINENUM = 1 TO NUMBEROFLINES
9020    LINE(NEWPOINTS(XCOORD,LINES(FROM,LINENUM)),
           NEWPOINTS(YCOORD,LINES(FROM,LINENUM))) -
           (NEWPOINTS(XCOORD,LINES(TO.,LINENUM)),
           NEWPOINTS(YCOORD,LINES(TO.,LINENUM)))
9030 NEXT
9100 RETURN
```

LINES(FROM,LINENUM) is the first point of line number **LINENUM**. Therefore, **NEWPOINTS(XCOORD,LINES(FROM,LINENUM))** is the x coordinate of this point. The rest of the terms in line **9020** evaluate similarly.

Now we have entered all the routines we need to draw lines. Only a few preparatory steps remain. First, we have to tell the computer we are going to plot graphics, and then, before we do the drawing, we need to clear the screen:

34 Two-Dimensional Line Graphics

```
400 '
401 'Prepare for graphics
402 '
410 SCREEN 2              'high resolution
420 KEY OFF

500 '
501 'Main Program
502 '
730     CLS
```

> To load in all the additions to **2DLG**, type:
>
> **MERGE** "3P2

Now run it. (You may want to go over the listing before you run it, to make sure you know what is happening.)

It's Wrong—The Problem of Dot Width

Look at the screen. The picture doesn't really look like the shuttle! It's all scrunched up. Well, don't junk the computer. The problem is that of *dot size*: the width of the dots is less than the height of the dots. Typically, the width of the screen is 4/3 that of its height. This is called the screen's *aspect ratio*. But, so many more dots are fit in horizontally than vertically that the width of a dot is less than its height. For example, suppose we are in high resolution. Then, there are 640 horizontal dots in 4/3 of the space that there are 200 vertical dots. So if we draw a square with 100 dots on each side, its width will be 5/12 (= 200/640 * 4/3) times its height. Fortunately, it is easy to adjust for this. We just multiply the Cartesian x coordinate by the maximum x value, divide by the maximum y value, and divide by the aspect ratio before converting to screen coordinates:

```
150 ASPECTRATIO = 4/3
8020    NEWPOINTS(XCOORD,POINTNUM) = MAXXRES/2 +
        NEWPOINTS(XCOORD,POINTNUM) * MAXXRES / MAXYRES /
        ASPECTRATIO
```

You may also want to add the following remarks for the sake of clarity:

```
720     GOSUB 8010     'adjust for dot width/convert to
        screen coordinate system
8001 'Adjust for dot width and convert to screen
     coordinate system
```

```
MERGE "3P3
```

If the ratio of width to height on your screen is not 4/3, appropriately change line **150**.

(One note: we could have adjusted the y coordinates instead of the x coordinate. But adjusting the x coordinate has two advantages: (1) all of our shapes are measured in terms of y dots—a constant in both high and medium resolution, and 2) objects drawn in high resolution will be the same size as if drawn in medium resolution.)

Now run the program: everything will be fine.

It is very easy to change to drawing on the medium-resolution screen. We simply change line **410** to

```
410 SCREEN 1
```

and line **140** to

```
140 MAXXRES = 320 : MAXYRES = 200
```

We will use the medium-resolution screen later.

2.4: TRANSLATION

Now that we can draw an object on the screen properly, we can get into animation, which is more exciting. But first we need to learn how to make objects move. We will begin with the simplest type of movement, *translation*. Translation is horizontal and/or vertical displacement. Imagine a ball bouncing from one side of the screen to the other or a car driving across the screen. Each step of these movements is a translation (Figure 2.17).

The equation for translation is very straightforward. Suppose we want to move an object **a** units to the right. Then we need to increase the x coordinate of every point by **a** units. So we simply add **a** to the x coordinate of every point. To move an object **a** units to the left, we decrease the x coordinate by **a** units. Similarly, we increase and decrease the y coordinates to move an object up and down. In other words, to move an object **a** units in the x direction and **b** units in the y direction:

$$(x,y)_{new} = (x_{old} + a, y_{old} + b)$$

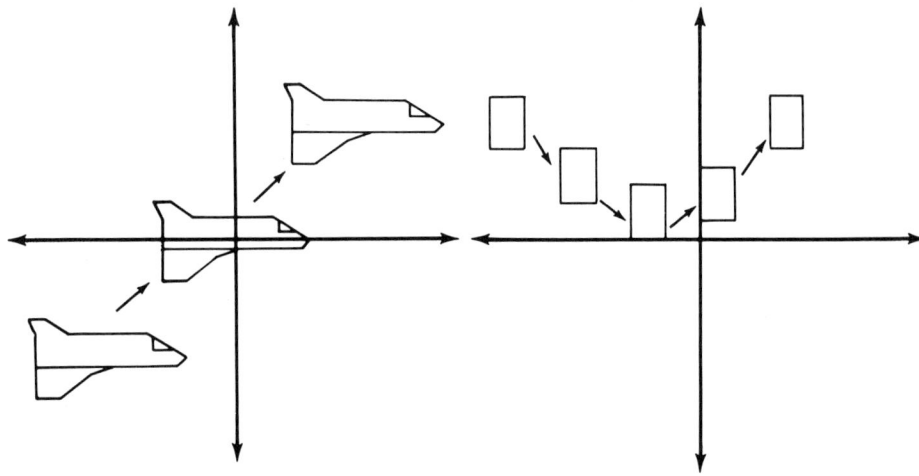

Figure 2.17
Two examples of translation: a shuttle moves across the screen; a box bounces.

So let's add a subroutine to our program to allow translation. First we add:

```
670     GOSUB 6010        'translate

6000 '
6001 'Translation
6002 '
6010 FOR POINTNUM = 1 TO NUMBEROFPOINTS
6020    NEWPOINTS(XCOORD,POINTNUM) = NEWPOINTS(XCOORD,
           POINTNUM) + XTRANSLATION
6030    NEWPOINTS(YCOORD,POINTNUM) = NEWPOINTS(YCOORD,
           POINTNUM) + YTRANSLATION
6040 NEXT
6100 RETURN
```

We also need to figure out **XTRANSLATION** and **YTRANSLATION** (the **a** and **b** just mentioned). Let's start simply. We will translate 15 units to the right and 5 units up:

```
660     GOSUB 6510        'get amount of translation

6500 '
6501 'get amount of translation
6502 '
6510 XTRANSLATION = XTRANSLATION + 15
6520 YTRANSLATION = YTRANSLATION + 5
6600 RETURN
```

```
MERGE "4P1
```

Note that we use a subroutine to find the amount of translation. This allows a lot of flexibility, as we will see later, especially when we deal with moving several objects at once.

Now run the program. The shuttle appears 15 units farther to the right and 5 units farther up. Experiment with taking out lines **660** and **670**, running the program, and then putting them back in, in order to see the difference. (One convenient way to do this is to insert a single quotation (') at the beginning of lines **660** and **670**. This mark makes them comment lines, and the computer will ignore them when the program is run. Then, to restore lines **660** and **670**, simply remove the '.) Because the amount of translation is so small you may want to increase it. For example, make **XTRANSLATION** increase by 100.

One further note: lines **6510** and **6520** add to a variable previously 0. It would be easier to simply set **XTRANSLATION** equal to 15 and **YTRANSLATION** equal to 5. But hold on! In a few paragraphs you will see why.

Animation

Translation is nice, but by itself it lacks excitement. What we need to do is to add *animation* to our program. We will make it so that the shuttle can fly across the screen.

Animation sounds a lot fancier and a lot more difficult than it really is. Instead of moving an object once, we move it several times in as rapid a succession as possible. Unfortunately, because we are using BASIC, *as rapid as possible* is often rather slow, so motion will seem choppy. In Chapter 4 we will make motion seem continuous.

To animate an object, place the main routine—the section of the code that calls up the movement and drawing subroutines (that is, lines **530** through **740**)—within a loop. Then, each time through the loop the translation values will change, and thus the object will move. We also need some way of terminating the program, as we don't want the object to move across (and probably off) the screen forever. So we will use a loop that stops when a Boolean (a variable that is either *true* or *false*), **FINISHED**, goes true. (If you are unfamiliar with Booleans, refer to Appendix A.) We will determine if **FINISHED** is true in a subroutine:

```
130 TRUE = -1 : FALSE = 0
```

38 Two-Dimensional Line Graphics

```
520 WHILE NOT FINISHED
760    GOSUB 10010    'evaluate finished
800 WEND

10000 '
10001 'See if finished
10002 '
10010 COUNTER = COUNTER + 1
10020 IF COUNTER = 10 THEN FINISHED = TRUE
10100 RETURN
```

MERGE "4P2

Lines **520** and **800** create the loop in which the main section is placed. Line **760** calls a subroutine to see if the loop should terminate. In this case our subroutine to evaluate **FINISHED** is very simple. We could make it much more complex, stopping the program if the object is in a certain area, or if, say, it crossed a bomb. Experiment with this later. Right now, let's keep it simple, so that each new technique will be clearly illustrated.

Just as we can change the subroutine that evaluates **FINISHED**, we can change the subroutine that computes translation values to make it much more complex. For example, the program could ask the user for translation values. Or, as we will discuss in a later chapter, the user could move the object about by pressing arrow keys. To be really fancy, the program could figure out translation differently according to the object's position or according to time. For example, try the following:

```
6510 IF COUNTER < 3 THEN XTRANSLATION = XTRANSLATION +
     20
6520 IF (COUNTER >= 3) AND (COUNTER < 6) THEN
     YTRANSLATION = YTRANSLATION - 20
6530 IF COUNTER > 5 THEN XTRANSLATION = XTRANSLATION -
     30 : YTRANSLATION = YTRANSLATION + 15
```

To load these lines, type:

MERGE "4P3

To restore lines **6510** and **6520** (see next paragraph), you can:

MERGE "4P1

After running this program, delete **6530** and restore **6510** and **6520** to their previous equations.

As we add more and more types of shape manipulations we will be able to make very complicated animated sequences. But you can probably already see that even with translation alone we can make an arcade game.

Relative and Absolute Translation

A quick note about terminology: there are two ways to specify the translation of an object. One is to supply the change in position relative to an absolute position—the object's initial position—as we just have. This is called *absolute translation*. Another method is *relative translation*, in which translation is specified relative to the object's current position. It is easy to convert from relative to absolute translation, and vice versa. In general, we will be using absolute translation.

2.5: SCALING

Now we are going to learn another simple type of object manipulation, *scaling*. Scaling means taking an object and stretching it—making it longer or shorter along its axes. For example, to get a little shuttle we could scale down our shuttle data; to get a big shuttle we could scale it up (Figure 2.18).

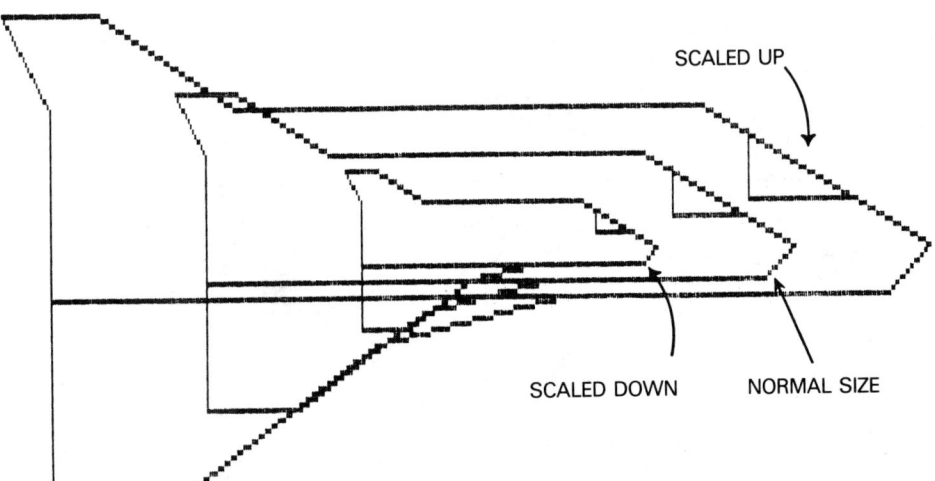

Figure 2.18
A normal sized, scaled up, and scaled down shuttle.

To scale an object, we simply multiply the x and y coordinates by a scaling factor. The scaling factor for the x coordinate can be different from that for the y coordinate. If it is different the object will be distorted. It will look stretched rather than shrunk or expanded. The formula is:

$(x,y)_{new} = (x_{old} * xscale, y_{old} * yscale)$

This is where choosing the center becomes important. Objects are expanded (or contracted) about the origin. Thus the origin is the only point remaining unchanged. This concept is easier to understand by looking at a drawing. Figure 2.19 (part a) shows a square centered about the origin and then scaled up by a factor of 2. Part b of this figure shows the same square, not centered about the origin, scaled by a factor of 2. Note how the coordinates of the square have changed after scaling. Scaling an object that is not centered about the origin is the same as scaling it about the origin and then translating it. So it can be difficult to figure out where the object ends up. This is especially troublesome if we want to translate it later. For this reason, if we want to scale and translate an object, we scale it first and then translate it.

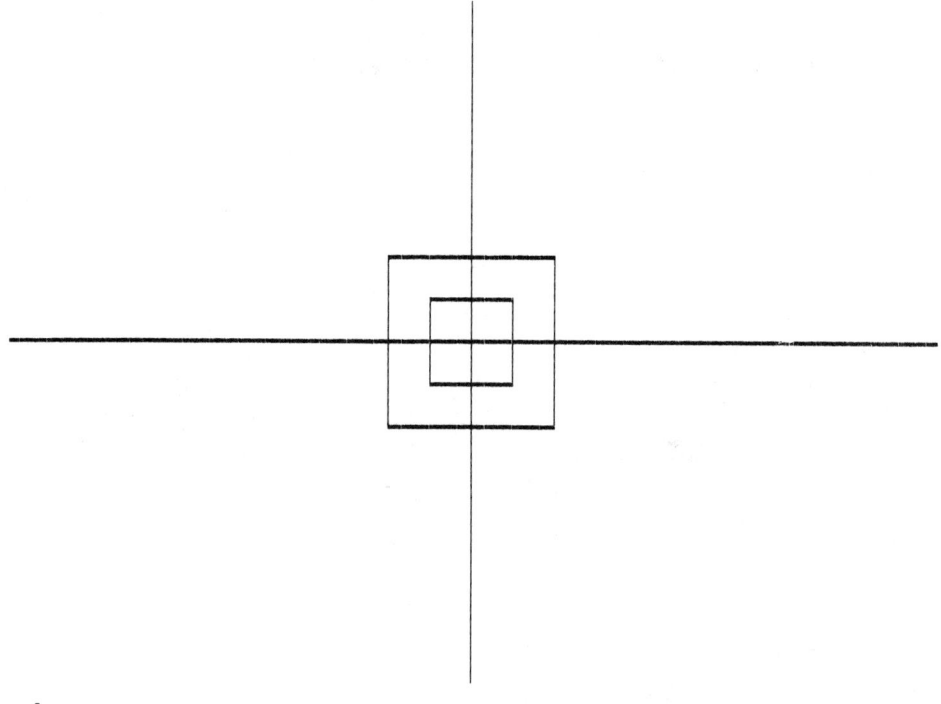

A.

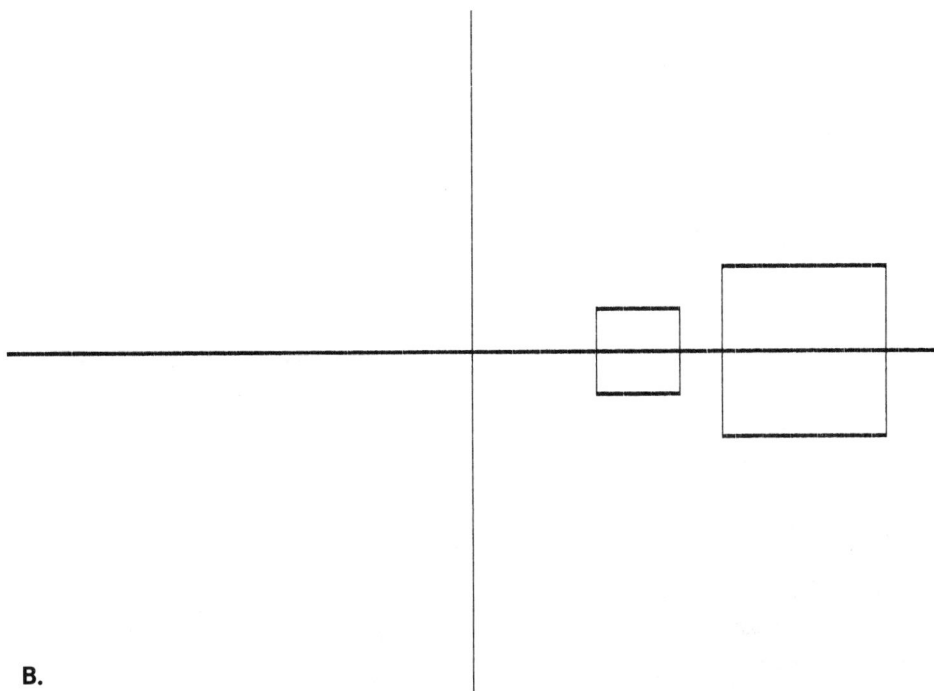

B.

Figure 2.19
Part a shows a square, centered about the origin, then scaled up by a factor of 2. Part b shows the same square, centered off the origin, scaled by a factor of 2. Note how the scaled square's center is different from that of the original square.

To incorporate scaling into our program, add the following:

```
550     GOSUB 3510          'get amount of scaling
560     GOSUB 3010          'scale

3000 '
3001 'Scale
3002 '
3010 FOR POINTNUM = 1 TO NUMBEROFPOINTS
3020    NEWPOINTS(XCOORD,POINTNUM) = NEWPOINTS(XCOORD,
        POINTNUM) * XSCALE
3030    NEWPOINTS(YCOORD,POINTNUM) = NEWPOINTS(YCOORD,
        POINTNUM) * YSCALE
3040 NEXT
3100 RETURN

3500 '
3501 'get scaling amount
```

```
3502 '
3510 XSCALE = XSCALE + .2
3520 YSCALE = XSCALE
3600 RETURN
```

> **MERGE "5**

Before running, remove lines **660** and **670**.

The subroutine for getting the x- and y-scaling values can be anything, just as it could be for translation. Experiment with using different algorithms. For example, to show stretching, make the following changes:

```
3510 XSCALE = XSCALE + .2
3520 YSCALE = YSCALE + .5
```

Now run it.

Before continuing, put lines **660** and **670** back in. You may want to make the subroutine for calculating translation the first one used—the one that increased x translation by 15 and y translation by 5 each time—and make line **3520** what it used to be.

2.6: OBJECT SPEED

Whenever we are animating an object, we are concerned not only with the movement of the object, but the rate at which the object moves. This rate is the object's *speed*. Any moving object has a speed associated with it. If we are trying to mimic the motion of an object, we have to be able to mimic its speed. There are two ways to do this. One way is to move the object a little bit and then pause for a variable number of time units before moving again. The other way is to change the amount of movement as speed changes.

If we want to use the first method, we could add the following line:

```
750 FOR DELAY = 1 TO SPEED : NEXT
```

If the speed is to increase, then **SPEED** should be decreased. For a decrease in speed, increase **SPEED**.

In general, however, this is not a good way to take care of speed. Programs are slow enough, especially in BASIC, that any further slowing down is more than unnecessary. You have seen this from the program we have been using so far. And, if we are moving more than one object, such a routine is pretty much useless.

The second way, changing the amount of translation, is much better. To make an object appear to travel slowly, use a small change in translation. To make it travel quickly, use a large change in translation.

Let's experiment with speed. First we'll save our program:

SAVE "2DLG

Now, let's make the following changes:
(if you haven't removed line **750** remove it now)

```
6510 XTRANSLATION = -80 + 4 * COUNTER ^ 2
6520 YTRANSLATION = XTRANSLATION - 20
```

Remove lines **550** and **560** and, if it is there, **6530**.

Run the program. As time goes on, the shuttle moves faster and faster.

Acceleration

The rate at which speed changes is called *acceleration*. In the above routine, acceleration is constant (the derivative of the equation in **6510** is linear). By changing the type of equation controlling an object's motion, we can make the object accelerate or decelerate.

Z Speed

Now, replace lines **550** and **560**, and temporarily remove lines **660** and **670**. Make line **3510** the following:

3510 XSCALE = XSCALE + .5

Run the program. It is pretty much the same as when scaling was introduced. But now imagine that the shuttle is flying towards you, as indicated by the increase in its size. The rate of change of scale, causing a change of size, can be used to make an object look like it is getting closer to or farther from the viewer. Changing the scale linearly makes the object move toward the viewer at constant velocity. Increasing at a faster than linear rate will make it accelerate toward the user.

Before continuing, reload **2DLG**.

2.7: COLOR

So far we have been drawing on the high-resolution screen; thus, all of our pictures are in black and white. As mentioned before, in medium resolution we have the option of drawing in four colors. Although resolution is sacrificed, it is usually prettier and more informative to draw objects with more than one color. We will now see how to do this.

The **LINE** command has an entry for color:

LINE [(x_1,y_1)] — (x_2,y_2) [, color]

color is a number ranging from 0 to 1 in high resolution and 0 to 3 in medium resolution. In high resolution, 0 means black, 1 means white. In medium resolution, **color** corresponds to the colors from the palette selected, as discussed in Section 1.2.

In high resolution we have been describing lines only by their end points. Now we must store a color for each line. To do this we add a dimension to **LINES** in which to store the color. Then, we retrieve the color for each line in the drawing subroutine. We also must add code to read in the new color values and make the appropriate changes to use the medium-resolution screen.

Before we add the code, let's use the shuttle example and make a table of the colors we want each line to be. We add another entry to our point-line data table (Figure 2.10), to get Figure 2.20.

Now we add the code. The color data appear in line **20050**:

```
20 DIM POINTS(2,100), NEWPOINTS(2,100), LINES(3,100)

120 FROM = 1 : TO. = 2 : COLOR. = 3
140 MAXXRES = 320 : MAXYRES = 200

370 FOR LINENUM = 1 TO NUMBEROFLINES     'read colors
380   READ LINES(COLOR.,LINENUM)
390 NEXT

410 SCREEN 1          'medium resolution
430 'use COLOR n to set background color
440 'use COLOR ,n to select different palette

3510 XSCALE = XSCALE + .1
3520 YSCALE = XSCALE

9020   LINE (NEWPOINTS(XCOORD,LINES(FROM,LINENUM)),
            NEWPOINTS(YCOORD,LINES(FROM,LINENUM))) -
```

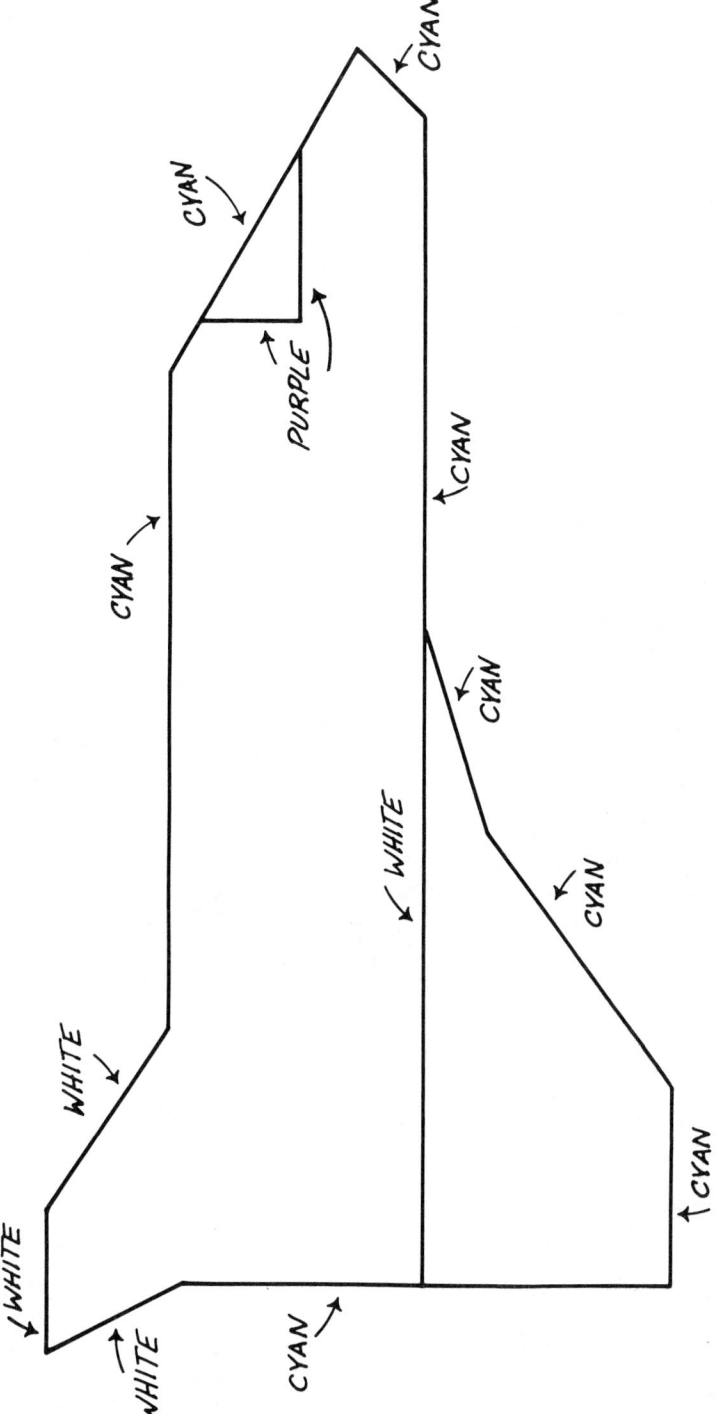

Figure 2.20
Decide what colors to make the shuttle's lines. Then make a table of these values.

```
            (NEWPOINTS(XCOORD,LINES(TO.,LINENUM)),
            NEWPOINTS(YCOORD,LINES(TO.,LINENUM))), LINES(
            COLOR.,LINENUM)
20050 DATA 1, 1, 3, 3, 3, 1, 1, 1, 1, 1, 1, 3, 2, 2
```

MERGE "7

Line **20** makes **LINES** three dimensional. Line **120** adds the constant **COLOR.**. Lines **140** and **410 — 440** are for medium resolution.

Now run the program.

Of course, this is a simple demonstration of color. Colored lines can make beautiful kaleidoscopes and fancy graphs and can add much to arcade games and structural models. Experiment with these on your own.

2.8: GRAPHICS DEFINITION LANGUAGE

So far it has been fairly easy to create, manipulate and display shapes. Despite the abundance of subroutines, the mathematics has been straightforward, and with some imagination you can figure new transformations of objects, as well as applications for what you have learned.

A major problem, however, has been speed. The *graphics definition language (GDL)* is the IBM PC's answer to this problem. This language consists of a set of simple commands that allow us to do most basic manipulations of two-dimensional figures, and to do them quickly. The messy math and subroutines are taken care of by BASIC.

Use of GDL centers around the **DRAW** command. A whole set of commands are used in conjunction with **DRAW**. The format of **DRAW** is simple:

DRAW "commands"

where **commands** is a string of valid GDL commands.

The Basic Movements

There are many different commands in GDL. The first and most basic command is the **M** command. Its format is:

M [+/−]x, [+/−]y

M is the move command. To start, assume the **+/−** option isn't being used. **M** draws a line from the last point drawn to **(x,y)**, where **(x,y)** is in the screen coordinate system. If **M** is the first command done after a **CLS** (or the very first GDL command executed), then a line is drawn from the center of the screen to **(x,y)**. Remember, in high resolution the center is (320,100), and in medium resolution it is (160,100). Let's try a quick example: (Note that we still follow the normal procedure for initializing the graphic screen.)

```
10 SCREEN 2
20 CLS
30 DRAW "M 320,50 M 400,50 M 400,100 M 320,100"
40 END
```

LOAD "8P1

Note how we used the draw command. We typed in a set of commands within double quotes. Also note that we can type a sequence of commands within the quotes. We don't need a separate **DRAW** for each command. Although commands don't need to be separated by spaces, it is much easier to read a command line if they are.

We have been using absolute movement. The **+/−** option specifies relative movement. In other words, suppose the last point drawn was (100,100). Then:

DRAW "M +20,−30"

will draw a line to (120,70).

We can't mix absolute and relative addressing. The type of addressing used for the first coordinate holds for the line.

There are eight other movement commands in addition to **M**, all in the form:

Command n

where **Command** is the command, and **n** is the number of units to move. Note that **n** must be an integer, or an **Illegal function call** error will occur.

48 Two-Dimensional Line Graphics

The other movement commands are:

Command	Movement direction
U	up
D	down
L	left
R	right
E	diagonally up and right
F	diagonally down and right
G	diagonally down and left
H	diagonally up and left

These movements are always relative to the last point drawn. As with **M**, if any of these are the first command executed after a **CLS** or the first GDL command executed, then movement is relative to the screen's center.

Let's try a program:

```
10 SCREEN 2
20 CLS
30 DRAW "U 20 R 48 D 20 L 48"
40 END
```

```
LOAD "8P2
```

This program highlights an inconvenience of the graphics definition language. So far we have been finding the points for objects in the Cartesian system and having the program take into account dot width. The GDL doesn't do this so we have to make the conversion ourselves. To draw a square, the horizontal sides must be $12/5$ths the size of the verticals in high resolution and $6/5$ths the size in medium resolution. (See Section 2.3 if you don't remember why.)

The Prefixes N and B

Now let's learn two commands that can be prefixes to any of the eight movement commands just introduced. These are the **B** and **N** commands. **B** is quite useful. When **B** precedes any command, the movement is made, but the line isn't drawn.

In other words, suppose we want to draw two parallel lines. We could do the following:

```
10 SCREEN 2
20 CLS
30 DRAW "U 20 BR 48 D 20"
40 END
```

LOAD "8P3

A line is drawn going 20 dots up. The cursor then moves right 48 dots without drawing, and finally a 20 dot line is drawn going down. As you will soon see, this command is even more useful when we draw several objects.

The **N** command, like the **B** command, precedes the movement commands. When it does so, the antecedent command is executed, but the cursor returns to its initial position. Suppose the last point drawn were (100,100). Then if we type:

DRAW "NU 20 M 20,20"

a line will be drawn from (100,100) to (100,80) and then from (100,100) to (20,20).

The following program uses **N** to draw a cross:

```
10 SCREEN 2
20 CLS
30 DRAW "NU 10 ND 10 NL 10 NR 10"
40 END
```

LOAD "8P4

Scaling and Translation—The Use of Variables

One nice feature of GDL is that instead of typing in numbers for distances, we can use variables. Two immediate uses of variables are for translating and stretching objects. The variables storing values can be either numeric or string. For numeric variables, we use the following format:

DRAW "Command = NumericVariable;"

50   Two-Dimensional Line Graphics

For string variables we omit the = :

DRAW "Command StringVariable;"

Now we will use variables to do translation:

```
10 SCREEN 2
20 KEY OFF
30 FOR COUNTER = 1 TO 10
40    XTRANSLATION = COUNTER * 10
50    CLS
60    DRAW "BR = XTRANSLATION; U 20 R 48 D 20 L 48"
70 NEXT
80 END
```

LOAD "8P5

Now we will use variables to stretch a rectangle:

```
10 SCREEN 2
20 KEY OFF
30 FOR COUNTER = 1 TO 20
40    HEIGHT = COUNTER * 5
50    WIDTH. = 20
60    CLS
70    DRAW "U = HEIGHT; R = WIDTH.; D = HEIGHT; L = WIDTH.;"
80 NEXT
90 END
```

LOAD "8P6

To scale a square we could make this change:

```
50    WIDTH. = HEIGHT * 12/5 '12/5 adjusts for dot width
```

Complex Shapes—The Shuttle

Another nice feature of GDL, if you haven't already guessed, is that we can continue commands over several lines. For example, the following is perfectly valid:

```
10 SCREEN 2
20 CLS
30 DRAW "M -30,-8 L 60 M -9,-5 L 21 M +6,+5 D 21 R 18 M
   +22,-8 M +24,-2 R 42"
40 DRAW "M +6,-3 BM -10,-3 L 14 U 5 BM -24,+11 L 66"
50 END
```

> LOAD "8P7

This object should look familiar. But note how much harder it is to figure out what the shape is from looking at the data. It is even harder to figure out the data from the shape. You should try converting the shuttle to GDL statements. Compare it to the above. (If your version differs, have you remembered to take into account dot width?)

The Real Power: X

The most powerful command of GDL is **X**, the execute command. Its format is:

X string

where **string** is a string variable containing a series of GDL commands. Not only does **X** make programs more readable, but it makes complex programs much simpler and more concise.

As an introductory example, suppose we want to draw two shuttles. Instead of typing in the shuttle data twice, we could use the following program:

```
10 SCREEN 2
20 CLS
30 SHUTTLE$ = "M -30,-8 L 60 M -9,-5 L 21 M +6,+5 D 21
   R 18 M +22,-8 M +24,-2 R 42 M +6,-3 BM -10,-3 L 14 U
   5 BM -24,+11 L 66"
40 DRAW "X SHUTTLE$; BR 280 X SHUTTLE$;"
50 END
```

> LOAD "8P8

52 Two-Dimensional Line Graphics

Because **SHUTTLE$** is a string, we don't use equal signs. Also note the use of **B**.

We can even nest **X** strings. For example:

TWOSHUTTLE$ = "X SHUTTLE$; BR 280 X SHUTTLE$;"

is a perfectly valid argument for **X**.

Scaling Revisited—The S Command

Previously, we showed scaling by using variables. Another method is to use GDL's own scaling command, **S**. Its format is:

S n

where **n** is an integer between 1 and 255 and represents 4 times the desired scaling. As you can guess, the default is 4. When **S** is placed in a line, any of the values plotted in commands following it are multiplied by **n/4**. An example appears in the next program.

A Speed Comparison

Let's put together the commands we have just learned to write a program that animates the shuttle, scaling and translating it along each step. This program will mimic almost exactly the program we wrote in the previous sections of this chapter. Pay particular attention to the difference in program length, and more importantly, the difference in speed.

```
10 SCREEN 2
20 KEY OFF
30 SHUTTLE$ = "M -30,-8 L 60 M -9,-5 L 21 M +6,+5 D 21
   R 18 M +22,-8 M +24,-2 R 42 M +6,-3 BM -10,-3 L 14 U
   5 BM -24,+11 L 66"
40 FOR COUNTER = 1 TO 10
50    XTRANSLATION = XTRANSLATION + COUNTER * 8
60    YTRANSLATION = COUNTER * 3
70    CLS
80    DRAW "BR = XTRANSLATION; BU = YTRANSLATION; S =
      COUNTER; X SHUTTLE$;"
90 NEXT
100 END
```

> **LOAD "8P9**

The difference in speed is impressive! (In fact, if you have BASIC 2.0, add:

```
510 STARTTIME = TIMER
810 PRINT "It took ";TIMER - STARTTIME;" seconds to
    run."
```

to **2DLG**, and

```
35 STARTTIME = TIMER
95 PRINT "It took ";TIMER - STARTTIME;" seconds to
    run."
```

to the program. You will find that **2DLG** took over 20 seconds to run; the latter program under 2 seconds!)

One More Command—Color

Several other commands exist in GDL. The only one we will deal with now is **C**—the color command. The antecedent to **C** is a number representing the color in the standard format for color: 0–3 is valid in medium resolution, and 0 or 1 in high resolution. All lines drawn following the **C** command will be in the color specified. Try this on your own.

A Final Example

Let's move two objects at once:

```
10 SCREEN 2
20 KEY OFF
30 SHUTTLE$ = "M -30,-8 L 60 M -9,-5 L 21 M +6,+5 D 21
   R 18 M +22,-8 M +24,-2 R 42 M +6,-3 BM -10,-3 L 14 U
   5 BM -24,+11 L 66"
40 FOR COUNTER = 1 TO 10
50    SHIP1X = COUNTER * 20 : SHIP2X = COUNTER * 10 + 50
60    CLS
70    DRAW "BR = SHIP1X; S 4 X SHUTTLE$;"
80    DRAW "BR = SHIP2X; BU 60 S 6 X SHUTTLE$;"
90 NEXT
100 END
```

> **LOAD "8P10**

3

Three-Dimensional Line Graphics

In this chapter we'll add depth to line graphics. This dimension will allow us to represent almost any real world object. Three-dimensional line graphics are very powerful. Their ability to communicate form gives them many applications, in fields such as architecture, chemistry, education, and engineering, to name a few.

We'll add new and exciting three-dimensional manipulations to our line graphics program.

3.1: DATA STRUCTURE

Converting a three-dimensional object to point-line data is similar to converting a two-dimensional object. Now we deal with another dimension—depth.

This time we will describe our objects with the three-dimensional Cartesian coordinate system (Figure 3.1). Instead of being represented by ordered pairs, points are represented by ordered triplets. Suppose we have a point 2 units to the right of the origin, 3 units above it, and 4 units out of the page (toward you, taking the origin as lying in the page). Then we call this point (2,3,4). A point going into the page 4 units, with the same x and y coordinates, would be represented by (2,3,−4). The third coordinate is called the z coordinate.

The process of creating point-line data is just the same as for two-dimensional objects: we break the object up into sets of lines, label the end points and make a table of their coordinates, then label the lines and make

56 Three-Dimensional Line Graphics

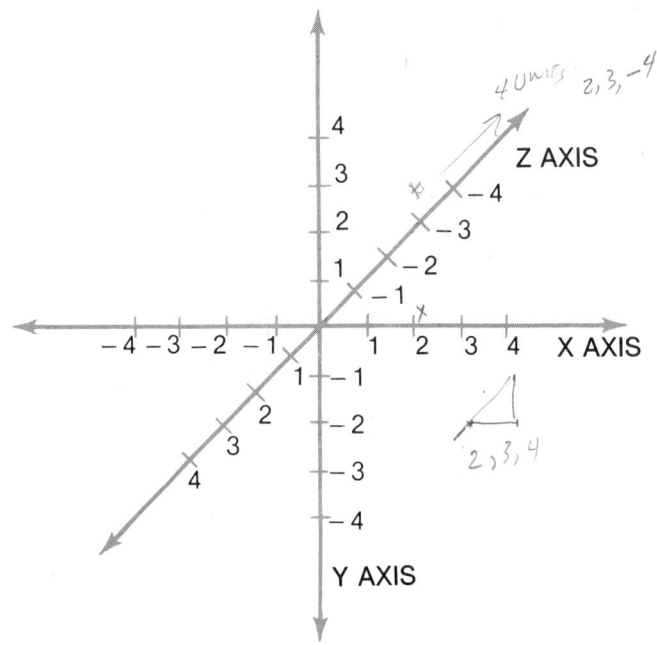

Figure 3.1
The three-dimensional Cartesian coordinate system.

a table of their end points. The only difference is that points have three coordinates. Storing data in the computer is also just the same; only **POINTS** needs to be a three-dimensional array.

Nonetheless, finding the coordinates of the end points and figuring how lines connect is much more difficult in three dimensions. It is hard to visualize what the object looks like, and angled shapes are especially difficult to break down. (You must use some crazy trigonometry or simplify such shapes. With luck, the coordinates may have been figured out before. For example, research institutions and crystallography magazines can be a great source for point-line data of molecules.)

An Example—The Cube

Perhaps the simplest object to describe is a cube (Figure 3.2). For more complex objects we may need to make drawings from several angles, but for a cube a perspective drawing is good enough. Place this drawing on three-dimensional coordinate axes with its center at the origin (Figure 3.3). What is the coordinate of the upper right forward point? It's 20 units to the right of the origin, 20 units up from the origin, and 20 units out of the page. So its coordinates are (20,20,20). Continuing in this manner we get all of the coordinates. Then we label the points (Figure 3.4).

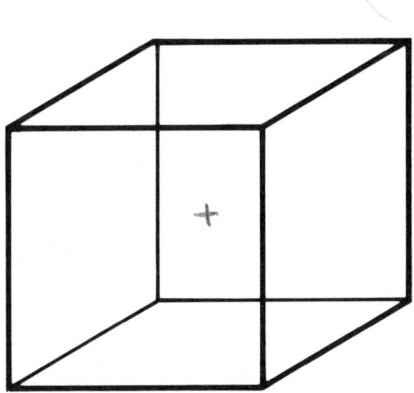

Figure 3.2
The cube.

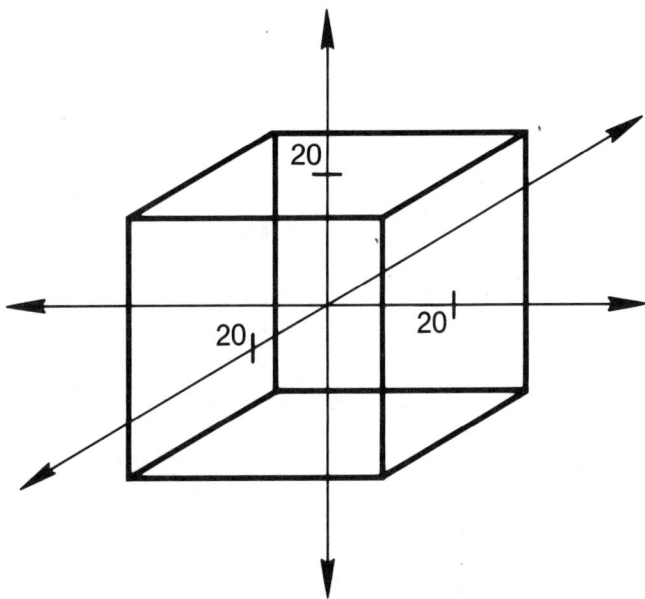

Figure 3.3
Place the object on coordinate axes.

58 Three-Dimensional Line Graphics

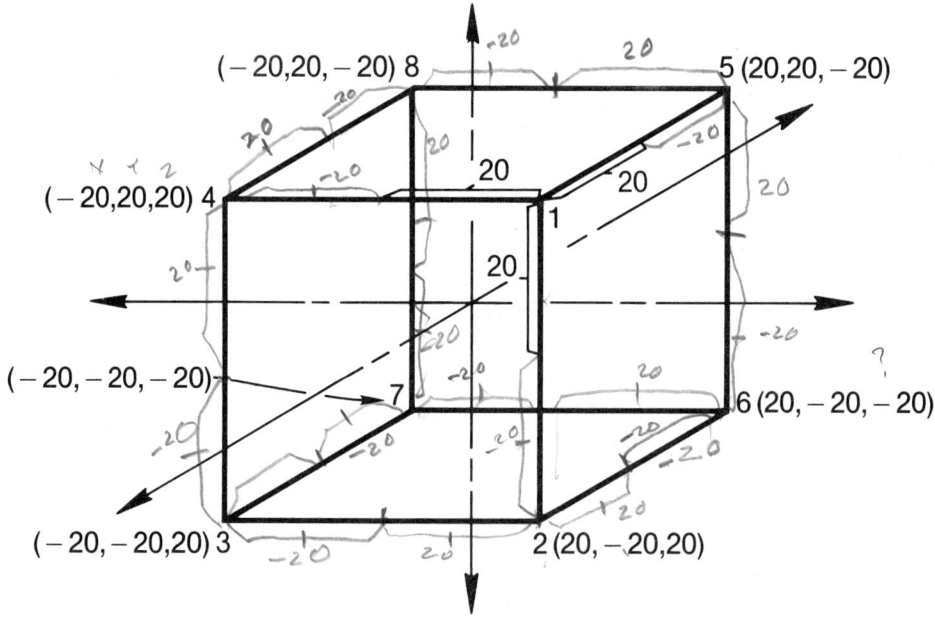

Figure 3.4
Find the coordinates and label the points.

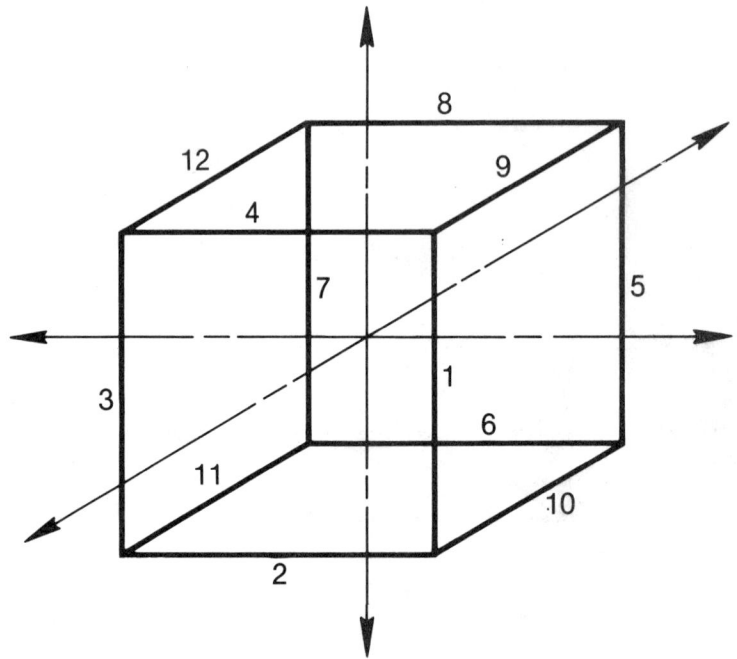

Figure 3.5
Label the lines.

Now label all of the lines (Figure 3.5). Remember, there is a total of 12 lines. Form a table of the points and lines (Figure 3.6).

POINT	COORDINATES
1	(20,20,20)
2	(20,−20,20)
3	(−20,−20,20)
4	(−20,20,20)
5	(20,20,−20)
6	(20,−20,20)
7	(−20,−20,−20)
8	(−20,20,−20)

LINE	END POINTS
1	1,2
2	2,3
3	3,4
4	4,1
5	5,6
6	6,7
7	7,8
8	8,5
9	1,5
10	2,6
11	3,7
12	4,8

Figure 3.6
Make a table of the point-line data.

Making The Program Three Dimensional

Let's modify our program to make it draw the cube. All we have to do is make **POINTS** three dimensional, read in the z coordinate, and use three-dimensional data. Load **2DLG**, then add:

```
20 DIM POINTS(3,100), NEWPOINTS(3,100), LINES(2,100)

110 XCOORD = 1 : YCOORD = 2 : ZCOORD = 3

320    READ POINTS(XCOORD,POINTNUM), POINTS(YCOORD,
       POINTNUM), POINTS(ZCOORD,POINTNUM)
```

```
20010 '3-D Cube
20020 DATA 8, 12
20030 DATA   20, 20, 20,    20, -20, 20,    -20, -20, 20,
           -20, 20, 20,    20, 20, -20,    20, -20, -20,
           -20, -20, -20,   -20, 20,-20
20040 DATA     1, 2,    2, 3,    3, 4,    4, 1,
              5, 6,    6, 7,    7, 8,    8, 5,    1, 5,    2,
              6,    3, 7,    4, 8
```

Finally, we make the routine that copies **POINTS** into **NEWPOINTS** operate in three dimensions:

```
1040    NEWPOINTS(ZCOORD,POINTNUM) = POINTS(ZCOORD,
        POINTNUM)
1050 NEXT
```

The programs in Chapter 3 are contained in the **CHAPTER3** directory. So the first thing to type is:

CHDIR "
CHDIR "CHAPTER3

You may wish to review the disk notes in Section 2.2 regarding loading files from a chapter's directory, and saving files while within a chapter's directory.

To load this section's program, type:

MERGE "1

Complex Shapes

It can be very difficult to break complex shapes into three-dimensional point-line data. You may need to draw several views of the object. Then, using trigonometry and geometry, you determine one coordinate (for example, the x) of some points from one view, the other coordinates from others. It is a long and tiring process.

3.2: TRANSLATION

Updating our program to translate in three dimensions is quite easy. Before, our coordinate system consisted of the x and y axes, and translation was a combination of a movement along the x axis with a movement along the y axis. Now we also have the z axis to consider. Suppose we want to move the object out of the screen—toward the viewer—by a distance **c**. We add **c** to the z coordinates of all the object's points. If we want to move the object into the page—away from the viewer—by a distance **c**, we subtract **c** from all of the points. So, our formula for translation becomes:

$(x,y,z)_{new} = (x_{old} + \text{xtranslation}, y_{old} + \text{ytranslation}, z_{old} + \text{ztranslation})$

Let's change our program so that it uses this formula instead of the two-dimensional translation formula. It is simple; just add a line to compute the new z coordinate:

```
6040    NEWPOINTS(ZCOORD,POINTNUM) = NEWPOINTS(ZCOORD,
        POINTNUM) + ZTRANSLATION
6050 NEXT
```

> **MERGE "2P1**

Let's try this. First, we'll make sure that the program translates in two dimensions properly. Our subroutine to get translation values is already set up for this, so just let it run. It works. A square translates across the screen. (Square? Thought it was a cube!)

Now let's try translating in the z direction. Add:

```
3510 XSCALE = 1
3520 YSCALE = 1

6510 XTRANSLATION = 0
6520 YTRANSLATION = 0
6530 ZTRANSLATION = ZTRANSLATION + 20
```

(Lines **3510** and **3520** are added to make the only changes be due to z translation.)

> **MERGE "2P2**

Run the program . . . hmmm, try it again. Nothing seems to happen. The square just stays put. And it doesn't look three dimensional at all. (Some

62 Three-Dimensional Line Graphics

of you may guess that we need to put the z coordinate in the line-drawing routine. Well, a z coordinate cannot be added to the line routine because the screen is only two dimensional. It looks like we are stuck.)

3.3: PERSPECTIVE

Halt. Don't press that Ctrl-Alt-Delete key! We haven't been able to draw three dimensionally yet, but a solution is at hand. So far we have been plotting only the x and y coordinates of the object. Translating in the z direction hasn't changed these, so of course z translation doesn't show up. If we can find a way so that the z coordinate makes a difference, then we are in business.

To do this we'll rely on an old trick of vision psychology. Look at the picture in Figure 3.7. Which house is closer? Number one of course! And does the road go off into the distance? Sure it does. What we are seeing is the effect of *linear perspective*, one of the most important psychological depth cues. Perspective is the decrease of image size as an object gets farther away. So the phone poles in Figure 3.7 get smaller. Airplanes look tiny when they are high up. Mountains get bigger as they get closer. When we see an object getting bigger, we assume it is getting closer. Now all we need is a way to add perspective to our program.

If you want to avoid some math, skip ahead and add the perspective routine, found at the end of this section. Otherwise, read on, and we will

Figure 3.7
An example of linear perspective. Note how the road and poles go off into the distance, and that house 1 seems closer than house 2.

mathematically derive the perspective algorithm. This process will be helpful not only in Chapter 5, but any time you want to develop new graphics algorithms.

The first thing we need to do is sketch a picture of the geometry of looking at an object in three space (Figure 3.8). If we want to show three-dimensional figures, we need to mimic this with the computer. So let's suppose the object doesn't really exist; but rather suppose we are observing it on the monitor. What would we see? We'd get something like Figure 3.9.

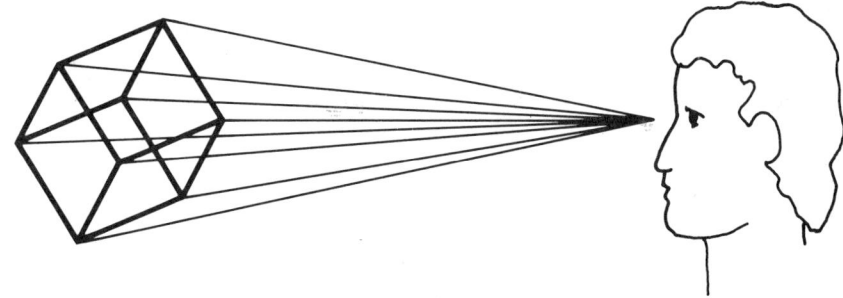

Figure 3.8
The geometry of looking at an object in three space.

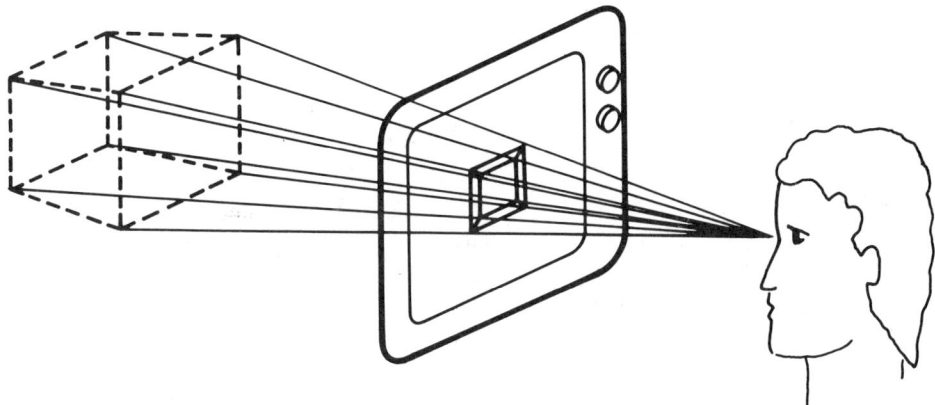

Figure 3.9
Looking at the cube on the computer monitor.

As viewers we're looking at the image of the cube as it is projected on the *focal plane* of the computer monitor. Thus, the size of the object, that is, the location of its end points, changes depending upon how far away it is. Objects in front of the focal plane are bigger than in real life (just like projecting a shadow), while objects behind the focal plane are smaller.

64 Three-Dimensional Line Graphics

We now need a formula to describe the change of coordinates caused by perspective as a function of the z coordinate. Figure 3.10, a top down flat picture of Figure 3.9, illustrates this. The point **a** is an end point of an object floating in three space; **a'** is the projection of **a** onto the focal plane. That is, **a'** is the point we want to draw to make the viewer think he is seeing **a**. So we need to figure out the coordinates of **a'**. To do this we need to make one assumption—that the viewer usually sits in the same spot. (Actually, this does not matter. It's just that the perspective change will be proper for the distance involved only when the viewer is at the spot assumed. Perspective will be just as effective from any other position, and really, as you will see from experimenting, won't make too much of a difference.) This assumption is fairly realistic. We will call this distance from the monitor **focal distance**, as labeled in Figure 3.11. Note that we have also indicated the x and z coordinates of **a** and **a'**.

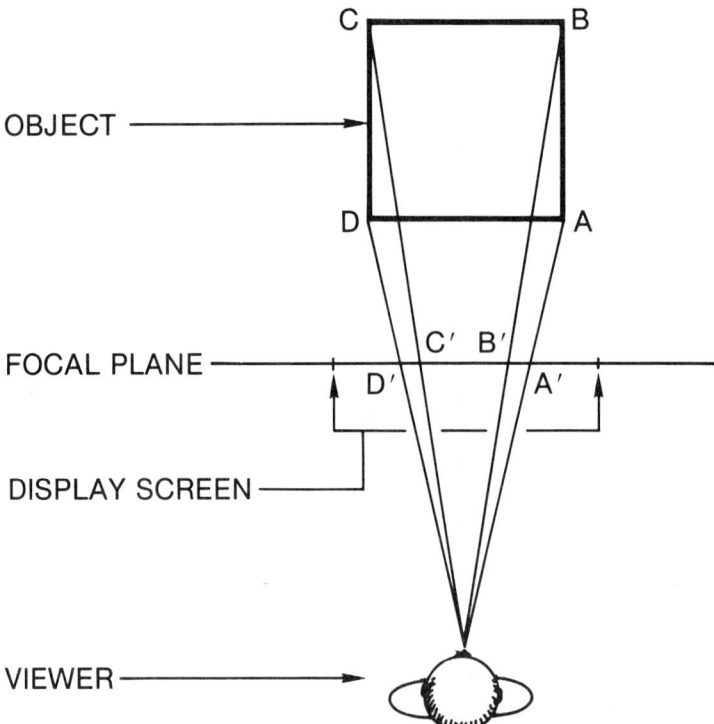

Figure 3.10
A top down view of looking at an object in three space through the focal plane of the computer monitor.

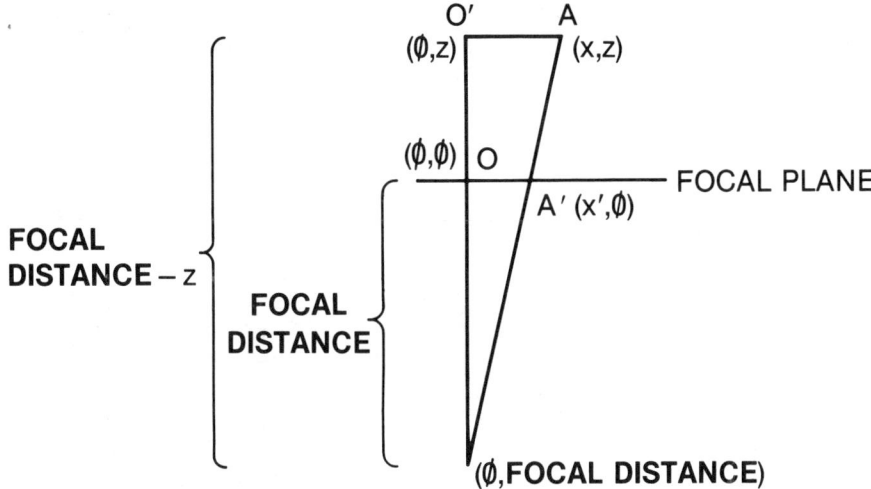

Figure 3.11
The viewer, at (0, focal distance), looks at part of the cube, (x,z), through the focal plane of the monitor. The point appears on the monitor as (x',0).

Now comes the mathematical part. By similar triangles, the ratio of **x/(focal distance − z)** is the same as **x'/focal distance**. (If you don't remember geometry, think of it this way: the angle formed by **o'**, the viewer, and **a** is the same as that formed by the origin, the viewer, and **a'**. So the tangent of this angle is the same no matter from which triangle it is determined. Tangent is just **y/x**. So **x/(focal distance − z) = x'/focal distance**.)

Solving this for **x'** yields:

x' = focal distance ∗ x / (focal distance − z)

By symmetry (that is, changing the x axis to the y axis and noticing that the drawing doesn't change), we find that the new y coordinate, **y'**, is:

y' = focal distance ∗ y / (focal distance − z)

The Perspective Routine

In our program we will always do perspective after all object movements and before converting to screen coordinates and adjusting for dot width. The routines after perspective only operate on the x and y coordinates. So

66 Three-Dimensional Line Graphics

after perspective we can ignore the z coordinate. Let's add a routine to do perspective:

```
160 FOCALDISTANCE = 400

710     GOSUB 7010        'perspective

7000 '
7001 'Perspective
7002 '
7010 FOR POINTNUM = 1 TO NUMBEROFPOINTS
7020    NEWPOINTS(XCOORD,POINTNUM) = FOCALDISTANCE *
        NEWPOINTS(XCOORD,POINTNUM)/(FOCALDISTANCE -
        NEWPOINTS(ZCOORD,POINTNUM))
7030    NEWPOINTS(YCOORD,POINTNUM) = FOCALDISTANCE *
        NEWPOINTS(YCOORD,POINTNUM)/(FOCALDISTANCE -
        NEWPOINTS(ZCOORD,POINTNUM))
7040 NEXT
7100 RETURN
```

> **MERGE "3**

Note that this routine just changes the x and y coordinates and leaves z alone. Also note that line **160** sets the focal distance.

Trying It Out—Translation Revisited

Now let's check our perspective routine. Just run the program—and watch the cube get closer. (Note: the object is now a cube.) Now change line **6530** so that the cube recedes into the distance. (That is, make z translation decrease each time.)

Experimentation—Changing the Focal Distance

Now try changing **FOCALDISTANCE**. Start off by making it much larger. For example, try 5,000. Then work back down to 400. Work the focal distance down even more, to around 50 or so. You will see a marked difference. The larger the focal distance, the less the effect of perspective. (Or rather, an object must be much closer to get the same effect.)

Each time you change focal distance, be sure to have the cube go through various z distances. You may want to do this:

```
6530 ZTRANSLATION = 1000 - 200 * COUNTER
```

Also, observe the effect of translating in the x and y direction.

Computing the Focal Distance

Although one way of choosing the focal distance is to experiment with a variety of values and choose the one that looks best, it is possible to calculate what it theoretically should be. Of course, if this value doesn't look good, choose another.

As mentioned before, focal distance should be the distance from the viewer to the screen, in the units we use to define our shapes, that is, vertical dots. To compute this, divide the height of your monitor by the number of vertical dots, yielding the size of a vertical dot. Now measure the normal viewing distance between you and your monitor. Divide this by the vertical dot size. In other words:

focal distance = viewing distance / (screen height / maxyres)

As an example, the height of my screen is 0.16 meters. I sit about 0.9 meters away from the screen. So I should use a focal distance of about 1,100. I like a stronger sense of perspective than this gives, however, so I use 400. It's a matter of taste.

3.4: SCALING

Now that we can draw in perspective, we are ready to continue with object manipulations. Before we learn new ones, we'll see how to scale in three dimensions. As with translation, upgrading from two dimensions is very simple. All we have to do is allow for a z-scaling factor.

We add:

```
3040   NEWPOINTS(ZCOORD,POINTNUM) = NEWPOINTS(ZCOORD,
       POINTNUM) * ZSCALE
3050 NEXT
```

Let's try this. You should realize x and y scaling will still work fine. So we'll isolate z scaling:

```
3510 XSCALE = 2
3520 YSCALE = 3
3530 ZSCALE = COUNTER
```

68 Three-Dimensional Line Graphics

```
6510 XTRANSLATION = 0
6520 YTRANSLATION = 0
6530 ZTRANSLATION = 0
```

MERGE "4

Run it. As you can see (with the help of perspective), the object, now a rectangular parallelpiped, is being scaled in the z direction.

3.5: ROTATION

So far we have seen how to do in three dimensions all of the object manipulations we learned in the last chapter. Now it's time to learn a new and very important manipulation—*rotation*. Rotation is the spinning of an object. Hold a bike wheel off the ground and spin it; that's rotation. (If it is on the ground, then it rotates and translates.) Some further examples of rotation are shown in Figure 3.12. Note that when rotating an object, just as when translating, the object's shape doesn't change; that is, none of the lengths of the lines connecting points change. In mathematical terms, this means rotation is an *isometry*.

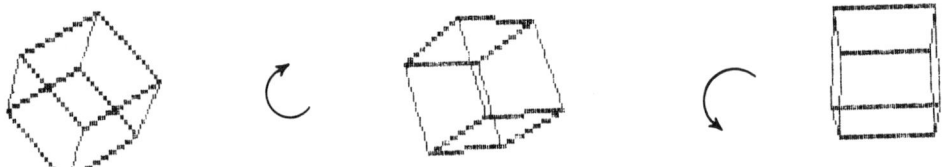

Figure 3.12
A rotating cube.

The Axis of Rotation

Rotation is a much more complicated manipulation than any of those we have learned so far. A few terms need to be understood before we can begin to add rotation to our program. Whenever we talk about rotation we talk of rotation about an *axis*. The axis functions like a pivot point. The object spins about this line.

For example, hold a ball between your thumb and middle finger. With your other hand, twirl it. The axis of rotation is a line connecting your two fingers. Figure 3.13 shows some axes of rotation.

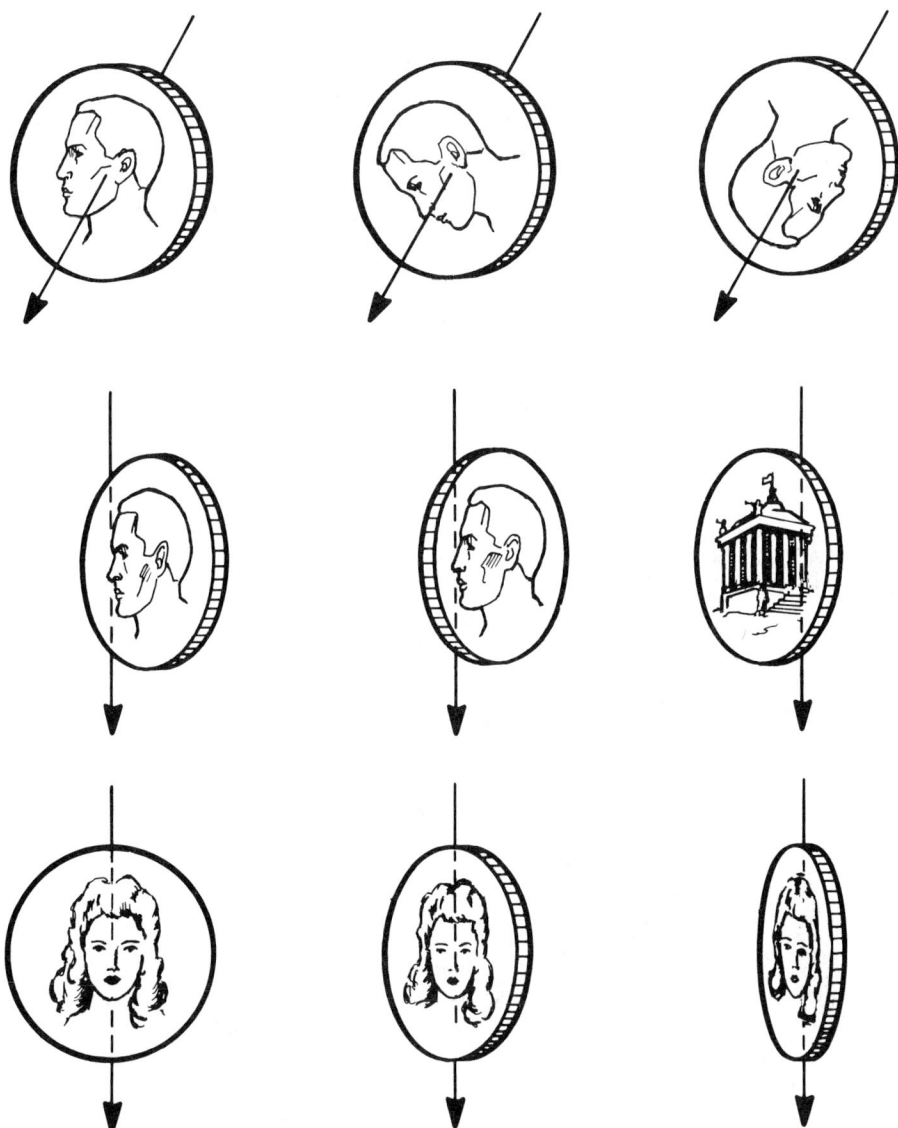

Figure 3.13
Three coins, rotating about different axes of rotation.

Angles

When we describe rotation we also need a way to state the amount of rotation. We do this with *angles*. Because we are dealing with three dimensions, there are many places from which we could measure angular

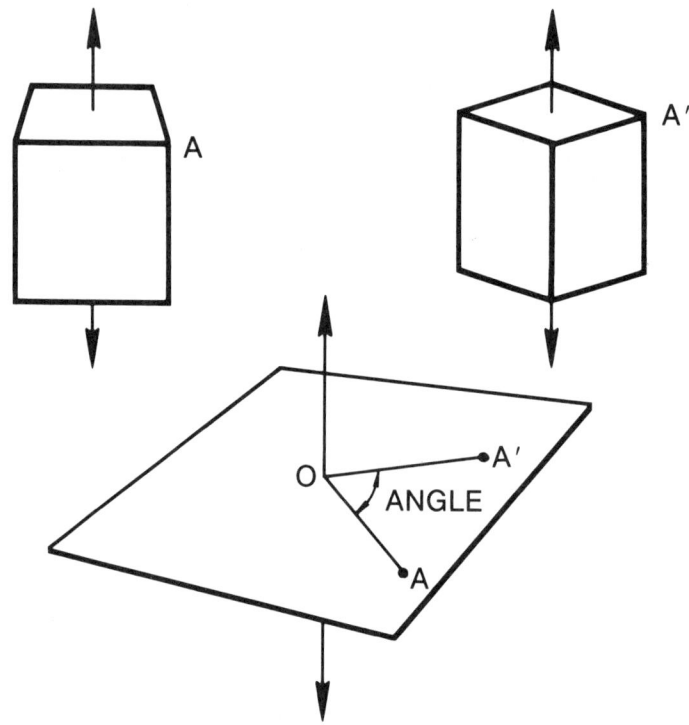

Figure 3.14
a rotates to **a'**. **aoa'**, indicated by the double arrow, is the angle by which the shape rotated.

change. We will measure it in a plane perpendicular to the axis of rotation. In other words, suppose **a** is a point on an object. After we rotate the object, **a** goes to **a'**. Now, draw a plane that intersects **a** and **a'** and also is perpendicular to the axis of rotation. If we call the point where the plane intersects the axis of rotation **o**, then the amount of rotation is the angle **aoa'** (Figure 3.14).

There are several units for measuring angles. The three standard ones are *degrees*, *radians*, and *grads*. Degrees are probably the most common unit of angular measurement, with which most of us are familiar. If someone were to tell you to spin 45 degrees, you would have no problem; but what if they asked you to spin $\pi/4$ radians?

Unfortunately, computers don't understand degrees. They prefer the radian system of angular measurement. This isn't to confuse users. Rather, the purpose is twofold. The primary reason is that to calculate *trigonometric functions* (see Appendix A) computers use limited term *Taylor series* expansions, and these require radians. (A Taylor series is a way of writing trigonometric functions—sine, cosine, and tangent, and actually most any function—as an infinite polynomial series. For example, the Taylor series expansion of sin(x) is $x - x^3/3! + x^5/5! - \ldots$) In addition, radians are more useful mathematically. They can be used in all kinds of equations, whereas degrees cannot. The radian and degree systems of measurement are illustrated in Figure 3.15.

Because the computer doesn't understand degrees, the arguments of trigonometric functions have to be in radians. So, sin(90) equals 0.893 instead of 1. If working in radians makes you uncomfortable, it's very easy to convert from radians to degrees and vice versa:

degrees = radians * 180/π
radians = degrees * π/180
(π = 3.1415926535 . . . .)

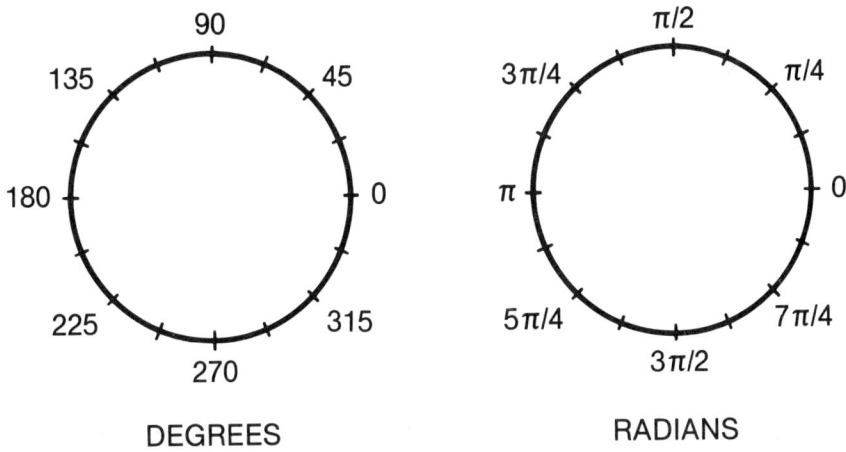

Figure 3.15
The degree and radian systems of measurement.

The Principal Axes of Rotation

Just as we could translate an object to any position by combining translations in the x, y, and z directions, we can rotate an object to any position by rotating about the x, y, and z axes. This concept is important. It means we only need to figure how to make our program rotate about these axes.

Let's look at some examples of rotating about these axes. Figures 3.16 b, c, and d show rotations about the x, y, and z axes, respectively. In Figures 3.16 e and f, the object is rotated about more than one axis. Now look

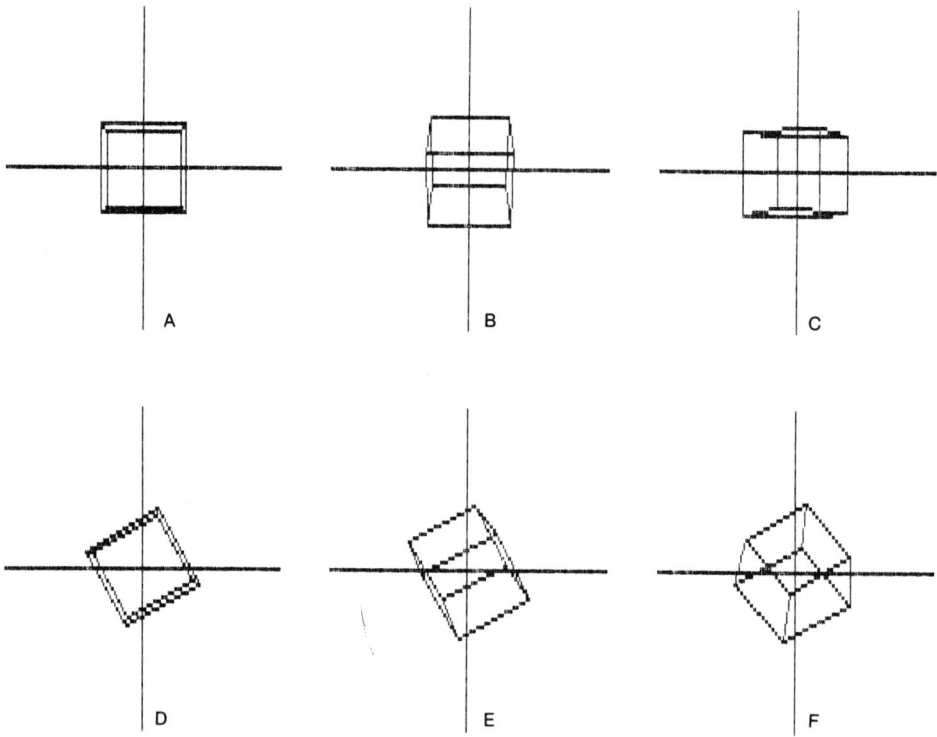

Figure 3.16
Part a is the cube. Part b is rotated about the x axis, c about the y axis, and d about the z axis. In part e, the cube is rotated about the x and y axes; if part f, the x, y, and z axes.

at Figure 3.17. Here we have the same object as in Figure 3.16, but its center is no longer at the origin. Figures 3.17 a–f show the same rotations as Figures 3.16 a–f—but look how different the results are. This comparison shows the importance of choosing the center of an object. Usually we want the center of the object at the origin. This way, rotation of objects will seem more natural, as they tend to rotate about their center of gravity. Sometimes, however, it simplifies matters to center an object off of the origin. For example, suppose we want a planet to revolve around the sun. If we center the sun on the origin and the planet away from it, any rotation will make it revolve (Figure 3.18).

Now that we have an idea of what rotation around the x, y, and z axes is all about, we are ready to examine the mathematics of rotation. Just as we only needed to figure how to translate in the x, y, and z directions, we will only figure out how to rotate about these three axes.

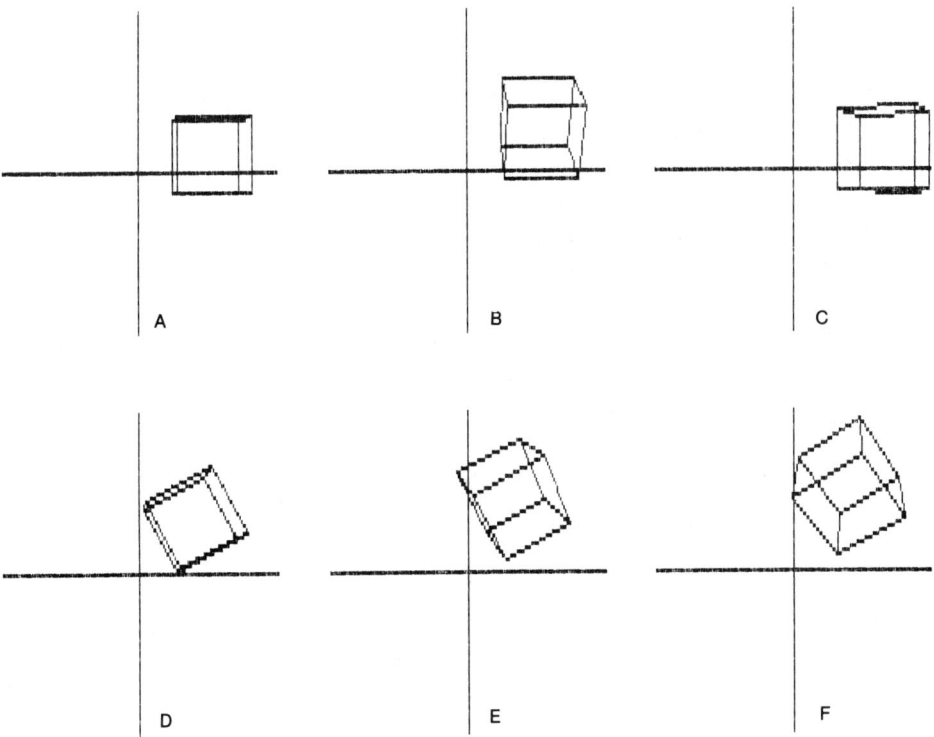

Figure 3.17
The cube, offset from the origin, rotated through the same angles as in Figure 3.18

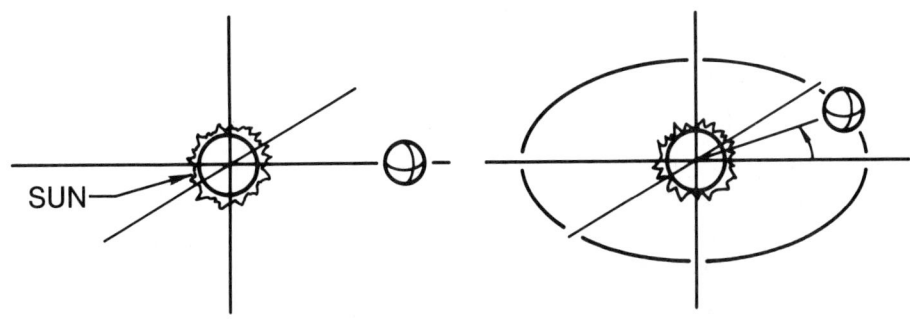

Figure 3.18
A planet is placed away from the origin. When it rotates, it revolves around the sun.

The Math of Rotation

Now we are ready to move to the complicated math—developing a formula to rotate objects. We'll start off figuring how to do this about the z axis. Because the z coordinates don't change when we rotate about the z axis (think about this), we will only show the x and y axes in our diagrams.

Let's begin by drawing some pictures. Figure 3.19 shows a point **a** on the x axis. Point **a'** is **a** rotated $\pi/2$ radians (90 degrees). Point **a''** is rotated some other amount: α. (It's traditional to use Greek letters for angle measures.) We can see that by rotating $\pi/2$ degrees, **(x,0)** maps to **(0,x)**—things could be simple! But how about **a'''**? Using trigonometry, we find that its coordinates are **(x∗cos(α), y∗sin(α))**.

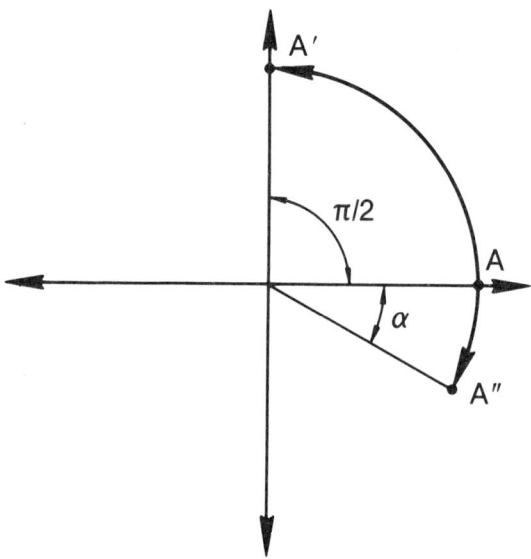

Figure 3.19
a rotates $\pi/2$ radians to **a'** and by angle α to **a''**.

But general rotations aren't as simple as this. Let's look at Figure 3.20. Here **b** doesn't lie on any axes. It is being rotated by an angle β about the z axis. If we can figure the coordinates for **b'**, then we'll have a general formula to do any rotation about the z axis.

Now, the length of **ob'** is equal to the length of **ob**, as they are radii of the same circle. We'll call this length **r**. By simple trigonometry, the x coordinate of point **b'** is **r∗cos($\beta + \theta$)**. Using the identity for cosine angle addition, we find that this equals **r ∗ (cos(β)∗cos(θ) − sin(β)∗sin(θ))**. But, by the definition of cosine and because of the geometry of Figure 3.20, cos(θ) =

x/r. Likewise, $\sin(\theta) = y/r$. Therefore, **x'** = $r*\cos(\beta)*x/r - r*\sin(\beta)*y/r$ = $x*\cos(\beta) - y*\sin(\beta)$. Using the same process, we find **y'** = $x*\sin(\beta) + y*\cos(\beta)$.

Let's write this out. Suppose **zangle** is the amount of rotation about the z axis. Then:

**(x,y,z)$_{new}$ = (x$_{old}$*cos(zangle) − y$_{old}$*sin(zangle),
x$_{old}$*sin(zangle) + y$_{old}$*cos(zangle), z$_{old}$)**

We can extend the process we used above to find the formulae for rotation about the other axes. If you want to do this, just use the x and z axes and the y and z axes where we used the x and y axes above. You will find that the other formulae are very similar to that for z axis rotation. They follow.

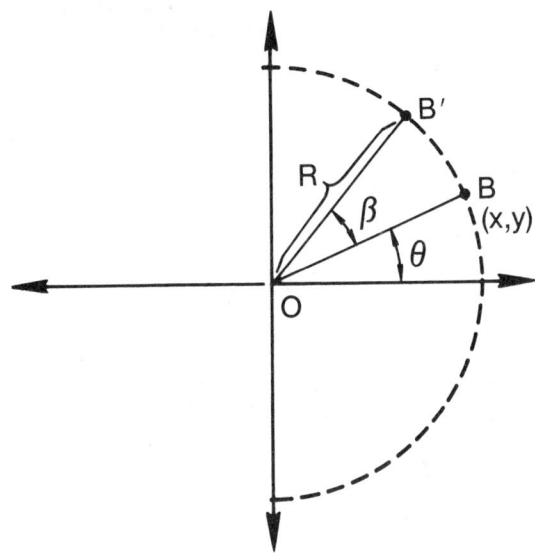

Figure 3.20
b is rotated by β to **b'**.

For rotation about the x axis:

**(x,y,z)$_{new}$ = (x$_{old}$, y$_{old}$*cos(xangle) − z$_{old}$*sin(xangle),
y$_{old}$*sin(xangle) + z$_{old}$*cos(xangle))**

For rotation about the y axis:

**(x,y,z)$_{new}$ = (x$_{old}$*cos(yangle) − z$_{old}$*sin(yangle), y$_{old}$,
x$_{old}$*sin(yangle) + z$_{old}$*cos(yangle))**

Adding Rotation to Our Program

Now we are ready to add rotation to our program. The first thing we need to do is add routines to do the actual rotation. We will simply put the formulae from above into BASIC code:

```
4000 '
4001 'Rotate x
4002 '
4010 FOR POINTNUM = 1 TO NUMBEROFPOINTS
4020     TEMPPT = NEWPOINTS(YCOORD,POINTNUM) *
         COS(XANGLE) - NEWPOINTS(ZCOORD,POINTNUM) *
         SIN(XANGLE)
4030     NEWPOINTS(ZCOORD,POINTNUM) = NEWPOINTS(YCOORD,
         POINTNUM) * SIN(XANGLE) + NEWPOINTS(ZCOORD,
         POINTNUM) * COS(XANGLE)
4040     NEWPOINTS(YCOORD,POINTNUM) = TEMPPT
4050 NEXT
4060 RETURN

4100 '
4101 'Rotate y
4102 '
4110 FOR POINTNUM = 1 TO NUMBEROFPOINTS
4120     TEMPPT = NEWPOINTS(XCOORD,POINTNUM) *
         COS(YANGLE) - NEWPOINTS(ZCOORD,POINTNUM) *
         SIN(YANGLE)
4130     NEWPOINTS(ZCOORD,POINTNUM) = NEWPOINTS(XCOORD,
         POINTNUM) * SIN(YANGLE) + NEWPOINTS(ZCOORD,
         POINTNUM) * COS(YANGLE)
4140     NEWPOINTS(XCOORD,POINTNUM) = TEMPPT
4150 NEXT
4160 RETURN

4200 '
4201 'Rotate z
4202 '
4210 FOR POINTNUM = 1 TO NUMBEROFPOINTS
4220     TEMPPT = NEWPOINTS(XCOORD,POINTNUM) *
         COS(ZANGLE) - NEWPOINTS(YCOORD,POINTNUM) *
         SIN(ZANGLE)
4230     NEWPOINTS(YCOORD,POINTNUM) = NEWPOINTS(XCOORD,
         POINTNUM) * SIN(ZANGLE) + NEWPOINTS(YCOORD,
         POINTNUM) * COS(ZANGLE)
4240     NEWPOINTS(XCOORD,POINTNUM) = TEMPPT
4250 NEXT
4260 RETURN
```

Let's briefly look at one of these routines—the one for x rotation. The first thing it does is use the formula for the new y coordinate to find a value for **TEMPPT**. Then the new z coordinate is computed, and finally, the new y coordinate gets the value of **TEMPPT**. But what is this **TEMPPT**? Well, suppose that we stored the new y coordinate in **NEWPOINTS** right away. Then when we get to line **4030** and need to use the old y coordinate to compute the new z, we will have the wrong value. This makes a strange distortion. To prevent this, we temporarily store the new y coordinate in **TEMPPT**.

We need to add subroutine calls to the rotation routines:

```
590    GOSUB 4010      'rotate x
610    GOSUB 4110      'rotate y
630    GOSUB 4210      'rotate z
```

Finally, we need a routine to get the amount of rotation. We'll start off simply:

```
580    GOSUB 4510       'get amount of rotation

4500 '
4501 'Get amount of rotation
4502 '
4510 XANGLE = XANGLE + .5
4520 YANGLE = 0
4530 ZANGLE = 0
4600 RETURN
```

This will rotate the cube about the x axis 0.5 radians (almost 30 degrees) each time through.

Before we try out the program, let's use scaling to make our cube a box (that is, a rectangular parallelpiped) so that we can see the effects of rotation more easily. Add:

```
3510 XSCALE = 1
3520 YSCALE = 1.5
3530 ZSCALE = 2
```

To add all the lines from this section, type:
MERGE "5

Trying It Out

Now run the program—pretty neat, huh? (Also pretty slow.) Now change line **4520** to

4520 YANGLE = YANGLE + .5

and **4510** to

4510 XANGLE = 0

And after running, make this change:

4520 YANGLE = 0
4530 ZANGLE = ZANGLE + .5

This will give you an idea of rotation about all of the axes. Now, combine rotations. For example, rotate about the x and z axes. Experiment.

The Routine's Speed

Rotation is slow. Part of the reason is that BASIC's sine and cosine routines are slow. We'll see how to solve this in Section 4.8. Furthermore, we call these trigonometric routines for every point in each of the rotation subroutines. This, combined with changing all the points in the scaling and translation routines, is very time consuming. The next two sections are devoted to solving this problem.

3.6: MATRICES

As promised, we are about to make our graphics program faster. To do this we will rely on *matrices*. (If you are unfamiliar with matrices, refer to Appendix A.) Matrices are two-dimensional arrays, a powerful form in mathematics. As you will see, they are very useful in computer graphics.

One of the great uses of matrices is representing *linear transformations*. Translation, scaling and rotation are all linear transformations.

A result of representing transformations as matrices is that by multiplying the matrices together we can get a new matrix doing the same thing as all the others put together. So far we have been figuring out scaling values, then scaling the points; figuring out rotation values, then rotating about each axis; and finally figuring out translation values, then translating the points. By combining matrices we can find one matrix, that is, *transform*, that does all of the above in one step. So our program reduces to computing this matrix, then transforming all of the points with it. The more points we have, the more time this saves, for we will replace five loops to change all of the points by one loop.

We will be able to represent all of our transformations—translation, scaling and rotation—by four-dimensional matrices. To manipulate a point, we simply multiply it by the transformation matrix. To do this, we will represent points by four-dimensional vectors of the form:

(x,y,z,1)

This really isn't any different from how we have been labeling points so far, except that we tack a 1 onto the end. The 1 allows us to do translation.

Suppose we have a point **(x,y,z)** and a transformation matrix **T**. Then the new point is:

(x,y,z,1) * T

It's probably a lot easier to understand if we just jump right in and look at some matrices.

Let's start with scaling. We can represent scaling by the following matrix:

XSCALE	0	0	0
0	YSCALE	0	0
0	0	ZSCALE	0
0	0	0	1

Now let's multiply a point—**(x,y,z,1)**—by this matrix. We get:

(x * XSCALE, y * YSCALE, z * ZSCALE, 1)

Just look at the first three coordinates. They are exactly what we got from our scaling routine before! So, matrices seem to work.

(Note: those familiar with matrix operations may be annoyed that we multiply the point by the matrix rather than vice versa, and that correspondingly we don't use a four by n dimensional point representation. Although such a format better suits the concept of matrices as transformations, using the above form results in a more familiar point format and makes multiple transformations easier to understand.)

Now we'll look at the translation matrix:

1	0	0	0
0	1	0	0
0	0	1	0
XTRANSLATION	YTRANSLATION	ZTRANSLATION	1

Again, multiply **(x,y,z,1)** by this. We get:

(x + XTRANSLATION, y + YTRANSLATION, z + ZTRANSLATION, 1)

— just what we want!

Now let's try doing two transformations—scaling and translation—at once. Call the scaling matrix **S** and the translation matrix **T**. To scale and translate simultaneously we find:

(x,y,z,1) * (S * T)

If we multiply the scaling matrix by the translation matrix, we get:

XSCALE	0	0	0
0	YSCALE	0	0
0	0	ZSCALE	0
XTRANSLATION	YTRANSLATION	ZTRANSLATION	1

Now, multiplying **(x,y,z,1)** by this, we get:

(x*XSCALE + XTRANSLATION, y*YSCALE + YTRANSLATION, z*ZSCALE + ZTRANSLATION, 1)

Once more, this is just what we would expect.

In a moment we will see how to rotate by using matrices. But first, let's see the advantage of this. Let our rotation matrices be R_x, R_y, and R_z. If we want to scale, rotate and translate a point, instead of calling routines doing each separately, we find:

X = S * R_x * R_y * R_z * T

and then to get our new points:

$point_{new}$ = $point_{old}$ * X

We can do this in one loop.

Now we are ready to see the rotation matrices. For rotating about the x axis, we have:

1	0	0	0
0	cos(XANGLE)	sin(XANGLE)	0
0	−sin(XANGLE)	cos(XANGLE)	0
0	0	0	1

For rotating about the y axis, the matrix is:

$$\begin{pmatrix} \cos(\text{YANGLE}) & 0 & \sin(\text{YANGLE}) & 0 \\ 0 & 1 & 0 & 0 \\ -\sin(\text{YANGLE}) & 0 & \cos(\text{YANGLE}) & 0 \\ 0 & 0 & 0 & 1 \end{pmatrix}$$

And the matrix for z rotation is:

$$\begin{pmatrix} \cos(\text{ZANGLE}) & \sin(\text{ZANGLE}) & 0 & 0 \\ -\sin(\text{ZANGLE}) & \cos(\text{ZANGLE}) & 0 & 0 \\ 0 & 0 & 1 & 0 \\ 0 & 0 & 0 & 1 \end{pmatrix}$$

Incorporating Matrices Into Our Program

Let's modify our program so that we use matrices instead of a lot of transformation subroutines. Before we do this, however, we need to do some general housekeeping. To start, save the program as it now stands. Call it **3DLG1**, for three-dimensional line graphics version 1. Next, delete routines we will no longer use. Get rid of lines **1000–1100**, **3000–3100**, **4000–4260**, and **6000–6100**. Also delete **530**, **560**, **590**, **610**, **630**, and **670**.

Now we can begin our new, matrix-based program. One important thing is that we want to set up our program to allow as much flexibility as possible, just as we did previously. This way, we can delete, debug, and reorder routines to our heart's content without having to do any messy patching.

For each type of transformation (scaling, translation, and rotation) we will:

1. get the movement values (such as **XSCALE**);
2. load the transformation into a temporary matrix; and
3. multiply a "running total" transformation matrix by this temporary matrix.

Let's call the "running total" matrix **TRANSFORM** and the temporary matrix **NEWTRANSFORM**. Then, for each routine we will load **NEWTRANSFORM**, and find **TRANSFORM** = **TRANSFORM** * **NEWTRANSFORM**. When we have finished multiplying all the matrices together, **TRANSFORM** will do all of the object manipulations we want. So, we will multiply the points by **TRANSFORM**.

82 Three-Dimensional Line Graphics

So that we can call up our routines in any order (that is, translate first, then rotate, then scale, or perhaps rotate, translate, then rotate again) we will first load **TRANSFORM** with the *identity matrix*. (Otherwise we would have to load **TRANSFORM** with the first matrix.)

First we will add some general matrix operating subroutines:

```
19000 '
19001 'Matrix Operations
19002 '
19005 'Move identity matrix to TRANSFORM
19006 '
19010 FOR ROW = 1 TO 4
19020   FOR COLUMN = ROW + 1 TO 4
19030     TRANSFORM(ROW,COLUMN) = 0
19040     TRANSFORM(COLUMN,ROW) = 0
19050   NEXT
19060   TRANSFORM(ROW,ROW) = 1
19070 NEXT
19080 RETURN

19100 '
19101 'Multiply TRANSFORM by NEWTRANSFORM to get
      TRANSFORM
19102 '
19110 FOR ROW = 1 TO 4      'do multiplication
19120   FOR COLUMN = 1 TO 4
19130     TEMP(ROW,COLUMN) = TRANSFORM(ROW,1) *
          NEWTRANSFORM(1,COLUMN) + TRANSFORM(ROW,2) *
          NEWTRANSFORM(2,COLUMN) + TRANSFORM(ROW,3) *
          NEWTRANSFORM(3,COLUMN) + TRANSFORM(ROW,4) *
          NEWTRANSFORM(4,COLUMN)
19140   NEXT
19150 NEXT
19160 FOR ROW = 1 TO 4      'copy TEMP to TRANSFORM
19170   FOR COLUMN = 1 TO 4
19180     TRANSFORM(ROW,COLUMN) = TEMP(ROW,COLUMN)
19190   NEXT
19200 NEXT
19210 RETURN

19300 '
19301 'Transform POINTS
19302 '
19310 FOR POINTNUM = 1 TO NUMBEROFPOINTS
19320   NEWPOINTS(XCOORD,POINTNUM) =
        POINTS(XCOORD,POINTNUM) * TRANSFORM(1,1) +
        POINTS(YCOORD,POINTNUM) * TRANSFORM(2,1) +
        POINTS(ZCOORD,POINTNUM) * TRANSFORM(3,1) +
        TRANSFORM(4,1)
```

```
19330      NEWPOINTS(YCOORD,POINTNUM) =
           POINTS(XCOORD,POINTNUM) * TRANSFORM(1,2) +
           POINTS(YCOORD,POINTNUM) * TRANSFORM(2,2) +
           POINTS(ZCOORD,POINTNUM) * TRANSFORM(3,2) +
           TRANSFORM(4,2)
19340      NEWPOINTS(ZCOORD,POINTNUM) =
           POINTS(XCOORD,POINTNUM) * TRANSFORM(1,3) +
           POINTS(YCOORD,POINTNUM) * TRANSFORM(2,3) +
           POINTS(ZCOORD,POINTNUM) * TRANSFORM(3,3) +
           TRANSFORM(4,3)
19350 NEXT
19360 RETURN
```

We also need to add the following to allow the new matrices to be used, to copy the identity into **TRANSFORM**, and to transform all of the points:

```
20 DIM POINTS(3,100), NEWPOINTS(3,100), LINES(2,100),
   TRANSFORM(4,4), NEWTRANSFORM(4,4), TEMP(4,4)

530      GOSUB 19010        'copy identity into TRANSFORM
700      GOSUB 19310        'transform POINTS
```

Now that we have these general routines, we just need the routines to load the transformation matrices into **NEWTRANSFORM**.

For scaling we add:

```
550      GOSUB 3510         'get scale values
560      GOSUB 3010         'load scale matrix into
                             NEWTRANSFORM
570      GOSUB 19110        'update TRANSFORM

3000 '
3001 'Load scale matrix into NEWTRANSFORM
3003 '
3010 NEWTRANSFORM(1,1) = XSCALE : NEWTRANSFORM(1,2) =
     0 : NEWTRANSFORM(1,3) = 0 : NEWTRANSFORM(1,4) = 0
3020 NEWTRANSFORM(2,1) = 0 : NEWTRANSFORM(2,2) =
     YSCALE : NEWTRANSFORM(2,3) = 0 : NEWTRANSFORM(2,4)
     = 0
3030 NEWTRANSFORM(3,1) = 0 : NEWTRANSFORM(3,2) = 0 :
     NEWTRANSFORM(3,3) = ZSCALE : NEWTRANSFORM(3,4) = 0
3040 NEWTRANSFORM(4,1) = 0 : NEWTRANSFORM(4,2) = 0 :
     NEWTRANSFORM(4,3) = 0 : NEWTRANSFORM(4,4) = 1
3100 RETURN
```

For rotation:

```
580      GOSUB 4510         'get rotation values
590      GOSUB 4010         'load x rotation matrix into
                             NEWTRANSFORM
```

```
600       GOSUB 19110       'update TRANSFORM
610       GOSUB 4110        'load y rotation matrix into
          NEWTRANSFORM
620       GOSUB 19110       'update TRANSFORM
630       GOSUB 4210        'load z rotation matrix into
          NEWTRANSFORM
640       GOSUB 19110       'update TRANSFORM

4000 '
4001 'load x rotation matrix into NEWTRANSFORM
4002 '
4010 NEWTRANSFORM(1,1) = 1 : NEWTRANSFORM(1,2) = 0 :
     NEWTRANSFORM(1,3) = 0 : NEWTRANSFORM(1,4) = 0
4020 NEWTRANSFORM(2,1) = 0 : NEWTRANSFORM(2,2) =
     COS(XANGLE) : NEWTRANSFORM(2,3) = SIN(XANGLE) :
     NEWTRANSFORM(2,4) = 0
4030 NEWTRANSFORM(3,1) = 0 : NEWTRANSFORM(3,2) =
     -SIN(XANGLE) : NEWTRANSFORM(3,3) = COS(XANGLE) :
     NEWTRANSFORM(3,4) = 0
4040 NEWTRANSFORM(4,1) = 0 : NEWTRANSFORM(4,2) = 0 :
     NEWTRANSFORM(4,3) = 0 : NEWTRANSFORM(4,4) = 1
4050 RETURN

4100 '
4101 'load y rotation matrix into NEWTRANSFORM
4102 '
4110 NEWTRANSFORM(1,1) = COS(YANGLE) :
     NEWTRANSFORM(1,2) = 0 : NEWTRANSFORM(1,3) =
     SIN(YANGLE) : NEWTRANSFORM(1,4) = 0
4120 NEWTRANSFORM(2,1) = 0 : NEWTRANSFORM(2,2) = 1 :
     NEWTRANSFORM(2,3) = 0 : NEWTRANSFORM(2,4) = 0
4130 NEWTRANSFORM(3,1) = -SIN(YANGLE) :
     NEWTRANSFORM(3,2) = 0 : NEWTRANSFORM(3,3) =
     COS(YANGLE) : NEWTRANSFORM(3,4) = 0
4140 NEWTRANSFORM(4,1) = 0 : NEWTRANSFORM(4,2) = 0 :
     NEWTRANSFORM(4,3) = 0 : NEWTRANSFORM(4,4) = 1
4150 RETURN

4200 '
4201 'load z rotation matrix into NEWTRANSFORM
4202 '
4210 NEWTRANSFORM(1,1) = COS(ZANGLE) :
     NEWTRANSFORM(1,2) = SIN(ZANGLE) :
     NEWTRANSFORM(1,3) = 0 : NEWTRANSFORM(1,4) = 0
4220 NEWTRANSFORM(2,1) = -SIN(ZANGLE) :
     NEWTRANSFORM(2,2) = COS(ZANGLE) :
     NEWTRANSFORM(2,3) = 0 : NEWTRANSFORM(2,4) = 0
4230 NEWTRANSFORM(3,1) = 0 : NEWTRANSFORM(3,2) = 0 :
     NEWTRANSFORM(3,3) = 1 : NEWTRANSFORM(3,4) = 0
```

```
4240 NEWTRANSFORM(4,1) = 0 : NEWTRANSFORM(4,2) = 0 :
     NEWTRANSFORM(4,3) = 0 : NEWTRANSFORM(4,4) = 1
4250 RETURN
```

And translation:

```
670       GOSUB 6010         'load translation matrix into
                              NEWTRANSFORM
680       GOSUB 19110        'update TRANSFORM

6000 '
6001 'load translation matrix into NEWTRANSFORM
6002 '
6010 NEWTRANSFORM(1,1) = 1 : NEWTRANSFORM(1,2) = 0 :
     NEWTRANSFORM(1,3) = 0 : NEWTRANSFORM(1,4) = 0
6020 NEWTRANSFORM(2,1) = 0 : NEWTRANSFORM(2,2) = 1 :
     NEWTRANSFORM(2,3) = 0 : NEWTRANSFORM(2,4) = 0
6030 NEWTRANSFORM(3,1) = 0 : NEWTRANSFORM(3,2) = 0 :
     NEWTRANSFORM(3,3) = 1 : NEWTRANSFORM(3,4) = 0
6040 NEWTRANSFORM(4,1) = XTRANSLATION :
     NEWTRANSFORM(4,2) = YTRANSLATION :
     NEWTRANSFORM(4,3) = ZTRANSLATION :
     NEWTRANSFORM(4,4) = 1
6100 RETURN
```

MERGE "6

Trying It Out

Save this program, calling it **3DLG2**, for three-dimensional line graphics version 2. Now run it.

3.7: MATRICES REVISITED OR "I THOUGHT YOU SAID THEY WERE FASTER?"

If you were patient enough to watch the program, you will realize that instead of being faster, as promised, the program took a lot longer to run. But it seemed logical that it would run faster. Actually, using matrices does make a program run faster, but only after objects reach a certain size. For small objects, it takes more time to figure out the matrices than it does to manipulate the points. With larger objects, matrices beat out the other

86 Three-Dimensional Line Graphics

method. If you want to verify this, try running the following sets of data on **3DLG1** and **3DLG2**.

The first set:

```
20010 'double 3-d cube
20020 DATA 16, 24
20030 DATA    20, 20, 20,   20, -20, 20,   -20, -20, 20,
         -20, 20, 20,   20, 20, -20,   20, -20, -20,
         -20, -20, -20,   -20, 20, -20
20040 DATA    25, 25, 25,   25, -25, 25,   -25, -25, 25,
         -25, 25, 25,   25, 25, -25,   25, -25, -25,
         -25, -25, -25,   -25, 25, -25
20050 DATA    1, 2,   2, 3,   3, 4,   4, 1,   5, 6,
         6, 7,   7, 8,   8, 5,   1, 5,   2, 6,   3, 7,
         4, 8
20060 DATA    9, 10,   10, 11,   11, 12,   12, 9,   13,
         14,   14, 15,   15, 16,   16, 13,   9, 13,   10,
         14,   11, 15,   12, 16
```

To use this test set, type:

MERGE "7P1

The second set:

```
20010 'four 3-d cube
20020 DATA 32, 48
20030 DATA    20, 20, 20,   20, -20, 20,   -20, -20, 20,
         -20, 20, 20,   20, 20, -20,   20, -20, -20,
         -20, -20, -20,   -20, 20, -20
20040 DATA    10, 10, 10,   10, -10, 10,   -10, -10, 10,
         -10, 10, 10,   10, 10, -10,   10, -10, -10,
         -10, -10, -10,   -10, 10, -10
20050 DATA    15, 15, 15,   15, -15, 15,   -15, -15, 15,
         -15, 15, 15,   15, 15, -15,   15, -15, -15,
         -15, -15, -15,   -15, 15, -15
20060 DATA    25, 25, 25,   25, -25, 25,   -25, -25, 25,
         -25, 25, 25,   25, 25, -25,   25, -25, -25,
         -25, -25, -25,   -25, 25, -25
20070 DATA    1, 2,   2, 3,   3, 4,   4, 1,   5, 6,
         6, 7,   7, 8,   8, 5,   1, 5,   2, 6,   3, 7,
         4, 8
20080 DATA    9, 10,   10, 11,   11, 12,   12, 9,
         13, 14,   14, 15,   15, 16,   16, 13,   9, 13,
         10, 14,   11, 15,   12, 16
```

```
20090 DATA    17, 18,    18, 19,    19, 20,    20, 17,
              21, 22,    22, 23,    23, 24,    24, 21,    17, 21,
              18, 22,    19, 23,    20, 24
20100 DATA    25, 26,    26, 27,    27, 28,    28,
              25, 29, 30,    30, 31,    31, 32,    32, 29,
              25, 29,    26, 30,    27, 31,    28, 32
```

> To use this test set, type:
>
> **MERGE "7P2**

The Speed Test

Now let's compare the speeds of **3DLG1**, **3DLG2**, and, for added interest, **Program X**—another program doing what the other two do:

Speeds for 10 Loops (seconds)

Program	1 cube	2 cubes	4 cubes
3DLG1	51.7	100.9	198.0
3DLG2	79.3	100.7	141.7
Program X	29.1	50.3	91.3

And the winner is . . . **Program X**. In a moment we will see what **Program X** was, but first, let's analyze the data. With the program using subroutines, **3DLG1**, the amount of time to draw the shapes doubled as the number of points doubled. The program using matrices, **3DLG2**, however, took about 2 seconds more per run every time another cube was added. In other words, for the first run it took 6 + 1*2 seconds per run, for the second it took 6 + 2*2 seconds, and for the third, it took 6 + 4*2 seconds. **Program X** increased in a fashion similar to **3DLG2**, only it took 1 + 1*2 seconds per run for one cube, 1 + 2*2 seconds per run for two cubes, and 1 + 4*2 seconds per run for four cubes.

Unveiling The Winner

Remember that I said matrices make things faster? Well, **Program X**, the winner of the speed test, uses matrices. The difference between **Pro-**

gram **X** and **3DLG2** is that instead of calculating **TRANSFORM** by multiplying matrices together each loop, **Program X** loads **TRANSFORM** with values just once. Recall that multiplying matrices together results in a transform doing everything that all of the other matrices did. **Program X** is based on this fact. It sacrifices the flexibility of **3DLG2** for speed.

Here's how it works: once we use our program for a while we will find an order of object manipulations we like most. Suppose this is scaling, rotating about the z axis, rotating about the x axis, rotating about the y axis, and then translating. (I suggest using this order.) We multiply these matrices out by hand, finding:

$$X = S * R_z * R_x * R_y * T,$$

Now, instead of taking time to multiply all of these matrices in the program, we can just load **X** into **TRANSFORM** and then multiply all of the points.

This will become clearer by doing it. First, let's find **X** (Figure 3.21). This is a messy, tedious, and time-consuming job (especially when more than five matrices are involved), and it is easy to make mistakes. You may want to write a symbolic matrix manipulation program to do the math for you. Even better, make it write out a program module to load **TRANSFORM**. (Such a program is on the optional disk. It makes the loss of flexibility virtually negligible.)

Putting in the Code

Let's put this idea to work in our program. First, get rid of all of those slow matrix multiplication calls. Delete lines **530**, **560**, **570**, **590–640**, **670**, and **680**. Also, delete lines **3000–3100**, **4000–4250**, **6000–6100**, and **19005–19210**.

Now add a subroutine that loads the total transformation matrix, **X**, into **TRANSFORM**:

```
17000 '
17001 'Load total transformation matrix into TRANSFORM
17002 '
17010 TRANSFORM(1,1) = XSCALE * (COS(ZANGLE) *
      COS(YANGLE) - SIN(ZANGLE) * SIN(XANGLE) *
      SIN(YANGLE))
17020 TRANSFORM(1,2) = XSCALE * SIN(ZANGLE) *
      COS(XANGLE)
```

XSCALE * (cos(ZANGLE) * cos(YANGLE) − sin(ZANGLE) * sin(XANGLE) * sin(YANGLE))	XSCALE * sin(ZANGLE) * cos(XANGLE)	XSCALE * (cos(ZANGLE) * sin(YANGLE) + sin(ZANGLE) * sin(XANGLE) * cos(YANGLE))	0
−YSCALE * (sin(ZANGLE) * cos(YANGLE) + cos(ZANGLE) * sin(XANGLE) * sin(YANGLE))	YSCALE * cos(ZANGLE) * cos(XANGLE)	YSCALE * (−sin(ZANGLE) * sin(YANGLE) + cos(ZANGLE) * sin(XANGLE) * cos(YANGLE))	0
−ZSCALE * cos(XANGLE) * sin(YANGLE)	−ZSCALE * sin(XANGLE)	ZSCALE * cos(XANGLE) * cos(YANGLE)	0
XTRANSLATION	YTRANSLATION	ZTRANSLATION	1

Figure 3.21
The matrix X. What a mess!

```
17030 TRANSFORM(1,3) = XSCALE * (COS(ZANGLE) *
      SIN(YANGLE) + SIN(ZANGLE) * SIN(XANGLE) *
      COS(YANGLE))
17040 TRANSFORM(1,4) = 0

17050 TRANSFORM(2,1) = -YSCALE * (SIN(ZANGLE) *
      COS(YANGLE) + COS(ZANGLE) * SIN(XANGLE) *
      SIN(YANGLE))
17060 TRANSFORM(2,2) = YSCALE * COS(ZANGLE) *
      COS(XANGLE)
17070 TRANSFORM(2,3) = YSCALE * (-SIN(ZANGLE) *
      SIN(YANGLE) + COS(ZANGLE) * SIN(XANGLE) *
      COS(YANGLE))
17080 TRANSFORM(2,4) = 0

17090 TRANSFORM(3,1) = -ZSCALE * COS(XANGLE) *
      SIN(YANGLE)
17100 TRANSFORM(3,2) = -ZSCALE * SIN(XANGLE)
17110 TRANSFORM(3,3) = ZSCALE * COS(XANGLE) *
      COS(YANGLE)
17120 TRANSFORM(3,4) = 0

17130 TRANSFORM(4,1) = XTRANSLATION
17140 TRANSFORM(4,2) = YTRANSLATION
17150 TRANSFORM(4,3) = ZTRANSLATION
17160 TRANSFORM(4,4) = 1

17200 RETURN
```

And we add this subroutine call:

```
690     GOSUB 17010      'load TRANSFORM
```

> **MERGE** *"7P3*
>
> Remember to first delete the lines just mentioned (**530**, **560**, etc.).

That's all! Notice how much simpler this is. Save it as **3DLG3**. Before trying it out, however, you may like to read the next section.

3.8: KEYBOARD INTERACTION

By now you are probably tired of typing those preplanned scaling, translation, and rotation changes in all those subroutines. And you are probably also frustrated with not being able to make the object move a little differently. It'd be nice to move things immediately. Now that our program goes fast enough, we can do this, by adding *keyboard interaction*.

Keyboard interaction means that as the program runs, we will type in movement commands from the keyboard. A few things need to be kept in mind. First, commands should be easy to type. Having to type "scale in the x direction by 4 units" would be inconvenient, especially in the two–six seconds we have. Second, we want commands that are intuitive and easy to remember. For example, if we use keys for translation, the key for right movement should be to the right of the key for left movement. Third, it shouldn't be necessary to enter a command for every movement. We should be able to start a trend and then watch it go. That is, instead of having to type in a command every time we want the object to rotate a little, we should be able to type a command to start it spinning. And finally, we don't want the program to stop running every pass to ask for a command.

All of these demands are easy to meet. Our commands will be one keystroke. Rather than having to remember all of the commands, we will organize them on the keyboard so that their location indicates their function. And we will have the commands for rotation, scaling and translation similarly organized so that only one setup needs to be learned. This will solve the first two requirements.

By arranging the function of the keys within each block, that is, the blocks for rotation, translation and scaling, in the proper fashion, we can solve the second part of demand two. Here is how to do it: we will break the keyboard up into three clusters of three-by-three blocks of keys, like tic-tac-toe boards. The upper block of keys will control x movement, the middle will control y, and the lower will control z. We will use the left column of keys to start movement in the negative direction, the middle to stop movement, and the right to start movement in the positive direction.

Let's look at an example—the rotation keys.

Rotation is a pretty important function, so we'll put it at a place easy to find quickly—the leftmost set of keys. We'll organize these as follows:

	Decrease Rotation	*Stop Rotation*	*Increase Rotation*
X	q	w	e
Y	a	s	d
Z	z	x	c

92 Three-Dimensional Line Graphics

How do we get the routine to increase and decrease rotation (and thus solve demand three)? We will keep a counter for each of the directions in the following fashion: each time a decrease key is pressed, the counter is decremented; each time an increase key is pressed, the counter is incremented; and whenever a stop key is pressed, the counter is set to zero. Then, in our routine to get rotation, we will add to the angle of rotation an amount proportional to the counter value. This accomplishes two things: once a key is pressed, motion continues until it is counteracted or stopped; and if a key is pressed more than once, the rate of motion changes.

We will do the same thing for scaling and translation. Scaling is a less often used function, so we will stick it in the middle of the keyboard—using keys r, t, y, f, g, h, v, b and n. Translation will be done with the next three-by-three block of keys.

Finally, we need to satisfy the fourth demand—not stopping the program for commands. We will do this by using the **INKEY$** command. This strobes the keyboard and returns any character that is pressed. If none is pressed, the program just continues. The only problem with this is that the IBM has a *type ahead buffer*. So if we press several keys as the program is drawing, it will read through each of these keys before reading new characters. Because this makes it harder to base decisions on the current output, we will add a line to clear the type ahead buffer.

The Routine

Let's look at the routine. First, we read the keyboard:

```
2000 '
2001 'Strobe keyboard for new command
2002 '
2003 'Positive change increments variable by 1
2004 'Negative change decrements variable by 1
2005 'Stop sets variable to 0
2006 'These variables will be read to determine amount
      of scaling, rotation, and translation
2007 '
2008 '           -         stop        +
2009 '                                          ROTATION
2010 'X          q          w          e
2011 '
2012 'Y          a          s          d
2013 '
2014 'Z          z          x          c
2015 '
```

```
2016 '
2017 'X          r         t         y
2018 '                                          SCALING
2019 'Y          f         g         h
2020 '
2021 'Z          v         b         n
2022 '
2023 '
2024 'X          u         i         o
2025 '                                          TRANSLATION
2026 'Y          j         k         l
2027 '
2028 'Z          m         ,         .
2029 '
2030 '
2031 '    SPACE BAR              =    stop all changes
2032 '    ESC                    =    quit
2033 '
2034 '
2040 COMMAND$ = INKEY$
2050 FOR DUMMY = 1 TO 10 : DUMMY$ = INKEY$ :
     NEXT   'clear the type ahead buffer
```

Then we analyze what is read:

```
2060 IF COMMAND$ = ""  THEN 2400
2070 IF COMMAND$ = "q" THEN XROT = XROT - 1 : GOTO 2400
2080 IF COMMAND$ = "w" THEN XROT = 0 : GOTO 2400
2090 IF COMMAND$ = "e" THEN XROT = XROT + 1 : GOTO 2400
2100 IF COMMAND$ = "a" THEN YROT = YROT - 1 : GOTO 2400
2110 IF COMMAND$ = "s" THEN YROT = 0 : GOTO 2400
2120 IF COMMAND$ = "d" THEN YROT = YROT + 1 : GOTO 2400
2130 IF COMMAND$ = "z" THEN ZROT = ZROT - 1 : GOTO 2400
2140 IF COMMAND$ = "x" THEN ZROT = 0 : GOTO 2400
2150 IF COMMAND$ = "c" THEN ZROT = ZROT + 1 : GOTO 2400
2160 IF COMMAND$ = "r" THEN XSCL = XSCL - 1 : GOTO 2400
2170 IF COMMAND$ = "t" THEN XSCL = 0 : GOTO 2400
2180 IF COMMAND$ = "y" THEN XSCL = XSCL + 1 : GOTO 2400
2190 IF COMMAND$ = "f" THEN YSCL = YSCL - 1 : GOTO 2400
2200 IF COMMAND$ = "g" THEN YSCL = 0 : GOTO 2400
2210 IF COMMAND$ = "h" THEN YSCL = YSCL + 1 : GOTO 2400
2220 IF COMMAND$ = "v" THEN ZSCL = ZSCL - 1 : GOTO 2400
2230 IF COMMAND$ = "b" THEN ZSCL = 0 : GOTO 2400
2240 IF COMMAND$ = "n" THEN ZSCL = ZSCL + 1 : GOTO 2400
2250 IF COMMAND$ = "u" THEN XTRN = XTRN - 1 : GOTO 2400
2260 IF COMMAND$ = "i" THEN XTRN = 0 : GOTO 2400
2270 IF COMMAND$ = "o" THEN XTRN = XTRN + 1 : GOTO 2400
2280 IF COMMAND$ = "j" THEN YTRN = YTRN - 1 : GOTO 2400
2290 IF COMMAND$ = "k" THEN YTRN = 0 : GOTO 2400
```

Three-Dimensional Line Graphics

```
2300 IF COMMAND$ = "l" THEN YTRN = YTRN + 1 : GOTO 2400
2310 IF COMMAND$ = "m" THEN ZTRN = ZTRN - 1 : GOTO 2400
2320 IF COMMAND$ = "," THEN ZTRN = 0 : GOTO 2400
2330 IF COMMAND$ = "." THEN ZTRN = ZTRN + 1 : GOTO 2400
2340 IF ASC(COMMAND$) = 32 THEN XROT = 0 : YROT = 0 :
     ZROT = 0 : XSCL = 0 : YSCL = 0 : ZSCL = 0 : XTRN =
     0 : YTRN = 0 = ZTRN = 0
2350 IF ASC(COMMAND$) = 27 THEN FINISHED = TRUE
2400 RETURN
```

We have added two other useful commands. First, the space bar stops all motion: scaling, rotation and translation. The space bar was chosen because it is large and easy to find and because it runs beneath all three keyboard groups. Because it is more convenient to stop the program when we please, rather than when a timer expires, the keyboard interaction routine checks for a key indicating program termination. In this case, the key is escape.

Now, we add the call to the keyboard interaction and delete **760**, the subroutine call to evaluate **FINISHED**:

```
540    GOSUB 2040       'read keyboard for new command
```

The final thing that remains is to change the routines that get the amount of scaling, translating and rotation so that they are dependent on the keyboard commands. I suggest the following:

```
200 '
201 'Initialize variables
202 '
210 XSCALE = 1 : YSCALE = 1 : ZSCALE = 1

3510 XSCALE = XSCALE + XSCL/8
3520 YSCALE = YSCALE + YSCL/8
3530 ZSCALE = ZSCALE + ZSCL/8

4510 XANGLE = XANGLE + XROT/10
4520 YANGLE = YANGLE + YROT/10
4530 ZANGLE = ZANGLE + ZROT/10

6510 XTRANSLATION = XTRANSLATION + XTRN * 5
6520 YTRANSLATION = YTRANSLATION + YTRN * 5
6530 ZTRANSLATION = ZTRANSLATION + ZTRN * 5
```

MERGE "8

Note that we initialize the scaling values to 1. This is so they don't start off as 0, which would result in all objects being drawn as points until the scaling keys are hit. Also notice the proportionality constants. These make the changes each time through more appropriate. You may wish to change these.

Experimenting

Now that we have added keyboard interaction, it will be much easier to experiment with all the manipulations. Try them out. Mix up rotations on all the axes, scalings, and translations. Perhaps use some different shapes. Have fun.

If you can't get keyboard interaction to work, check the Caps Lock key; the program only checks for lower case characters.

Before continuing, type:

SAVE "3DLG3

(You may want to save it with a different name.)

3.9: ROTATION COMPLICATIONS

In Section 3.7 I mentioned that once we have figured out a favorite order of manipulations, we should multiply the individual transforms to get the faster matrix routine. Well, there are two reasons we need to pick the order.

First, if we want to be fancy, we can do more than five manipulations. In fact, it is often helpful, as we will see in Section 6.3, to do two sets of rotations, scalings, and translations. These result in a different matrix than the one we have computed. Also, we will learn a few more transformations. You may wish to add these to your sequence.

The second reason has to do with rotation. Unfortunately, the order in which we do rotation affects the results of the rotation. In other words, rotating first about the z axis and then the x and y is different from rotating first about the x axis and then the y and z (Figure 3.22).

As mentioned before, I like rotating first about the z axis, and then the x and y. This method allows an object to turn right or left, then bank up and spin. But you should experiment to see what suits you best. There are two ways to do this. First, you could use our subroutine-based program, **3DLG1**, or our first matrix program, **3DLG2**. By adding and moving around subroutines or matrix loading, you can easily generate whatever order of manipulations you want. Then, you can watch the outputs to see what the effects are. The only problem is that as these programs are pretty slow, it may be hard to see what is going on. The alternative is to multiply out the matrices you are interested in, and use **3DLG3**. This will be much nicer when it comes to looking at results, and it is no imposition if you use a module-generating software tool, such as the one on the optional disk.

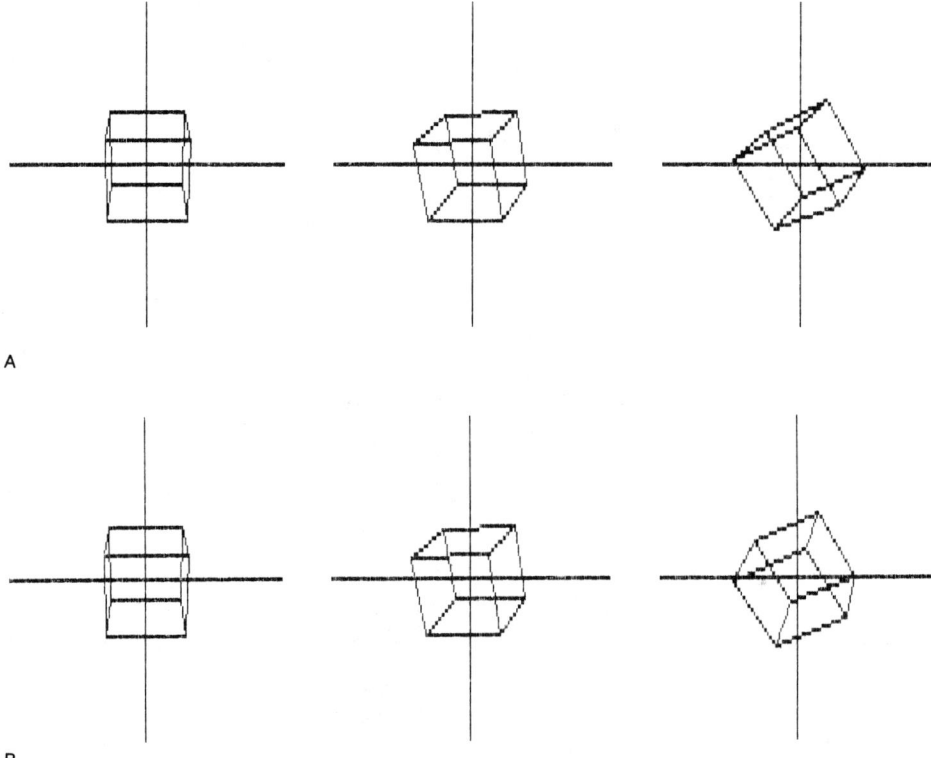

A

B

Figure 3.22
In part a, rotation is in the order z, x, y. Part b shows the same rotations, but in the order x, y, z. Both sequences start by rotating .4 radians about the x axis, then .4 radians about the y axis, then .4 radians about the z axis. The difference can be seen in the last rotations of each sequence.

3.10: REFLECTION

We have covered most all of the major concerns of three-dimensional line drawing. But before we go on to some complicated aspects—*variable perspective* and *clipping*—we'll look at two more transformations. The first of these is *reflection*.

You should already have a good idea of what reflection does from its name. It is what happens when you look in a mirror—all the points on one side of a plane are flipped to the other. We will only deal with flipping about the xy, yz, and xz planes (Figure 3.23).

Reflecting is very easy mathematically. Suppose we want to reflect about the yz plane. We simply multiply all x coordinates by -1. Reflection about the other two planes requires multiplying either the y or z coordinates by -1. To reflect about more than one plane, we multiply more than one coordinate by -1. It's that simple.

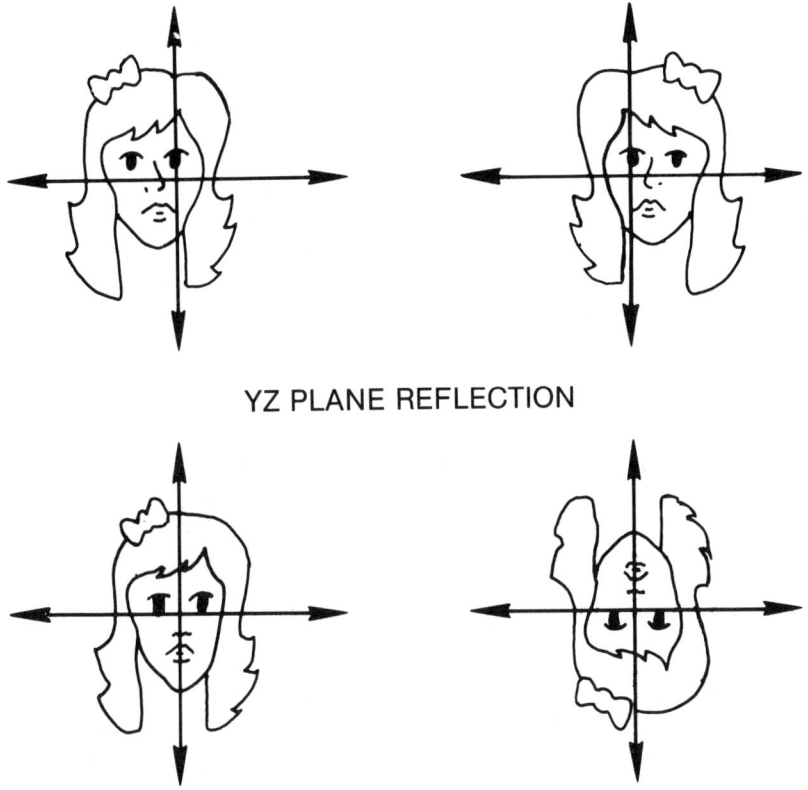

YZ PLANE REFLECTION

XZ PLANE REFLECTION

Figure 3.23
Reflections.

Adding reflection to our program is almost as simple as the math. The first thing we will do is set up three Boolean variables, **XYREFLECT**, **XZREFLECT**, and **YZREFLECT**, to tell us when we need to do reflection.

Then, if any of these are true, we make the corresponding scale factor negative. In other words, suppose we want to reflect about the yz plane. Then all we need do is make **XSCALE** negative. The folowing routine does this:

```
650      GOSUB 5000        'determine what reflections to do

3540 IF XYREFLECT THEN ZSCALE = - ABS(ZSCALE)
3550 IF YZREFLECT THEN XSCALE = - ABS(XSCALE)
3560 IF XZREFLECT THEN YSCALE = - ABS(YSCALE)

5000 '
5001 'Determine what reflections to do
5002 '
5100 RETURN
```

MERGE "10

The routine to determine what reflections to do, located between **5002** and **5100**, can be anything. Instead of using it, you may want to add keys to the keyboard interaction program to toggle the reflection variables.

The Matrices

The program above does reflection at the same time it does scaling. If we wish to reflect at a different time, such as after translation, the above program will not work. Instead, we will need to use matrices. These are listed here:

To reflect about the xy plane use:

```
1   0    0  0
0   1    0  0
0   0   -1  0
0   0    0  1
```

To reflect about the yz plane use:

```
-1  0  0  0
 0  1  0  0
 0  0  1  0
 0  0  0  1
```

To reflect about the xz plane use:

1	0	0	0
0	−1	0	0
0	0	1	0
0	0	0	1

If all of the reflections are done at the same time, you could make **XYRE-FLECTION**, etc., be set to −1 if a reflection should occur, and 1 otherwise. Then, instead of using three separate matrices, you could use:

YZREFLECTION	0	0	0
0	XZREFLECTION	0	0
0	0	XYREFLECTION	0
0	0	0	1

3.11: SHEARING

Shearing, the last transformation we will learn, is an interesting special effect. Imagine that our cube is made out of a block of Jello. Glue the bottom to a table. Now, put your hand on the top and push forward. The cube will distort into an elongated, somewhat diamond-shaped solid. This is shearing (see Figure 3.24).

Shearing is adding to one coordinate a number proportional to the other two. For example, one shear would be to add **2y + 3z** to the x coordinate.

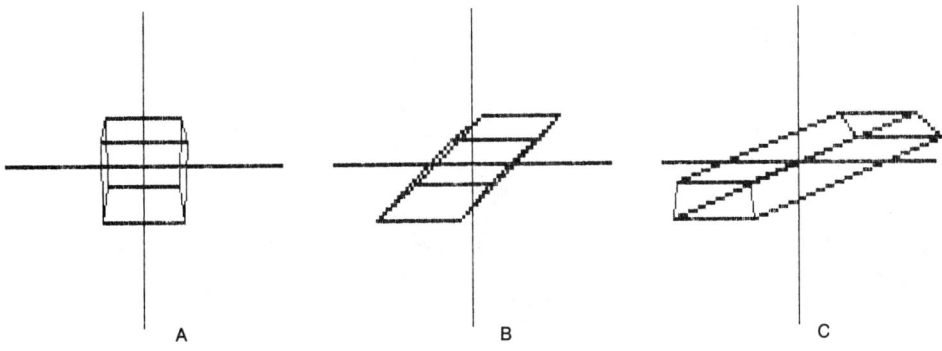

Figure 3.24
Part a is the cube. Part b is the same cube, but with XSHEARY set to 1. In part c, XSHEARY = 3 and XSHEARZ = 1.

Another would be to add **−2x** to the z coordinate. This can be done anywhere in the series of transformations. I like to shear before rotating.

To get a better feel for shearing, try it out yourself. The matrices for shearing are presented below. I would recommend going through the hassle of using **3DLG3**, because as the program will be faster, it will be easier to play with shearing.

For changing the x coordinate as a function of y and z:

1	0	0	0
XSHEARY	1	0	0
XSHEARZ	0	1	0
0	0	0	1

For changing the y coordinate as a function of x and z:

1	YSHEARX	0	0
0	1	0	0
0	YSHEARZ	1	0
0	0	0	1

For changing the z as a function of x and y:

1	0	0	ZSHEARX
0	1	0	ZSHEARY
0	0	1	0
0	0	0	1

If we set the shearing variables to zero, the matrix becomes the identity matrix, and thus has no effect on the shape.

You may also want to add commands to the keyboard interaction program to adjust the shearing values. I would suggest starting with one shearing matrix only.

3.12: A STEP BACK—MATRICES FOR TWO-DIMENSIONAL GRAPHICS

In the rest of this chapter we will not be using matrices. Before going on, let's see how to use them for two-dimensional graphics. There is really no difference between using them for three dimensions and two, except that we have fewer degrees of movement, and our matrices will be three by three. Our points will be in the form **(x,y,1)**. Adjusting the matrix operation routines to handle these sizes is pretty straightforward.

Scaling:

XSCALE	0	0
0	YSCALE	0
0	0	1

Translation:

1	0	0
0	1	0
XTRANSLATION	YTRANSLATION	1

In two dimensions, only the z axis can be used for rotation. Therefore, there is only one rotation matrix:

cos(ANGLE)	sin(ANGLE)	0
−sin(ANGLE)	cos(ANGLE)	0
0	0	1

X axis reflection:

1	0	0
0	−1	0
0	0	1

Y axis reflection:

−1	0	0
0	1	0
0	0	1

X shearing:

1	0	0
XSHEAR	1	0
0	0	1

Y shearing:

1	YSHEAR	0
0	1	0
0	0	1

With these matrices you can make a matrix-driven, two-dimensional line graphics system.

3.13: ROTATION IN THE GRAPHICS DEFINITION LANGUAGE

While we are wrapping up two-dimensional line graphics, we also should learn how to do rotation using the graphics definition language (GDL). There are two commands for this.

The first of these commands is **A**. Its format is:

A n

where **n** is either 0, 1, 2, or 3. **A** rotates any of the lines drawn following the command by the amount **n** indicates. If **n** is 0, the object is rotated 0 degrees; 1 causes 90-degree rotation; 2 causes 180-degree rotation; and 3 causes 270-degree rotation. When using the **A** command, the shapes are automatically adjusted for dot width after rotation.

In other words, if we do:

DRAW "A 1 U 20 R 48 D 20 L 48"

the shape drawn will still be a square, despite the fact that due to the rotation the longer lines are now drawn with bigger dots.

The second command is only available in BASIC 2.0. It is the turn angle command, **TA**. Its format is:

TA n

where **n** ranges from -360 to 360 degrees. Like **A**, any lines drawn following this command are rotated, but they can be rotated any amount. Negative angle measures result in clockwise turns; positive measures result in counterclockwise turns. Line size is automatically adjusted for dot width. Rotation is done about the last point referenced before **TA**.

The following is a quick demonstration of **TA**:

```
10 SCREEN 2
20 KEY OFF
30 SHUTTLE$ = "M -30,-8 L 60 M -9,-5 L 21 M +6,+5 D 21
   R 18 M +22,-8 M +24,-2 R 42 M +6,-3 BM -10,-3 L 14 U
   5 BM -24,+11 L 66"
40 FOR ANGLE = 0 TO 360 STEP 5
```

```
50    CLS
60    DRAW "TA = ANGLE; X SHUTTLE$;"
70 NEXT
80 END
```

> LOAD "13

After you run it, remove line **50**, and run it again.

3.14: VARIABLE PERSPECTIVE

So far we have discussed perspective from a fixed viewpoint. That is, we have assumed that the viewer has been looking straight at the origin. Now we will simulate what happens if the viewer moves about or looks elsewhere.

Translational Change of Perspective

The viewer's perspective can change in two ways. First, the viewer can walk around. Instead of staring straight at the origin, he stares straight ahead, but at another point. Try this out. Step a few feet back from the computer, and stare straight at the monitor. Now, move to the left, still staring straight ahead. Everything that you saw before has shifted to the right. In a similar fashion, you can move up and down, toward or away from the computer (Figure 3.25).

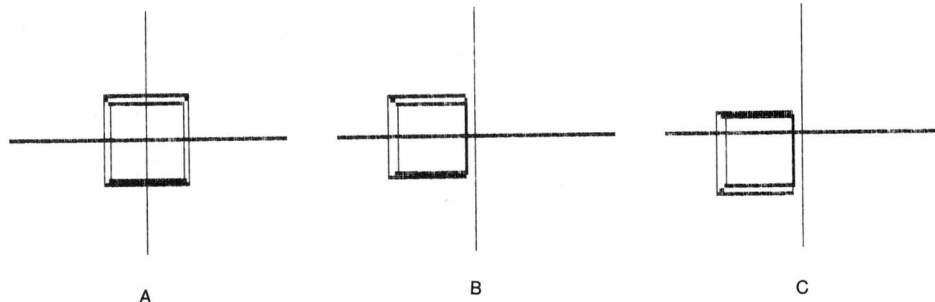

Figure 3.25
Part a shows the cube viewed from the normal viewpoint. In part b, the cube is viewed from 25 units to the right, and in c, from 25 units to the right, 10 units up.

104 Three-Dimensional Line Graphics

One way to account for such motion would be to rewrite the perspective routine. But after doing so we would come to the following conclusion: the visual change due to the viewer translating is the same as if all of the objects in the visual scene translated in an equal and opposite direction. In other words, suppose we are looking at a cube. Now, let's move two units to the right and two units down. What we will see is the same scene as before with the cube translated two units left and two units up.

To allow translational movement, add the following matrix after all other movement matrices:

1	0	0	0
0	1	0	0
0	0	1	0
−VIEWERXCHANGE	−VIEWERYCHANGE	−VIEWERZCHANGE	1

Rotational Change of Perspective

The other way viewpoint can change is that the viewer can keep the same position, but look elsewhere. For example, look straight at the monitor. Now, move only your head so that you look higher and higher. This is a rotational change of perspective (Figure 3.26).

Accounting for rotational change is harder than accounting for translational change. For translational change, we could simply translate all objects. But suppose to account for rotational change we rotated all objects? Well, when we rotate, we rotate everything about the origin. But, as viewers, we are not located at the origin. So when we rotate our heads, we are not rotating about the origin, but we are rotating relative to our position.

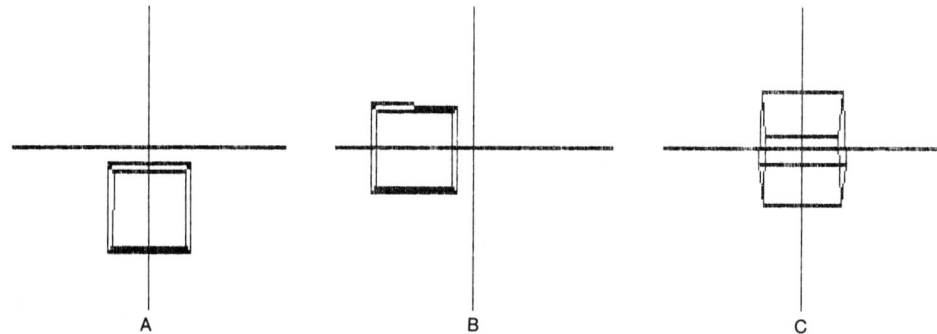

A   B   C

Figure 3.26
Part a shows the cube viewed when looking up .1 radians. Part b is viewed looking .1 radians to the right. In figure c, the viewer has walked in a circular path above the cube, keeping his eyes centered on the cube.

To account for this, we need to move the Cartesian system so that the origin is where the viewer is. But at the same time, all old distances need to be preserved (Figure 3.27). Then, we rotate everything by the amount the viewer rotates, but in the opposite direction (Figure 3.28). Finally, we move the viewpoint to its normal position: **(0, 0, focal distance)** (Figure 3.29).

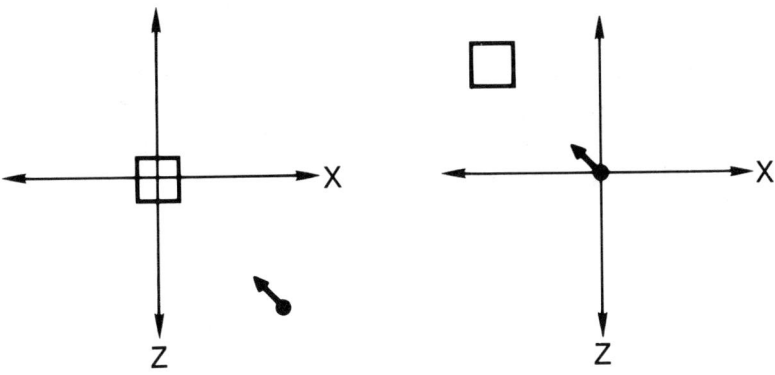

Figure 3.27
Move the viewpoint to the origin.

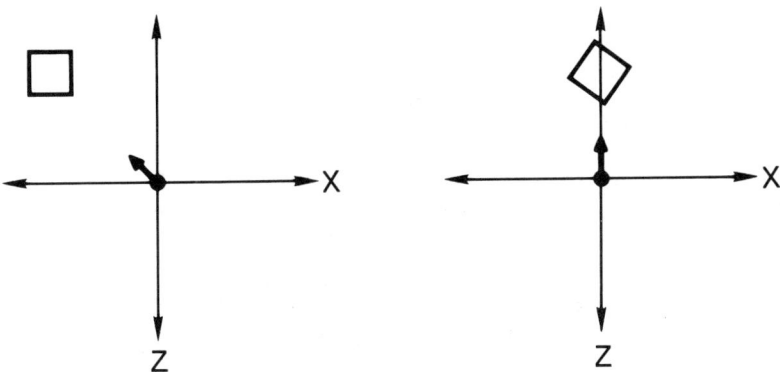

Figure 3.28
Rotate by negative the amount the viewer rotates.

So, suppose **X** was our old total transform matrix. To adjust for rotational change of viewpoint, we find:

$$X * T_{o \text{ to } v} * R_v * T_{v \text{ to } o}$$

where $\mathbf{T_{o\ to\ v}}$, the matrix to translate the origin to the viewer's position is:

1	0	0	0
0	1	0	0
0	0	1	0
−VIEWERXCHANGE	−VIEWERYCHANGE	−(FOCAL DISTANCE + VIEWERZCHANGE)	1

$\mathbf{R_v}$, the matrix to adjust for the viewer's rotation is the multiplication of the three rotation matrices we learned before, with **−VIEWERXANGLE**, **−VIEWERYANGLE**, and **−VIEWERZANGLE** substituted for **XANGLE**, **YANGLE**, and **ZANGLE**.

Finally, the matrix to move the viewpoint, $\mathbf{T_{v\ to\ o}}$, is:

1	0	0	0
0	1	0	0
0	0	1	0
0	0	FOCAL DISTANCE	1

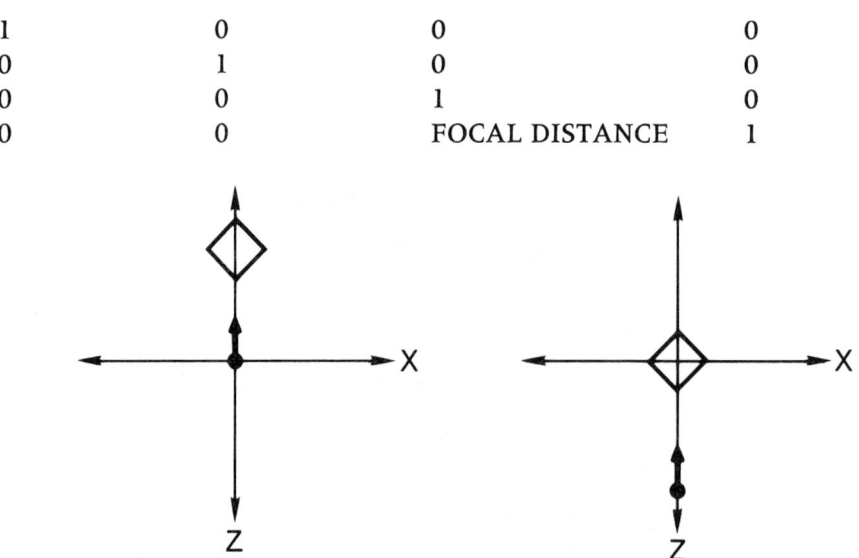

Figure 3.29
Restore the viewpoint to the normal viewpoint.

Trying It Out

Before trying out this routine, you need to add subroutines to set the viewer's translational and rotational changes. Either make the viewpoint change with time or add keys to the keyboard interaction subroutine to change viewpoint. Experiment with walking around objects, and also with having objects moving at the same time you are.

3.15: CLIPPING

Any graphics system needs some way to cope with shapes that go off of the screen. The process of only drawing the parts of lines that are on the screen is called *clipping*. Those with BASIC 2.0 will already be familiar with clipping.

There are two basic types of clipping—*xy clipping* and *z clipping*. Xy clipping cuts lines whose end points' x and y coordinates exceed certain bounds. If we want to keep lines from going off the screen, we use xy clipping. Those with BASIC 1.1 will want to add this type of clipping. Z clipping, on the other hand, clips lines whose z coordinates go out of bounds. Neither BASIC 1.1 or BASIC 2.0 does z clipping.

Boundaries

The previous paragraph dealt with bounds. But what are they? Well, a *boundary* divides the screen into what can and what cannot be drawn. We will be dealing with six boundaries—the minimum x, y, and z planes, and the maximum x, y, and z planes. Any line with end points having coordinates less than the minimum values or greater than the maximum values needs to be clipped (Figure 3.30). When a coordinate lies on the wrong side of a boundary, we'll say that it *exceeds the boundary*.

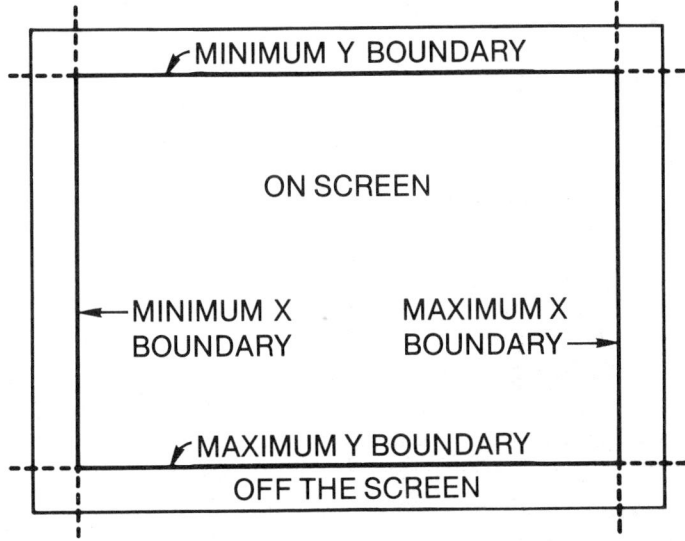

Figure 3.30
Boundary lines.

Xy Clipping

We will start by learning how to do xy clipping. Let the minimum x coordinate boundary line be **x = xmin**, the maximum x line be **x = xmax**, the minimum y line be **y = ymin**, and the maximum y line be **y = ymax**. (Because we are just interested in the xy plane, we can consider boundaries to be lines rather than planes.) Now, suppose we are given two points, **a** and **b**, with coordinates (x_a, y_a) and (x_b, y_b), respectively. If both of these points are within the boundary lines, we have nothing to worry about. But suppose they are not? Then we have to find what segment of line **ab** can be seen.

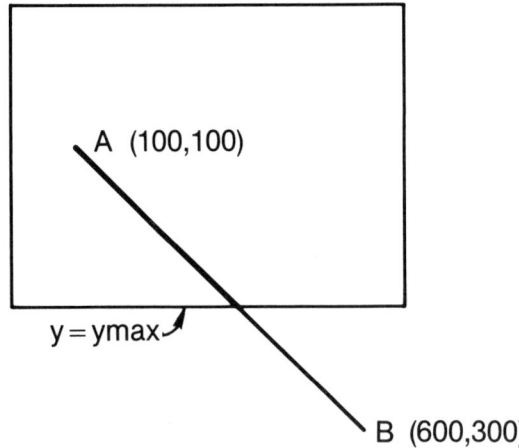

Figure 3.31
Line **ab** goes off the screen.

A line going outside the boundaries is shown in Figure 3.31. The viewable segment—the one we want to find—is highlighted. Note that its end points are at the intersection of **ab** and the boundary lines **ab** crosses. This will hold for any line that needs to be clipped. To be more explicit, suppose **xmin** and **ymin** are 0, **xmax** is 640, **ymax** is 200, **a** is (100,100), and **b** is (600,300). Then, **a** is within bounds; **b** isn't—it crosses **y = ymax**. To clip **ab**, we find the point where it intersects **y = ymax**. Call this point **b'**. The clipped line is **ab'**.

Figure 3.32a shows a more complicated case. Both **a** and **b** are out of bounds, and what's more, they cross more than one boundary line. From visual inspection we know to which boundary line to clip. But this isn't so easy for the computer. For example, in Figure 3.32b, the points exceed the same boundary lines as the line in Figure 3.32a, but this time different boundary lines intersect the end points of the clipped line. And in Figure 3.32c, no part of the line can be seen.

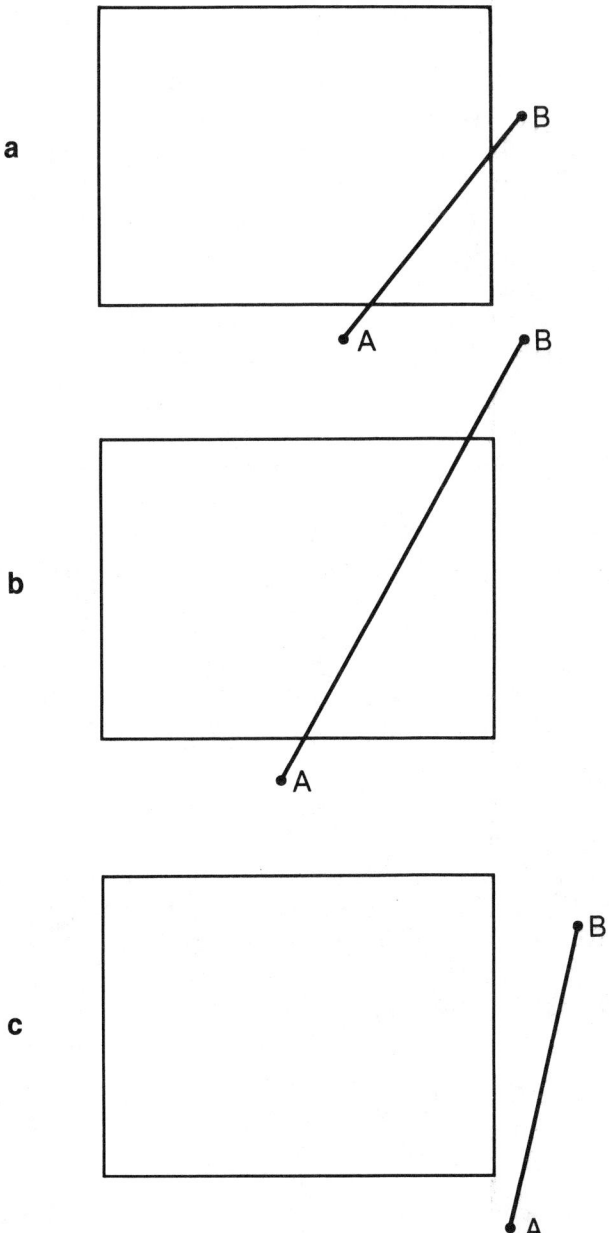

Figure 3.32
Point **a** always has y coordinate too large. Point **b** always has x coordinate too large. But **ab** crosses different boundaries in parts a, b, and c.

Clipping Routine Logic

It could be very difficult to write a subroutine that takes all these possibilites into account. To get around this bind, we will use recursion. We want our subroutine to do one of two things: either it will return with the end points of the line to plot, or it will tell us not to plot the line. So the first thing we'll do is check if the line can't be seen at all, or if both end points are within the boundaries. If either of these conditions are met, we don't need to do clipping.

In other words, we'll see if the first point needs to be changed. If it exceeds an x boundary, then we will find its point of intersection with the boundary, and call our clipping subroutine again. If one of the first two conditions (the line can be plotted or cannot be seen at all) isn't met, we will need to check the first point again, to see if its y coordinate needs changing. If so, we find the intersection with the proper y boundary and start all over again. If we don't need to change the y coordinate, then the first point is OK. We then go through the whole process for the second point.

As a result, either we'll find that no part of the line can be seen, or we will find the end points of the segment that can be seen. Only three problems remain: how do we know if a line can't be seen; how do we know if both end points are within the boundaries; and how do we find the intersection of the line with a boundary line?

Figure 3.33 gives several examples of lines that go off the screen. Common to all of them is this: either both end points are on the wrong side of the same boundary line, or, when the segment is clipped to a boundary line it exceeds, both end points exceed the same boundary line. For example, both end points of line 1 are outside the line **y = ymax**. Likewise, both end points of line 2 are outside **x = xmin**. When we find the intersection of line 3 with the boundary lines, then if point **a** is clipped to **y = ymin**, both end points exceed **x = xmax**; if point **b** is clipped to **x = xmax**, both end points exceed **y = ymin**.

Thus, a line (or its intersection with boundaries it exceeds) is off the screen if:

((x_a > xmax) AND (x_b > xmax)) OR ((x_a < xmin) AND (x_b < xmin)) OR ((y_a > ymax) AND (y_b > ymax)) OR ((y_a < ymin) AND (y_b < ymin)).

Figure 3.34 shows several lines completely on the screen. We conclude that a line is completely on the screen if both of its end points are within the boundaries.

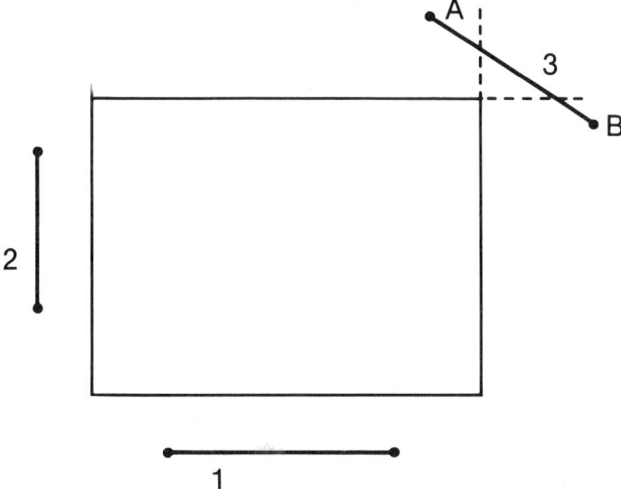

Figure 3.33
Several lines that are off the screen.

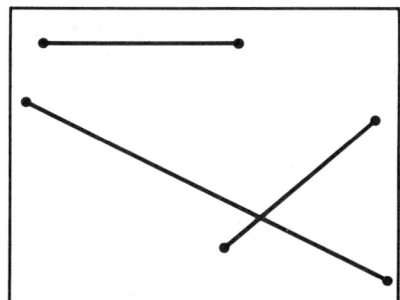

Figure 3.34
Several lines completely on the screen.

Now we need to figure how to find where two lines intersect. This amounts to solving two simultaneous equations: the equation for the boundary line and the equation for the line **ab**. Perhaps the most common equation form for a line is:

y = mx + b

where **m** is the *slope* and **b** is the *y intercept*. This is called *slope-intercept form*. The slope, **m**, is defined to be $(y_b - y_a)/(x_b - x_a)$. To solve for the y intercept, we need only substitute a point. Let's put in the coordinates for **a**.

112 Three-Dimensional Line Graphics

We get $y_a - mx_a$. Putting these back into the equation and solving for y, we find:

$$y_{new} = y_a + (x_{new} - x_a) * (y_b - y_a) / (x_b - x_a)$$

To find where **ab** crosses $x = xmax$, all we need to do is set $x_{new} = xmax$ and solve for y_{new}.

If we want to find the intersection with a y boundary, the above equation won't work. Instead, we use:

$$x_{new} = x_a + (y_{new} - y_a) * (x_b - x_a) / (y_b - y_a)$$

For finding the intersection with the maximum y line we set y_{new} equal to **ymax**. For intersecting the minimum y line, we set y_{new} equal to **ymin**.

The Routine

Now we are ready to design a clipping routine. We will call it with the end points of the first point in **X(1)**, **Y(1)** and the end points of the second point in **X(2)**, **Y(2)**. On return, **SKIP** will be true if the line should not be drawn. Otherwise, **SKIP** will be false, and **X(1)**, **Y(1)** and **X(2)**, **Y(2)** will be the coordinates of the line to draw.

To start, we need a subroutine to see if the end points are out of bounds. First:

LOAD "3DLG3

Then add:

```
11500 '
11501 'Set booleans indicating if point is off screen
      in x and y directions
11502 '
11510 IF X(POINT.) > XMAX THEN XTOOBIG(POINT.) = TRUE
      ELSE XTOOBIG(POINT.) = FALSE
11520 IF Y(POINT.) > YMAX THEN YTOOBIG(POINT.) = TRUE
      ELSE YTOOBIG(POINT.) = FALSE
11530 IF X(POINT.) < XMIN THEN XTOOSMALL(POINT.) = TRUE
      ELSE XTOOSMALL(POINT.) = FALSE
11540 IF Y(POINT.) < YMIN THEN YTOOSMALL(POINT.) = TRUE
      ELSE YTOOSMALL(POINT.) = FALSE
11550 RETURN
```

Now, we need to call up this subroutine for each point and then see if the line can be drawn, is off the screen, or needs clipping. In case it needs clipping, we will set **POINT.** to 1. This indicates whether we are finding new coordinates for the first or second point. Also, we will compute **DELTAX** and **DELTAY**. **DELTAY/DELTAX** is the slope. We will use these terms in any clipping; it will save time to compute them only once. We add:

```
11000 '
11001 'Clip to screen boundaries
11002 '
11003 'XMIN = minimum x allowed     XMAX = maximum x
      allowed
11004 'YMIN = minimum y allowed     YMAX = maximum y
      allowed
11005 '     these are in screen coordinates
11006 '
11007 '
11010 POINT.= 2 : GOSUB 11510 : POINT. = 1 : GOSUB
      11510 : DELTAX = X(2) - X(1) : DELTAY = Y(2) -
      Y(1)

11020 IF (XTOOBIG(1) AND XTOOBIG(2)) OR (XTOOSMALL(1)
      AND XTOOSMALL(2)) OR (YTOOBIG(1) AND YTOOBIG(2))
      OR (YTOOSMALL(1) AND YTOOSMALL(2)) THEN SKIP =
      TRUE : RETURN

11030 IF NOT (XTOOBIG(1) OR XTOOBIG(2) OR XTOOSMALL(1)
      OR XTOOSMALL(2) OR YTOOBIG(1) OR YTOOBIG(2) OR
      YTOOSMALL(1) OR YTOOSMALL(2)) THEN SKIP = FALSE :
      RETURN
```

Line **11020** determines if the line cannot be drawn. Line **11030** sees if the line is ready to be drawn.

Now, if the line needs clipping, we have to find the new coordinates. To do this we add:

```
11040 IF XTOOBIG(POINT.) THEN Y(POINT.) = Y(1) + (XMAX
      - X(1)) * DELTAY / DELTAX : X(POINT.) = XMAX :
      GOSUB 11510 : GOTO 11020 ELSE IF
      XTOOSMALL(POINT.) THEN Y(POINT.) = Y(1) + (XMIN -
      X(1)) * DELTAY / DELTAX : X(POINT.) = XMIN :
      GOSUB 11510 : GOTO 11020

11050 IF YTOOBIG(POINT.) THEN X(POINT.) = X(1) + (YMAX
      - Y(1)) * DELTAX / DELTAY : Y(POINT.) = YMAX :
      GOSUB 11510 : GOTO 11020 ELSE IF
      YTOOSMALL(POINT.) THEN X(POINT.) = X(1) + (YMIN -
      Y(1)) * DELTAX / DELTAY : Y(POINT.) = YMIN :
      GOSUB 11510 : GOTO 11020

11060 POINT. = 2 : GOTO 11020
```

Line **11040** adjusts the x coordinate; line **11050** adjusts the y coordinate. Line **11060** tells the program to start working with the second end point.

Before we can run this, we also need to add the following lines to set up **X(1)**, **Y(1)**, **X(2)**, and **Y(2)**, and to call the clipping routine:

```
9020     X(1) = NEWPOINTS(XCOORD,LINES(FROM,LINENUM))
9030     Y(1) = NEWPOINTS(YCOORD,LINES(FROM,LINENUM))
9040     X(2) = NEWPOINTS(XCOORD,LINES(TO.,LINENUM))
9050     Y(2) = NEWPOINTS(YCOORD,LINES(TO.,LINENUM))
9060     GOSUB 11010      'CLIP
9070     IF NOT SKIP THEN LINE (X(1),Y(1)) - (X(2),Y(2))
9080 NEXT
```

Note that the call is done from within the line drawing subroutine.

The final step is to set **XMAX**, **XMIN**, **YMAX**, and **YMIN**. Because we clip just before drawing, these should be in screen coordinates. Set these at line **170**. To start, use the following:

```
170 XMAX = 500 : XMIN = 50 : YMAX = 150 : YMIN = 50
```

MERGE "15P1

Now run the program. Move the object across all screen boundaries to see how it gets cut. Then, change the clipping boundaries.

Advanced Techniques

To be fancy, we can clip to a nonrectangular border. We can form the boundary out of lines with any slope as long as they intersect to form a closed space. If such changes are made, lines **11040**, **11050**, and **11510–11540** will need to be changed accordingly.

Z Clipping

Although z clipping is similar to xy clipping, there are two important differences. First, because we are only dealing with two boundary planes, it will be simpler to see if lines need to be clipped or not, and we will be able to clip them without recursion. Second, instead of dealing with just the x and y coordinates already in screen coordinates, we will be dealing with x, y, and z Cartesian coordinates. Thus, the line equations we will solve will be three-dimensional line equations.

We will need to do z clipping before figuring out perspective. This requires major changes. Because we do z clipping for each line, we will call the z clipping subroutine from the line-drawing subroutine. But, we then need to do perspective, adjust for dot width, and convert to screen coordinates. To speed things up, we will do these in the line routine, right after calling z clipping.

The Z Clipping Routine

Let's look at the code to do z clipping. First, we check to see if the line cannot be seen, or if no clipping is necessary. As with xy clipping, we will set **SKIP** appropriately:

```
11600 '
11601 'z clip
11602 '
11603 'ZMIN = minimum z value         ZMAX = maximum z
      value
11604 '
11605 '
11610 IF (Z(1) < ZMAX) AND (Z(1) > ZMIN) AND (Z(2) <
      ZMAX) AND (Z(2) > ZMIN) THEN SKIP = FALSE : GOTO
      11700
11620 IF ((Z(1) > ZMAX) AND (Z(2) > ZMAX)) OR ((Z(1) <
      ZMIN) AND (Z(2) < ZMIN)) THEN SKIP = TRUE : GOTO
      11700
```

If clipping is needed, we do it:

```
11630 SKIP = FALSE
11640 IF Z(1) > ZMAX THEN NEWZ = ZMAX : GOSUB 11810 :
      X(1) = NEWX : Y(1) = NEWY : Z(1) = NEWZ ELSE IF
      Z(1) < ZMIN THEN NEWZ = ZMIN : GOSUB 11810 : X(1)
      = NEWX : Y(1) = NEWY : Z(1) = NEWZ

11650 IF Z(2) > ZMAX THEN NEWZ = ZMAX : GOSUB 11810 :
      X(2) = NEWX : Y(2) = NEWY : Z(2) = NEWZ ELSE IF
      Z(2) < ZMIN THEN NEWZ = ZMIN : GOSUB 11810 : X(2)
      = NEWX : Y(2) = NEWY : Z(2) = NEWZ

11700 RETURN

11800 '
11801 'Compute new z coordinate
11802 '
11810 T = (NEWZ - Z(1))/(Z(2) - Z(1))
```

116 Three-Dimensional Line Graphics

```
11820 NEWX = X(1) + (X(2) - X(1)) * T
11830 NEWY = Y(1) + (Y(2) - Y(1)) * T
11840 RETURN
```

We find the intersection point by finding the intersection of the plane **z** = **NEWZ** and the three-dimensional line equation of the line connecting the end points. This is done in the subroutine at **11810**. Note how we get around recursion by using the temporary variables **NEWX**, **NEWY**, and **NEWZ**.

Now, we need to set up the variables for z clipping, and then call the z clipping subroutine:

```
9020      X(1) = NEWPOINTS(XCOORD,LINES(FROM,LINENUM))
9030      Y(1) = NEWPOINTS(YCOORD,LINES(FROM,LINENUM))
9040      Z(1) = NEWPOINTS(ZCOORD,LINES(FROM,LINENUM))
9050      X(2) = NEWPOINTS(XCOORD,LINES(TO.,LINENUM))
9060      Y(2) = NEWPOINTS(YCOORD,LINES(TO.,LINENUM))
9070      Z(2) = NEWPOINTS(ZCOORD,LINES(TO.,LINENUM))
9080      GOSUB 11610       'zclip
```

Following this, either we don't draw, or we do perspective, adjust for dot width, convert to screen coordinates, and xy clip:

```
9090      IF SKIP THEN 9220
9100      'perspective
9110      X(1) = FOCALDISTANCE * X(1) / (FOCALDISTANCE -
          Z(1))
9120      X(2) = FOCALDISTANCE * X(2) / (FOCALDISTANCE -
          Z(2))
9130      Y(1) = FOCALDISTANCE * Y(1) / (FOCALDISTANCE -
          Z(1))
9140      Y(2) = FOCALDISTANCE * Y(2) / (FOCALDISTANCE -
          Z(2))
9150      'adjust for dot width and convert to screen
          coordinates
9160      X(1) = X(1) * MAXXRES / MAXYRES / ASPECTRATIO +
          MAXXRES/2
9170      X(2) = X(2) * MAXXRES / MAXYRES / ASPECTRATIO +
          MAXXRES/2
9180      Y(1) = MAXYRES/2 - Y(1)
9190      Y(2) = MAXYRES/2 - Y(2)
9200      GOSUB 11010       'xy clip
9210      IF NOT SKIP THEN LINE (X(1),Y(1)) - (X(2),Y(2))
9220 NEXT
9500 RETURN
```

> **MERGE "15P2**

These program lines are all additions to the line drawing subroutine.

Finally, we set the z boundaries, remove the calls to the perspective routine and the routine to adjust for dot width, and convert to screen coordinates. Delete **710** and **720** and add:

```
180 ZMIN = -500 : ZMAX = 500
```

Remember that these are Cartesian coordinates.

Trying It Out

Run the program and move the object back and forth until it gets clipped. Place it back at the origin, and then scale so that one side is very long. Now, rotate about the x axis. As the object rotates, different sections will be clipped. Experiment with using different z clipping boundaries.

3.16: SPECIAL BASIC 2.0 COMMANDS

You have now learned everything necessary to make a really good, thorough three-dimensional graphics program. In this section, we will explore two graphics commands only available in BASIC 2.0.

WINDOW

The first of these is the **WINDOW** statement. **WINDOW** allows us to change what BASIC considers the coordinates of the screen. Normally, BASIC uses (0,0) as the upper left corner, and, assuming high resolution,

WINDOW [[SCREEN] (x_1,y_1) — (x_2,y_2)]

Let x_{min} be the smaller of the x coordinates, and x_{max} the larger of the x coordinates. Define y_{min} and y_{max} similarly. After:

WINDOW (x_1,y_1) — (x_2,y_2)

is executed, the lower left corner is considered to be (x_{min},y_{min}) and the upper right corner is considered (x_{max}, y_{max}) (Figure 3.35).

As an example, suppose we type:

WINDOW (−320,−100) − (320,100)

Then, if we type:

LINE (0,0) − (320,−100)

a line will be drawn from the center of the screen to the bottom right corner. This is a Cartesian coordinate system. By making $x_{max} - x_{min}$ four-thirds as much as $y_{max} - y_{min}$, we no longer need to convert to screen coordinates and adjust for dot width. We can just plot Cartesian coordinates directly.

Let's try this. Add:

```
450 WINDOW (-133,-100) - (133,100)
```

and delete **720**. (If you have added z clipping, delete lines **9150–9200**.) Now run the program. It works just as before, but quicker.

We can use **WINDOW** to achieve two special effects—*scaling* and *panning*. If we make the end points of the screen larger, any object being drawn occupies less of the screen. Likewise, by decreasing the coordinates of the screen, any object takes up more of the screen. We can also change the part of the screen to which the origin corresponds. This change has the effect of panning. If we make the origin 20 units to the right of the center, all shapes will be drawn 20 units more to the right. And points that went off of the left side before may show up. Experiment with these two techniques.

If the **SCREEN** option is included, (x_{min}, y_{min}) will correspond to the upper left corner, and (x_{max}, y_{max}) will correspond to the lower right corner. This layout is the same as the screen coordinate system; only we can change the coordinates of the corners.

Remember that whenever we use **WINDOW**, BASIC sorts the coordinates so that the smaller and larger coordinates are put together. So:

WINDOW SCREEN (100,20) − (10,100)

is the same as:

WINDOW SCREEN (10,20) − (100,100)

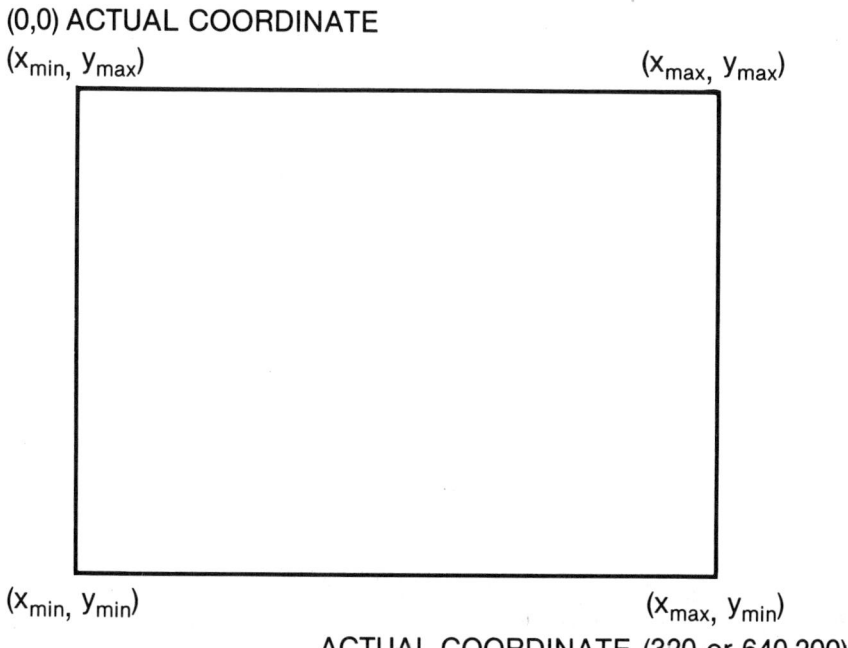

Figure 3.35
The effect of **WINDOW**.

WINDOW without any arguments, **SCREEN**, and **RUN** negate the effects of any previous **WINDOW**.

VIEW

The **VIEW** command is another exciting graphics command unique to BASIC 2.0. It defines what part of the screen gets used for graphics.
The format for **VIEW** is:

VIEW [[SCREEN] (x_1,y_1) − (x_2,y_2) [,[color] [,[boundary]]]]]

(x_1,y_1) and (x_2,y_2) are given in screen coordinates. Define x_{min}, y_{min}, x_{max}, and y_{max} as for **WINDOW**. **VIEW** makes (x_{min},y_{min}) the upper left corner of the graphics screen and (x_{max},y_{max}) the lower right corner. Only points within these bounds will be plotted. **color** and **boundary** are numbers between 0 and 3. If **color** is specified, the part of the screen within the viewport—the area set up for graphics by **VIEW**—will be filled with that color. If **boundary** is given, the boundary of the viewport will be drawn with **color**.

(640,200) as the lower right corner. This was why we needed the routine to convert from Cartesian to screen coordinates. **WINDOW** lets us get around this. Its format is:

For example, type:

WINDOW   (to remove the effects of any previous **WINDOW**)
VIEW (10,10) — (630,190),,1

This draws a rectangle 10 units in from all sides of the screen. From now on, only points within this rectangle can be accessed. For example, type:

LINE (0,0) — (220,190)

Now try:

CLS

The only part of the screen cleared is that within the rectangle.

If we use **VIEW** with **WINDOW**, whatever type of coordinate system is defined by **WINDOW** will be mapped to the viewport defined by **VIEW** (Figure 3.26). Type:

WINDOW SCREEN (0,0) — (640,200)
LINE (5,5) — (5,195)

A line will be drawn slightly below the top of the rectangle to slightly above the bottom of the rectangle, instead of from the actual (5,5) to the actual (5,195).

VIEW can be used for scaling: by decreasing the part of the screen used for graphics, all objects will seem smaller.

The **SCREEN** option means that all coordinates plotted will be relative to the normal viewport, but only those points within the **VIEW** defined viewport will be plotted. For example, to do xy clipping, delete **11010 — 11550**, and add:

```
9200 VIEW SCREEN (XMIN,YMIN) - (XMAX,YMAX)
```

Note how much time this saves.

A more powerful use of **VIEW** is to create windows on the screen. For example, we could use the upper left part of the screen to display a top view of an object, the upper right to display a side view, the lower left to display a front view, and the lower right to display data about the shape or, perhaps, command options.

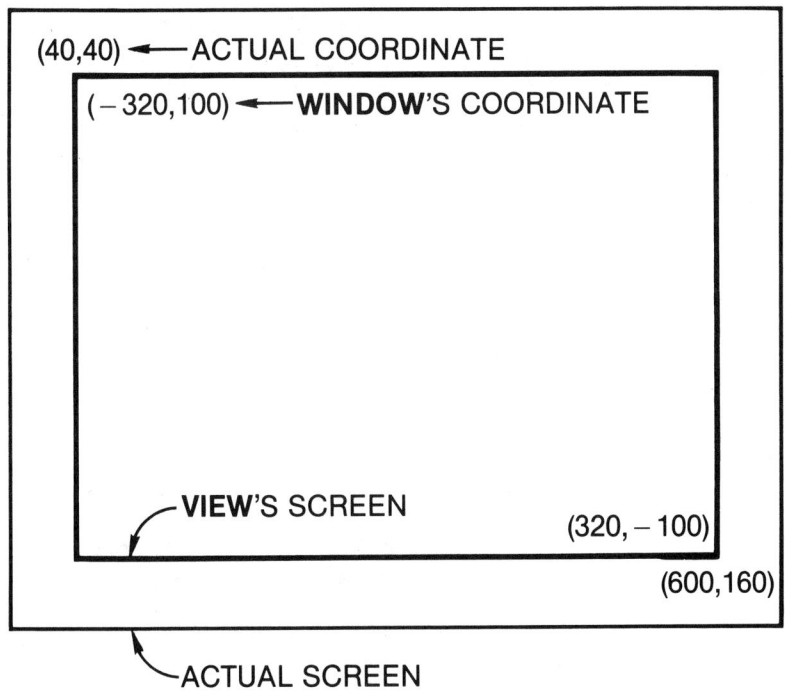

Figure 3.36
The effect of **VIEW** and **WINDOW** combined. In this case, **VIEW (40,40) — (600,160):WINDOW (−320,100) — (320,−100)**

Let's look at a more simple example of windowing. We will split the screen into two parts. Every cycle through, we will plot our object in the window not used immediately before. Drawing will go back and forth between screens. As a result, we will always be able to see the last move as well as the current move. Add:

```
220 CHECK = 1
450 WINDOW (-200,-295) - (200,295)
460 VIEW (5,5) - (315,195),,1
```

Delete **9200**, then as the last step of the line drawing subroutine, add:

```
CHECK = -CHECK : IF CHECK < 0 THEN VIEW (325,5) -
(635,195),,1 ELSE VIEW (5,5) - (315,195),,1
```

VIEW without parameters causes the full screen to be used as a viewport.

4

Assembly Language Line Graphics

So far we have been programming in BASIC. This has been great for software development; we have been able to experiment with different algorithms and immediately see the effects of changing our program. Unfortunately, BASIC doesn't give us the speed and flexibility we often desire. This chapter is the first on graphics programming in Assembly Language, a language that gives us complete control over the computer and operates at breathless speed.

We will start with some basics: using the graphics screen, plotting dots, clearing the screen, and drawing lines. Then, we will see how to put these together to form a three-dimensional line graphics program like **3DLG3.BAS**.

A NOTE ON PROGRAMS

Almost every section in this chapter presents a program. The variables each routine needs, presented before each procedure, should be placed within the data segment. Most procedures need extra code to run them. They tie into the main program developed throughout the chapter. It is not hard to write routines to test them separately.

When procedures are long and repetitive, I will leave sections for you to complete. Such sections are clearly indicated and can be filled in easily

4.1: SETTING THE GRAPHICS MODES

Before we can draw pictures, we need to set the graphics mode. In BASIC we did this with the **SCREEN** command. There are a couple of ways to do this in Assembly Language; the easiest is to use *interrupts*.

Interrupts are a set of Machine Language subroutines provided by IBM through DOS and BIOS that are accessed by using the **int** command. They perform a wide variety of functions, from displaying characters on the screen to reading data from the disk.

We use **interrupt 10H** to set the graphics mode. This interrupt has several capabilities. Among others, it can change the cursor, output characters, and plot dots. For more information on this and the other interrupts, see the *DOS Manual* and the *Technical Reference Manual*.

To set the graphics mode, we call **interrupt 10H** with the following:

AH = 0
AL = 4 for medium-resolution graphics (color)
     = 5 for medium-resolution graphics (black and white)
         Use this if your graphics monitor is not a color monitor.
     = 6 for high-resolution graphics

If we are using medium-resolution graphics, we may want to change the palette. To do this, we call **interrupt 10H** with:

AH = 11
BH = 1
BL = 0 for palette 0
     = 1 for palette 1

The Routine

Let's write a procedure to set the graphics mode. Use the following variable definitions:

```
;
mode                    db              2       ;default to high res
palette                 db              0
;
```

Then,

```
;
;set graphics mode
; called with:
;    mode = 1 for medium resolution
;         = 2 for high resolution
;    if mode = 1 then
;         palette = 0 for green/red/yellow
;                 = 1 for cyan/magenta/white
;
set_mode        proc    near
                cmp     mode,2
                je      set_high_res
; set medium res
                mov     ah,0            ;set mode
                mov     al,4
                int     10h
                mov     ah,11           ;set palette
                mov     bh,1
                mov     bl,palette
                int     10h
                jmp     short s_m_end
;
set_high_res:
                mov     ah,0
                mov     al,6
                int     10h
;
s_m_end:
                ret
;
set_mode        endp
```

The programs in this chapter are in the **CHAPTER4** directory. The Assembly Language programs are stored as text files, with the variables section first and the code section second. Any routines in the text left for the reader to complete appear in full in the disk programs. You may want to edit and merge the Assembly Language files to create utilities or a large three-dimensional (3-D) program.

Source code for a complete 3-D Assembly Language program, incorporating all the features of Chapter 4 as well as some from Chapters 5 and 7, appears in the file **3D.ASM**, in the main directory. Look over it to see how the programs from the chapter fit together. (Variations are due to the additional features.)

3D.EXE is the executable form of **3D.ASM**. Be sure to experiment with it after reading this chapter (or before to give you incentive)—simply type **3D**. It uses the keyboard interaction commands developed in Section 3.8.

For Assembly Language programs, the program disk notes will simply tell the name of the file in which the source code is located.

The first **set_dot** routine is located in **1P1.ASM**

To use this procedure you need to incorporate it into a full Assembly Language program. For example, you could use:

```
title               test set mode
;
stack               segment para stack 'stack'
                    db          64 dup (?)
stack               ends
;
variables           segment
mode                db          1
palette             db          0
variables           ends
;
code                segment
                    assume cs:code,ss:stack,ds:variables
testit              proc        far
                    push        ds          ;set up stack for return from
                    mov         ax,0        ;program
                    push        ax
                    mov         ax,variables    ;make DS point to
                    mov         ds,ax           ;the variables
                    call        set_mode
                    ret
testit              endp

;
;PUT set_mode HERE
;

;
code                ends
                    end         testit
```

> **1P2.ASM**

4.2: PLOTTING POINTS

Now that we can set the graphics mode, let's see how to plot points. We'll start by using interrupts. We call **interrupt 10H** with the following:

AH = 12
CX = x coordinate
DX = y coordinate
AL = color

The x and y coordinates are in the screen coordinate system.
So, as a procedure:

```
;
x                       dw      100     ;100 is just to test the routine
y                       dw      100     ;100 is for testing the routine
color                   db      1
;

;
;set dot using interrupts
;
;called with:
;   x = x coordinate
;   y = y coordinate
;   color = 0 - 1   if high res
;         = 0 - 3   if medium res
;
set_dot                 proc    near
                        mov     ah,12
                        mov     dx,y
                        mov     cx,x
                        mov     al,color
                        int     10h
;
                        ret
set_dot                 endp
```

2P1.ASM

That's all. Run the program and a dot will appear at (**x,y**). Be careful; this interrupt does not check to see if the x and y coordinate values are valid. If you try to plot a dot off the screen you may end up wiping out an important section of memory.

Memory Map

While using interrupts is convenient, we can do faster and fancier graphics by directly accessing the graphics screen.

The graphics screen is *memory mapped*. This means that an area of memory is set aside for graphics. Every dot on the screen corresponds to one or more bits in this memory. By changing these bits, we can make a dot appear or disappear and change its color. As we will later see, by moving data around the graphics screen memory, we can move pictures across the screen.

Let's experiment with this. Use **set_mode** to display the high-resolution screen. (Use an assembled version of the test program and run it directly or load it in DEBUG and enter **g**.) Now, get into DEBUG, and type:

e b800:646 ff ff 01 80

A bunch of dots will appear on the screen. Now, type:

e b800:2646 ff ff 01 80

The same dots will appear directly beneath the old ones.

The graphics screen is divided into 200 rows of 80-byte-sized columns. Depending upon resolution, each byte holds information for four or eight dots. The 100 even rows are stored in memory starting at B8000H, and the 100 odd rows in memory starting at BA000H (Figure 4.1).

In the high-resolution mode, each byte stores eight dots. The leftmost bit (high order) represents the leftmost dot in the column; the rightmost bit (low order) represents the rightmost dot (Figure 4.2). If a bit is set (=1), then a dot is plotted. Otherwise, the space is left blank.

In the medium-resolution mode, it takes two bits to represent each dot. These two bits, taking values between 0 and 3, store the color of the dot. Using color 0 has the effect of plotting no dot (Figure 4.3).

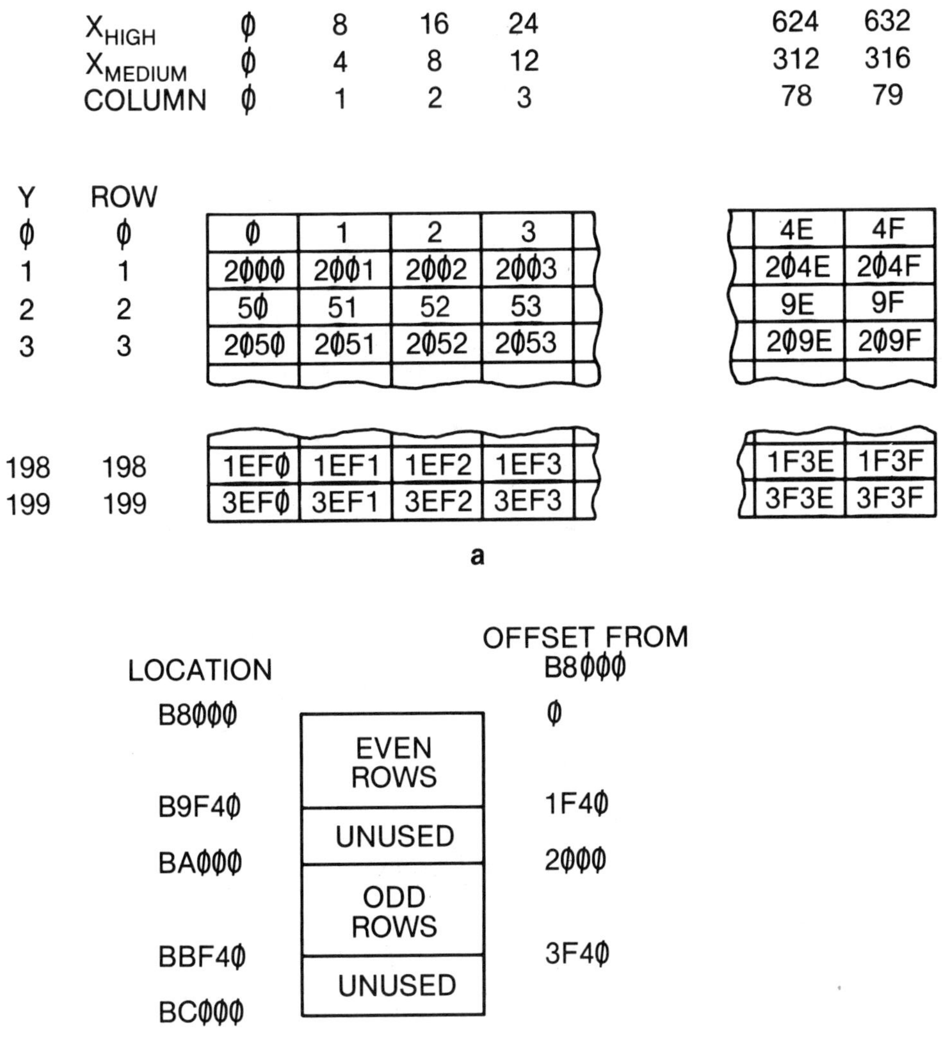

X$_{HIGH}$	0	8	16	24		624	632
X$_{MEDIUM}$	0	4	8	12		312	316
COLUMN	0	1	2	3		78	79

Y	ROW	0	1	2	3		4E	4F
0	0							
1	1	2000	2001	2002	2003		204E	204F
2	2	50	51	52	53		9E	9F
3	3	2050	2051	2052	2053		209E	209F

198	198	1EF0	1EF1	1EF2	1EF3		1F3E	1F3F
199	199	3EF0	3EF1	3EF2	3EF3		3F3E	3F3F

a

LOCATION		OFFSET FROM B8000
B8000	EVEN ROWS	0
B9F40	UNUSED	1F40
BA000	ODD ROWS	2000
BBF40	UNUSED	3F40
BC000		

b

Figure 4.1
The memory map of the graphics screen. All row and column positions are given in decimal; all memory locations are given in hex. All of the location values in part a are offset from B8000H.

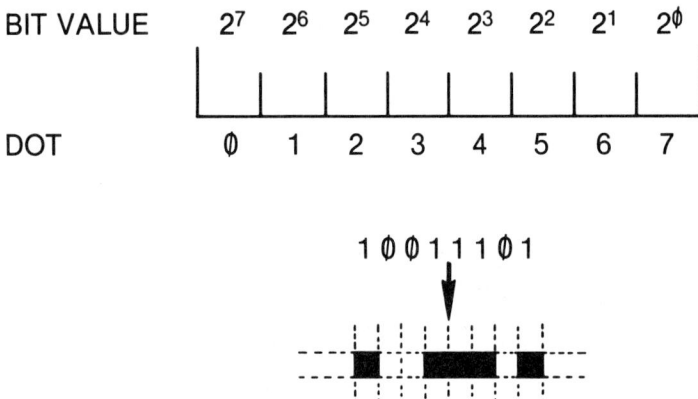

Figure 4.2
In high resolution each bit represents one dot. The high order bit stores data for the left most dot; the low order, the right most. If a bit is set, the dot appears. The figure shows what dots 10011101B would set in a column.

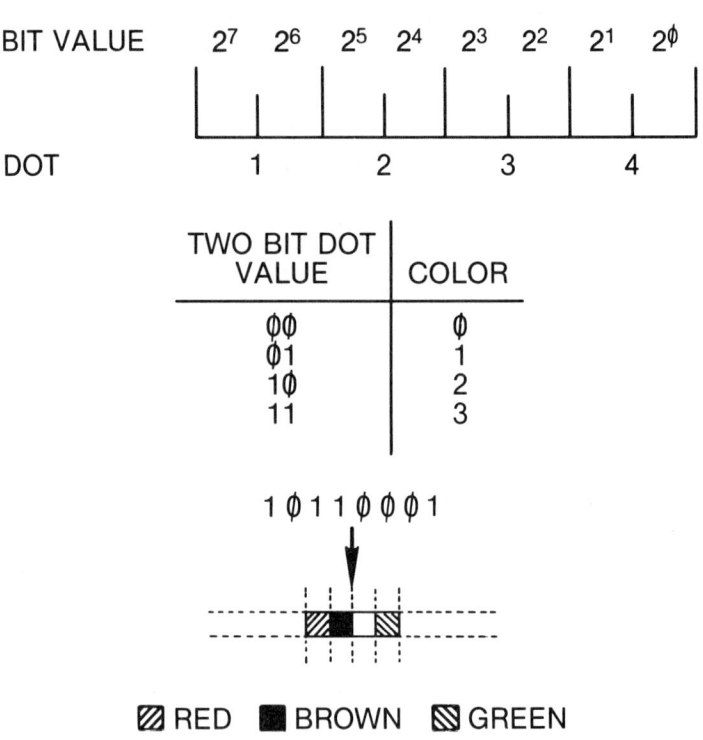

Figure 4.3 (PALETTE 0)

In medium resolution, every two bits represent one dot. The value of these two bits tells the color number.

Calculating Dot Position Given (x,y) Coordinates

To plot a dot to the screen, we need to know which byte contains information about that dot and what bits to set in that byte.

Instead of finding the actual byte, we will find its offset from B8000H. Therefore, we will call the first byte in the graphics screen byte zero. This makes calculations easier. We can then access the graphics screen relative to a segment register set to B800H.

We start by finding the beginning byte of the row in which the dot is located. Note that odd rows start 2000H bytes after even ones. Each even row starts 80 bytes after the previous even row; each odd row starts 80 bytes after the previous odd. So, to find the row's beginning, we divide the y coordinate by 2 and multiply the integral part by 80. (Dividing by 2 tells the number of even or odd rows before the row. For example, row 7 has 7 div 2 = 3 odd rows before it.) If y is odd, we add 2000H to this number.

Then, we need to find in which byte in the row the dot is located. In high resolution, we divide the x coordinate by 8 (dots per byte); in medium resolution, we divide the x coordinate by 4. The integral result tells the byte in which the dot is located; the remainder tells which dot in the byte we need to set.

For example, suppose we are in high resolution and want to plot (21,31). First, we find the row's starting byte. INT(31/2) = 15. 15 * 80 = 1,200. Because 31 is odd, we add 8,192 (2000H). Thus, the row starts at 9,392. Now, 21/8 = 2 with a remainder of 5. So, we want to set dot 5 (the sixth over) in the second byte—byte 9,394.

The Data to Plot

Once we know the dot position and byte location, we have to figure out what data to put in the byte. There are a couple of ways to do this. The quickest is to use a look-up table.

We will have *color* and *mask* tables. When we **AND** the number corresponding to the color with the mask corresponding to the dot, we get the value to store in the byte.

We need separate tables for medium and high resolution. The color table has an entry for each color. This entry is the byte that would cause every dot to have the particular color. For example, in medium resolution, the byte for color 1 would be 01010101B (Figure 4.4).

The mask table has an entry for every dot position in a byte. This entry has ones where data for that dot would be stored, and zeros elsewhere (Figure 4.5).

COLOR TABLES

HIGH RESOLUTION

COLOR	TABLE VALUE
0	00000000
1	11111111

MEDIUM RESOLUTION

COLOR	TABLE VALUE
0	00000000
1	01010101
2	10101010
3	11111111

Figure 4.4
The color table entries. Values are in binary.

MASK TABLES

HIGH RESOLUTION

DOT	TABLE VALUE
0	10000000
1	01000000
2	00100000
3	00010000
4	00001000
5	00000100
6	00000010
7	00000001

MEDIUM RESOLUTION

DOT	TABLE VALUE
0	11000000
1	00110000
2	00001100
3	00000011

Figure 4.5
The mask table entries. Values are in binary.

As an example, suppose we are in medium resolution and want to find the data to plot with color 2 the third dot in a byte. We find that the color entry is 10101010B, and the mask for the third dot (dot 2) is 00001100B. If we **AND** these, we get 00001000B. Looking at the way medium-resolution dots are stored, we see that this is correct.

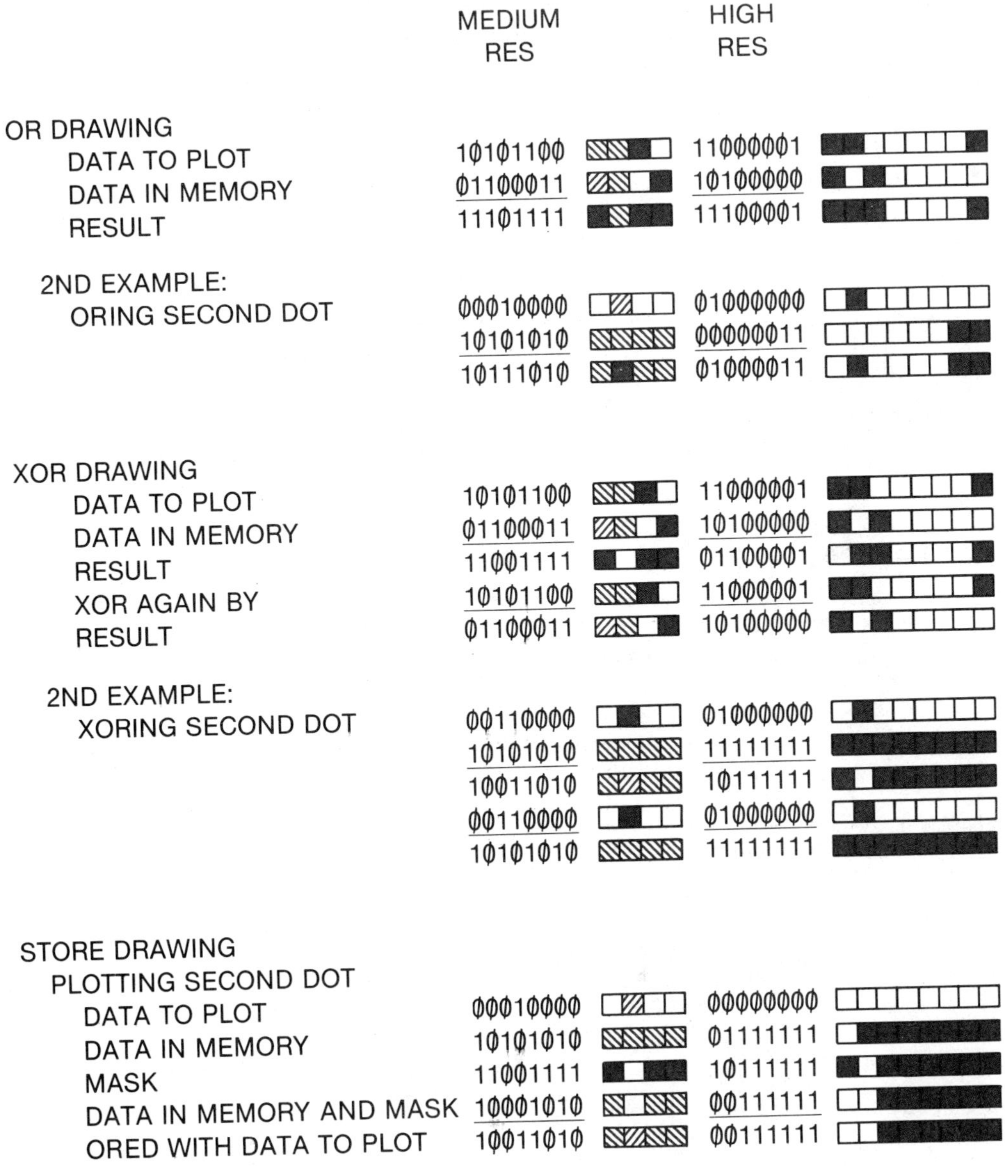

	MEDIUM RES	HIGH RES
OR DRAWING		
DATA TO PLOT	10101100	11000001
DATA IN MEMORY	01100011	10100000
RESULT	11101111	11100001
2ND EXAMPLE:		
ORING SECOND DOT	00010000	01000000
	10101010	00000011
	10111010	01000011
XOR DRAWING		
DATA TO PLOT	10101100	11000001
DATA IN MEMORY	01100011	10100000
RESULT	11001111	01100001
XOR AGAIN BY	10101100	11000001
RESULT	01100011	10100000
2ND EXAMPLE:		
XORING SECOND DOT	00110000	01000000
	10101010	11111111
	10011010	10111111
	00110000	01000000
	10101010	11111111
STORE DRAWING		
PLOTTING SECOND DOT		
DATA TO PLOT	00010000	00000000
DATA IN MEMORY	10101010	01111111
MASK	11001111	10111111
DATA IN MEMORY AND MASK	10001010	00111111
ORED WITH DATA TO PLOT	10011010	00111111

THE MASK IS THE INVERSE OF THE MASK FROM FIG 4.5.

Figure 4.6 OR, XOR, and store drawing.

Plotting It

Now that we know what data to plot, we need a way to put it on the screen. There are several ways to do this. The first way, and perhaps the most useful, is to **OR** it to the screen. **OR**ing keeps all dots that used to be set in the byte set. And if dots of two different colors are **OR**ed together, the resulting dot is the blend of the two colors.

Another method is to **XOR** the data. The main reason for **XOR**ing is that if we **XOR** a byte twice with the same data, the original data returns. So, for example, if we have a picture on the screen and **XOR** a line over it, **XOR**ing the the same line again restores the original picture.

We can also store the dot directly. First, we mask out the dot from the screen byte (using the inverse of the dot mask) and **OR** the result with the dot data. This results in the dot being plotted over any other dot present. For example, suppose we have a green line on the screen. If we then *store draw* a red line over it, where the two lines intersect, only the red will show. Drawing in the background color will erase lines. BASIC's **LINE** store draws.

These three styles of plotting are illustrated in Figure 4.6.

The Routine

Now let's write a routine to plot a dot given its color and x and y screen coordinates. We will use the **OR**ing method of plotting:

```
;
x               dw      100             ;for testing the routine x = 100
y               dw      100             ;set to 100 for testing purposes
color           db      1
resolution      db      3               ;default to hi res
color_table     dw      ?               ;these need to be loaded by another
mask_table      dw      ?               ;procedure
colors_high     db      00000000b, 11111111b
mask_high       db      10000000b, 01000000b, 00100000b, 00010000b
                db      00001000b, 00000100b, 00000010b, 00000001b
colors_med      db      00000000b, 01010101b, 10101010b, 11111111b
mask_med        db      11000000b, 00110000b, 00001100b, 00000011b
;

;
;set dot by calculating position
;
;called with:
;   x = x coordinate
;   y = y coordinate
;   color = 0 - 1 for high res
```

```
;                = 0 - 3 for med res
;    resolution = 3 for high res
;               = 2 for med res
;                 (mode + 1)
;
;    mask_table should point to the mask table for current screen
;    color_table should point to the color table for current screen
;    ES should point to the graphics screen - B800H
;
set_dot             proc        near
                    mov         ax,y
                    mov         bx,0
;see if odd or even line
                    shr         ax,1
                    jnc         mult_by_80
;odd
                    mov         bx,2000h
;multiply by 80 to determine memory location of first byte in row
mult_by_80:         mov         dx,ax
                    shl         ax,1        ; * 2
                    shl         ax,1        ; * 4
                    add         ax,dx       ; * 5
                    shl         ax,1        ; * 10
                    shl         ax,1        ; * 20
                    shl         ax,1        ; * 40
                    shl         ax,1        ; * 80
                    add         bx,ax       ;BX = first byte in line
;find position in line
                    mov         ax,x
                    mov         cl,resolution
                    shr         ax,cl       ;AX = byte position in line
                    add         bx,ax       ;BX points to byte in which to plot
                    mov         bp,bx       ;find what to plot
                    shl         ax,cl
                    xor         ax,x        ;AX = dot within byte
                    mov         bx,mask_table
                    xlat        mask_high
                    mov         ch,al
                    mov         bx,color_table
                    mov         al,color
                    xlat        colors_high
                    and         ch,al
plot_it:            or          es:[bp],ch  ;change this to XOR or store plot
;
                    ret
set_dot             endp
```

2P2.ASM

To use this procedure, we need to have previously set **resolution**, **mask_table**, and **color_table**. For medium resolution, make **mask_**

table point to **mask_med** and **color_table** to **colors_med**; for high resolution, make **mask_table** point to **mask_high** and **color_table** to **colors_high**.

Testing It Out

You may want to test out this routine. You will find it runs much faster than our interrupt driven routine. (Of course, you need to run it a great many times to see the difference.) The following table compares the two dot-setting routines:

Routine	*Time for 36,864 Executions*
Interrupt Driven	12 seconds
Calculation Driven	3.9 seconds

4.3: CLEARING THE SCREEN

Perhaps two of the most important graphics functions are *clearing the screen* and *drawing lines*. Before we are able to develop a line graphics system, we will have to program procedures to do both. We will start with the easier of the two—clearing the screen.

We have already seen that graphics information is stored through the graphics memory map. You noticed that for both medium and high resolutions, no dots are drawn if a byte contains zero. We will use this fact to clear the screen—we will put a zero in every memory location in the graphics screen. Let's look at a routine:

```
;
;clear the screen
;
;   assumes that ES points to graphics screen (B800H)
;
clear_screen    proc    near
                mov     ax,0    ;to fill with a color, put
                mov     di,ax   ;color value in ax, 0 in di
                mov     cx,1fa0h
                cld
                rep     stosw
;
                ret
clear_screen    endp
```

> **3.ASM**

We repeat the **stosw** 1FA0H times. The graphics screen takes up 16K of continuous memory, but only 16,000 of these bytes are used for graphics—8,000 bytes for even lines, and 8,000 bytes for odd lines. To save time, this routine stops after it has filled up all but the last 192 bytes with zeros. These last 192 bytes are the unused portion of the odd line half of graphics memory. Thus, we repeat (16,384 − 192)/2 = 1FA0H times.

If we want to fill the screen with a color, we change the value stored in every location. For example, to fill the medium-resolution screen with color 1, move 01010101 01010101B into **AX**. To make the screen striped, set **AX** to a word representing several colors, such as 11000110 10010011B.

4.4: DRAWING LINES

Drawing lines is a bit more complicated than clearing the screen. We no longer can just fill the whole screen with a value; we have to figure out every dot that needs to be lit. Line drawing can be broken into two processes: figuring out what points to plot and plotting them. We have already seen how to plot.

Given the two end points of a line segment, we can calculate the slope: $(y_2 - y_1)/(x_2 - x_1)$. Let's call $(x_2 - x_1)$ **delta_x**, and $(y_2 - y_1)$ **delta_y**. Now, suppose **c** is a positive number less than 1. Then, $(x_1 + c * $ **delta_x**, $y_1 + c * $ **delta_y**) will be a point on the line, falling between (x_1,y_1) and (x_2,y_2) (Figure 4.7).

If we want to draw a line between (x_1,y_1) and (x_2,y_2), we need to figure out the coordinates of every point between these end points and plot them. Actually, doing so would be pretty inefficient. There are an infinite number of points between the end points. We only need to know the coordinates of the points we can see.

If we are given a point on the line, we want to find a number to add to the x coordinate and a number to add to the y coordinate to find the coordinates of the next point. If we pick numbers that are too large, our line will skip around. If we choose numbers that are too small, our routine will bog down in plotting points on top of each other (Figure 4.8).

138 Assembly Language Line Graphics

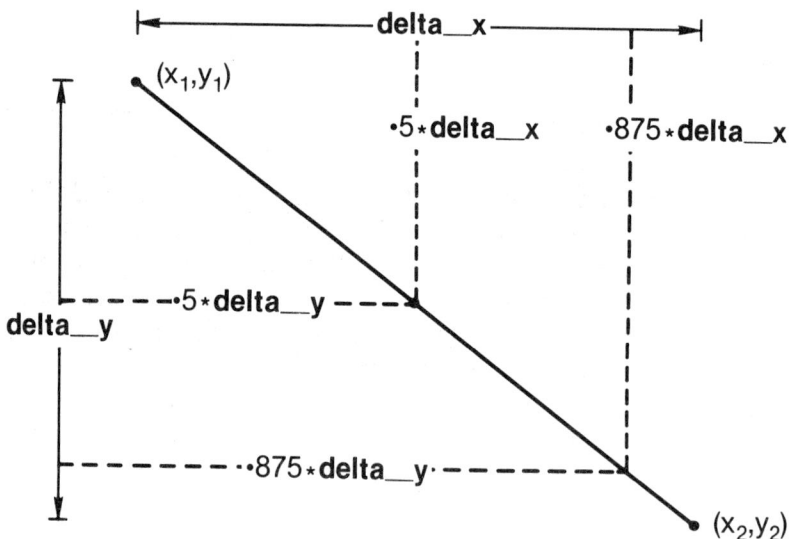

Figure 4.7
Points of the form $(x_1 + C * \text{delta}\_x, y_1 + c * \text{delta}\_y)$ fall on the line segment between (x_1, y_1) and (x_2, y_2).

So, the numbers must satisfy four conditions:

1. The x increment must be of the form **c * delta_x**.
2. The y increment must be of the form **c * delta_y**.
3. Neither the x coordinate nor the y coordinate can change by more than one each time the increments are added.
4. At least one of the coordinates should change by one each time the increments are added.

In this manner, all the points we calculate will lie on the line segment, and our points will neither skip parts of the line nor plot over the same dot twice.

Finding such numbers is a lot easier than it sounds. Call the number added to the x coordinate **inc_x**, and that added to the y coordinate **inc_y**. If we want one of the coordinates to always change by one, we need to divide **delta_x** and **delta_y** by the absolute value of either **delta_x** or **delta_y**. So that no coordinate changes by more than 1, we divide by the larger of the two absolutes. In other words, call the maximum of the absolute value of **delta_x** and the absolute value of **delta_y**, **max_delta**. Then:

inc_x = delta_x / max_delta
inc_y = delta_y / max_delta

Assembly Language Line Graphics 139

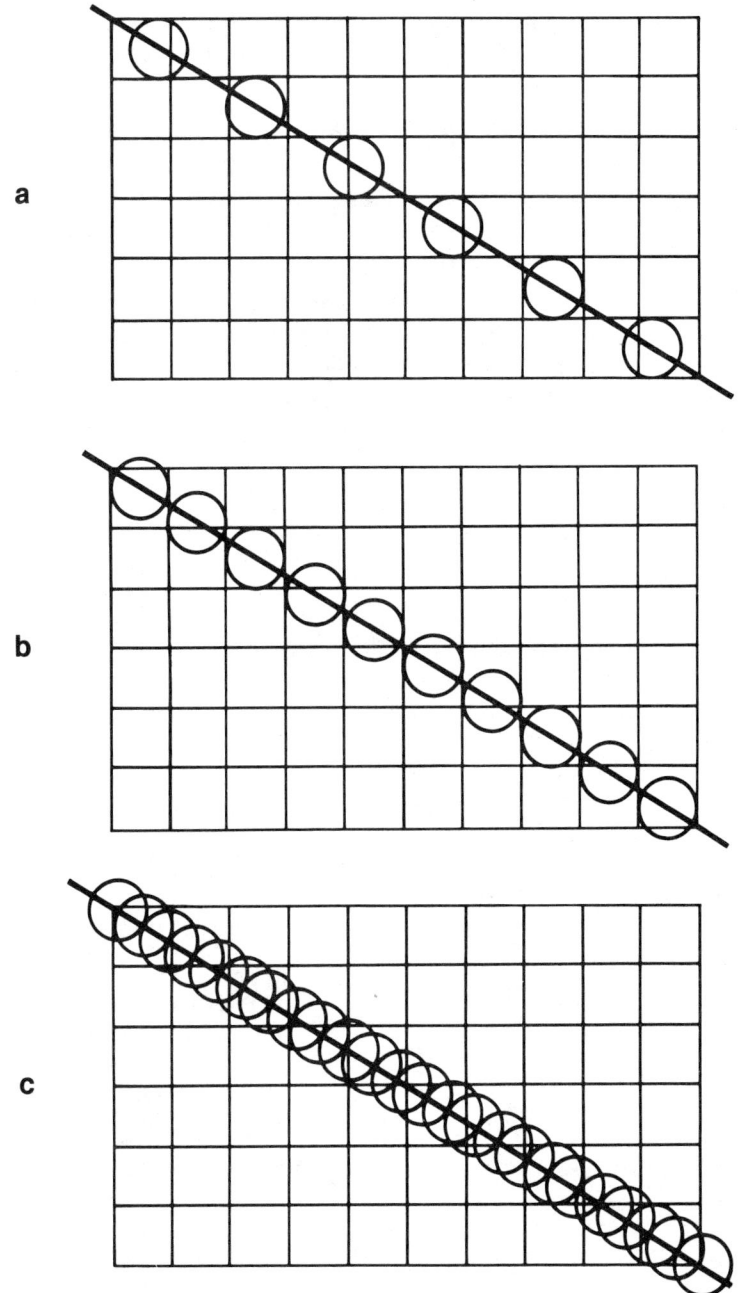

Figure 4.8
In part a, increments are too large, thus the line skips. In part b, the increments are correct. In part c, the increments are too small, thus dots are plotted over each other.

Once we have these increments, we start with the first end point and add **inc_x** and **inc_y** until we get to the second end point, and we plot all of the points between. One way to tell when we reach the second point is to compare our current point against the second end point. But because of round-off errors, this isn't always safe. (The line could overshoot the second point, and thus never stop.) Because of the way we have computed the increments, the number of points we will be plotting is **max_delta**. So, we just loop through our routine **max_delta** times.

We will break our coordinates and increments into two parts: a fractional and an integral part. We will add the fractional increment part to the fractional coordinate part; the integral increment part to the integral coordinate part. The integral coordinate parts tell where to plot. Storing the fractional parts as bytes and the integral parts as words gives us the accuracy we need.

The Routine

Now let's look at a procedure to draw lines:

```
;
;the following are input by user
x1                  dw          0           ;coordinates of the end points
x2                  dw          0
y1                  dw          0
y2                  dw          0
;
;the following are computed by the program
xl                  db          ?           ;fractional and integral parts
xh                  dw          ?           ;of current x coordinate
yl                  db          ?           ;fractional and integral parts
yh                  dw          ?           ;of current y coordinate
incxl               db          ?           ;fractional and integral parts
incxh               dw          ?           ;of x increment
incyl               db          ?           ;fractional and integral parts
incyh               dw          ?           ;of y increment
;
;draw a line between (x1,y1), (x2,y2)
;
;       this procedure calls set_dot
;           set_dot must be modified to operate on xh,yh instead of
;           x,y
;

draw_line           proc        near
;compute delta x
                    mov         bp,0
```

```
                        mov     ax,x2
                        sub     ax,x1
                        jg      compute_delta_y ;the calculations are easier using
                        or      bp,1    ;positives. This marks that delta_x should
                        neg     ax      ;be negative, then takes the absolute value
compute_delta_y:
                        mov     bx,y2
                        sub     bx,y1
                        jg      check_not_0 ;see above note
                        or      bp,2            ;indicate that delta_y is negative
                        neg     bx
check_not_0:
;if both deltas are zero, no line need be drawn.
                        mov     cx,ax   ;this check prevents division by 0
                        or      cx,bx   ;errors
                        jnz     set_up  ;OK
                        jmp     d_l_end ;Not OK
set_up:
                        mov     cx,x1   ;the first point to plot is x1,y1
                        mov     xh,cx
                        mov     xl,0
                        mov     cx,y1
                        mov     yh,cx
                        mov     yl,0
;see whether delta x or delta y is bigger
                        cmp     ax,bx
                        jl      y_bigger
;x bigger
                        mov     cx,ax   ;CX stores max_delta
                        jmp short d_l_1
y_bigger:
                        mov     cx,bx   ;CX stores max_delta
d_l_1:                  mov     di,cx   ;set counter
;compute x and y increments
                        mov     dh,0    ;multiply delta_x by 256 first
                        mov     dl,ah   ;so that will have a fractional
                        mov     ah,al   ;part after division
                        mov     al,dh
                        div     cx      ;delta_x / max_delta
                        shr     bp,1    ;see if delta_x was negative
                        jnc     d_l_2   ;if so, negate result of division
                        neg     ax
d_l_2:                  cwd
                        mov     dl,ah   ;integral part of division
                        mov     incxl,al ;fractional part of division
                        mov     incxh,dx
;now do the same thing for y
                        mov     ax,bx
                        mov     dh,0
                        mov     dl,ah
                        mov     ah,al
                        mov     al,dh
                        div     cx
                        shr     bp,1    ;see if delta_y was negative
                        jnc     d_l_3
                        neg     ax
d_l_3:                  cwd
                        mov     dl,ah
                        mov     incyl,al
                        mov     incyh,dx
```

```
;now we are ready to begin the main loop
;we will plot each point, and if it's not the last, compute the
;next one by adding the x and y increments to the current x and y
;coordinates
;
plot_the_point:
                        call        set_dot
;see if finished
                        cmp         di,0            ;remember that DI contains the number
                        je          d_l_end         ;of points to plot
                        dec         di
;find next point
                        mov         al,incxl        ;new x coordinate
                        add         xl,al
                        mov         ax,incxh
                        adc         xh,ax
                        mov         al,incyl        ;new y coordinate
                        add         yl,al
                        mov         ax,incyh
                        adc         yh,ax
;
                        jmp short   plot_the_point
d_l_end:
                        ret
;
draw_line               endp
```

4.ASM

The Time Test

Drawing a 30-dot line 4,096 times takes about 20 seconds. We can take advantage of the fact that the x and y positions never change by more than one to create a faster line-drawing routine; but such a routine will be less versatile, especially when we try to clip.

4.5: PUTTING TOGETHER A THREE-DIMENSIONAL LINE GRAPHICS PACKAGE

Now that we can do the basic graphics functions, let's create a three-dimensional line-drawing program just like **3DLG3.BAS.**

As with our BASIC program, our program can be broken into a series of subroutines, and each can be called from a main loop. Take a look at this main loop and then at each of the subroutines.

```
;
finished            db          1           ; = 0 when finished
;

;
;main loop
;
main_loop           proc        near
                    call        read_keyboard
                    call        get_movement_values
                    call        load_trig_values
                    call        get_matrix
                    call        transform_points
                    call        perspect_to_screen
                    call        clear_screen
                    call        draw_the_lines
                    cmp         finished,0
                    jne         main_loop
;
                    ret
main_loop           endp
```

5.ASM

read_keyboard will scan the keyboard for commands (**3DLG3.BAS** subroutine **2000**); **get_movement_values** will update the amount of scaling, rotation and translation to be done (**3DLG3.BAS** subroutines **3500**, **4500**, and **6500**); **load_trig_values** will get the sines and cosines of the angles; and then **get_matrix** will use these in computing the transform matrix (**3DLG3.BAS** subroutine **17000**). **transform_points** will use this matrix to transform the points (**3DLG3.BAS** subroutine **19300**). **perspect_to_screen** will do perspective and then convert the points to screen coordinates, taking into account dot width (**3DLG3.BAS** subroutines **7000** and **8000**). We have already seen **clear_screen**; **draw_the_lines** will take the end points of all lines and feed them into **draw_line** (**3DLG3.BAS** subroutine **9000**).

4.6: READING COMMANDS FROM THE KEYBOARD

The first procedure we will look at is **read_keyboard**, a routine that reads and analyzes commands from the keyboard. As with our BASIC subroutine, we don't want to stop the program to wait for input, but rather to check if any key has been pressed. We will do this with BIOS **interrupt 16H**. We call it with **AH** = 1. If a key has been pressed, the **zero flag** is cleared and the key code is returned in **AX**. Otherwise, the **zero flag** is set. The character is not removed from the keyboard buffer.

Once we have read a character, we will analyze it and adjust our scaling, rotation, and translation counters, just as we did in our BASIC subroutine. We will use the same command keys and variables.

Then we will clear the keyboard buffer. We'll do this with DOS **function 6**. It reads the keyboard buffer, and if a key is pressed, removes it from the buffer, clears the **zero flag**, and returns the key code in **AL**. To call this function, invoke **interrupt 21H** with:

AH = 6
DL = FFH

We'll call this until the **zero flag** is set.

The main difference between BIOS **interrupt 16H** and DOS **function 6** is that the BIOS interrupt can read extended character codes and doesn't clear the buffer, while the DOS function clears the buffer but can't read extended character codes.

The Routine

```
;
xrot            db      0
yrot            db      0
zrot            db      0
xscl            db      0
yscl            db      0
zscl            db      0
xtrn            db      0
ytrn            db      0
ztrn            db      0
;

;
;read the keyboard for command
;adjust counters appropriately
;
read_keyboard   proc    near
;read it
                mov     ah,1
                int     16h
;analyze it
                jnz     ckq             ;a key has been hit
                jmp     r_k_end         ;no key pressed
```

```
ckq:            cmp     al,'q'          ;see if q
                jne     ckw             ;if not, check for next command
                dec     xrot
                jmp     clear_buffer
ckw:            cmp     al,'w'          ;see if w
                jne     cke
                mov     xrot,0
                jmp     clear_buffer
cke:            cmp     al,'e'          ;see if e
                jne     cka
                inc     xrot
                jmp     clear_buffer
;
;CONTINUE HERE, CHECKING FOR THE Y AND Z ROTATION COMMANDS, AND
;THEN FOR THE SCALING AND TRANSLATION COMMANDS
;
;this routine would be called by the last z translation checking routine
ckspace:        cmp     al,' '          ;see if space bar pressed
                jne     ckesc
                mov     al,0            ;clear all of the counters
                mov     xrot,al
                mov     yrot,al
                mov     zrot,al
                mov     xscl,al
                mov     yscl,al
                mov     zscl,al
                mov     xtrn,al
                mov     ytrn,al
                mov     ztrn,al
                jmp     clear_buffer
ckesc:          cmp     al,27           ;see if escape pressed
                jne     clear_buffer
                mov     finished,0      ;time to stop program
;
clear_buffer:   mov     ah,6
                mov     dl,0ffh
c_b_loop:       int     21h             ;read buffer
                jnz     c_b_loop        ;until no keys left
r_k_end:
                ret
read_keyboard   endp
```

6.ASM

4.7: GETTING THE MOVEMENT VALUES

The next step in our program is to update the movement values: **xangle**, **yangle**, **zangle**, **xscale**, **yscale**, **zscale**, **xtranslation**, **ytranslation**, and

ztranslation. We call this procedure **get_movement_values**.

As with our BASIC routine, we could really do anything here. Because the Assembly Language program will run so quickly we do not need to multiply the rotation and translation changes by proportionality constants. Scaling will be four times the amount actually scaled; that is, a scaling value of eight means scale by two. We won't take that into account here—it will be taken care of in the routine to load the matrix.

The Routine

```
;
xscale            db      4       ;set these initially to 4. As these values
yscale            db      4       ;are four times the scaling amount, there
zscale            db      4       ;will be no scaling initially
xangle            db      0       ;start with no rotation
yangle            db      0
zangle            db      0
xtranslation      dw      0       ;translation needs to be word sized
ytranslation      dw      0
ztranslation      dw      0
;

;
;adjust the movement values
;
get_movement_values  proc   near
;get scale values
                  mov     al,xscl
                  add     xscale,al
                  mov     al,yscl
                  add     yscale,al
                  mov     al,zscl
                  add     zscl,al
;get translation values
                  mov     al,xtrn
                  cbw                     ;sign extend it to a word
                  add     xtranslation,ax ;to add to translation
                  mov     al,ytrn
                  cbw
                  add     ytranslation,ax
                  mov     al,ztrn
                  cbw
                  add     ztranslation,al
;get rotation values
                  mov     al,xrot
                  add     xangle,al
                  mov     al,yrot
                  add     yangle,al
                  mov     al,zrot
                  add     zangle,al
;
                  ret
get_movement_values  endp
```

> **7.ASM**

We will allow for 256 different angles of rotation. When we increase an angle so that it exceeds 255, its value will fall around 0. This gives us the same wraparound we get when an angle that exceeds 2 π.

4.8: GETTING THE TRIG VALUES

Before we can do rotation, we need to find the sine and cosine of **xangle**, **yangle**, and **zangle**. Assembly Language doesn't have trigonometric functions. We could program them in by using Taylor series, but such routines would take too long. Instead, we will use look-up tables.

The idea is that if the number of possible angles is limited, then we can make tables of the sine and cosine values of all the angles. We need enough angles to make rotation smooth, but not so many that angular change is unnoticeable. Therefore 256 is a good amount, especially since this gives us wraparound when angle byte values exceed 255.

Cosine and sine values are never greater than 1; 1 is the smallest value we can store in a byte. So we will have to multiply the trigonometric values by a proportionality constant. Then, whenever we use these trigonometric values, we will have to divide by this constant. As division by factors of 2 is much quicker than division by any other numbers, we will multiply our trigonometric values by 128. This will allow us to store the trig values as one byte signed integers.

MAKING THE TABLES

Now we are ready to make the tables. We need to find the sine and cosine values of 256 evenly spaced angles covering the range between 0 and 2 π. Every angle will be 2 * π / 256 radians greater than the last. We will multiply the sine and cosine values by 128, and change any +/− 128 values to +/− 127 values.

Instead of making this table by hand, the computer can do it for us. The following BASIC program finds the trigonometric values and creates a text file of them in a form we can merge into our Assembly Language program:

```
10 TORADIANS = 2 * 3.141592 / 256
20 DEF FNANGLE = (LINE. * 8 + ITEM) * TORADIANS
30 OPEN "a:trigtbl.dat" FOR OUTPUT AS #1
40 PRINT #1, ";"
```

148 Assembly Language Line Graphics

```
50 PRINT #1, ";Sine data"
60 PRINT #1, ";"
70 PRINT #1, "sine";
80 FOR LINE. = 0 TO 31
90     PRINT #1, SPC(15 + (LINE. = 0) * 4);"db";SPC(8);
100    FOR ITEM = 0 TO 6
110       GOSUB 1000
120       PRINT #1, X;", ";
130    NEXT
140    ITEM = 7
150    GOSUB 1000
160    PRINT #1, X
170 NEXT
180 PRINT #1, ";"
190 PRINT #1, ";Cosine data"
200 PRINT #1, ";"
210 PRINT #1, "cosine";
220 FOR LINE. = 0 TO 31
230    PRINT #1, SPC(15 + (LINE. = 0) * 6);"db";SPC(8);
240    FOR ITEM = 0 TO 6
250       GOSUB 2000
260       PRINT #1, X;", ";
270    NEXT
280    ITEM = 7
290    GOSUB 2000
300    PRINT #1, X
310 NEXT
320 CLOSE #1
330 END
1000 X = INT(SIN(FNANGLE)*128)
1010 IF X = 128 THEN X = 127 ELSE IF X = -128 THEN X =
     -127
1020 RETURN
2000 X = INT(COS(FNANGLE)*128)
2010 IF X = 128 THEN X = 127 ELSE IF X = -128 THEN X =
     - 127
2020 RETURN
```

8P1.BAS

The output of the program looks like:

```
;
;Sine data
;
sine               db        0 ,  3 ,  6 ,  9 , 12 , 15 , 18 , 21
                   db       24 , 28 , 31 , 34 , 37 , 40 , 43 , 46
                   db       48 , 51 , 54 , 57 , 60 , 63 , 65 , 68
                     .
                     .
                     .
                   db      -25 ,-22 ,-19 ,-16 ,-13 ,-10 , -7 , -4
;
;Cosine data
;
```

```
cosine          db      127 , 127 , 127 , 127 , 127 , 127 , 126 , 126
                db      125 , 124 , 124 , 123 , 122 , 121 , 120 , 119
                db      118 , 117 , 115 , 114 , 112 , 111 , 109 , 108
                    .
                    .
                    .
                db      125 , 126 , 126 , 127 , 127 , 127 , 127 , 127
```

Loading the Values

Now that we have a table of trigonometric values, we are ready to access them. If, for example, we want the sine of the fiftieth angle, we load the fiftieth entry of the sine table. We will store the sine and cosine of the angles in **sinx**, **cosx**, **siny**, **cosy**, **sinz**, and **cosz**:

```
;
cosx                db      0
sinx                db      0
cosy                db      0
siny                db      0
cosz                db      0
sinz                db      0
;

;
;load the trig values
;
;   requires a table of sine and cosine values
load_trig_values    proc    near
                    mov     bh,0                    ;convert xangle to word to
                    mov     bl,xangle               ;index table
                    mov     di,bx
                    mov     al,cosine[di]           ;load the value
                    mov     cosx,al
                    mov     al,sine[di]
                    mov     sinx,al
                    mov     bl,yangle               ;load y values
                    mov     di,bx
                    mov     al,cosine[di]
                    mov     cosy,al
                    mov     al,sine[di]
                    mov     siny,al
                    mov     bl,zangle               ;load z values
                    mov     di,bx
                    mov     al,cosine[di]
                    mov     cosz,al
                    mov     al,sine[di]
                    mov     sinz,al
```

150 Assembly Language Line Graphics

```
;
                        ret
load_trig_values        endp
```

8P2.ASM

4.9: LOADING THE TRANSFORMATION MATRIX

Now we can load the transformation matrix. This is a long section to program because we need to program the formulae to determine the values for each entry of the matrix. To keep fractions in the matrix, we will make all entries except the last row 128 times larger than they should be (remember that the trigonometric values are 128 times larger than their real values). The last row needn't be scaled because it is the row causing translation, and fractions will be too small to have an effect.

There is really nothing tricky to programming this section, it is just a lot of work. Be careful not to make mistakes. They will cause strange distortions.

The routine below uses a matrix that scales, does z, x, then y rotation and finally translates. You may wish to use a different matrix.

The Routine

```
;
mat11                   dw              0               ;transform(1,1)
mat12                   dw              0               ;transform(1,2)
mat13                   dw              0               ;transform(1,3)
mat14                   dw              0               ;transform(1,4)
mat21                   dw              0               ;transform(2,1)
mat22                   dw              0               ;transform(2,2)

;
;SET UP VARIABLES FOR THE REST OF THE TRANSFORM MATRIX ENTRIES
;

mat43                   dw              0               ;transform(4,3)
mat44                   dw              1               ;transform(4,4) always = 1
;

;
;load the tranformation matrix
;
```

Assembly Language Line Graphics 151

```
;       scale * z rotation * x rotation * y rotation * translation
;
get_matrix              proc            near
                        mov             cl,7            ;for dividing by 128
;transform(1,1)
                        mov             al,cosz
                        mov             bl,cosy
                        imul            bl
                        mov             dx,ax           ;temporarily store cosz*cosy
                        mov             al,sinz
                        mov             bl,sinx
                        imul            bl
                        sar             ax,cl           ;divide by 128, preserving sign
                        mov             bl,siny         ;now get sinz*sinx*-siny
                        neg             bl              ;-siny
                        imul            bl
                        add             ax,dx           ;add in cosz*cosy
                        sar             ax,cl           ;divide by 128
                        mov             bl,xscale       ;multiply by scale
                        imul            bl
                        sar             ax,1            ;adjust for scale being 4 times
                        sar             ax,1            ;its actual value
                        mov             mat11,ax        ;store the value in the matrix
;transform(1,2)
                        mov             al,sinz         ;sinz * cosx
                        mov             bl,cosx
                        imul            bl
                        sar             ax,cl
                        mov             bl,xscale       ;xscale * sinz * cosx
                        imul            bl
                        sar             ax,1
                        sar             ax,1
                        mov             mat12,ax
;
;CONTINUE, CALCULATING THE VALUES FOR ALL THE OTHER MATRIX ENTRIES
;
;transform(4,3)
                        mov             ax,ztranslation
                        mov             mat43,ax
;
                        ret
get_matrix              endp
```

9.ASM

4.10: TRANSFORMING THE POINTS

Now we are ready to transform the points. First, however, we need a structure for storing and accessing the points. We will separate the x, y, and z coordinates into three arrays and store each coordinate as a word (Figure 4.9).

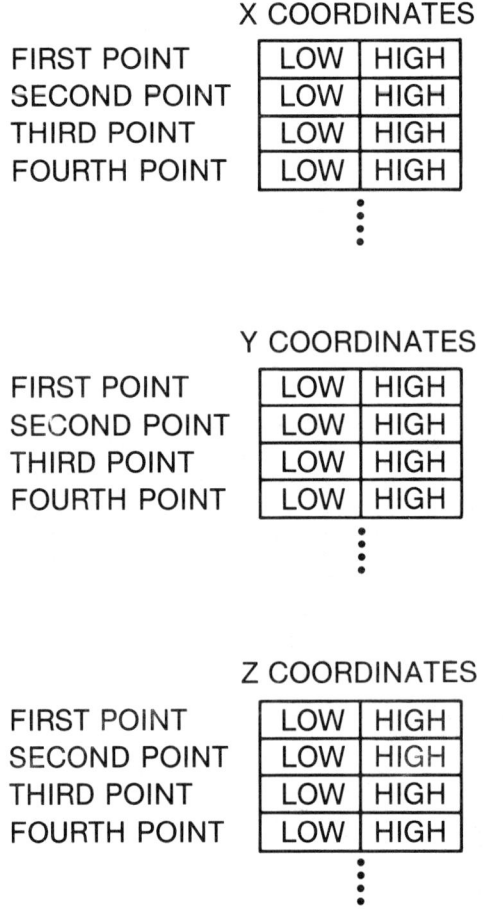

Figure 4.9
We will separate the x, y, and z coordinates into three arrays.

Let's see how to reference the points. The first point starts at byte 0. Each point is two bytes (one word) long. So, the nth point starts at byte $2*(n-1)$ (Figure 4.10).

To transform the points, we load the x, y, and z coordinate values for each point and multiply them by the transformation matrix.

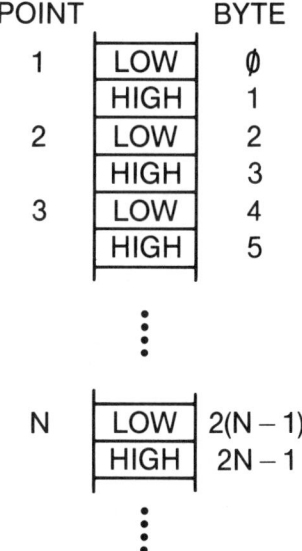

Figure 4.10
The nth point starts at byte $2*(n - 1)$.

The Routine

Now let's look at the procedure. We first load the coordinates of the point to be modified into temporary variables, **x**, **y**, and **z**. This saves time, as the coordinates need to be used several times. The approach for finding each of the new coordinates is the same—we multiply the coordinates of the old point by either the first, second, or third columns of the transformation matrix. Therefore, we will create a procedure that does this multiplication—**get_new_coord**—and call it three times, once for each coordinate. We will store the new x, y, and z coordinates in arrays called **newxpoints**, **newypoints**, and **newzpoints**.

We will enter the coordinates of the points directly into the program as we did in our BASIC program. The point-line data should be placed last in the variable declaration list. As we will use the cube, we will reserve eight words for each coordinate array.

```
;
x               dw      0           ;for temporarily holding coordinates
y               dw      0
z               dw      0
mat1            dw      0           ;for holding the current column
mat2            dw      0           ;of transform to be used for
mat3            dw      0           ;multiplication
mat4            dw      0
```

154   Assembly Language Line Graphics

```
;
newxpoints          dw          8 dup (0)
newypoints          dw          8 dup (0)
newzpoints          dw          8 dup (0)
;
number_of_points    dw          16          ;2 * 8 points
;
;data for the cube
;
xpoints             dw          20, 20, -20, -20, 20, 20, -20, -20
ypoints             dw          20, -20, -20, 20, 20, -20, -20, 20
zpoints             dw          20, 20, 20, 20, -20, -20, -20, -20
;

;
;transform the points
;
transform_points    proc        near
                    mov         di,number_of_points
t_p_loop:           cmp         di,0        ;see if finished
                    je          t_p_end     ;if so, end
                    dec         di          ;point to beginning of point to modify
                    dec         di
;load the coordinates of the current point into x, y, and z
                    mov         ax,xpoints[di]
                    mov         x,ax
                    mov         ax,ypoints[di]
                    mov         y,ax
                    mov         ax,zpoints[di]
                    mov         z,ax
;find the new x coordinate
                    mov         ax,mat11    ;first load the first column of
                    mov         mat1,ax     ;transform into mat1 - mat4
                    mov         ax,mat21
                    mov         mat2,ax
                    mov         ax,mat31
                    mov         mat3,ax
                    mov         ax,mat41
                    mov         mat4,ax
                    call        get_new_coord           ;now find the new x coordinate
                    mov         newxpoints[di],ax       ;store it in newxpoints

;REPEAT, LOADING IN THE NEXT TWO COLUMNS OF THE TRANSFORMATION MATRIX
;IN ORDER TO FIND THE NEW Y AND Z COORDINATES

;
                    jmp         t_p_loop    ;go on to next point
t_p_end:            ret
transform_points    endp
```

DI keeps track of the starting byte of the point we are currently processing. We decrement it by two each time through the loop so that it will point to the beginning of the next point to modify. Because we decrement it twice each time, **number_of_points** needs to store twice the number of points in the shape—it represents the number of bytes each coordinate array uses. As you can see, this makes accessing the data much easier.

Instead of starting with the first point and working to the last, we start with the last and work to the first. This doesn't affect the results, but it makes checking when the last point has been processed easier.

get_new_coord

Now let's look at **get_new_coord**. It multiplies the first three coordinates by the first three matrix column entries and then divides by 128. It adds these together with the last entry of the matrix column. Instead of shifting to divide by 128, it divides by 256, by using simple byte moves, then shifts left once. This process saves time, but it results in the loss of one bit of accuracy, which is an insignificant amount.

```
;
;multiply point vector by a column of the transformation matrix to
;get the new coordinate
;
; the matrix column is given in mat1 - mat4
; the point coordinates are given in x, y, z
; the new coordinate is returned in AX
;
get_new_coord   proc    near
                mov     ax,x            ;x * mat1
                mov     bx,mat1
                imul    bx
                push    dx              ;save for finding sum later
                push    ax
                mov     ax,y            ;y * mat2
                mov     bx,mat2
                imul    bx
                push    dx
                push    ax
                mov     ax,z            ;z * mat3
                mov     bx,mat3
                imul    bx
                pop     bx              ;add this to y*mat2
                add     ax,bx           ;the low byte first
                pop     bx              ;now the high
                adc     dx,bx
                pop     bx              ;now add in x*mat1
                add     ax,bx
                pop     bx
                adc     dx,bx
                mov     al,ah           ;divide by 128
                mov     ah,dl
                sal     ax,1
```

```
                        add             ax,mat4         ;now add in mat4
;
                        ret
get_new_coord           endp
```

> **transform_points** and **get_new_coord** are in **10.ASM**

4.11: ACCOUNTING FOR PERSPECTIVE AND DOT WIDTH AND CONVERTING TO SCREEN COORDINATES

Next we need to do perspective, adjust for dot width, and convert to screen coordinates. In our BASIC programs we did this in two steps; here we will do it in one.

This procedure uses four new variables. You should already be familiar with **maxxres**, **maxyres**, and **focal_distance**. The fourth variable, **width_factor**, is the number by which we multiply the x coordinate to account for dot width. Instead of computing it each time through the loop, we'll set it when we set the graphics mode. To maintain accuracy, we scale it by a factor of 16. Therefore, we need to divide by 16 after accounting for dot width. The width factor is found by:

width_factor = INT (16 * maxxres / (maxyres * aspect ratio))

The points are accessed just as they were in **transform_points**.

The Routine

Let's look at the routine:

```
;
focal_distance          dw      400         ;for perspective
maxxres                 dw      640         ;320 for medium res
maxyres                 dw      200
width_adjust            dw      39          ;20 for medium res
;

;
;do perspective, adjust for dot width, and convert to
;screen coordinates
;
perspect_to_screen proc          near
```

```
                        mov     di,number_of_points
p_t_s_loop:             cmp     di,0        ;see if finished
                        je      p_t_s_end
                        dec     di          ;point to starting byte of point
                        dec     di
;compute (focal_distance - z)
                        mov     cx,focal_distance
                        sub     cx,newzpoints[di]
                        jne     get_new_x   ;if 0, increment so that division
                        inc     cx          ;by 0 errors are avoided
get_new_x:
                        mov     ax,newxpoints[di]    ;perspective
                        mov     bx,focal_distance
                        imul    bx          ;x*focal_distance
                        idiv    cx          ;x*focal_distance/(focal_distance - z)
;adjust for dot width
                        mov     dx,width_adjust
                        imul    dx
                        sar     ax,1        ;divide by 16 because of the
                        sar     ax,1        ;proportionality factor
                        sar     ax,1
                        sar     ax,1
;convert to the screen system
                        mov     dx,maxxres
                        sar     dx,1        ;maxxres/2
                        add     ax,dx       ;this is ready to be plotted
                        mov     newxpoints[di],ax    ;store the new x
;
;now get the new y
;
                        mov     ax,newypoints[di]    ;perspective
                        imul    bx
                        idiv    cx
;convert to screen
                        mov     dx,maxyres
                        sar     dx,1
                        sub     dx,ax
                        mov     newypoints[di],dx    ;store the new y
;
                        jmp     short p_t_s_loop
p_t_s_end:              ret
perspect_to_screen endp
;
```

11.ASM

4.12: DRAWING THE LINES

Now we are ready to draw the lines. We need to load the end points from a line data base, find the coordinates, and send them to **draw_line**.

We will set up our line data base in this fashion: for each line we will

158 Assembly Language Line Graphics

have a word giving the number of the first point, then a word giving the number of the second point (Figure 4.11). We will call the first point 0, the second point 1, and so on. Then, once we have the point number, multiplying it by two gives the starting address of the point's coordinates.

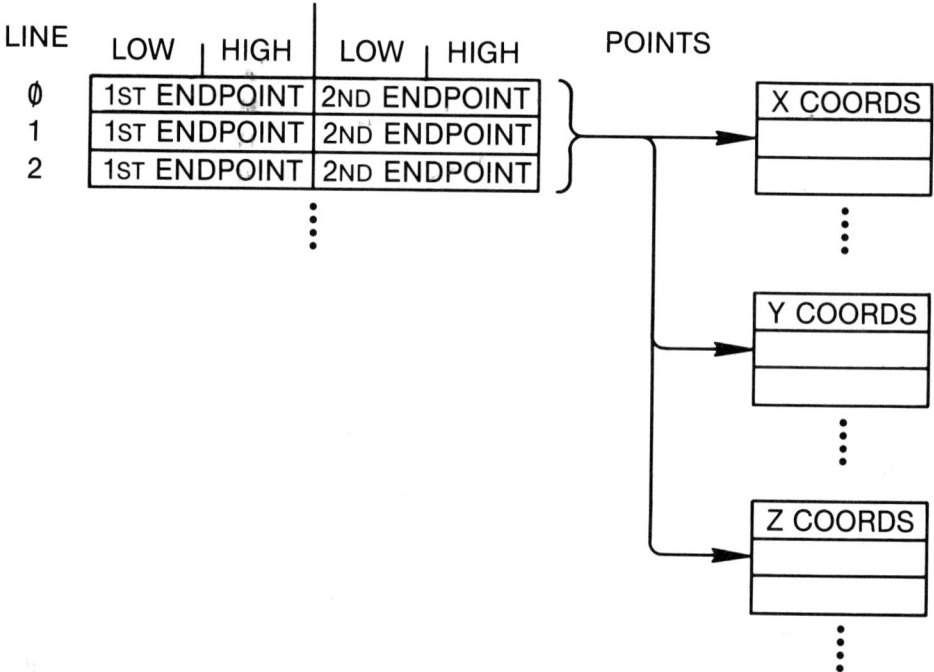

Figure 4.11
The line data are stored in an array. Each line has a word pointing to the first end point, and a word pointing to the second end point.

As with points, we will put the line data in as data statements. This data should appear, along with the point data, at the end of the variables section. The variable **number_of_lines** will hold four times the number of lines—the number of bytes used to represent lines. This makes accessing the line data easier.

Our routine to draw the lines will be simple. For each line we will find the point numbers of its end points, pass the coordinates of these points to **draw_line**, and call **draw_line**. Let's look at it:

```
;
number_of_lines    dw      48          ;4 * 12 lines
;
lines              dw      0,1, 1,2, 2,3, 3,0, 4,5, 5,6  ;for the cub
                   dw      6,7, 7,4, 0,4, 1,5, 2,6, 3,7
;
```

```
;
;draw the lines
;
;   load the line data from the data base and pass it to
;   the draw_line procedure
;
draw_the_lines     proc      near
                   mov       di,number_of_lines
d_t_l_loop:        cmp       di,0
                   je        d_t_l_end
                   dec       di              ;point to current line
                   dec       di
;
                   mov       si,lines[di]    ;first end point
                   shl       si,1            ;point to start of point data
                   mov       ax,newxpoints[si]  ;load x coordinate
                   mov       x1,ax           ;pass to draw_line
                   mov       ax,newypoints[si]  ;load y coordinate
                   mov       y1,ax
                   dec       di              ;point to next end point
                   dec       di
                   mov       si,lines[di]    ;second end point
                   shl       si,1
                   mov       ax,newxpoints[si]
                   mov       x2,ax           ;pass to draw_line
                   mov       ax,newypoints[si]
                   mov       y2,ax
;
                   push      di              ;save this before calling draw_line
                   call      draw_line       ;draw the line
                   pop       di              ;get back the line pointer
;
                   jmp short d_t_l_loop      ;do it again
d_t_l_end:         ret
draw_the_lines     endp
;
```

12.ASM

4.13: CLIPPING

To prevent possible memory overwrites and distortions on the graphics screen, we will add clipping to our line routine. Instead of using a set of calculations, as we did in BASIC, we will just check to see if each point is on the screen before we call **set_dot**.

The Routine

Let's see how to do this. Before **plot_the_point**, add:

```
ck_if_in_bounds:
            mov         cx,xh           ;check x
            cmp         cx,maxxres
            jae         find_next_point
            mov         cx,yh           ;check y
            cmp         cx,maxyres
            jae         find_next_point
```

13.ASM

then, change:

`;find next point`

to:

`find_next_point:`

and change:

`            jmp short plot_the_point`

to:

`            jmp short ck_if_in_bounds`

It may seem at first that we are only checking if the coordinates exceed the maximum boundaries. But remember that our numbers are stored as signed integers. The command **jae** compares unsigned numbers. If a coordinate is less than 0, that is, below a minimum boundary, then its value will be greater than 8000H. And certainly, 8000H is greater than **maxxres** and **maxyres**.

Unlike the BASIC clipping routine, the decrease in speed is unnoticeable.

4.14: THE FINAL TOUCHES

Now only two things remain. First, we need a routine to start up the program. This has to prepare the stack for returning after the program runs, set up the data and extra segment registers, and call the routine to set the graphics mode. Here it is:

```
;
;start up graphics program
;
;   assumes the data segment is called variables
;
start_it            proc       far
                    push       ds              ;for returning from program
                    mov        ax,0
                    push       ds
                    mov        ax,variables    ;set up data segment
                    mov        ds,ax
                    mov        ax,0b800h       ;set up extra segment
                    mov        es,ax           ;to point to graphics memory
                    call       set_mode
                    call       main_loop
;
                    ret                        ;it's all finished
start_it            endp
```

Second, we need to update **set_mode**:

```
set_mode            proc       near
                    cmp        mode,2          ;see if high res
                    je         set_high_res
;set medium res
                    mov        ah,0            ;set mode
                    mov        al,4
                    int        10h
                    mov        ah,11           ;set palette
                    mov        bh,1
                    mov        bl,palette
                    int        10h
;   set up data for set_dot
                    mov        ax,offset colors_med   ;indicate what color table
                    mov        color_table,ax         ;to use for set_dot
                    mov        ax,offset mask_med     ;indicate what mask table
                    mov        mask_table,ax          ;to use for set_dot
                    mov        resolution,2           ;2^2 points per line
;   set up data for perspect_to_screen
                    mov        width_adjust,20
                    mov        maxxres,320
;
                    mov        color,1
                    jmp short  s_m_end
;
set_high_res:
                    mov        ah,0            ;set mode
                    mov        al,6
                    int        10h
;   set up data for set_dot
                    mov        ax,offset colors_high  ;indicate what color table
                    mov        color_table,ax         ;to use for set_dot
                    mov        ax,offset mask_high    ;indicate what mask table
                    mov        mask_table,ax          ;to use for set_dot
                    mov        resolution,3           ;2^3 points per line
;   set up data for perspect_to_screen
                    mov        width_adjust,39
```

```
                        mov     maxxres,640
;
                        mov     color,1
s_m_end:
                        ret
;
set_mode                endp
```

14.ASM

We're finished. Put together all of the procedures, set up a stack and the data segment (containing all of the variables), and assemble the program.

Now run it. Notice how fast it goes. In fact, it will do 100 loops in under 14 seconds—over 20 times faster than **3DLG3.BAS**! The only problem with the routine is flicker. We will see how to eliminate flicker in Chapter 7.

5

True Three-Dimensional Graphics

So far we have drawn two-dimensional projections of three-dimensional objects and have been relying on perspective to give the illusion of depth. In this chapter we will learn how to fool the eyes into seeing three dimensions by using stereoscopic images. Objects will seem to pop right out of the screen.

We will start by briefly examining how the eye perceives depth, and then we will see how to program true three-dimensional graphics—first in BASIC, then in Assembly Language.

5.1: A BRIEF INTRODUCTION TO HOW WE PERCEIVE DEPTH

Several major factors contribute to depth perception. These can be divided into two groups: *physiological depth cues*—cues that are due to an actual physical response—and *pyschological depth cues*—cues that we learn signify depth. Physiological depth cues are most important and are missing from conventional graphics displays. Psychological depth cues are also very important and are often quite convincing at portraying depth. Unfortunately, they can be misleading.

The Physiological Depth Cues

There are four major physiological depth cues: *binocular parallax, disparity, convergence* and *accommodation*.

Binocular parallax is caused by the difference in what the left and right eyes see when looking at an object. Hold a pen with a clip about one-half of a meter away. Close your left eye and rotate the pen so that the clip just barely sticks out from the left side. Now, close your right eye and open your left. Blink back and forth a couple of times. Each eye will see a slightly different image.

Disparity is the doubling of images on the retina. When the eye focuses on an object, the image falls onto the most sensitive part of the retina, the fovea. Any objects that are not being focused appear doubled, because they fall onto the left and right retinae at different distances from the foveae. For example, hold one finger about one-third of a meter away from your eyes and another finger about two-thirds of a meter away. Focus on the farther one. Now, without switching to focus on the closer, count how many times you see the closer finger—you should see it twice. Now, focus on the closer one, and see how many times you see the farther finger.

Convergence arises from the muscular tension caused by rotation of the eyes in focusing on an object. For the image to fall on the fovea, the eye needs to rotate—to converge onto the object. Hold your finger an arm's length in front of you and focus on it. Slowly bring your finger towards your nose, focusing on the finger as it comes closer. Soon you will feel yourself going cross-eyed, and at some point your eyes might begin to hurt. You are feeling your eyes converging.

Accommodation refers to the muscular tension caused by the eye's ciliary body adjusting the focal length of the crystalline lens (Figure 5.1).

We will be adding binocular parallax, disparity, and convergence to our graphics display. We won't be able to add accommodation, as the eyes always accommodate to the monitor—the place where the images actually appear.

Pyschological Depth Cues

There are many psychological depth cues (painters have relied upon them for centuries to convey depth). The most important are *linear perspective, overlap* and *shading and shadows*.

Linear perspective is the decrease in an image's size as its distance from the viewer increases. You are already quite familiar with it; it has been the basis for our perspective routine.

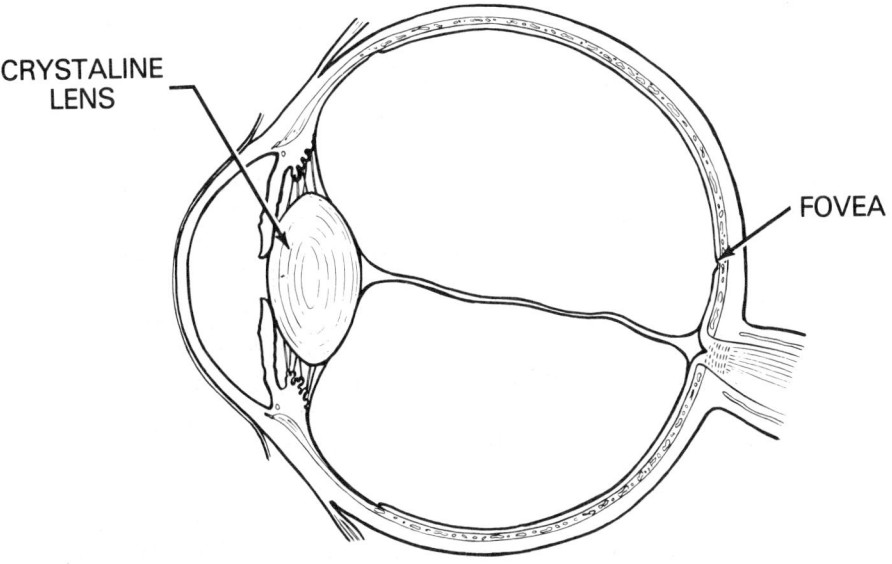

Figure 5.1
The eye.

Overlap is the blocking of part of an object because another object appears in front of it. When we see lines cut off by others, we assume the blocked lines are farther off. But this can be misleading.

Shading and shadows are extremely important cues. *Shading* is the difference in intensity of light falling on parts of an object because of the object's contours. Generally, parts of an object perpendicular to a light source are brightest; those at angles are dimmer. *Shadows* are caused by an object being between the light source and the viewed object. They are quite effective in communicating depth, but very difficult to program.

The only psychological depth cue we will use is linear perspective.

5.2: MAKING TRUE THREE-DIMENSIONAL IMAGES

Now we need to find a way to add physiological depth cues to the graphics display. It's a lot simpler than it sounds. We have only to figure what each eye would see if an object really were three dimensional, and then make sure that each eye sees only this image. The eyes will thus be fooled into thinking the object has depth. This approach is called *stereoscopy*.

Finding the Images

First let's determine what the left and right eyes see. Let's imagine an object floating in three space, and try to draw what each eye would see, as projected on to the focal plane of the monitor, just as we did for our perspective algorithm. Only now, instead of finding the view from a point on the z axis, we need to determine what is seen from two points in the xz plane (Figure 5.2).

Let's call the distance between each eye and **(0, 0, focal distance) pupil distance**. Suppose we are looking at the point **(x,y,z)**. Then from the right eye we see the projection **(x_{right}, y_{right})**, and from the left eye we see **(x_{left}, y_{left})** (Figure 5.3). Using similar triangles, we find:

(pupil distance − x_{right}) = focal distance * (pupil distance − x) / (focal distance − z)

y_{right} = focal distance * y / (focal distance − z)

Solving for **x_{right}**, we get:

x_{right} = pupil distance − focaldistance * (pupil distance − x) / (focal distance − z)

Similarly, by substituting **−pupil distance** for **pupil distance,** we find:

x_{left} = −pupil distance − focal distance * (−pupil distance − x) / (focal distance − z)

y_{left} = focal distance * y / (focal distance − z)

The distance between the pupils is fairly constant among humans—about 6.5 centimeters. **pupil distance** needs to be half of this, in terms of screen dots. You can compute it by:

pupil distance = (.065 / 2) * maxyres / screen height

screen height is the height of the screen in meters. For my screen, I set **pupil distance** to 40. You may want to measure your interpupillary distance and use it instead of 6.5 centimeters. Unless the difference is major, the change won't be necessary.

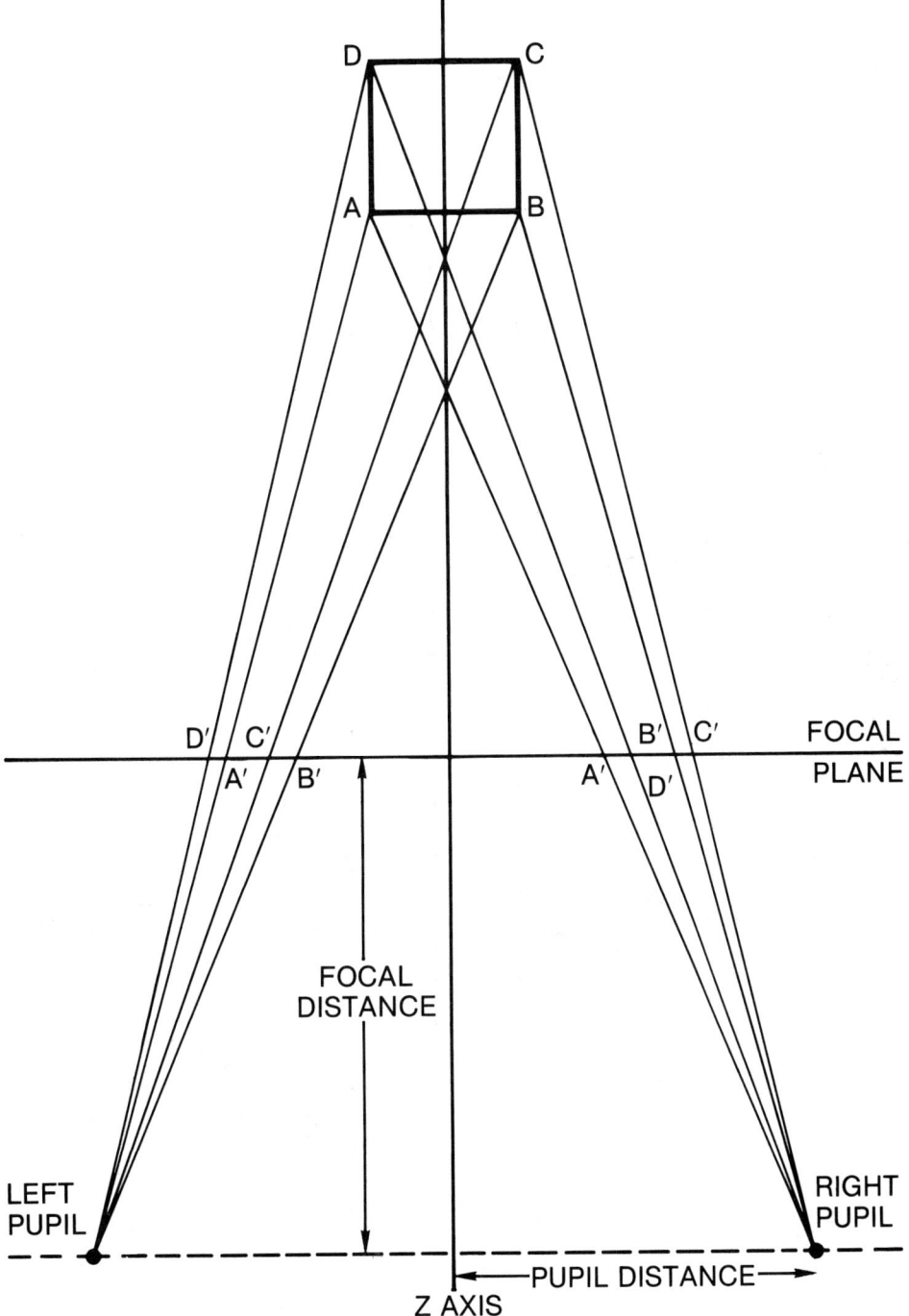

Figure 5.2
A top down view of looking at an object through the focal plane of the monitor, as seen by the left and right eye pupils.

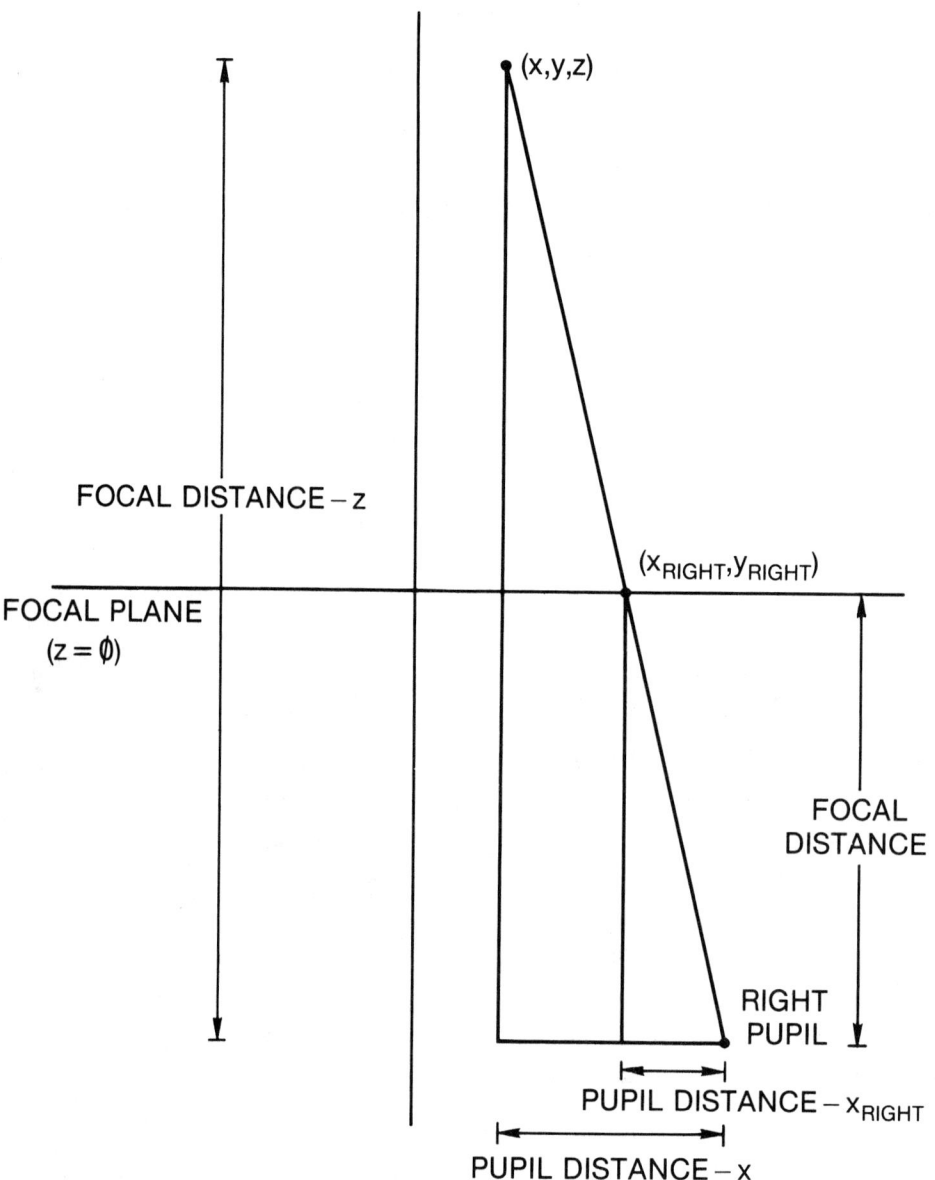

Figure 5.3
The right eye sees point (x,y,z) as (X_{right}, Y_{right}).

Displaying the Images

There are many ways to display and filter the two images so that each eye sees only its appropriate image. One is to move the images apart and have the viewer merge them together by rotating his eyes, with or without the help of lenses. This method is most useful for generating printed outputs of three-dimensional pictures. For screen display, however, it can be cumbersome, as it is hard to merge the images if they are moving. Its advantages are that it requires no outside equipment and will work with any monitor.

Another approach is to filter the images with *polarizers*. One image is displayed on the upper half of the screen, the other on the lower, and they are merged by a *beam splitter*. They are viewed with a pair of polarized filters. The advantages of this system are many: it causes no eyestrain; there is no color distortion; and it is very easy to merge the images. However, it requires optical hardware (the beam splitter and polarizers) and the vertical resolution of the screen is halved.

A third method is to use *colored filtering*. The left and right eye images are displayed in complementary colors. They are viewed with a pair of glasses colored so that each eye sees only its respective image. With this method, the only additional hardware needed is a pair of colored glasses. Images are a little harder to merge than with the polarizing method, and extended use of the glasses can cause eyestrain. We need to use the medium-resolution screen to get color; thus, our horizontal resolution is limited. But more importantly, colored filtering works best only on red-green-blue (RGB) screens. Composite monitors can cause too much distortion when they plot in color; black and white screens won't work at all.

5.3: MORE ON COLORED FILTERING

We'll approach three-dimensional graphics first with the colored filter method. In both color palettes, colors 1 and 2 are complementary. Every now and then three-dimensional movies using colored filters play in theaters or on TV. These filters use red and green lenses. You can probably find a pair of these glasses; therefore, we will draw with palette 0. Its green and red match the glasses' green and red quite well.

Ordinarily, the glasses have a red filter for the right eye and a green filter for the left eye. So, if we look through the right eye, we are unable to see anything green. Looking through the left, we can't see anything red. Therefore, we will draw the left eye image in green and the right in red.

170 True Three-Dimensional Graphics

After drawing the left and right eye views, look at the screen wearing the colored glasses. Each eye sees only what it would if a three-dimensional object really were present. Instead of seeing two separate two-dimensional images, we see one three-dimensional image.

Because of the filtering, we will not be able to give any color to the objects.

Making Glasses

If you are unable to find a pair of colored filter glasses, make them yourself. Art supply stores sell transparent colored films. Get film to match the green and red of your screen. Then, cut glasses from cardboard and stretch the filters over the appropriate eyeholes.

5.4: TRUE THREE-DIMENSIONAL IMAGES FROM BASIC—THE COLORED FILTER APPROACH

Now let's change **3DLG3** so that it does true three-dimensional graphics. We'll use the colored lens method.

First we'll add code to compute the left and right eye images. We will do this in the perspective routine. To save the results, we need to add two more dimensions to our **NEWPOINTS** array. Let's do this:

```
20 DIM POINTS(3,100), NEWPOINTS(5,100), LINES(2,100)

190 PUPILDISTANCE = 40 : LEFTX = 4 : RIGHTX = 5

7001 'Determine left and right eye views
7020 NEWPOINTS(LEFTX,POINTNUM) = -PUPILDISTANCE -
     FOCALDISTANCE * (-PUPILDISTANCE -
     NEWPOINTS(XCOORD,POINTNUM))/(FOCALDISTANCE -
     NEWPOINTS(ZCOORD,POINTNUM))
7040 NEWPOINTS(RIGHTX,POINTNUM) = PUPILDISTANCE -
     FOCALDISTANCE * (PUPILDISTANCE -
     NEWPOINTS(XCOORD,POINTNUM))/(FOCALDISTANCE -
     NEWPOINTS(ZCOORD,POINTNUM))
7050 NEXT
```

We also have to adjust the subroutine to convert to screen coordinates to work on the left and right x coordinates:

```
8020 NEWPOINTS(LEFTX,POINTNUM) = MAXXRES/2 +
     NEWPOINTS(LEFTX, POINTNUM) * MAXXRES / MAXYRES /
     ASPECTRATIO
```

```
8040 NEWPOINTS(RIGHTX,POINTNUM) = MAXXRES/2 +
     NEWPOINTS(RIGHTX, POINTNUM) * MAXXRES / MAXYRES /
     ASPECTRATIO
8050 NEXT
```

Then, we need to set up the program to work with the medium-resolution screen:

```
140 MAXXRES = 320 : MAXYRES = 200

410 SCREEN 1
440 COLOR,0
```

Finally, we need to change the line drawing subroutine to draw the left and right lines in the appropriate colors:

```
9020 LINE (NEWPOINTS(LEFTX,LINES(FROM,LINENUM)),
     NEWPOINTS(YCOORD,LINES(FROM,LINENUM))) -
     (NEWPOINTS(LEFTX,LINES(TO.,LINENUM)),NEWPOINTS
     (YCOORD,LINES(TO.,LINENUM))),1    'draw left line
9030 LINE (NEWPOINTS(RIGHTX,LINES(FROM,LINENUM)),
     NEWPOINTS(YCOORD,LINES(FROM,LINENUM))) -
     (NEWPOINTS(RIGHTX,LINES(TO.,LINENUM)),NEWPOINTS
     (YCOORD,LINES(TO.,LINENUM))),2    'draw right line
9040 NEXT
```

All the programs for Chapter 5 are in the **CHAPTER5** directory. Type:

CHDIR "
CHDIR "CHAPTER5

To add the code, type:

MERGE "4P1

Try it out. The two cubes will appear on the screen, each in a different color. But looking at them through the glasses is confusing. The cubes don't seem at all three dimensional!

It Doesn't Work—The Line Problem

Here's the problem: suppose we want to see a left and right eye line in the same place. Then, in that place, the line must be both green and red.

If we use color 3—a mixture of green and red—then we will be able to see the line through both lenses. But look at the screen. Wherever any lines overlap, the last color drawn is what shows. This is because BASIC uses store drawing. For our purposes, we need **OR** drawing. We learned how to do this in the last chapter. We'll use **draw_line** instead of BASIC's **LINE**. We will call it with **CALL**—a command that executes Machine Language subroutines.

We'll make some minor modifications to our line drawing routine, place it in a framework that we can call from BASIC, and then see how to use it from BASIC.

Modifying the Line Routine

We'll add a routine allowing us to call **draw_line** from BASIC, and we'll simplify **set_dot**. Rather than going through these routines step-by-step, let's just look at them. Those interested in Assembly Language can analyze all of the changes and additions made. (If you don't have an Assembler, the routine is presented in ready to **BLOAD** form on the optional disk. If you have this disk, you may wish to skip to the subsection **Doing It**.):

```
;
maxxres                 equ      320
maxyres                 equ      200
;
variables segment
;
;the following are input from BASIC
x1                      dw       0
x2                      dw       0
y1                      dw       0
y2                      dw       0
color                   db       0
;
;the following are computed by the program
;
xl                      db       0
xh                      dw       0
yl                      db       0
yh                      dw       0
incxl                   db       0
incxh                   dw       0
incyl                   db       0
incyh                   dw       0
;
color_table             db       00000000b, 01010101b, 10101010b, 11111111b
mask_table              db       11000000b, 00110000b, 00001100b, 00000011b
;
variables ends
;
code segment
```

```
                        assume  cs:code,ds:variables
draw_it                 proc    far
                        push    bp                      ;save these for return to BASIC
                        push    ds
                        push    es
                        mov     ax,variables            ;set up data segment
                        mov     ds,ax
                        mov     ax,0b800h               ;ES points to graphics page
                        mov     es,ax
                        call    draw_line               ;draw the line
                        pop     es                      ;restore ES, DS, and BP for
                        pop     ds                      ;return to BASIC
                        pop     bp
                        ret
draw_it                 endp
;
;PUT draw_line HERE
;

;set dot
;
;called with:
;   xh = x coordinate
;   yh = y coordinate
;   color = 0 - 3 for med res
;
set_dot                 proc    near
                        mov     ax,yh
                        mov     bx,0
;see if odd or even line
                        shr     ax,1
                        jnc     mult_by_80
;odd
                        mov     bx,2000h
;multiply by 80 to determine memory location of first byte in row
mult_by_80:             mov     dx,ax
                        shl     ax,1
                        shl     ax,1
                        add     ax,dx
                        shl     ax,1
                        shl     ax,1
                        shl     ax,1
                        shl     ax,1
                        add     bx,ax           ;BX = first byte in line
;find position in line
                        mov     ax,xh
                        shr     ax,1
                        shr     ax,1
                        add     bx,ax           ;BX points to byte in which to plot
                        mov     bp,bx
;find what to plot
                        shl     ax,1
                        shl     ax,1
                        xor     ax,xh           ;AX = dot within byte
                        mov     bx,ax
                        mov     al,mask_table[bx]
                        mov     ch,al
                        mov     al,color
                        mov     bx,ax
```

```
                    mov      al,color_table[bx]
                    and      ch,al
plot_it:            or       es:[bp],ch
;
                    ret
set_dot             endp
;
code                ends
                    end      draw_it
```

> This file is located in **DRWLNBAS.ASM**. If you don't have the Assembler, skip to the subsection **Doing It**, as all you need is already on the program disk.

Let's call this program **DRWLNBAS.ASM**. Assemble it. Now, link it with LINK, using the high option:

LINK DRWLNBAS/HIGH

This option will place it at the top of memory. Thus, if possible, it will be far away from BASIC. Get a list file (the one with the extension **.MAP**). **DRWLNBAS.MAP**, appearing here, tells us how long the sections of our program are. Don't worry about the **No STACK** warning:

Warning: No STACK segment

Start	Stop	Length	Name	Class
00000H	0011CH	011DH	CODE	
00120H	0013CH	001DH	VARIABLES	

Origin   Group

Program entry point at 0000:0000

Interfacing with BASIC

Now we are ready to interface with BASIC. If you are familiar with the BASIC manual, you may have read how to interface the **CALL** command with Assembly Language routines (*BASIC Manual* Appendix C). Passing data through the stack, as they suggest, is a bit cumbersome. All of the variable offsets are relative to BASIC's data segment, while we need to store the incoming data in a data segment of our own. To avoid a lot of segment overrides, we will **POKE** the coordinates and the color value directly into **DRWLNBAS**'s data segment.

To use the routine in BASIC, we need to load it with **BLOAD**. But to do this, we need to have **BSAVE**d it. Here's how:

First, type:

debug basica.com

This loads in BASIC. See what all of the registers are by typing:

r

This tells where BASIC is loaded. Copy down the **CS**, **IP**, **SS**, and **SP** values. For me, they were:

CS = 905   SS = 905   IP = 100   SP = FFFE

Now, put your program disk in drive A. (Or you can do it from drive B.) Type:

n drwlnbas.exe
l

This will load **DRWLNBAS.EXE** into memory. To find out where it is placed, type:

r

and copy down **CS** and **IP**; for me they were 2F94H and 0, respectively.

Now, we restore the registers so that they point to BASIC. To do this, type in **r** followed by the register and its value after we loaded BASIC. I had to type:

r cs

then (after the computer spits out a few lines of data):

905

r ip

then:

100
r ss

then:

905
r sp

then:

fffe

Now, we will get into BASIC. Type:

g

You should see the BASIC start-up.

As a result of our actions, BASIC is running, and the routine is in memory. We're now ready to **BSAVE** it. First, we point to the segment in which the routine is located:

DEF SEG = &H2F94

The value above, 2F94H, is where my program was loaded. Your program's load location may be different. It is the number to which the **CS** register was set after **DRWLNBAS.EXE** was loaded.
Then, do:

BSAVE "DRWLNBAS",0,&H13D

DRWLNBAS is the name we have given the program. You can change it to whatever you want. Zero is the value from **IP** after we loaded **DRWLNBAS.EXE**, &H13D is the length of the routine, equal to one plus the location of the end of the variables segment (found from **DRWLNBAS.MAP**).

To use the routine, we use **DEF SEG** to point to where we loaded the routine—the **DEF SEG** declaration we used to **BSAVE** the program. Then, we **BLOAD** the routine by using an offset of 0.

Each time we want to draw a line we need to **POKE** the coordinates of the end points and the color into the routine's data segment. From **DRWLNBAS.MAP**, we see that the data segment starts 120H bytes after the start of **DRWLNBAS**. Therefore, we do all of our pokes relative to that value. For example, to set **X1** to 10, do:

POKE &H120,10 : POKE &H121,0

Finally, we call the routine with:

DRWLN = 0
CALL DRWLN

We can use any variable set to 0; it is not necessary to use one called **DRWLN**.

If you don't have more than 96K in your computer, you will need to set aside some of BASIC's memory for **DRWLNBAS**. To do this, use the **CLEAR** command. (See Appendix C of the *BASIC Manual* for more information.)

Doing It

Now let's incorporate our new line-drawing function into our true three-dimensional program. First, we'll **BLOAD** in the routine:

```
30 DEF SEG = &H2F94
40 BLOAD "drwlnbas",0
```

Use the appropriate value for **DEF SEG**.

If you didn't make your own assembled version of **draw_line**, you can use one from the program disk. There are three versions available. If you have a 192K (or more) memory machine, the machine code (that created above and stored in **DRWLNBAS**) is stored in **DRWLNBAS**. Either keep the program disk in the default drive when you run the program, or copy **DRWLNBAS.BAS** to the disk in the default drive.

If you have a 128K machine, use **DRWLN128** instead of **DRWLNBAS**. Change the file name in line **40** to **DRWLN128**, and **DEF SEG** to &H1F94 in line **30**.

If your machine is 64K, use **DRWLN64** instead of **DRWLNBAS**. Change the file name in line **40** to **DRWLN64**. Then, add:

1 CLEAR, &HA000

DEF SEG to &HA00 instead of &H2F94 in line **30**.

> You'll have to make the above changes (if necessary) after you load the BASIC code for this section. I'll explain how to do that in the next program disk box. (It will appear shortly.)

Now we'll define a variable **VARSTART**, which points to the start of the data segment for our Assembly Language routine:

```
50 VARSTART = &H120
```

When we **POKE** numbers in the computer, they need to be in the form low-byte, high-byte. To figure out these values, we define:

```
60 DEF FNHIGH(X) = INT(X/256) - 256 * (X < 0)
70 DEF FNLOW(X) = INT(X - INT(X/256)*256) - 256 * (X < 0)
```

Now, we delete **9030**, and use the following instead of the **LINE** command in **9020**:

```
9020 GOSUB 18010   'draw the left and right eye lines
```

This subroutine pokes in the end points' x and y coordinates and the color and calls our line-drawing routine for the left and right eye lines:

```
18000 '
18001 'Poke end points and draw left and right eye
      lines
18002 '
18010 POKE VARSTART,FNLOW(NEWPOINTS(LEFTX,LINES(FROM,
      LINENUM))) : POKE VARSTART + 1,FNHIGH(NEWPOINTS
      (LEFTX,LINES(FROM,LINENUM)))    'x1
18020 POKE VARSTART + 2,FNLOW(NEWPOINTS(LEFTX,LINES
      (TO.,LINENUM))) : POKE VARSTART + 3,FNHIGH
      (NEWPOINTS (LEFTX,LINES(TO.,LINENUM )))    'x2
18030 POKE VARSTART + 4,FNLOW(NEWPOINTS(YCOORD,LINES
      (FROM,LINENUM))) : POKE VARSTART + 5,FNHIGH
      (NEWPOINTS(YCOORD,LINES(FROM, LINENUM)))    'y1
18040 POKE VARSTART + 6,FNLOW(NEWPOINTS(YCOORD,LINES
      (TO.,LINENUM))) : POKE VARSTART + 7,FNHIGH
      (NEWPOINTS(YCOORD,LINES(TO.,LINENUM)))    'y2
18050 POKE VARSTART + 8,1
18060 CALL DRWLN          'draw the left eye line
18070 POKE VARSTART,FNLOW(NEWPOINTS(RIGHTX,LINES
      (FROM,LINENUM))) : POKE VARSTART + 1,FNHIGH
      (NEWPOINTS(RIGHTX,LINES(FROM,LINENUM)))    'x1
18080 POKE VARSTART + 2,FNLOW(NEWPOINTS(RIGHTX,LINES
      (TO.,LINENUM))) : POKE VARSTART + 3,FNHIGH
      (NEWPOINTS(RIGHTX,LINES(TO.,LINENUM)))    'x2
```

```
18090 POKE VARSTART + 4,FNLOW(NEWPOINTS(YCOORD,LINES
      (FROM,LINENUM))) : POKE VARSTART + 5,FNHIGH
      (NEWPOINTS(YCOORD,LINES(FROM,LINENUM)))    'y1
18100 POKE VARSTART + 6,FNLOW(NEWPOINTS(YCOORD,LINES
      (TO.,LINENUM))) : POKE VARSTART + 7,FNHIGH
      (NEWPOINTS(YCOORD,LINES(TO.,LINENUM)))     'y2
18110 POKE VARSTART + 8,2
18120 CALL DRWLN          'draw the right eye line
18200 RETURN
```

MERGE "4P2

Trying It Once More

Run the program. At first you may have some difficulty merging the images. This problem should go away with practice. (If you are completely unable to merge the two, close one eye at a time to make sure your glasses filter the images properly. If they do, and you still have problems, try moving the object a bit and change your viewing position. If it still doesn't work, have someone else try it out. It's possible that you can't see stereoscopically.)

5.5: ADDING TRUE THREE DIMENSIONS TO OUR ASSEMBLY LANGUAGE PROGRAM

Now that we can do stereoscopic three-dimensional graphics in BASIC, let's add it to our Assembly Language program. Rather than modify old routines, we'll add a key to switch between regular and stereoscopic drawing. We need to make the following additions: a routine to determine what the left and right eyes see, a routine to draw these views in the correct colors, and additions to the main loop and keyboard reading procedures to handle true three-dimensional graphics.

We will use **true_three_d** to indicate whether to plot stereoscopically or not. Zero will indicate regular mode, and one will indicate stereoscopic three-dimensional mode. We will change **main_loop** to check it:

```
;
true_three_d      db         0           ;initially regular mode
;
main_loop         proc       near
```

180 True Three-Dimensional Graphics

```
                    call        read_keyboard
                    call        get_movement_values
                    call        load_trig_values
                    call        get_matrix
                    call        transform_points
                    cmp         true_three_d,1      ;1 indicates sterescopic mode
                    jne         regular
                    call        left_right          ;find the left and right eye
                    call        clear_screen        ;views, clear the screen, and
                    call        draw_left_right     ;draw them
                    jmp         m_1_1
regular:            call        perspect_to_screen
                    call        clear_screen
                    call        draw_the_lines
m_1_1:              cmp         finished,0
                    jne         main_loop
;
                    ret
main_loop           endp
```

Let's use the F1 key to toggle between the regular and stereoscopic mode. When it is pressed, we need to switch to whatever mode we weren't in; that is, if **true_three_d** were 1, we make it 0, and vice versa. For now, let's have regular mode always be in high resolution. Stereoscopic mode needs to be in medium resolution. You may want to add a command to switch to medium resolution while in the regular graphics mode.

When a function key is pressed, **interrupt 16H** returns with **AL = 0** and the extended key code in **AH**. For F1, **AH** will be 3BH.

Let's check for it:

Change:

```
                    jne         ckesc
```

to:

```
                    jne         ckf1
```

in **read_keyboard**'s **ckspace**.

Then add:

```
ckf1:               cmp         ax,3b00H            ;see if F1 pressed
                    jne         ckesc
                    xor         true_three_d,1      ;toggle between true and false
                    xor         mode,3              ;toggle between med and high
                    call        set_mode            ;res and make the change
                    jmp         clear_buffer
```

Now we need to add a routine to compute the left and right eye views, adjust for dot width, and convert to screen coordinates. This is very similar to the routine **perspect_to_screen**, only we need to do two x perspectives by using our stereoscopic formulae:

```
;
pupil_distance         dw              40
;
left                   dw              8 dup (0)       ;place these with newpoints
right                  dw              8 dup (0)
;

;
;determine left and right eye views, account for dot width, and
;convert to screen coordinates
;
left_right             proc            near
                       mov             di,number_of_points
l_r_loop:              cmp             di,0
                       jne             l_r_1           ;l_r_end to far away for je l_r_end
                       jmp             l_r_end
l_r_1:                 dec             di
                       dec             di
;compute focal_distance - z
                       mov             cx,focal_distance
                       sub             cx,newzpoints[di]
                       jne             get_left        ;make sure not 0
                       inc             cx
get_left:              mov             ax,pupil_distance
                       neg             ax
                       sub             ax,newxpoints[di]   ;-p_d - x
                       mov             bx,focal_distance
                       imul            bx                  ;f_d * (-p_d - x)
                       idiv            cx                  ;f_d*(-p_d - x)/(f_d - z)
                       add             ax,pupil_distance   ;p_d+f_d*(-p_d - x)/(f_d - z)
                       neg             ax                  ;left x coordinate
                       mov             dx,width_adjust     ;now adjust width
                       imul            dx
                       sar             ax,1
                       sar             ax,1
                       sar             ax,1
                       sar             ax,1
                       mov             dx,maxxres          ;convert to screen coords
                       sar             dx,1
                       add             ax,dx
                       mov             left[di],ax
;get right eye view
                       mov             ax,pupil_distance
                       sub             ax,newxpoints[di]   ;p_d - x
                       imul            bx
                       idiv            cx
                       sub             ax,pupil_distance   ;(p_d-x)*f_d/(f_d-z) - p_d
                       neg             ax                  ;right x coordinate
                       mov             dx,width_adjust     ;now adjust width
                       imul            dx
                       sar             ax,1
                       sar             ax,1
                       sar             ax,1
                       sar             ax,1
                       mov             dx,maxxres          ;convert to screen coords
                       sar             dx,1
                       add             ax,dx
                       mov             right[di],ax
;get y coordinate
                       mov             ax,newypoints[di]
                       imul            bx
```

182 True Three-Dimensional Graphics

```
                idiv    cx
                mov     dx,maxyres
                sar     dx,1
                sub     dx,ax
                mov     newypoints[di],dx
;
                jmp     l_r_loop
l_r_end:
                ret
left_right      endp
```

Finally, we need a routine to draw the left and right eye lines in their appropriate colors. This is just like **draw_the_lines**, only we need to account for twice as many lines:

```
;
;draw the left and right eye images of the object
;the left lines are in green, the right in red
;
draw_left_right proc    near
                mov     di,number_of_lines
d_l_r_loop:     cmp     di,0
                je      d_l_r_end
                dec     di
                dec     di
                mov     si,lines[di]
                shl     si,1
                mov     ax,left[si]         ;first the left lines
                mov     x1,ax
                mov     ax,newypoints[di]
                mov     y1,ax
                mov     ax,right[si]   ;load it while we are pointing to it
                dec     di
                dec     di
;now for the second endpoint
                mov     si,lines[di]
                shl     si,1
                push    di      ;so that draw_line doesn't destroy it
                push    ax      ;for later use
                mov     ax,left[si]
                mov     x2,ax
                mov     ax,newypoints[di]
                mov     y2,ax
                mov     ax,right[si]        ;get it while we point there
                push    ax                  ;for later use
                mov     color,1             ;draw in green
                call    draw_line           ;draw the left line
                pop     ax                  ;the second right x coordinate
                mov     x2,ax
                pop     ax                  ;the first right x coordinate
                mov     x1,ax
                mov     color,2             ;draw in red
                call    draw_line           ;draw the right line
                pop     di                  ;restore line counter
;
                jmp     short d_l_r_loop
d_l_r_end:
                ret
draw_left_right endp
```

> All code in this section is stored in **5P1.ASM**.

Try it out. Run the program and after a moment, press F1. Toggle back and forth. Translate and rotate the object in all directions.

Problems

I had some trouble seeing these images in three dimensions. Besides the flicker problem, which we'll get rid of in Chapter 7, my glasses could no longer filter out the colors. The colors were too bright. But how could this be? The colors were fine in BASIC.

If you look carefully, you will see that the colors being displayed are in high intensity. Run our BASIC three-dimensional program. The colors are less bright. Break out of it in the middle and type:

COLOR 16

All the lines change to high-intensity colors—the colors we get from the Assembly Language program. Now type:

COLOR 0

They are back to the regular-intensity colors. My glasses filter these better. So we need to switch intensities in our Assembly Language program. As the BIOS interrupts don't support intensity change, we'll have to program the color graphics board directly. Programming this will be discussed in detail in Chapter 7. For now, to get regular-intensity graphics, replace the call to **interrupt 10H** by setting the palette (in the medium-resolution setting section of **set_mode**) with:

```
        mov     al,palette      ;set up AX for programming
        cbw                     ;the color graphics intensity
        shl     ax,1            ;control
        shl     ax,1
        shl     ax,1
        shl     ax,1
        mov     dx,3d9h
        out     dx,ax           ;program it
```

184 True Three-Dimensional Graphics

> **5P2.ASM**

Now run the program. The images will be in regular intensity and much easier to filter.

If you are still having problems fusing the images, there could be two reasons. First, the filters might not be strong enough. Second, your eye muscles may not be used to the excercise through which you are putting them. It can take a bit of stretching to make the two images come together. Try to relax your eyes so that the two images merge. After a while you should get used to it.

5.6: PRINTING THREE-DIMENSIONAL IMAGES

Sometimes we may want to print out images for viewing in three dimensions. Or we may want to view them on the screen without having to use glasses. To do either, we split the screen into two halves, drawing the left eye images on the left side of the screen, and the right eye images on the right side of the screen. Then, by relaxing our eyes we fuse the two separate pictures together and get the stereoscopic effect. A printed example appears in Figure 5.4. Look at it and try to relax your eyes so that one

Figure 5.4
A printed 3-D output. By relaxing your eyes, try to merge the two images.

image superimposes itself on the other. The picture should all of a sudden take on three dimensions. When you look at it, though, you will see three images—the left and right views, as well as the merged image. Now, place a thin divider over the line separating the drawings, and place your nose against this, as shown in Figure 5.5. Merge the images again. This time you will see only the three-dimensional image.

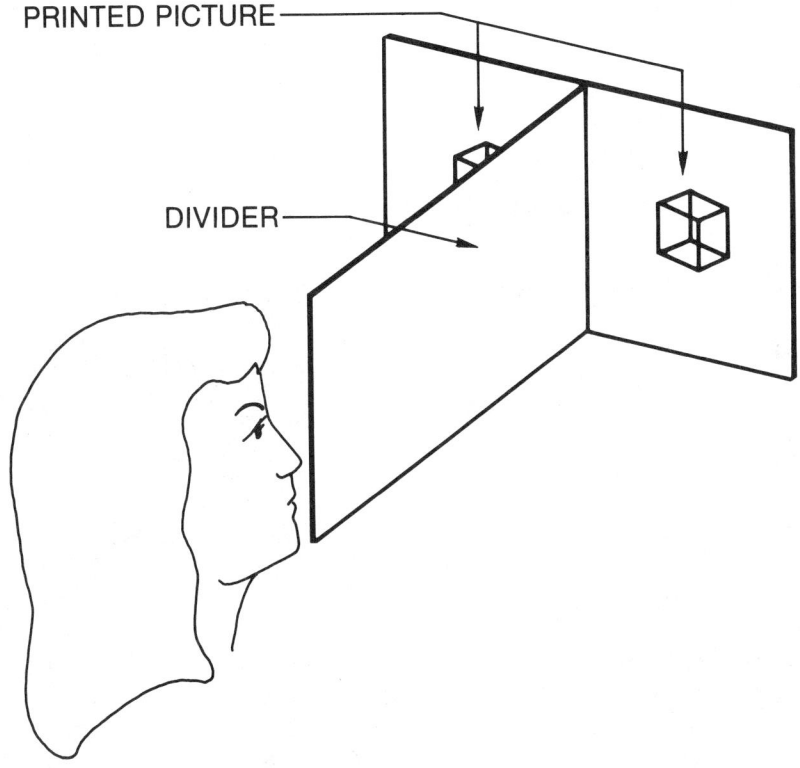

Figure 5.5
Place a thin divider over the lines separating the two eye views. Place your nose against the divider and look at the 3-D picture.

To create a left and right area for plotting, we will divide the screen into two viewports. We can't just divide the screen in any way though. We must carefully choose the viewport size. Here's why. It is very difficult for the eyes to spread apart more than they do when looking at an object an infinite distance away. For an object at this distance, the eyes look straight ahead. So the largest separation of the left and right images is the interpupillary distance, 6.5 centimeters. When we draw images, they reach their farthest distance apart at infinity—when they move toward the pupil view points. This matches what the eyes do. So when we define our viewports, the distance between the pupil points in each cannot exceed 6.5 centimeters (Figure 5.6).

186 True Three-Dimensional Graphics

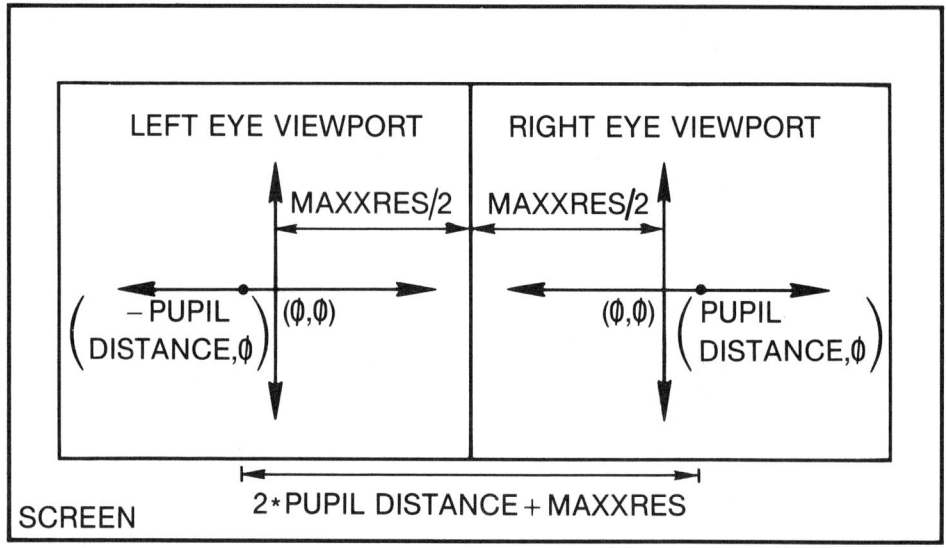

Figure 5.6

The distance between the pupil points must be less than 6.5 cm. The left pupil appears at (−pupil distance, 0) in the left viewport; the right, at (pupil distance, 0) in the right viewport. The distance between the origins of each viewport is maxxres. Thus, 2∗pupil distance + maxxres must be less than 6.5 cm.

We have to make **2 ∗ pupil distance + maxxres**, in terms of vertical viewport dots, less than 6.5 centimeters. To start, we'll compute the maximum width of our viewport. It's easier to keep an aspect ratio of 4/3, find the height, and then find the width from this. The screen width in terms of vertical dots is:

maxxres ∗ aspect ratio

The size of dots in the viewport in terms of physical vertical dots is:

(view height / maxyres) ∗(screen height / maxyres)

where **view height** is in physical dots and **screen height** is in meters.
 Therefore, we want:

view height = .065 ∗ maxyres ∗ maxyres / (screen height ∗ (aspect ratio ∗ maxyres + 2 ∗ pupil distance))

For my screen, **view height** turns out to be 47 dots—about one-quarter of the normal screen size. The width of each viewport is thus **47 * maxxres / maxyres**. If you are getting printouts, you need to do the calculation with respect to the size of the printout rather than the screen. If you are using an Epson printer, you should use a viewport with a vertical size of around 47.

So, now let's see how to put this in our program. We will use the BASIC 2.0 commands **WINDOW** and **VIEW**. If you are not using BASIC 2.0, you will have to scale and translate before drawing to get the same effects. We'll be using the algorithms presented in Section 5.4, but not the function definitions, **BLOAD** and drawing routines. So, if you have entered all of the code from Section 5.4, delete lines **30 − 70, 9020**, and **18000 − 18200**. If you haven't entered the code from Section 5.4, add Section 5.4's lines **20, 7001 − 7050**, and **8020 − 8050**. Now add:

```
190 PUPILDISTANCE = 40 : VIEWHEIGHT = 47 : LEFTX = 4 :
    RIGHTX = 5
```

If the above calculation gave you a different view height, substitute it here.

We also need to figure out the width of the viewing screen:

```
30 DEF FNVIEWWIDTH = VIEWHEIGHT / MAXYRES * MAXXRES
```

Now we make changes to the line-drawing section. We first use **WINDOW** to make the whole screen map into each viewport. If you have already used **WINDOW** to map directly in Cartesian coordinates, place the **WINDOW** statement you used here instead. I have assumed that **WINDOW** wasn't used before, and that, therefore, we want to map with screen coordinates:

```
9020 WINDOW SCREEN (0,0) - (MAXXRES,MAXYRES)
```

Next, we set up the left viewport:

```
9030 VIEW (MAXXRES/2 - FNVIEWWIDTH, MAXYRES/2 -
     VIEWHEIGHT/2) - (MAXXRES/2, MAXYRES/2 +
     VIEWHEIGHT/2)
```

This centers the viewport vertically and right justifies it against the horizontal center.

Now, we draw the left line:

```
9040 LINE (NEWPOINTS(LEFTX,LINES(FROM,LINENUM)),
     NEWPOINTS(YCOORD,LINES(FROM,LINENUM))) -
     (NEWPOINTS(LEFTX,LINES(TO.,LINENUM)),NEWPOINTS
     (YCOORD,LINES(TO.,LINENUM)))
```

We then set up the right viewport and place it adjacent to the left one:

```
9050 VIEW (MAXXRES/2, MAXYRES/2 - VIEWHEIGHT/2) -
     (MAXXRES/2 + FNVIEWWIDTH, MAXYRES/2 + VIEWHEIGHT/
     2)
```

And draw the right line:

```
9060 LINE (NEWPOINTS(RIGHTX,LINES(FROM,LINENUM)),
     NEWPOINTS(YCOORD,LINES(FROM,LINENUM))) -
     (NEWPOINTS(RIGHTX,LINES(TO.,LINENUM)),NEWPOINTS
     (YCOORD,LINES(TO.,LINENUM)))
9070 NEXT
```

Finally, before we clear the screen, we must reset the viewport to the whole screen. So we add:

```
730 VIEW : CLS
```

MERGE "6
to add the code in this section. Remember to do the deletions.

Now run it. Rotate the image a little, then try to merge the two together. After some practice, you should have no trouble, but you may experience a little eyestrain.

To print out the pictures, load the GRAPHICS module from DOS before you start BASIC (enter **graphics** before typing **basica**). Then, when you want to print what is on the screen, type Shift-PrtSc, just as you would for printing text.

5.7: USING A POLARIZER FILTERING SYSTEM

The third way to filter and mix stereo pairs is to use polarizers. This method gives the least eyestrain, the most effective filtering, and allows full use of colors. To use it, we halve the screen horizontally. The upper half of the screen displays one eye's image; the bottom displays the other. We place orthogonally polarized sheets over these two screens, and a beam splitter (one-way mirror) perpendicular to and against the screen along the dividing line (Figure 5.7).

Let's put the left eye image on the top and the right eye image on the bottom. We view the screen by looking down through the beam splitter at the bottom image. We see the right eye image through the beam splitter,

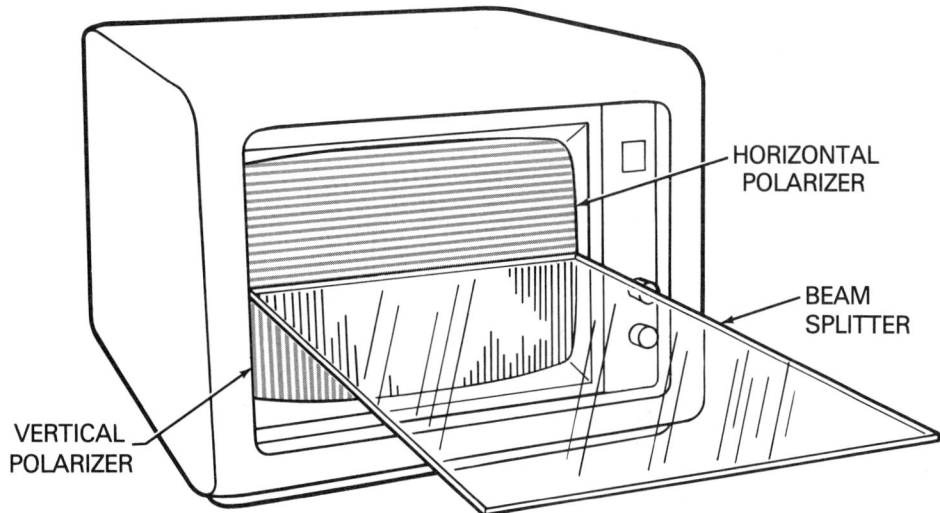

Figure 5.7

Place a horizontal polarizer over the upper half of the screen, a vertical polarizer over the lower, and a beam splitter perpendicular to and against the center of the screen.

while at the same time seeing the reflection of the left eye image superimposed (Figure 5.8).

Because of partial polarization due to reflection, we orient the upper polarizing sheet horizontally. We make the lower polarizing sheet a vertical polarizer. We then view the screen wearing glasses having a horizontal polarizer in the left eye and a vertical polarizer in the right. Thus, the left eye sees only the left eye image, the right eye sees only the right.

To display the images we need to define viewports for the upper and lower parts of the screen. The upper image must be flipped upside down. Then, when it reflects off the beam splitter, it will have the same orientation as the lower image.

We will do this by using the same approach as for printing the images. First, we set up the screen for the left eye image:

```
9020 WINDOW (0,0) - (MAXXRES,MAXYRES)
9030 VIEW (0,0) - (MAXXRES - 1,MAXYRES/2),,1
```

Note that we use **WINDOW** without the **SCREEN** option; this reflects the upper image. (If you are using **WINDOW** to map directly into Cartesian coordinates, use that **WINDOW** statement here, but add the **SCREEN** option.)

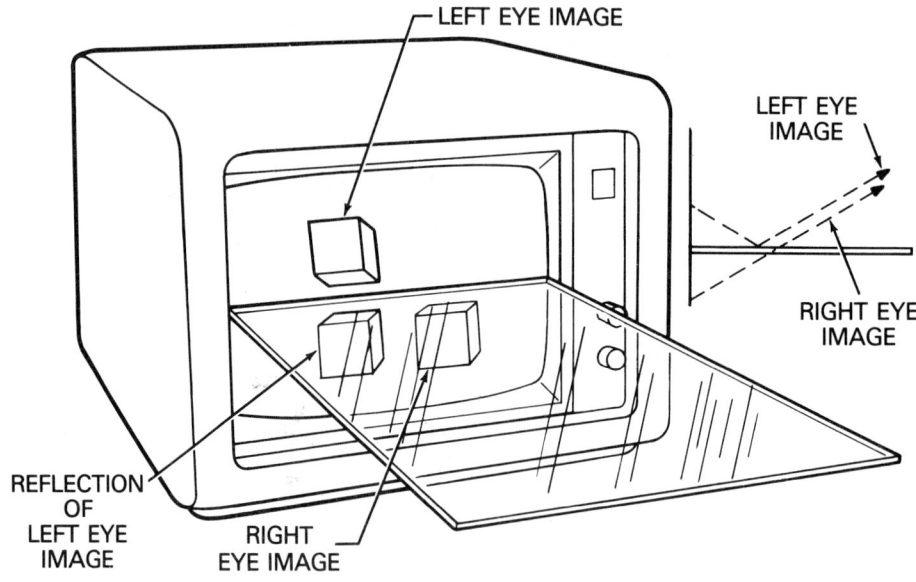

Figure 5.8

The left eye image reflects off the beam splitter. The right eye image transmits through the beam splitter.

We draw the left line:

```
9040 LINE (NEWPOINTS(LEFTX,LINES(FROM,LINENUM)),
     NEWPOINTS(YCOORD,LINES(FROM,LINENUM))) -
     (NEWPOINTS(LEFTX,LINES(TO.,LINENUM)),NEWPOINTS
     (YCOORD,LINES(TO.,LINENUM)))
```

Then we set up the right eye viewport:

```
9050 WINDOW SCREEN (0,0) - (MAXXRES,MAXYRES)
9060 VIEW (0,MAXYRES/2) - (MAXXRES - 1,MAXYRES - 1)
```

and draw the line:

```
9070 LINE (NEWPOINTS(RIGHTX,LINES(FROM,LINENUM)),
     NEWPOINTS(YCOORD,LINES(FROM,LINENUM))) -
     (NEWPOINTS(RIGHTX,LINES(TO.,LINENUM)),NEWPOINTS
     (YCOORD,LINES(TO.,LINENUM)))
9080 NEXT
```

Because we have split the screen in two horizontally, the aspect ratio for each viewport is 8/3. (Multiply the initial aspect ratio by 2. Yours may not have initially been 4/3.) To adjust we make:

```
150 ASPECTRATIO = 8/3
```

As with screen printing, we need to change **730** to:

`730 VIEW : CLS`

MERGE "7

If you have entered all the code from Section 5.4, delete lines **30 — 70**, and **18000 — 18200**. If you haven't entered any code from Section 5.4, add Section 5.4's lines **20**, **7001 — 7050**, and **8020 — 8050**.

Now try it out. You can use the line dividing the two viewports as a guide for aligning the polarizing sheets and the beam splitter.

The Hardware

To create your three-dimensional display, you need polarizing sheets and a beam splitter. The polarizers should be neutrally toned; gray filters work well. The closer the beam splitter's transmission/reflection ratio is to 1, the better. Both items are available from science supply stores and should cost under $50.

You also need a way to maintain the position of the polarizers and beam splitter. I tape the polarizers to the screen and use a four-pole sliding assembly to hold and align the beam splitter (Figure 5.9).

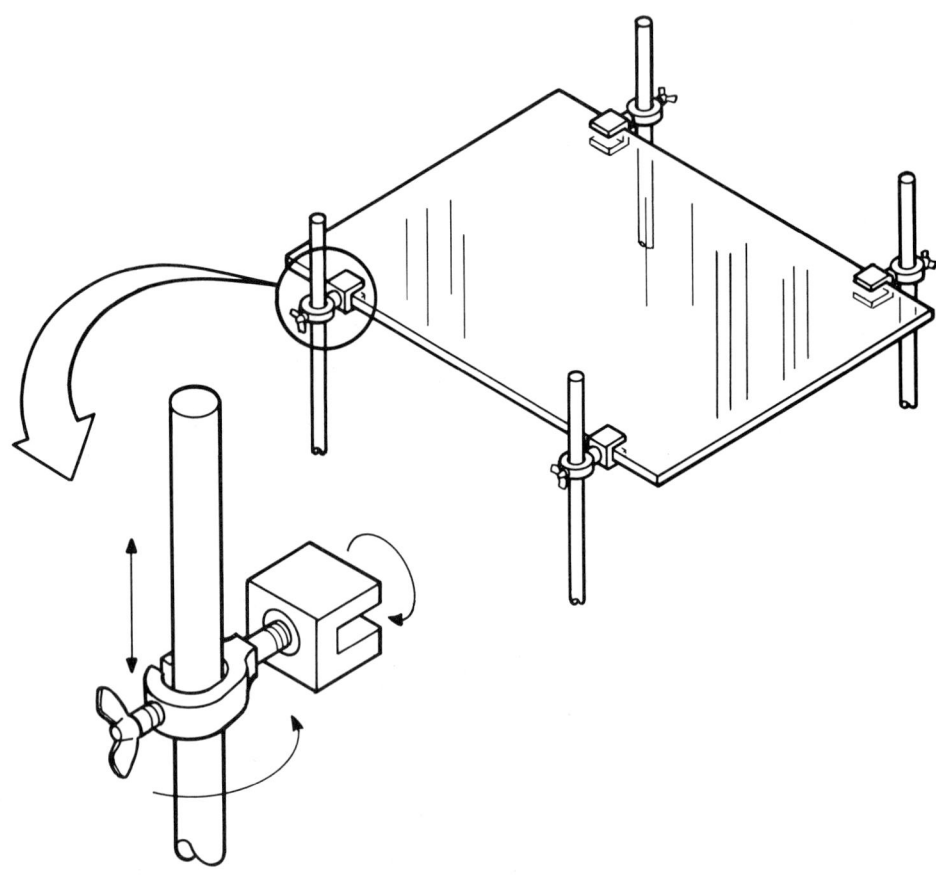

Figure 5.9
I hold the beam splitter with a four pole sliding assembly. The lower figure is a close up of the grip. The grip can slide up and down on the pole, and rotate about the pole's and grip's axes.

6

Multiple and Structured Objects

Displaying several objects would greatly increase the usefulness of our programs. We'll see how to do this in this chapter.

6.1: MULTIPLE OBJECTS

When dealing with multiple objects, we need to learn how to store and access the data, and how to manipulate the data.

Data Structure

So far we have been storing points and lines in two-dimensional arrays. One index represented what was being stored, for example, the x coordinate; the other told for which point or line the data was stored. Now we add a third dimension to indicate to which object the data belongs.

As a result, we have to turn several variables into arrays. For example, we need to store the number of points and lines in each object. Thus, to read the data we do:

```
300 READ NUMBEROFOBJECTS
310 FOR OBJECTNUM = 1 TO NUMBEROFOBJECTS
320   READ NUMBEROFPOINTS(OBJECTNUM),
      NUMBEROFLINES(OBJECTNUM)
330   FOR POINTNUM = 1 TO NUMBEROFPOINTS(OBJECTNUM)
340     READ POINTS(OBJECTNUM,XCOORD,POINTNUM),
```

194 Multiple and Structured Objects

```
             POINTS(OBJECTNUM,YCOORD,POINTNUM),
             POINTS(OBJECTNUM,ZCOORD,POINTNUM)
350    NEXT
360    FOR LINENUM = 1 TO NUMBEROFLINES(OBJECTNUM)
370      READ LINES(OBJECTNUM,FROM,LINENUM),
             LINES(OBJECTNUM,TO.,LINENUM)
380    NEXT
390  NEXT
```

We need to add an index for the object number everywhere we have used **LINES**, **POINTS** and **NEWPOINTS**, as well as **NUMBEROFLINES** and **NUMBEROFPOINTS**. It is easiest to do this using EDLIN. From BASIC, save your program as an ASCII file. (**SAVE "file name",A**) Then load it into EDLIN. For example, suppose we are modifying **3DLG3.BAS**. We type:

SAVE "3DLG3",A

To get into DOS:

SYSTEM

And to edit the program:

EDLIN 3DLG3.BAS

Now, we use the replace command to change the array indexing. First, we change **POINTS** and **NEWPOINTS**. We will replace every occurrence of "POINTS(" with "POINTS(OBJECTNUM,". Thus, both the **POINTS** and **NEWPOINTS** arrays will be changed:

1RPOINTS(^ZPOINTS(OBJECTNUM,

You can get ^Z by hitting F6 or by holding down Ctrl and typing Z. Now we change the lines:

1RLINES(^ZLINES(OBJECTNUM,

And index **NUMBEROFPOINTS** and **NUMBEROFLINES**:

1RNUMBEROFPOINTS^ZNUMBEROFPOINTS(OBJECTNUM)
1RNUMBEROFLINES^ZNUMBEROFLINES(OBJECTNUM)

To save these changes type:

From either BASIC or EDLIN, you need to change line **20** to **DIM** the new arrays and add an extra dimension to the old. Depending upon how much memory you have and how many objects you plan to load, you may have to decrease the number of points and lines allowed per object.

Manipulating the Objects

The objects can be manipulated in two ways. The first method is to allow all objects to change position simultaneously. That is, each object can move each time through the main loop. This allows very complicated animation and is easy to program. Its disadvantage is that it is hard to interact with the system. All of the calculations take up a lot of time, and besides, we have already used most of the keyboard just to manipulate one object. What would we do to control several? Of course, we can always use algorithms to control movement.

The second way is to manipulate only one object at a time. We add a command to choose which object to manipulate, and move the object with keyboard commands, keeping all other objects' positions constant. This allows interaction and is faster than the above method. But, it also sacrifices the potential for moving all objects simultaneously.

Method 1: Moving All of the Objects

If we are moving all of the objects each frame, we need to store the movement values—**XANGLE, YANGLE, ZANGLE, XTRANSLATION,** etc.—for each object. So, we change these variables to arrays indexed by **OBJECTNUM**. We need to **DIM** these at the beginning of the program.

Then, we account for all of the objects within our main loop. First, we find the new positions of each object:

```
525 FOR OBJECTNUM = 1 TO NUMBEROFOBJECTS
725 NEXT
```

Then we draw them:

```
735 FOR OBJECTNUM = 1 TO NUMBEROFOBJECTS
745 NEXT
```

We use two separate loops to make the animation smoother. If we were to calculate and then draw each object one by one, we would see the full picture for a short time, then spend most of our time watching the picture being drawn object by object. Using the two loops allows us to look at the whole picture while the next is computed. Then, the new picture is drawn all at once.

You need a subroutine to change the movement values for each object.

Method 2: Moving Only One Object

When moving only one object at a time, we need to select which object to move, and then modify only its movement values. We then add a loop to draw all of the objects. To be able to draw all of the other objects (the ones not currently being modified), their coordinates for drawing need to be in the **NEWPOINTS** array. We add a loop to do this:

```
505 FOR CURRENTOBJECT = 1 TO NUMBEROFOBJECTS : GOSUB
       16010 : GOSUB 7010 : GOSUB 8010 : NEXT

16000 '
16001 'Copy POINTS into NEWPOINTS
16002 '
16010 FOR POINTNUM = 1 TO NUMBEROFPOINTS(CURRENTOBJECT)
16020    FOR COORDINATE = 1 TO 3
16030       NEWPOINTS(CURRENTOBJECT,COORDINATE,POINTNUM)
              = POINTS(CURRENTOBJECT,COORDINATE,POINTNUM)
16040    NEXT
16050 NEXT
16100 RETURN
```

Add this, and lines **735** and **745** from below, by typing:

MERGE "CHAPTER6\1

Subroutine **16000** does the same thing as multiplying **POINTS** by the identity matrix, **7000** does perspective, and **8000** accounts for dot width and converts to screen coordinates.

CURRENTOBJECT, just introduced, is used throughout the program to point to the object currently being manipulated. All of the procedures called before line **730**—the **CLS**—need to be indexed by **CURRENTOBJECT** (rather than **OBJECTNUM**).

To draw all of the objects we add:

```
735 FOR OBJECTNUM = 1 TO NUMBEROFOBJECTS
745 NEXT
```

Note that we do not transform all of the objects.

We also need to add a way to change **CURRENTOBJECT**; a keyboard command is a good method. We also need a way to change the movement values for **CURRENTOBJECT**. The keyboard commands we have already used can be used for this. (Although we only need to keep track of one set of movement values at a time, it is better to store the current movement values for each object. That way, after switching to manipulating a new object, the new object will not suddenly jump from its old position.)

6.2: MULTIPLE OBJECTS IN ASSEMBLY LANGUAGE

To handle multiple objects in Assembly Language we follow the same idea used for handling them in BASIC. Only we need to index three-dimensional arrays differently. We will set up a table of the starting locations of **xpoints**, **ypoints**, **zpoints**, **newxpoints**, **newypoints**, **newzpoints**, and **lines** for each object (Figure 6.1). We will call these

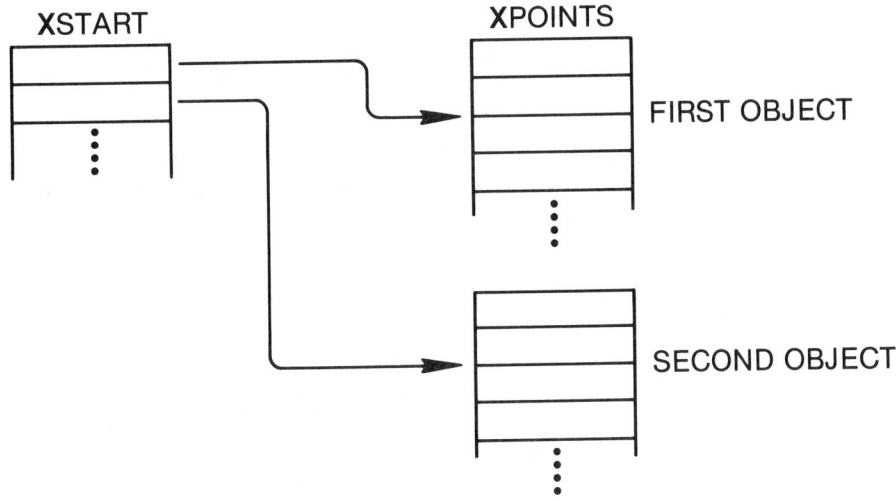

Figure 6.1
xstart points to the start of each object's **xpoints**.

arrays **xstart**, **ystart**, **zstart**, **newxstart**, etc. Whenever we switch the object on which we are operating (whether in a loop for moving all the objects or by command), we need to load the location values for the current object:

```
;
;Find starting location of xpoints, ypoints, zpoints, newxpoints,
;newypoints, newzpoints, and lines. The object for which they
```

198 Multiple and Structured Objects

```
;are loaded is indicated by current_object.
;
get_starts       proc      near
                 mov       di,current_object
                 shl       di,1         ;to point to start of word
                 mov       ax,xstart[di]
                 mov       xpoints,ax
                 mov       ax,ystart[di]
                 mov       ypoints,ax
;
;CONTINUE HERE, LOADING STARTING LOCATIONS OF zpoints, newxpoints,
;newypoints, and newzpoints

                 mov       ax,linesstart[di]
                 mov       lines,ax
;
                 ret
get_starts       endp
```

To access the data arrays, we need to use base-indexed addressing. For example, to load the x coordinate of point 6, we would use:

```
                 mov       di,6             ;for point 6
                 shl       di,1
                 mov       bx,xpoints       ;find x coordinate
                 mov       ax,[bx][di]      ;load it
```

We also need to set up the movement values as arrays. But rather than modify all of our routines, we will make a procedure to load the movement values for the current object into the variables we have used before. We call up this procedure when we change **current_object**:

```
;
;get the movement values for the current object
;
get_cur_obj_vals proc      near
                 mov       di,current_object
                 mov       al,xanglearray[di]
                 mov       xangle,al
                 mov       al,yanglearray[di]
                 mov       yangle,al
;
;CONTINUE HERE FOR zangle AND THE SCALING FACTORS
;
                 shl       di,1          ;point to word start
                 mov       ax,xtransarray[di]
                 mov       xtranslation,ax
                 mov       ax,ytransarray[di]
                 mov       ytranslation,ax
                 mov       ax,ztransarray[di]
```

```
                    mov         ztranslation,ax
;
                    ret
get_cur_obj_vals    endp
```

> **2.ASM** in **CHAPTER6** directory.

We also need to change accordingly the structure of our variables in the data segment.

6.3: STRUCTURED OBJECTS

Because we have the ability to display multiple objects we can go one step higher in the definition of objects: we can define basic building blocks and then combine these to form objects. For example, we could define a window and a cube as building blocks. Then, we could describe a room as the cube plus several windows.

To manipulate such an object, we need to find the points of each of the building blocks; scale, rotate and translate them; then scale, rotate and translate the whole object. This involves two transformation matrices.
We also need to change our loops and arrays to point from objects to building blocks to points and lines.
A diagram of the data structure for structured objects appears in Figure 6.2.

6.4: STORING AND RETRIEVING OBJECTS FROM DISK

With multiple, and especially structured, objects, it is cumbersome to load the point-line data from data statements. Rather, it is much easier and quicker to create an object editor that saves data on disk files. These disk files should save the point-line data in the same format with which it is **READ**. Then, we can just replace **READ** with **INPUT #**, and add code to control the disk files. In Assembly Language, we add a procedure that uses disk reading interrupts.

200 Multiple and Structured Objects

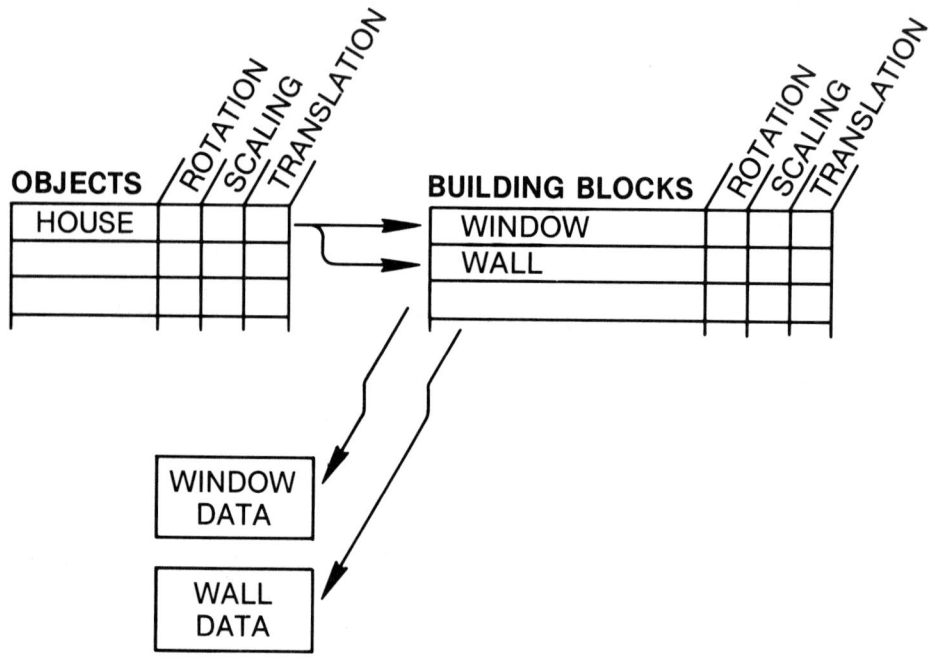

Figure 6.2
The data structure of structured objects. Each object, which can be rotated, translated, and scaled, points to the building blocks composing it, and indicates by how much to rotate, translate, and scale the building blocks. The building blocks point to their point-line data.

7

Advanced Graphics Techniques

This chapter presents some advanced graphics techniques. It has two main divisions. The first section shows how to smooth animation by removing flicker and discusses picture storage and retrieval; the second section discusses how to program the graphics board directly, which allows us to fully exploit the power of the IBM PC's graphics.

7.1: PREVENTING FLICKER

The main problem of our Assembly Language graphics program has been flicker. Regular line images look stroboscopic; stereoscopic images are hard to fuse.

Flicker occurs because the screen is always changing. A lot of time is spent clearing the screen. Then the lines are drawn. But no sooner is the last line drawn, then the screen is cleared again. (That is why the last couple of lines drawn seem to flash on and off more than the others.)

While the changes to the screen are fast, they are not so fast that we don't see them. And so much time is spent clearing the screen that we see a blank or partially filled screen more often than the complete picture.

Movies don't have flicker, because they display an image for a short time, then rapidly replace it with the next complete image. We will use this idea to prevent flicker. While we are displaying the complete picture, we will draw the next picture—but in a place where it can't be seen. Then, we will instantly replace the displayed picture with the new one. This is called *two-page graphics*.

A *page* is just one graphics screen, or rather a graphics screen's worth of memory. We will use two pages—one for displaying and one for drawing. The display page is the one we have always used: B8000H to BC000H. We will set up a second 16K area of memory for the drawing page, and treat it just as if it were the regular graphics screen. We will clear it and draw all of the lines on it; but when the picture is complete, we will move it to the displayed page. Thus, none of the stroboscopic screen clearing and redrawing will be seen. One picture will abruptly switch to the next. The effect is fantastic; let's see how to do it.

First, we need to create the undisplayed second page, a block of memory the same size as the graphics screen: 3F40H bytes (2000H for even lines and extra + 1F40H for odd lines):

```
;
page_2                  segment
                        db              3f40h dup (?)
page_2                  ends
;
```

We want to draw to and clear **page_2** instead of the displayed page. In all of our routines, **ES** has pointed to the graphics screen. So before we draw and clear, we will change **ES** to point to **page_2**. To do this, add the following before calls to **clearscreen**:

```
mov                     ax,page_2
mov                     es,ax
```

Once we have finished drawing the new picture, we need to move it to the displayed page. After the picture is completed (that is, after calling **draw_the_lines** or **draw_left_right**), call this procedure:

```
;
;move the undisplayed page to the displayed graphics page
;
;   assumes ES points to page_2
;
display_page_2  proc    near
                push    ds              ;save it for return
                mov     ax,es           ;page_2
                mov     ds,ax
                mov     ax,0b800h       ;displayed page
                mov     es,ax
;
                mov     di,0            ;clear for string move
                mov     si,0            ;command
                cld
                mov     cx,1fa0h        ;number of words in the screen
                rep     movsw           ;copy page_2 to displayed page
;
```

```
                    pop     ds        ;restore DS
                    ret
display_page_2      endp
;
```

> All files in this chapter are in the **CHAPTER7** directory. The file for this section is in **1.ASM**.

Though this routine is short and straightforward, it will have a remarkable effect. Flicker will be completely eliminated, and movement will look very smooth. Fusing stereoscopic images should be much easier. The only disadvantage of adding the routine to prevent flicker is a slight slowdown in speed.

7.2: SAVING AND LOADING THE GRAPHICS SCREEN

It is important to be able to save the graphics screen. Saving it allows later modification and display, and lets a picture be transported from one machine to another. (For example, you could make a picture on your computer and then print it on a computer having a color plotter.)

Saving and Retrieving the Normal Way

We can always save the graphics screen from BASIC or DEBUG as a 16,192 byte binary file. In BASIC we do this by:

DEF SEG = &HB800
BSAVE "file name",0,&H3F40

and in DEBUG by:

n file name
r bx
3f40
r cx
3f40
w b800:0

Then, to load the screen, we do:

DEF SEG = &HB800
BLOAD "file name",0

or in DEBUG:

n file name
l
r
m (put value displayed in **CS** here)**:100 l 3f40 b800:0**

Compacting It

But this isn't efficient. It takes a lot of disk space to save each picture; 10 will fill one side of a disk. And it takes a long time to load the pictures. It's much more efficient to compact the screen first.

A great deal of the screen is usually blank or repetitious. Even long horizontal lines are the repetition of one value. Instead of saving the same data over and over again, we only need to tell how many times to repeat one element. For example, instead of saving a blank screen, we can tell the computer to move 0 to consecutive graphics screen memory locations 3F40H times. When data aren't repeated, we can just save it as is.

We'll compact the data as follows: if the data repeats, we will store a word telling the number of repetitions, followed by the datum to repeat; if the data doesn't repeat, we will store a code marking that there is no repetition, followed by a word indicating for how long there is no repetition, followed by the data; if the data is the last data, we will follow it by an end code.

The number of repeating elements can never be greater than 3F40H, the size of the screen. Normally numbers are stored in low-byte, high-byte format. But if we store the number of repeating elements in high-byte, low-byte format, we guarantee that the first byte never exceeds 3FH. We can then use any larger numbers as codes. We will use FEH to signal nonrepetitious data and FFH to signal the end of the data. In other words, repetitious data will be encoded as:

number of reps$_{\text{high byte}}$ number of reps$_{\text{low byte}}$ datum to repeat

and nonrepetitious data will be encoded as:

FEH length of data$_{\text{low byte}}$ length of data$_{\text{high byte}}$ data

For example, suppose the first 40 bytes of the screen are blank, followed by 0F FF F0. The compacted data for this would be:

00 28 00 FE 03 00 0F FF F0

We would thus store 43 bytes of data in nine bytes. The first two bytes are the high and low bytes of the number of times to repeat the third byte. The fourth byte indicates that nonrepetitious data follows. The next two bytes are the low and high bytes of how much nonrepetitious data follows, and the next three bytes are the data. Because FFH signals the end of data only when it follows a sequence of data, the FFH is not taken as an end indicator.

The Routine

Let's look at a program to compact the graphics screen. First, we set up an area in which to hold the compacted data. In some, but very rare, circumstances, the compacted data will be longer than the original screen. (If this occurs, just save the original screen.) In the worst case, the compacted screen will take 24K. We will allow for this:

```
;
page_1              equ         0b800h      ;points to data to compact
;
;set up area in which to save compacted data
;
compact_screen      segment
                    db          6000h dup (?)
compact_screen      ends
;
```

Now we are ready for the procedure:

```
;
;compact the graphics screen
;
;   repetitions indicated by     low number reps   high number reps   datum
;   nonrepetitions indicated by FE    length of nonrep section     data
;   end indicated by                FF
;
;   On exit, SI indicates length of compacted data (in bytes)
;
compact         proc        near
                mov         ax,page_1              ;ES points to graphics screen
                mov         es,ax
                mov         ax,compact_screen      ;DS points to compacted
                mov         ds,ax                  ;data
                mov         si,0                   ;points to location in compact screen
                mov         di,0                   ;points to location in graphics screen
;see if finished compacting the screen
```

```
ck_end:         cmp     di,3f40h
                jb      scan            ;if not finished, examine next bytes
;at end of screen
                mov     al,0ffh         ;store end code
                mov     [si],al         ;at end of compact screen
                inc     si              ;point to next byte in compact screen
                jmp     c_end
;
;look for repetitions in the graphics screen
;
scan:
                cld
                push    di              ;save starting location
                mov     al,es:[di]      ;byte against which to compare
                inc     di              ;start looking at next byte
                mov     cx,3f40h        ;don't look past end of screen
                sub     cx,di
                mov     dx,di           ;for calculating length
;search until end of screen or until mismatch
                repe    scasb
                sub     dx,di           ;find length of repeating data
                neg     dx              ;DX = number of repeating bytes
                jcxz    repeats         ;if at end of screen
                cmp     dx,1            ;1 indicates no repetitions
                jne     repeats
;
;see for how long no repetition of data
;
                dec     di              ;point to first byte to check
check:
                mov     al,es:[di]      ;load the data
                inc     di
                cmp     al,es:[di]      ;compare to next data
                loopne  check
;a repetition has been found
                mov     cx,di           ;calculate length of non
                dec     cx              ;repeating section
                pop     di              ;beginning of section
                sub     cx,di
                mov     al,0feh         ;store nonrepeat code
                mov     [si],al
                inc     si
                mov     [si],cx         ;store length
                inc     si
                inc     si
                push    ds              ;switch ES and DS registers,
                push    es              ;SI and DI pointers, to move data
                pop     ds              ;from graphics screen to compact
                pop     es              ;screen
                xchg    si,di
                cld
                rep     movsb           ;move it
                xchg    si,di           ;restore registers and pointers
                push    ds
                push    es
                pop     ds
                pop     es
                jmp     ck_end          ;ready to go on
```

```
;
repeats:
                cmp       cx,0            ;CX = 0 means at end of screen
                jne       r_1
                inc       dx
r_1:            mov       [si],dh         ;store length in high low format
                inc       si
                mov       [si],dl
                inc       si
                mov       [si],al         ;data to repeat
                inc       si
                pop       di              ;find next data to examine
                add       di,dx
                jmp       ck_end          ;ready to go on
;
c_end:
                ret
compact         endp
;
```

Sample Runs

The following are results of a few trial runs; more complex pictures would result in larger compacted lengths:

Picture	Compact Length	Percent Saved
All green	4	99.9
Cube	57F	91
3-D box with words	D2E	79
Two large cubes	12DF	70

Uncompacting the Picture

Now we need a routine to uncompact the data. The routine will load the data from the compacted screen, check for nonrepeat and end codes, and repeat or move data accordingly:

```
;
uncompact       proc      near
                mov       ax,page_1
                mov       es,ax
                mov       ax,compact_screen
                mov       ds,ax
                mov       di,0
                mov       si,0
                cld
```

```
;check byte
ck_byte:        mov     ch,[si]         ;will be either code or repeat
                inc     si              ;length high byte
                cmp     ch,0ffh         ;see if end
                je      up_end
                cmp     ch,0feh         ;see if nonrepeat
                je      up_no_repeat
;unpack repeating data
                mov     cl,[si]         ;get low byte of length
                inc     si
                mov     al,[si]         ;get datum to repeat
                inc     si
                rep     stosb           ;store it on graphics screen
                jmp     ck_byte         ;go on to next data
;unpack nonrepeating data
up_no_repeat:
                mov     cx,[si]         ;get length of nonrepeating data
                inc     si
                inc     si
                rep     movsb           ;move the data to the graphics screen
                jmp     ck_byte         ;go on to next data
;
up_end:
                ret
uncompact       endp
;
```

> **compact** and **uncompact** are in **2P1.ASM**.

Try this. The uncompacted picture will appear almost instantly.

Animation

You can use picture compacting and uncompacting to efficiently store screens; a fancier use is short sequence animation. Suppose you want to animate a set of pictures that take a great deal of time to create. If you compact and save each, you can load several of the compacted pictures into memory at the same time. Then, if you uncompact each in rapid succession, the pictures will seem to be animated. If the pictures are loaded contiguously, then the start of one immediately follows the end code of the previous. So if we remove the line in **uncompact** which sets **SI** to 0, then after executing **uncompact**, **SI** will point to the start of the next picture. Thus, to animate the pictures, we could use:

```
;
;animate a sequence of compacted pictures
;
;   assumes uncompact does not set SI to 0
;
```

```
animate_picture     proc        near
                    mov         si,0
                    mov         cx,number_of_pictures
a_p_1:              push        cx
                    call        uncompact
                    pop         cx
                    loop        a_p_1
;
                    ret
animate_picture     endp
;
```

2P2.ASM

7.3: PROGRAMMING THE COLOR GRAPHICS CONTROLLER

In this section we will explore various programming features of the color graphics board. There are two main programmable parts: the *6845 CRT controller*, which controls the parameters of the video signal transmission, and the *mode* and *color select registers*, which control how the graphics data are decoded. The extreme flexibility in programming the 6845 and other registers allows many special effects, including color high-resolution graphics and 160-by-100 resolution, sixteen color graphics.

The controller is programmed by using the **OUT** command to access four different input/output ports. From BASIC, this is done with:

OUT location,data

and in Assembly Language with:

```
mov         dx,location
mov         ax,data
out         dx,ax
```

Because interaction is easier in BASIC, the rest of this section will use BASIC commands and programs. Incorporating the ideas into Assembly Language is straightforward.

A Warning

Throughout this chapter we will use the graphics controller in a nonstandard fashion. If at any time you are unable to get your display back, or you are uncomfortable with the way your screen looks or monitor sounds, don't hesitate to immediately hit Ctrl-Alt-Delete or turn off your computer.

Starting Off Simply—Screen Position

Before we go to more advanced features, let's look at a simple demonstration of programming the graphics board. Perhaps your display appears too far to the left or right, and thus you have had to use MODE to justify it. If so, you will have noticed that **SCREEN**, as well as the mode setting interrupt, knocks out any adjustments you have made. (If you haven't had this problem, feel fortunate, and read on anyway.)

The 6845 controls the horizontal and vertical position of the display with two synchronization registers (discussed in detail later). For now, we need only know that the horizontal sync register is register 2, and the vertical sync register is register 7. To change their value, we first **OUT** the register's number to port 3D4H. Then, we **OUT** the data to port 3D5H.

For graphics, the horizontal sync is usually set to 2DH, and the vertical sync is set to 70H. If we increase the horizontal sync value, the screen moves left; decreasing it moves the screen right. If we increase the vertical sync value, the screen moves up; decreasing it moves the screen down.

Let's experiment with these registers, by using the following BASIC program to move the screen:

```
10 'change the screen's position by programming the
   6845 sync registers
20 'a moves left; s moves right; w moves up; z moves
   down
30 'any other key stops the program and prints the
   register values
40 HORIZSYNC = &H2D : VERTSYNC = &H70
50 SCREEN 2          'display high res page
60 OUT &H3D4,2 : OUT &H3D5,HORIZSYNC : OUT &H3D4,7 :
   OUT &H3D5, VERTSYNC
70 FOR CHAR = 1 TO 80 : PRINT STR$(CHAR MOD 10); : NEXT
   : PRINT 'print a test line
80 PRINT "Enter command to move screen: " : INPUT "a =
   left s = right w = up z = down"; COMMAND$
90 IF COMMAND$ = "a" THEN HORIZSYNC = HORIZSYNC + 1 :
   GOTO 60 ELSE IF COMMAND$ = "s" THEN HORIZSYNC =
   HORIZSYNC - 1 : GOTO 60
100 IF COMMAND$ = "w" THEN VERTSYNC = VERTSYNC + 1 :
    GOTO 60 ELSE IF COMMAND$ = "z" THEN VERTSYNC =
    VERTSYNC - 1 : GOTO 60
```

```
110 PRINT "horizontal sync = "; HEX$(HORIZSYNC); "
    vertical sync = "; HEX$(VERTSYNC)
120 END
```

> Load this program with:
>
> **LOAD** "3P1
>
> Remember, you must first be in the **CHAPTER7** directory.

If you had a screen position problem, align your screen using this program and note the proper sync values. Then, to keep your screen aligned later, follow any **SCREEN** command or mode setting interrupt by **OUT** statements to adjust the sync values.

The Color Select Register

The first register we will examine in depth is the color select register, a write-only register located at port 3D9H. This register controls various aspects relating to color, depending on the graphics mode. To access it, type:

OUT &H3D9,data

Only six bits have effect.

Let's start by examining its function in medium resolution.

Bits 0–3 define the background color. Bit 0 controls blue, 1 controls green, 2 controls red, and 3 controls intensity. If a bit is set, then the color is added. If bit 3 is set, the colors are more intense. Combined, these four bits give the sixteen standard colors (Figure 1.1).

Experiment with moving values from 0 to FH to the color select register. For example, try:

OUT &H3D9, 9

This will set the background color to intense blue.

We have used *bit 4* in our stereoscopic Assembly Language program. This bit controls the intensity of the foreground colors. If it is set, the colors are intense; otherwise, they are normal. Draw a couple of lines in colors 1, 2, and 3. Then, do:

OUT &H3D9,&H10

and after noting the colors, try:

OUT &H3D9,0

If you want the background to be colored while you change the intensity bit, just add 10H to the value of the background color.

Bit 5 selects the palette. If it is set, then palette 1 is used. If it is 0, palette 0 is used. Add 20H to the last value you placed in port 3D9H—then go back to the old value. Make sure to try adding 0H, 10H, 20H, and 30H to the background color. This will show you the four available palettes (the normal two, plus the normal two in intense colors).

In high resolution, only the first four bits have effect. So far, all lines we have drawn in high resolution have been white. *Bits 0-3* can change this; they control the color of high-resolution dots. The color is selected the same way the medium-resolution background color is, by storing the color number (Figure 1.1) in port 3D9H.

Draw a couple of lines in high resolution, then experiment with changing the color. **OUT** the numbers between 0 and FH to port 3D9H. One application is to change the color of text on the high resolution screen. Amber and green cause less eyestrain than white. Note that the background will always be black and only one color will appear at a time.

If you are using a composite monitor, you won't see any color changes. The low-intensity colors will be barely visible; the high-intensity colors will show up well. But they will always be white on a black background.

The effects of the bits in the color select register are summarized in Figure 7.1.

The Mode Select Register

Now we are ready to look at another register, the mode select register. This register controls the display mode. It's a write-only register located at port 3D8H. Six of its bits are meaningful (Figure 7.2).

Let's start with *bit 5*, the blink bit. If it is set, blink is allowed. Blink is primarily useful in text modes, but let's fool with it anyway. In medium resolution, port 3D8H normally contains AH. So let's put 2AH there instead—setting the blink bit. Return to normal by restoring port 3D8H to AH. (From high resolution use 3EH instead of 2AH, and use 1EH to return to normal.) The result is interesting, but pretty useless for graphics.

Advanced Graphics Techniques   213

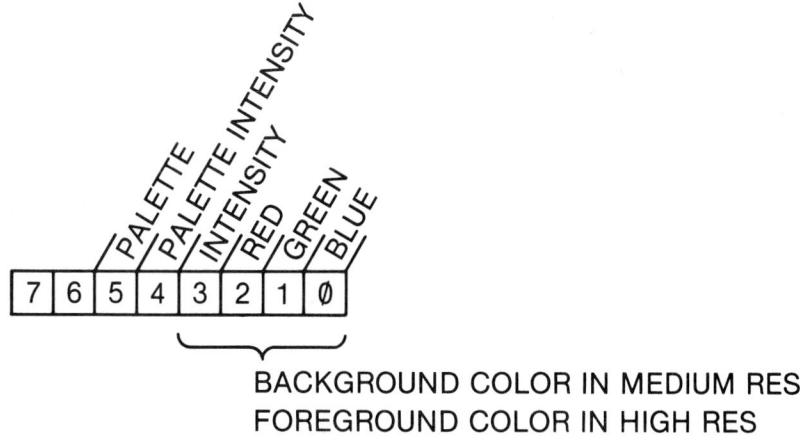

Figure 7.1
The color select register's bits.

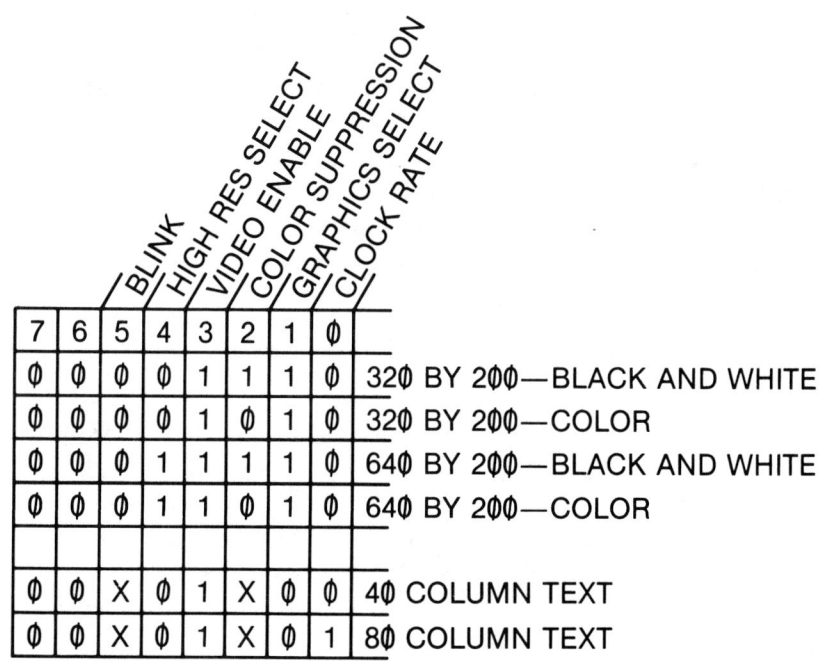

Figure 7.2
The mode select register's bits.

Next let's look at *bit 0*, the clock-rate bit. If it is set, the dot clock, which controls at what rate dots are drawn on the screen, goes at 14 megahertz (MHz). Otherwise it goes at 7 MHz. The 14-Mhz clock is only used for 80-column text. When used with graphics, it provides an interesting but unusable effect. If you are in high resolution, try:

OUT &H3D8,&H1F

and do:

OUT &H3D8,&H1E

to get back. In medium resolution use BH and AH instead of 1FH and 1EH.

Bit 3 is a very useful bit, the video-enable bit. If it is set, the screen is displayed. If it is 0, no video signal is sent to the monitor; thus, the screen is blanked. This bit can be used to save your monitors' phosphor, by shutting off the screen after it has not been used for a while.

Let's experiment with bit 3. Do:

OUT &H3D8,&H2

The screen will disappear. To get back to medium resolution send AH to port 3D8H; to get back to high resolution send 1EH to port 3D8H.

Now we are ready to examine two very important bits, *1* and *4*, the graphics mode selection bits. Setting bit 1 causes graphics to be displayed. If bit 4 is 0, the medium-resolution graphics mode will be selected. If bit 4 is 1, high-resolution graphics will be selected. So, if we want medium-resolution graphics we need to set bit 1 to select the mode and bit 3 to display the screen. That is, we do:

OUT &H3D8,&HA

Before we set high resolution, let's look at *bit 2*—the color-suppression bit. When it is set, the color burst is not sent to composite monitors; thus, the display is black and white. This bit does not affect RGB monitors.

In the high-resolution mode we have been using so far, the one set by the mode setting interrupt or by **SCREEN 2**, color has been suppressed. Let's switch into the high-resolution mode to which we are accustomed. It has bits 1 and 4 set to select high resolution, 3 set to display the screen, and 2 set to prevent color. Thus, we enter:

OUT &H3D8,&H1E

The good, old, high-resolution graphics screen will appear.

Now let's try black and white medium-resolution graphics. We set bit 1 to select medium-resolution graphics, bit 3 to display the screen, and bit 2 to select black and white graphics. So, we do:

OUT &H3D8,&HE

On an RGB monitor, nothing will happen. But on a composite monitor, any lines we draw, no matter their color, will appear as white on a black background. Experiment (using port 3D9H) with changing the background color. If you set the background-intensity bit, the display flips colors: black lines will be drawn on a white background.

Now let's try the last graphics mode combination—color high-resolution graphics. To do this, we type:

OUT &H3D8,&H1A

On RGB monitors nothing happens. But try it on a composite monitor. Draw a few lines. They will appear in a myriad of colors. Now, try the following program:

```
10 'generate colors in high-resolution color mode
20 DEF SEG = &HB800
30 INPUT EVENLEFT, EVENRIGHT, ODDLEFT, ODDRIGHT
40 FOR ROW = 1 TO 10 : POKE ROW*80, EVENLEFT : POKE
   ROW*80 + 1, EVENRIGHT : POKE ROW*80 + &H2000,
   ODDLEFT : POKE ROW*80 + &H2001, ODDRIGHT : NEXT
50 GOTO 20
```

LOAD "3P2

Enter a wide variety of numbers for **EVENLEFT**, **EVENRIGHT**, **ODDLEFT**, and **ODDRIGHT**. Start with all four variables the same, then mix numbers. These four variables determine what high resolution dots to plot, using the standard high res bit map. Two columns are plotted. **EVENLEFT** is placed in the left column of even rows; **ODDLEFT** in the left columns of odd rows. Likewise, **EVENRIGHT** and **ODDRIGHT** are placed in the right columns of even and odd rows, respectively.

You'll get an incredible assortment of colors. Some combinations result in patchiness, others result in very thick colors. As you can see, this technique is quite useful in getting many more than the standard sixteen colors.

Advanced Graphics Techniques

Also try changing the high-resolution foreground color. This change will have a slight effect on the colors.

The 6845 Registers

We're now ready to examine the eighteen 6845 registers. We have already used two of them—the horizontal and vertical sync registers. A list of the registers' functions and their default values appears in Figure 7.3. To program any of the registers, we first do:

OUT &H3D4,register number

then:

OUT &H3D5,value

register number tells in which register to place the next datum sent to port 3D5H. Thus we can access 18 different registers through only two ports.

These registers let us control all the parameters of screen display. Let's start off simply. If you have both a monochrome and color display, you can program the 6845 so that you can use the monochrome monitor for text and the color monitor for graphics at the same time. To do this, set the 6845 registers to their default graphics values, and set the mode select register for the resolution you want. From BASIC you would use:

```
10 'view color display, but operate from monochrome
   display
20 FOR REGISTER = 0 TO 13 : READ VALUE : OUT &H3D4,
   REGISTER : OUT &H3D5, VALUE : NEXT
30 'set 3d8H here for either high or medium res
   graphics
40 END
50 DATA &H38, &H28, &H2D, &HA, &H7F, 6, &H64, &H70, 2,
   1, 6, 7, 0, 0
```

You will be unable to draw to the screen with any BASIC graphics commands because the graphics commands are not activated if the monochrome display is in use. But direct memory access works fine. To switch completely to the color screen, and thus be able to use BASIC's graphics commands, use DOS's MODE or the program appearing in Appendix I of the *BASIC Manual*.

Register Number	Register Type	40 x 25 Alpha	80 x 25 Alpha	Graphics
0	horizontal total	56	113	56
1	horiztonal displayed	40	80	40
2	horizontal sync position	45	90	45
3	horizontal sync width	10	10	10
4	vertical total	31	31	127
5	vertical total adjust	6	6	6
6	vertical displayed	25	25	100
7	vertical sync position	28	28	112
8	interlace mode	2	2	2
9	maximum scan line address	7	7	1
10	cursor start	6	6	6
11	cursor end	7	7	7
12	start address (H)	0	0	0
13	start address (L)	0	0	0
14	cursor address (H)	x	x	x
15	cursor address (L)	x	x	x
16	light pen (H)	x	x	x
17	light pen (L)	x	x	x

Figure 7.3
The function of and default values for the 6845 registers.

Now let's examine each of the registers. We'll start with *registers 14 and 15*. These control the cursor position. The cursor only appears in text modes. The value given is the position within the screen at which to draw the cursor, in number of characters. For 80-column text, multiply the row by 80 and add the column; in 40-column text, multiply the row by 40 and add the column. The low byte is given in register 15; the high byte is given in register 14.

The largest number of characters that can appear on the screen at once is 100 * 80 = 8,000. Thus, if we program the cursor registers to a larger number, no cursor will appear. Setting register 14 to 32 guarantees that the cursor will always be off the screen.

Registers 10 and 11 control the shape of the cursor.

Registers 16 and 17 tell the character position of the light pen. Register 16 is the high byte; 17 is the low byte.

Registers 12 and 13 tell the location in graphics memory with which to start drawing. In other words, the number stored in these registers tells what byte to map to the upper left corner of the screen. This value is given in terms of character positions. In 80-column-text mode, we can scroll the screen up by adding 80 to the starting location. In 40-column-text mode, we add 40 to the location to scroll up. In graphics modes, every increase of 40 moves the screen two rows higher.

Register 13 gets the low byte of the address; register 12 gets the high byte. Experiment with changing them. The larger the number, the higher and the more to the left the screen moves (in barber-pole fashion).

Before examining the other registers, we need to review some television fundamentals. Dots are drawn on monitors by a beam of electrons scanning from left to right, top to bottom. When the beam hits the right side of the screen, it is shut off, and pulled all the way to the left—readying it for drawing a new scan line. The pull back is called the *horizontal retrace*. When the beam hits the bottom of the screen, it is turned off and pulled to the upper left corner of the screen, readying it to draw the screen again. This is called the *vertical retrace*.

The remaining 6845 registers control the speed and size of the horizontal and vertical scans.

Register 0 tells the amount of time to take to draw a horizontal scan line and retrace. It is given one less than the number of characters that can be drawn during this time. Monitors usually draw 15,734 horizontal scan lines per second. With the 40-column dot clock (used for 40-column text and graphics), 7.16 million dots are drawn a second. With the 80-column dot clock, 14.3 million dots are drawn per second. Characters take 8 dots to draw. So, for graphics or 40-column text, there are:

7.16×10^6 dots per second / (8 dots per character * 15,734 lines per second) = 57 characters per line

and thus register 0 gets 56.

In 80-column text, 14.3 million dots are drawn per second. This gives 114 characters per line, so register 0 gets 113.

If you give register 0 a slightly higher value, the screen moves right, the monitor whines, and the colors get brighter. Decreasing register 0 slightly causes the screen to move left and the monitor to whine. Changing it by large amounts causes the screen to scramble.

Register 1 gets the number of characters actually displayed per line. For 40-column text and graphics, this amount is 40; for 80-column text, this amount is 80.

If you give register 1 a slightly smaller or larger value, the screen shears to the left or to the right, respectively. This gives way to major distortion for values largely different than that expected.

We have already played with *register 2*, the horizontal sync position. This register tells at what character position to place the *horizontal sync*—a pulse that initiates horizontal retrace. Register 2 should be set to the character position about 5 microseconds after the last displayed character. For 40 column text and graphics, this is:

40 characters + 5 × 10^{-6} seconds * (7.16 × 10^6 dots per second / 8 dots per character) = 45

In 80 columns:

80 + 5 * 14.3 / 8 = 89 (The *Technical Reference Manual* recommends 90)

Register 3 controls the width of the horizontal sync pulse. It is given as a time, measured in terms of characters. For most monitors, register 3 should be set to 10. 'Making it less than 10 moves the screen right; making it greater moves the screen left.

Registers 4 and 5 set the amount of time to take to display a whole screen and retrace vertically. The measuring unit is the time it takes to draw one row of characters. Register 4 gets the number of character rows per screen, minus 1. If this value exceeds 127, register 4 is set to 127. Register 5 serves as fine tuning for register 4.

To figure the number of character rows per screen, we first need to compute the number of horizontal scan lines per screen. Register 0 plus 1 tells us the time it takes to draw one scan line, in terms of characters. So if we divide this by the clock frequency and multiply by the number of dots per horizontal character, we find the number of seconds it takes to draw each line. Color monitors draw the screen every one-sixtieth of a second. If we divide this time period by the number of seconds to draw each scan line, we get the number of scan lines per screen. Now all we need to do is divide this number by the number of scan lines per character row, and we'll have the number of character rows per screen. In text modes there are eight scan lines per character; in graphics modes, there are two scan lines.

So, for 40-column text, the number of scan lines per screen is:

(1/60) seconds per screen / [(56 + 1) characters per line * 8 dots per character / 7.16 × 10⁶ dots per second] = 261.7

and the number of character rows per screen is:

261.7 scan lines per screen / 8 scan lines per character = 32.7

Thus, register 4 gets 33 − 1 = 32.

For 80-column text, both the clock rate and register 0 plus one are doubled, so there are also 32.7 character rows per screen.

For graphics, there are 261.7 scan lines per screen and 130.8 character rows per screen. Because 130.8 exceeds 128, register 4 is set to 127.

If the number of character rows per screen is less than or equal to 128, register 5 gets:

scan lines per screen MOD scan lines per character row.

Thus, for 40- and 80- column text, register 5 gets 262 mod 8 = 6.

If the number of character rows per screen exceeds 128, then register 5 gets:

(scan lines per screen MOD scan lines per character row) + scan lines per character row * (character rows per screen MOD 128)

For graphics this is:

(262 mod 2) + 2 * (131 mod 128) = 6.

Changing register 4 slightly completely throws off vertical hold, making the screen unintelligible. Changing register 5 moves the screen up and down a little.

Register 6 gets the number of characters displayed vertically. For text this is 25, for graphics this is 100. Decreasing it cuts off the bottom rows.

Register 7 controls the position of the vertical sync pulse. This is the character row position 1,524 microseconds after the last displayed character. For text this is:

25 character rows + 1,524 microseconds / (63.4 microseconds per line * 8 lines per character row = 28 character rows.

The time used to draw one line is found from register 0. For standard text modes, it is 63.4 microseconds per line.

For graphics, register 7 gets:

100 + 1,524 / (63.4 * 2) = 112

Register 8 gets the interlace mode. Normally this is set to 2. Setting it to 3 doubles the numbers of rows that can be displayed but causes a little bit of bounce. Doubling the vertical resolution requires more memory than the graphics card has.

Register 9, the maximum scan line address, gets one less than the number of scan lines per character row. For text, this value is 7, for graphics, this value is 1.

Other Graphics Modes

We can program the 6845 directly to create new graphics resolutions. Because of memory decoding considerations, we program these as text modes. We control the horizontal resolution by programming the number of columns, resulting in either 40- or 80-dot horizontal resolution. Remember to adjust 3D8H accordingly. (Use 10H for 40 column graphics, 11H for 80 column graphics.) We then program the vertical resolution, which can range from 25 to 100.

For example, to get 80-by-100 resolution graphics, we use the register values shown in Figure 7.4.

Consult Chapter 10 for doing graphics on the text screens. That chapter also discusses doubling text-screen resolution, resulting in up to 80-by-200 or 160-by-100 sixteen color graphics.

6845 REGISTER	VALUE
0	113
1	80
2	90
3	10
4	127
5	6
6	100
7	112
8	2
9	1
10	32

MODE SELECT REGISTER = 9

Figure 7.4
The values of the 6845 registers for 80 by 100 graphics.

8

Block Graphics

    Block graphics differs greatly from line graphics. We no longer consider objects as points and lines but rather as a group of dots. We determine the data to represent these dots, and move it around the graphics screen as a block of memory.

    Block graphics are best for solid two-dimensional objects. Most video games, including Pac-Man and Space Invaders, use block graphics.

8.1: CONVERTING OBJECTS TO BLOCK DATA

    As with line graphics, we need to represent *block objects* in a way the computer can understand. Suppose we want to convert Figure 8.1 to block data. First, we draw it on graph paper (Figure 8.2). Each square will represent one dot. Now, we examine every graph square covered by the pic-

Figure 8.1
A female face.

Block Graphics

Figure 8.2
Draw the face on graph paper.

ture. If the square is more than halfway filled in, we color it completely. For medium-resolution pictures, we fill each square with one of the four colors; for high-resolution pictures, we either fill or don't fill each square (Figure 8.3). Now, we draw the smallest possible box containing all the points. Calling the upper left corner of this box row 1, column 1, we number the remaining rows and columns (Figure 8.4). Finally, we make a table of the color values in each element of the box (Figure 8.5).

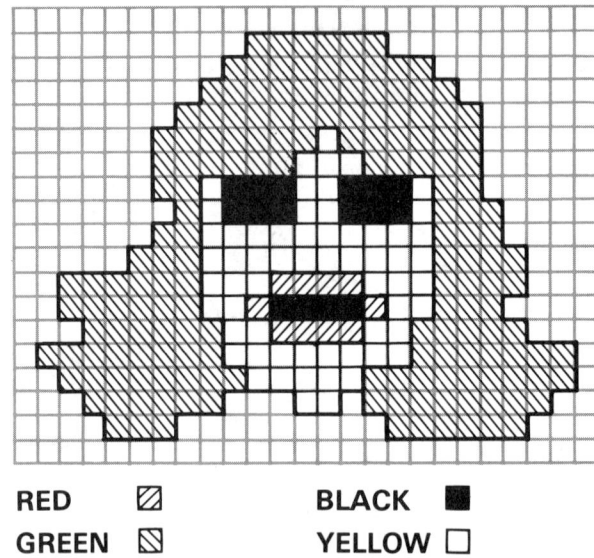

Figure 8.3
If a square is more than half way covered, fill it in completely.

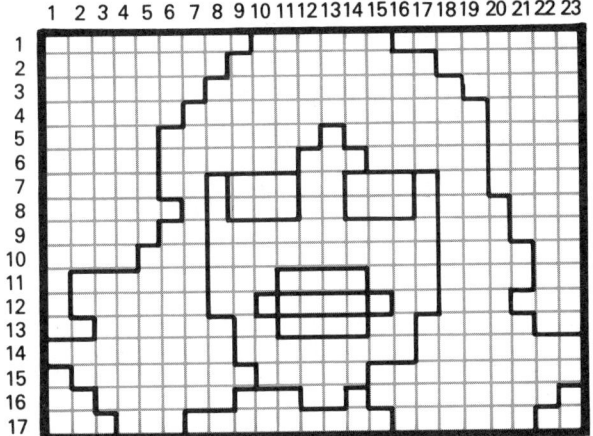

Figure 8.4
Draw the smallest rectangle containing the figure. Label the rows and columns, starting at the upper left corner.

0	0	0	0	0	0	0	0	0	1	1	1	1	1	1	0	0	0	0	0	0	0	0
0	0	0	0	0	0	0	0	1	1	1	1	1	1	1	1	0	0	0	0	0	0	0
0	0	0	0	0	0	0	1	1	1	1	1	1	1	1	1	1	0	0	0	0	0	0
0	0	0	0	0	0	1	1	1	1	1	1	1	1	1	1	1	0	0	0	0	0	0
0	0	0	0	0	1	1	1	1	1	1	3	1	1	1	1	1	1	0	0	0	0	0
0	0	0	0	0	1	1	1	1	1	1	3	3	3	1	1	1	1	0	0	0	0	0
0	0	0	0	0	1	1	3	0	0	0	3	3	0	0	0	3	1	1	0	0	0	0
0	0	0	0	0	0	1	3	0	0	0	3	3	0	0	0	3	1	1	1	0	0	0
0	0	0	0	0	1	1	3	3	3	3	3	3	3	3	3	3	1	1	1	0	0	0
0	0	0	0	1	1	1	3	3	3	3	3	3	3	3	3	3	1	1	1	1	0	0
0	1	1	1	1	1	1	3	3	3	2	2	2	2	3	3	3	1	1	1	1	0	0
0	1	1	1	1	1	1	3	3	2	0	0	0	0	2	3	3	1	1	1	0	0	0
0	0	1	1	1	1	1	3	3	2	2	2	2	2	2	3	1	1	1	1	1	0	0
1	1	1	1	1	1	1	3	3	3	3	3	3	3	3	1	1	1	1	1	1	1	1
0	1	1	1	1	1	1	1	3	3	3	3	3	1	1	1	1	1	1	1	1	1	1
0	0	1	1	1	1	1	0	0	0	3	3	0	1	1	1	1	1	1	1	1	1	0
0	0	0	1	1	1	0	0	0	0	0	0	0	0	1	1	1	1	1	0	0	0	0

Figure 8.5
Make a table of the color values of each dot in the object.

Dot Size

Standard graph paper grids are square; screen dots are rectangular. Remember to take this into account when drawing shapes on graph paper. You may want to make graph paper with rectangular grids proportional in size to screen dots.

8.2: BLOCK GRAPHICS FROM BASIC

Warning—this section gets rather complicated. Beginners may wish to skip to the subsection **The Routine**. If you read on, it would be helpful to have read Section 4.2, which discusses the screen memory map.

PUT

In BASIC, block graphics revolves around **PUT**—a command that moves block data from an array to the graphics screen. Its format is:

PUT (x,y), array name, option

We'll start by seeing how to store **PUT** data in an array. There are many ways to do this. I will discuss the simplest.

Storing the Data

We will store our data in a one-dimensional integer array. Each entry in an integer array is one word (two bytes) long. Figure 8.6 shows the format of the data: the first two entries tell the width and height of the object; the remaining entries are the shape data, compressed into word-size chunks.

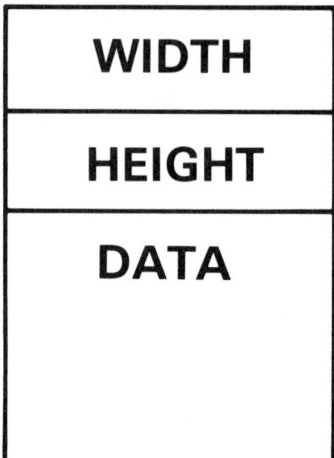

Figure 8.6
The data format of PUT arrays.

PUT stores on the screen the numbers from the array. Suppose array entries 1 and 2 indicate that there are **a** rows of data that are each **b** array entries (words) wide. Then, **PUT** will move **b** entries of data to the screen, starting with entry 3, skip down one row, move the next **b** entries of data to the screen, skip down a row, and so on, until all **a** rows have been moved. (A total of **a** times **b** entries will be moved.) Figure 8.7 should make this clearer.

So, for **PUT** to use shape data, we need to break our data into words telling what dots to set on the screen (see Figures 4.2. and 4.3). First, we divide our data table into columns one word wide. For medium resolution, this means every eight dots, for high resolution, every 16 dots (Figure 8.8). Now, we find the value to store to the screen to make the dots in each table entry appear. In medium resolution, we multiply the leftmost dot's color value by 2^{14}, add it to the next dot's color value multiplied by 2^{12}, and continue the process for all eight dots. In high resolution, we multiply the first dot's value by 2^{15}, add it to the second multiplied by 2^{14}, and continue for all 16 dots. Or, we can consecutively write the hex digit for every four bits of dots (two medium-resolution dots; four high-resolution dots) in each entry. Both methods of computing the word values are shown in Figure 8.9.

For example, to compute the word value for the following medium-resolution table entry:

3 3 2 2 0 1 0 1

we find $3 \times 2^{14} + 3 \times 2^{12} + 2 \times 2^{10} + 2 \times 2^8 + 0 \times 2^6 + 1 \times 2^4 + 0 \times 2^2 + 1 \times 2^0 = 64,017$.

Before we can store the table entry data in an array, we need to make two adjustments. Integers are stored in low-byte, high-byte format, but **PUT** transfers data in high-byte, low-byte format. Thus, we need to reverse the order of the bytes in each word of data before placing it in the array. For example, suppose we want to store 12,837 in our array. 12,837 is 3225H: the high byte is 32H, the low byte is 25H. We now flip these bytes and get 2532H. In decimal, this is 9,552. But suppose we want to store 8,849. If we switch the high and low bytes, we get 37,154 (9122H). This amount is too large to store as an integer; we will get an **Overflow** error (remember that integers cannot exceed $2^{15} - 1 = 32,767$). So how can we store numbers with the sixteenth-bit set? Well, the most significant bit of an integer tells its sign. To get numbers over 32,767, we need to find a negative integer with the same low 15 bits set. Suppose **old number** is greater than 32,767. The integer value to store is:

new number = − (65,536 − **old number**).

228 Block Graphics

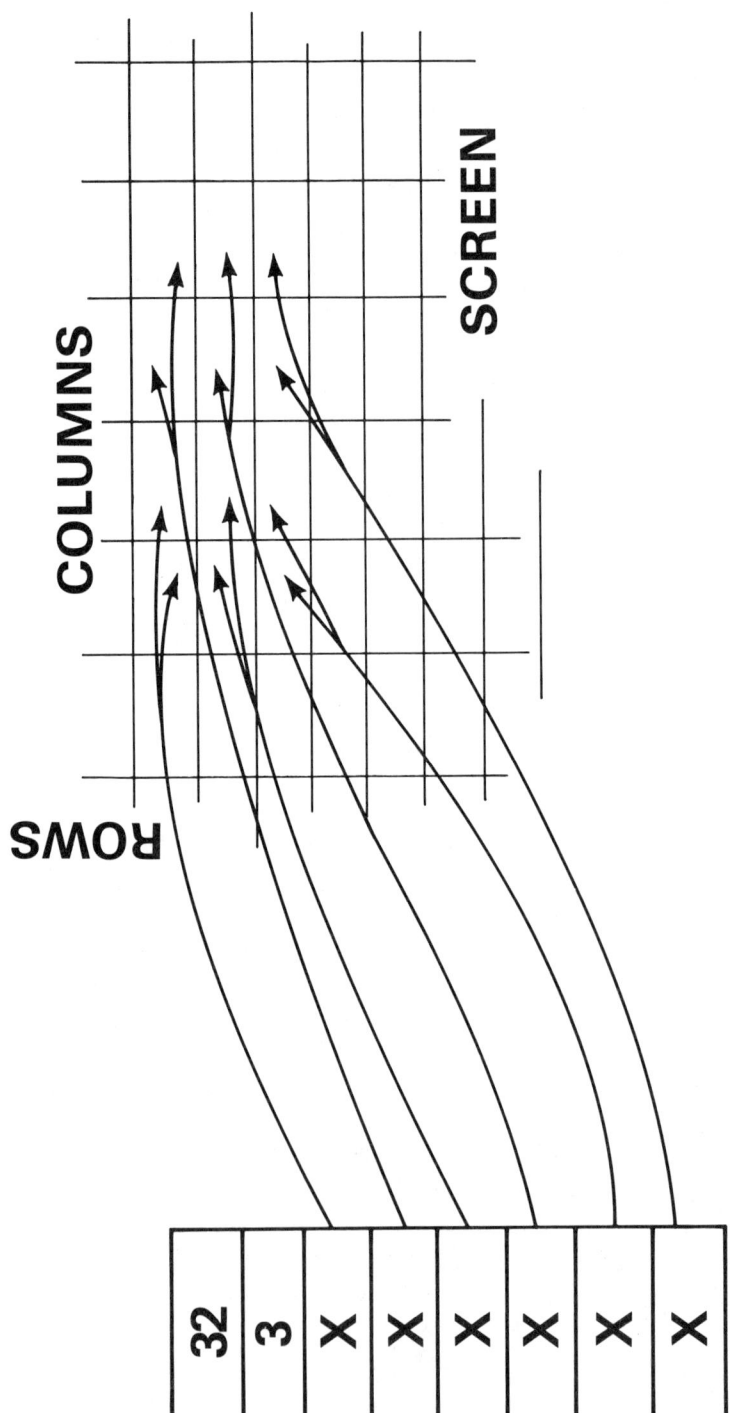

Figure 8.7
This PUT array holds data for an object 32 bits wide and 3 bits high. Row by row, the array entries are moved to the screen. Each array entry holds data for two graphics columns.

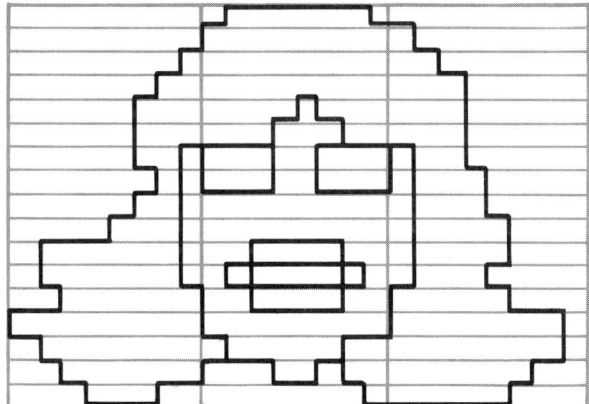

Figure 8.8
Divide the object into columns, each one word of dot data wide.

To continue our example, instead of storing 37,154, we store −(65,536 − 37,154) = −28,382.

Having switched the high and low bytes and made sign adjustments to prevent overflow, we can now store the values in an array. One row at a time and moving left to right, we read the numbers from each column and store them in the array, starting with the third array element.

We also need to tell **PUT** the size of our data. We place the number of rows in array entry two. In array entry 1, we place the width of our data in bits, which is the number of words times 16. For example, suppose we have medium-resolution data 23 dots across and 17 rows high. Then array entry 2 gets 17, and array entry 1 gets 48 (23 dots * 2 bits per dot = 46 bits; 46 bits needs 3 words; 3 * 16 = 48).

Making the Computer Convert the Data

For all but the smallest of shapes, the process of converting dot data to an array we can **PUT** is difficult, time consuming, error prone and boring. So, rather than converting dot data manually, the computer can do it.

We'll feed the dot data into a matrix (we'll call this the *dot matrix*) and convert it to an array for **PUT**ting (we'll call this the *PUT array*). Giving the computer the dot matrix data has several advantages: we don't have to do any calculations; it's easy to correct data (just looking at the matrix data gives us an idea of the shape); and we can create new shapes by manipulating the data (for example, by scaling).

The Routine

Our program needs to start by loading the dot matrix data. To increase flexibility, we'll do this in a subroutine. We'll place the dot matrix in an integer array, **SHAPEMAT%**. **NUMROWS** and **NUMCOLUMNS** tell the size of the data:

```
10 OPTION BASE 1
300 GOSUB 1010 'read shape data
1000 '
1001 'read shape data
1002 '
1010 READ NUMROWS, NUMCOLUMNS
1030 DIM SHAPEMAT%(NUMROWS,NUMCOLUMNS)
1040 FOR ROW = 1 TO NUMROWS
1050    FOR COLUMN = 1 TO NUMCOLUMNS
1060       READ SHAPEMAT%(ROW,COLUMN)
1080    NEXT
1090 NEXT
1900 RETURN
```

Now we put in the data taken from Figure 8.1:

```
20000 '
20001 'shape data
20002 '
20003 '
20004 'female face
20005 '
20010 DATA 17,23
20020 DATA 0, 0, 0, 0, 0, 0, 0, 0, 0, 1, 1, 1, 1, 1, 1, 0, 0, 0, 0, 0, 0, 0, 0
20030 DATA 0, 0, 0, 0, 0, 0, 0, 0, 1, 1, 1, 1, 1, 1, 1, 1, 0, 0, 0, 0, 0, 0, 0
20040 DATA 0, 0, 0, 0, 0, 0, 0, 1, 1, 1, 1, 1, 1, 1, 1, 1, 1, 0, 0, 0, 0, 0, 0
20050 DATA 0, 0, 0, 0, 0, 0, 1, 1, 1, 1, 1, 1, 1, 1, 1, 1, 1, 0, 0, 0, 0, 0, 0
20060 DATA 0, 0, 0, 0, 0, 1, 1, 1, 1, 1, 1, 3, 1, 1, 1, 1, 1, 0, 0, 0, 0, 0, 0
20070 DATA 0, 0, 0, 0, 0, 1, 1, 1, 1, 1, 1, 3, 3, 3, 1, 1, 1, 1, 0, 0, 0, 0, 0
20080 DATA 0, 0, 0, 0, 0, 1, 1, 3, 0, 0, 0, 3, 3, 0, 0, 0, 3, 1, 1, 0, 0, 0, 0
20090 DATA 0, 0, 0, 0, 0, 1, 1, 3, 0, 0, 0, 3, 3, 0, 0, 0, 3, 1, 1, 1, 0, 0, 0
20100 DATA 0, 0, 0, 0, 0, 1, 1, 3, 3, 3, 3, 3, 3, 3, 3, 3, 3, 1, 1, 1, 0, 0, 0
20110 DATA 0, 0, 0, 0, 1, 1, 1, 3, 3, 3, 3, 3, 3, 3, 3, 3, 1, 1, 1, 1, 0, 0, 0
20120 DATA 0, 1, 1, 1, 1, 1, 1, 3, 3, 3, 2, 2, 2, 2, 3, 3, 3, 1, 1, 1, 1, 0, 0
20130 DATA 0, 1, 1, 1, 1, 1, 1, 3, 3, 2, 0, 0, 0, 0, 2, 3, 3, 1, 1, 1, 0, 0, 0
20140 DATA 0, 0, 1, 1, 1, 1, 1, 3, 3, 2, 2, 2, 2, 3, 3, 1, 1, 1, 1, 0, 0, 0
20150 DATA 1, 1, 1, 1, 1, 1, 1, 3, 3, 3, 3, 3, 3, 3, 1, 1, 1, 1, 1, 1, 1, 1, 1
20160 DATA 0, 1, 1, 1, 1, 1, 1, 1, 3, 3, 3, 3, 3, 1, 1, 1, 1, 1, 1, 1, 1, 1, 1
20170 DATA 0, 0, 1, 1, 1, 1, 1, 1, 0, 0, 0, 3, 3, 0, 0, 1, 1, 1, 1, 1, 1, 1, 0
20180 DATA 0, 0, 0, 1, 1, 1, 0, 0, 0, 0, 0, 0, 0, 0, 1, 1, 1, 1, 1, 1, 0, 0
```

If you look at lines **20020 − 20180** from an angle or a bit back from the screen, you should be able to pick out the face.

We are now ready to convert the dot matrix to a **PUT** array. We will make the conversion subroutine convert a dot matrix called

NEWSHAPEMAT% to a **PUT** array called **NEWSHAPE%**. Before conversion, the main program needs to move a dot matrix to **NEWSHAPEMAT%**, and after conversion, move **NEWSHAPE%** to another array. This generalizes the subroutine—we can convert many dot matrices to **PUT** arrays with one subroutine.

First, we set up **NEWSHAPEMAT%**:

```
30   DIM NEWSHAPEMAT%(1,1), NEWSHAPE%(1)
1010 READ NUMROWS, NUMCOLUMNS : NUMNEWROWS = NUMROWS :
     NUMNEWCOLUMNS = NUMCOLUMNS
1020 ERASE NEWSHAPEMAT%
1030 DIM SHAPEMAT%(NUMROWS,NUMCOLUMNS), NEWSHAPEMAT%(
     NUMROWS, NUMCOLUMNS)
1070     NEWSHAPEMAT%(ROW,COLUMN) = SHAPEMAT%(ROW,
         COLUMN)
```

Then, we call the subroutine to convert the data:

```
1100 GOSUB 2010     'convert newshapemat% to newshape%
```

The subroutine first computes the size of the array in which to store the data—two plus the number of words per row times the number of rows. Then, it fills in the array, starting with the third entry.

Line **2040** reads each row. Line **2050** moves through the rows one word at a time. The loop at **2090** examines each dot in a column and allows line **2100** to compute the value of the word. Note that **2100** is the process we used to convert dot data to words (Figure 8.9). In medium resolution, the exponent goes from 14 to 0 in steps of two; in high resolution, the exponent goes from 15 to 0 in steps of one. Line **2070** makes sure that the matrix is not read beyond its bounds. If there are not enough dots to fill a word, the absent dots are assumed to be zeros:

```
2000 '
2001 'convert newshapemat% to newshape%
2002 'newshapemat% is in matrix format
2003 ' newshape% is in PUTable format
2004 '
2010 NEWSIZE = INT(NUMNEWCOLUMNS / (2 * RESOLUTION) +
     .99) * NUMNEWROWS + 2
2020 ERASE NEWSHAPE% : DIM NEWSHAPE%(NEWSIZE)
2030 POSITION = 2
2040 FOR ROW = 1 TO NUMNEWROWS
2050    FOR COLUMN = 1 TO NUMNEWCOLUMNS STEP 2 *
        RESOLUTION
```

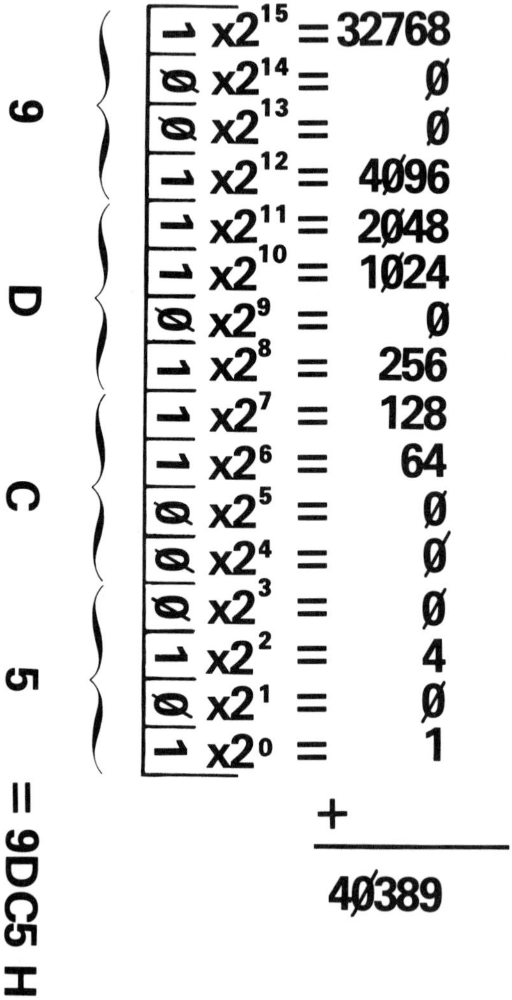

Block Graphics

$$
\left.\begin{array}{l}
1 \times 2^{15} = 32768 \\
0 \times 2^{14} = 0 \\
0 \times 2^{13} = 0 \\
1 \times 2^{12} = 4096 \\
1 \times 2^{11} = 2048 \\
1 \times 2^{10} = 1024 \\
0 \times 2^{9} = 0 \\
1 \times 2^{8} = 256 \\
1 \times 2^{7} = 128 \\
1 \times 2^{6} = 64 \\
0 \times 2^{5} = 0 \\
0 \times 2^{4} = 0 \\
0 \times 2^{3} = 0 \\
1 \times 2^{2} = 4 \\
0 \times 2^{1} = 0 \\
1 \times 2^{0} = 1
\end{array}\right\} \quad \begin{array}{c} 9 \\ D \\ C \\ 5 \end{array} = 9DC5\ H
$$

$$+ \overline{40389}$$

Figure 8.9
Two ways to compute numeric values for a word of dot data.

```
2060       POSITION = POSITION + 1
2070       IF COLUMN + 2*RESOLUTION > NUMNEWCOLUMNS THEN
           ENDDOT = NUMNEWCOLUMNS - COLUMN + 1 ELSE
           ENDDOT = 2*RESOLUTION
2080       VALUE = 0
2090       FOR DOT = 1 TO ENDDOT
2100          VALUE = VALUE + NEWSHAPEMAT%(ROW,COLUMN +
              DOT - 1) * 2^((2*RESOLUTION - DOT) * 8/
              RESOLUTION)
2110       NEXT
2120       IF FNVALUE < 32767 THEN NEWSHAPE%(POSITION) =
           FNVALUE ELSE NEWSHAPE%(POSITION) = -(65536! -
           FNVALUE)
```

```
2130    NEXT
2140    NEXT
2150    NEWSHAPE%(1) = 16 * INT(NUMNEWCOLUMNS/
        (2*RESOLUTION) + .99)
2160    NEWSHAPE%(2) = NUMNEWROWS
2200    RETURN
```

FNVALUE switches the high and low bytes. This is used in 2120, which also sign adjusts. **RESOLUTION** tells the number of dots per byte. In medium resolution this is 4, in high resolution, 8:

```
100 DEF FNVALUE = INT(VALUE/256) + (VALUE - INT(VALUE/
    256)*256) *256
200 RESOLUTION = 4
```

Once we return from the conversion subroutine, we need to copy **NEWSHAPE%** to another array:

```
1110 DIM SHAPE%(NEWSIZE)
1120 FOR POSITION = 1 TO NEWSIZE : SHAPE%(POSITION) =
     NEWSHAPE%(POSITION) : NEXT    'copy newshape% to
     shape%
```

We are now ready to display the shape. First, we'll pick a location:

```
210 X = 50 : Y * 50
```

Then, we'll set the graphics mode, clear the screen, and call a subroutine to draw the shape:

```
400 '
401 'set graphics mode
402 '
410 IF RESOLUTION = 4 THEN SCREEN 1 : COLOR 1,0 ELSE
    SCREEN 2
420 KEY OFF

500 '
501 'main loop
502 '
530     CLS
540     GOSUB 6010          'draw the shape
700 END
```

Finally, we'll draw it:

```
6000 '
6001 'draw the shape
6002 '
6010 PUT (X,Y), SHAPE%
6100 RETURN
```

234 Block Graphics

> Switch into Chapter 8's directory with:
> **CHDIR** "\
> **CHDIR** "CHAPTER8
>
> Then:
>
> **LOAD** "2

Run the program. The face will appear at (50,50).

8.3: EXPERIMENTING WITH PUT

While we have our face data in a **PUT** array, let's experiment with **PUT**. First, type:

CLS

We'll start by seeing how **PUT** justifies the dot matrix data. Move the cursor to a few rows above the bottom of the screen. Type:

PUT (0,0), SHAPE%

As you can see, **PUT** places the dot from row 1, column 1 of the dot matrix at **(x,y)**.
Now try:

PUT (315,0), SHAPE%

This will result in an **Illegal function call** error. This error occurs whenever you try to **PUT** part of an array off of the screen.
Now, print the value of **SHAPE%(1)**. Add 9 to this before **PUT**ting. Subtract 9 from the original value and **PUT**. Now restore the original value and print **SHAPE%(2)**. Increase and decrease its value by 2, **PUT**ting after each change. Restore **SHAPE%(2)**.
If you have BASIC 2.0, change the **WINDOW** and **VIEW**. The size of the **PUT** shape will not change, but what locations cause **Illegal function call** errors will.

The PUT Options

PUT can draw objects five different ways. So far we have been using the default—**XOR** drawing. If we **XOR** the same drawing twice, it disappears. Let's try this. Type:

PUT (20,30), SHAPE%

Now, type it again:

PUT (20,30), SHAPE%

The face will disappear. Type some text in the area where you drew the face. Again, do:

PUT (20,30), SHAPE%

The face will appear over the text. The colors will be different where it hits the text. **PUT** the face in the same place again. The text will reappear, unchanged.

Four other drawing style options are available. To use them, follow the array name by a comma and one of:

OR
AND
PSET
PRESET

For **XOR** drawing, either omit **option**, or follow the array name by a comma and **XOR**.

OR causes the shape data to be **OR**ed to the screen. Let's try it:

PUT (20,60), SHAPE%, OR

Retype the line, and the shape remains. Now, try:

PUT (20,70), SHAPE%, OR

Note the color changes. Consult the *BASIC Manual,* under **PUT (graphics)** to see how **OR**ing affects color.

AND causes the data to be **AND**ed with the screen's contents before being plotted. Thus, if no dots have been set on the screen, no picture will appear. Try it out:

PUT (20,95), SHAPE%, AND

Nothing will appear. Now, do:

PUT (20,70), SHAPE%, AND

Fill some text over this area. Do:

PUT (20,70), SHAPE%, AND

Refer to the *BASIC Manual* to see the effect of **AND** on color.

PSET causes the shape data to be stored on the screen directly. Any dots appearing behind the shape are ignored; the only data appearing are that of the shape. Try:

PUT (20,75), SHAPE%, PSET

Note the border cleared around the shape. This is from the zeros surrounding the face.

PRESET also directly stores the dot data, but after taking the inverse. So in medium resolution, color 0 is plotted as color 3, color 1 is plotted as color 2, color 2 is plotted as color 1, and color 3 is plotted as color 0. Let's try it:

PUT (40,30), SHAPE%, PRESET

The shape's border can be seen very clearly.

8.4: ANIMATION

Animating block figures is easy. All we need to do is change the x and y coordinates in the **PUT** command. For example, try:

FOR POSITION = 1 TO 20 : CLS : PUT (POSITION * 4, 10), SHAPE% : NEXT

The face will move very rapidly across the screen.

Let's add animation to our program. We'll put the call to the drawing subroutine, along with a subroutine to move the shape, within a **WHILE** loop. As with our line programs, we'll have a subroutine to see when to exit the **WHILE** loop. The translation subroutine that follows is quite simple. You may want to fancy it:

```
210 TRUE = -1 : FALSE = 0
510 WHILE NOT FINISHED
520     GOSUB 3010      'move the shape
550     GOSUB 7010      'evaluate finished
600 WEND

3000 '
3001 'move the shape
3002 '
3010 GOSUB 3510         'get amount of translation
3020 X = X + XTRANSLATION
3030 Y = Y + YTRANSLATION
3100 RETURN

3500 '
3501 'get amount of translation
3502 '
3510 XTRANSLATION = 10
3520 YTRANSLATION = 1
3600 RETURN

7000 '
7001 'evaluate finished
7002 '
7010 IF COUNTER = 10 THEN FINISHED = TRUE ELSE COUNTER
    = COUNTER + 1
7100 RETURN
```

MERGE ″4

Run it. Note that translation is very fast, but computing the shape data is very slow.

8.5: MULTIPLE OBJECTS

Drawing multiple objects is simple. We just keep track of each object's position, and use a separate **PUT** statement for each object. For example, to move a block of six faces, try:

```
6020 PUT (X + 40, Y), SHAPE%
6030 PUT (X + 80, Y), SHAPE%
6040 PUT (X, Y + 40), SHAPE%
6050 PUT (X + 40, Y + 40), SHAPE%
6060 PUT (X + 80, Y + 40), SHAPE%
```

MERGE "5

Of course, we can use more than one shape.

8.6: MANIPULATING OBJECTS

Anytime we want to change the appearance of an object, we need to change its dot matrix and recompute the **PUT** array. Directly changing the **PUT** array is too difficult. You have seen how long it takes to convert a dot matrix to a **PUT** array. If we were to compute the new **PUT** array in the middle of drawing, smooth animation would be impossible. Therefore, we need to compute data for all the shapes we will use before we draw any of them.

For example, suppose we want a shape to fly from the upper left corner to the right side of the screen, flip 90 degrees clockwise, fly to the bottom, flip another 90 degrees clockwise, fly to the left border, flip 90 degrees again, return to its starting position, and flip to its original orientation. We wouldn't rotate the shape each time it hit a boundary. Rather, we would compute all four **PUT** arrays at the beginning of the program, and whenever a boundary is hit, switch which **PUT** array we draw.

We use the same technique if we want parts of a shape to move. For example, to make the shape in Figure 8.10 walk, we compute **PUT** arrays for both stages of walking shown. Then, as the shape moves, we flip between each **PUT** array.

When parts of an object move, we need to recompute the dot matrix by hand. But when the whole object is manipulated, such as if it is scaled or rotated, we can have the computer determine the new dot matrix.

8.7: ROTATING A DOT MATRIX

As I mentioned, the computer can be made to do block rotation. We will restrict ourselves to rotating in 90-degree increments. (Otherwise, rotation is very messy. To avoid negative indices, the rotated dot matrix must be

Figure 8.10
A shape walking. To animate it, determine dot matrices for each stage of walking.

dimensioned very large, and then translated twice—once while rotating, then afterwards to align the data with the matrix boundary. But there will still be an offset, causing the shape to rock wildly when rotating.) Figure 8.11 shows a small dot matrix rotated 0, 90, 180, and 270 degrees clockwise.

Let's examine 90-degree rotation. Note that the number of columns of the rotated matrix is the same as the number of rows of the original matrix; the number of rows of the rotated matrix is the same as the number of columns of the original.

The 1 in position (1,1) moves to (1,5) (Figure 8.11). And the 2 in (5,3) moves to (3,1). Examining the rest of the entries, we get the following formula:

ROTATEDMATRIX(row, column) = OLDMATRIX(number of rotated columns − column + 1, row)

Remember, because **row** is between 1 and the number of old columns, and **number of rotated columns − column + 1** is between 1 and the number of old rows, there will be no **Subscript out of range** errors.

We can similarly derive formulae for rotating 180 and 270 degrees.

The Routine

Let's look at a routine to rotate dot matrices. We will rotate the matrix in **NEWSHAPEMAT%** by the amount specified by **ANGLE**, an integer

240 Block Graphics

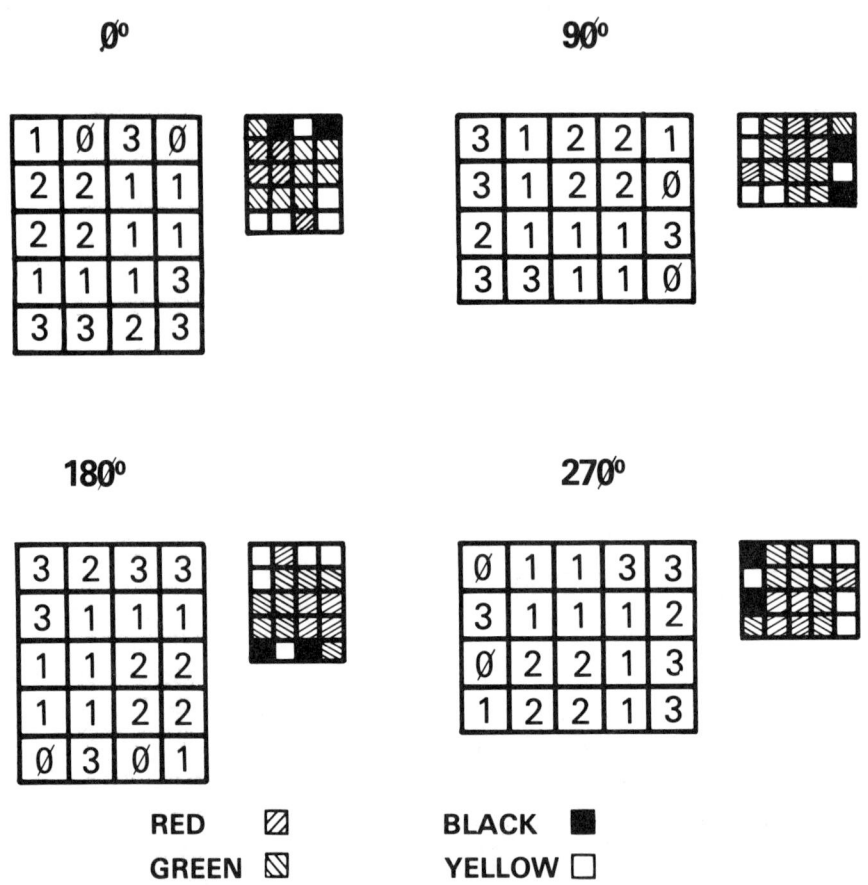

Figure 8.11
A small dot matrix, rotated 0, 90, 180, and 270 degrees.

between 0 and 3. **ANGLE** equals the amount of rotation divided by 90 degrees. The rotated matrix will be returned in **NEWSHAPEMAT%**, its **PUT** array in **NEWSHAPE%**.

First, we set the angle and call a routine to rotate the shape. Because we create all **PUT** arrays before animation, we don't get **ANGLE** from a subroutine.

The shape must already be in **NEWSHAPEMAT%**:

```
1130 ANGLE = 1
1140 GOSUB 5010        'rotate the shape
```

If **ANGLE** is zero, we skip over most of the rotation section. Otherwise, we figure the size of the rotated matrix, **ROTATEDMAT%**, and **DIM** it:

```
5000 '
5001 'rotate the shape
```

```
5002 '   angle = 0        means 0 radians rotation
5003 '         = 1        means pi/2 radians rotation
5004 '         = 2        means pi radians rotation
5005 '         = 3        means 3pi/2 radians rotation
5006 '
5010 IF ANGLE = 0 THEN 5200
5020 IF (ANGLE = 1) OR (ANGLE = 3) THEN DIM
     ROTATEDMAT%(NUMNEWCOLUMNS,NUMNEWROWS) :
     NUMROTATEDROWS = NUMNEWCOLUMNS : NUMROTATEDCOLUMNS
     = NUMNEWROWS
5030 IF ANGLE = 2 THEN DIM ROTATEDMAT%(NUMNEWROWS,
     NUMNEWCOLUMNS) : NUMROTATEDROWS = NUMNEWROWS :
     NUMROTATEDCOLUMNS = NUMNEWCOLUMNS
```

Now, we load each entry of **ROTATEDMAT%** with the appropriate entry of **NEWSHAPEMAT%**:

```
5040 FOR ROW = 1 TO NUMROTATEDROWS
5050    FOR COLUMN = 1 TO NUMROTATEDCOLUMNS
5060       IF ANGLE = 1 THEN ROTATEDMAT%(ROW,COLUMN) =
           NEWSHAPEMAT%(NUMROTATEDCOLUMNS + 1 - COLUMN,
           ROW)
5070       IF ANGLE = 2 THEN ROTATEDMAT%(ROW,COLUMN) =
           NEWSHAPEMAT%(NUMROTATEDROWS + 1 - ROW,
           NUMROTATEDCOLUMNS + 1 - COLUMN)
5080       IF ANGLE = 3 THEN ROTATEDMAT%(ROW,COLUMN) =
           NEWSHAPEMAT%(COLUMN,NUMROTATEDROWS + 1 - ROW)
5090    NEXT
5100 NEXT
```

We copy **ROTATEDMAT%** to **NEWSHAPEMAT%**, compute the **PUT** array, **ERASE ROTATEDMAT%** to conserve space, and return to the main program:

```
5110 'copy rotatedmat% to newshapemat%
5120 NUMNEWROWS = NUMROTATEDROWS : NUMNEWCOLUMNS =
     NUMROTATEDCOLUMNS
5130 ERASE NEWSHAPEMAT% : DIM NEWSHAPEMAT%(NUMNEWROWS,
     NUMNEWCOLUMNS)
5140 FOR ROW = 1 TO NUMNEWROWS
5150    FOR COLUMN = 1 TO NUMNEWCOLUMNS
5160       NEWSHAPEMAT%(ROW,COLUMN) = ROTATEDMAT%(
           ROW,COLUMN)
5170    NEXT
5180 NEXT
5190 ERASE ROTATEDMAT%
5200 GOSUB 2010      'convert newshapemat% to newshape%
5400 RETURN
```

Finally, we copy the **PUT** array to **ROTATEDSHAPE%**:

```
1150 DIM ROTATEDSHAPE%(NEWSIZE)
1160 FOR POSITION = 1 TO NEWSIZE : ROTATEDSHAPE%(
     POSITION) = NEWSHAPE%(POSITION) : NEXT      'copy
     newshape% to rotatedshape%
```

and draw it:

```
6020 PUT (X + 50, Y + 50), ROTATEDSHAPE%
```

MERGE "7

Trying It Out

Experiment with changing **ANGLE**. Then get all four rotations of the shape at once. Try writing the program discussed in Section 8.6.

8.8: SCALING THE SHAPE

In block graphics, scaling is more difficult than rotating. We can't just multiply the position of every dot by a scaling factor to determine its position in the scaled dot matrix. This would make the scaled object full of holes. Rather, our scaling routine must do the following:

1. If the scaling factor is greater than one, every dot in the old matrix must be replicated several times.
2. If the scaling factor is less than one, dots in the old matrix must be skipped over.

To do this, we break scaling into two parts: we first scale in the x direction, then in the y.

For example, suppose our dot matrix is:

1 1 0 0 3 3

and our x-scaling factor is 0.5, and our y-scaling factor is 2. First, we scale in the x direction getting:

1 0 3

Then, we scale in the y direction getting:

1 0 3
1 0 3

The Routine

Let's put this into a routine. We'll start by setting the scaling factors and calling the scaling subroutine:

```
1130 XSCALE = 2 : YSCALE = 1.5
1140 GOSUB 4010        'scale the shape
```

We'll x scale the dot matrix **NEWSHAPEMAT%** into **SCALEDMAT%**. Then, we'll y scale **SCALEDMAT%** into **NEWSHAPEMAT%**.

First, we'll find the size of the scaled matrix and set up **SCALEDMAT%**. As **SCALEDMAT%** holds the result of x scaling, its column dimension is **NUMSCALEDCOLUMNS**:

```
4000 '
4001 'scale the shape
4002 '
4010 NUMSCALEROWS = INT(NUMNEWROWS * YSCALE + .5)
4020 NUMSCALECOLUMNS = INT(NUMNEWCOLUMNS * XSCALE + .5)
4030 DIM SCALEDMAT%(NUMNEWROWS,NUMSCALECOLUMNS)
```

Now we'll x scale each row and examine the row's contents dot-by-dot. We'll set up a pointer, **OLDCOL**, telling the last column filled in **SCALEDMAT%**, then figure to what column in **SCALEDMAT%** to repeat the value being examined in **NEWSHAPEMAT%**. We'll fill **SCALEDMAT%**, then update **OLDCOL**:

```
4040 'do x scaling
4050 FOR ROW = 1 TO NUMNEWROWS
4060    OLDCOL = 1
4070    FOR COLUMN = 1 TO NUMNEWCOLUMNS
4080       NEWCOL = XSCALE * COLUMN
4090       FOR REPEAT = OLDCOL TO NEWCOL
4100          SCALEDMAT%(ROW,REPEAT) =
                 NEWSHAPEMAT%(ROW,COLUMN)
4110       NEXT
4120       IF NEWCOL > 1 THEN OLDCOL = NEWCOL
4130    NEXT
4140 NEXT
```

244 Block Graphics

Line **4120** is a little tricky. If **XSCALE** is greater than 1, **OLDCOL** will be updated. But, if **XSCALE** is less than 1, **OLDCOL** will never fall below 1. This prevents **Subscript out of range** errors.

Scaling in the y direction is similar to scaling in the x direction:

```
4150 'do y scaling
4160 ERASE NEWSHAPEMAT%
4170 DIM NEWSHAPEMAT%(NUMSCALEROWS,NUMSCALECOLUMNS)
4180 FOR COLUMN = 1 TO NUMSCALECOLUMNS
4190    OLDROW = 1
4200    FOR ROW = 1 TO NUMNEWROWS
4210       NEWROW = YSCALE * ROW
4220       FOR REPEAT = OLDROW TO NEWROW
4230          NEWSHAPEMAT%(REPEAT,COLUMN) =
               SCALEDMAT%(ROW,COLUMN)
4240       NEXT
4250       IF NEWROW > 1 THEN OLDROW = NEWROW
4260    NEXT
4270 NEXT
```

Now, we erase **SCALEDMAT%**, and convert **NEWSHAPEMAT%** to a **PUT** array:

```
4280 ERASE SCALEDMAT%
4290 NUMNEWROWS = NUMSCALEROWS : NUMNEWCOLUMNS =
     NUMSCALECOLUMNS
4300 GOSUB 2010      'convert newshapemat% to newshape%
4400 RETURN
```

Finally, we copy this **PUT** array into **SCALEDSHAPE%**, and draw it:

```
1150 DIM SCALEDSHAPE%(NEWSIZE)
1160 FOR POSITION = 1 TO NEWSIZE : SCALEDSHAPE%(
     POSITION) = NEWSHAPE%(POSITION) : NEXT      'copy
     newshape% to scaledshape%
6020 PUT (X + 50, Y + 50), SCALEDSHAPE%
```

MERGE "8

Trying It Out

Run this (be patient, it will take a while). Use scaling factors greater and less than 1. Try rotating and scaling (it will be faster to rotate first).

You can use scaling to adjust for dot width.

8.9: MASKING

Figure 8.12
A male face.

Now let's experiment with another shape, Figure 8.12. We want his hair to be black (color 0), so we'll code it with zeros outlined by threes (Figure 8.13). Add the following code:

```
1130 READ NUMROWS2, NUMCOLUMNS2 : NUMNEWROWS = NUMROWS2
     : NUMNEWCOLUMNS = NUMCOLUMNS2
1140 ERASE NEWSHAPEMAT%
1150 DIM SHAPEMAT2%(NUMROWS2,NUMCOLUMNS2),
     NEWSHAPEMAT%(NUMROWS2, NUMCOLUMNS2)
1160 FOR ROW = 1 TO NUMROWS2
1170    FOR COLUMN = 1 TO NUMCOLUMNS2
1180       READ SHAPEMAT2%(ROW,COLUMN)
1190       NEWSHAPEMAT%(ROW,COLUMN) =
           SHAPEMAT2%(ROW,COLUMN)
1200    NEXT
1210 NEXT
1220 GOSUB 2010      'convert newshapemat% to newshape%
1230 DIM SHAPE2%(NEWSIZE)
1240 FOR POSITION = 1 TO NEWSIZE : SHAPE2%(POSITION) =
     NEWSHAPE%(POSITION) : NEXT      'copy newshape% to
     shape2%

3040 X2 = 150 - X
3050 Y2 = Y

6020 PUT (X2,Y2), SHAPE2%

20190 '
20191 'male face
```

246 Block Graphics

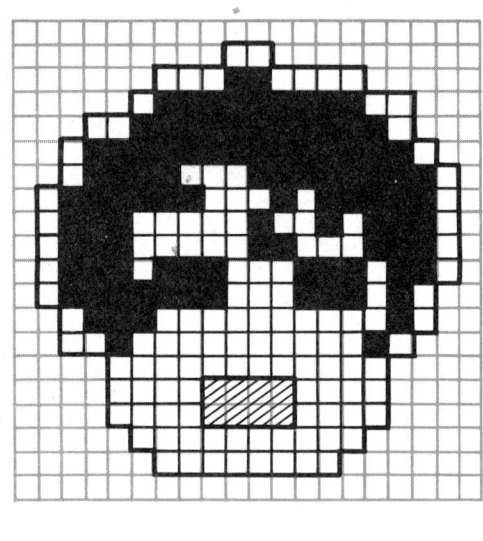

RED ▨ BLACK ■
GREEN ▧ YELLOW □

Figure 8.13
To make the figure's hair black, we'll code it as zeros surrounded by color 3.

```
20192 '
20200 DATA 18,18
20210 DATA 0, 0, 0, 0, 0, 0, 0, 3, 3, 0, 0, 0, 0, 0,
      0, 0, 0
20220 DATA 0, 0, 0, 0, 0, 3, 3, 3, 0, 0, 3, 3, 3, 3, 0,
      0, 0, 0
20230 DATA 0, 0, 0, 0, 3, 0, 0, 0, 0, 0, 0, 0, 0, 0, 3,
      3, 0, 0
20240 DATA 0, 0, 3, 3, 0, 0, 0, 0, 0, 0, 0, 0, 0, 0, 0,
      3, 0, 0
20250 DATA 0, 3, 0, 0, 0, 0, 0, 0, 0, 0, 0, 0, 0, 0, 0,
      0, 3, 0
20260 DATA 0, 3, 0, 0, 0, 0, 3, 3, 3, 0, 0, 0, 0, 0, 0,
      0, 0, 3
20270 DATA 3, 0, 0, 0, 0, 0, 0, 3, 3, 3, 0, 3, 0, 0, 0,
      0, 0, 3
20280 DATA 3, 0, 0, 0, 3, 3, 3, 3, 3, 0, 3, 3, 0, 3, 0,
      0, 0, 3
20290 DATA 3, 0, 0, 0, 3, 3, 3, 3, 3, 0, 0, 3, 3, 3, 0,
      0, 0, 3
20300 DATA 3, 0, 0, 0, 3, 0, 0, 0, 3, 3, 3, 0, 0, 0, 3,
      0, 0, 3
20310 DATA 3, 0, 0, 0, 0, 0, 0, 0, 3, 3, 3, 0, 0, 0, 3,
      0, 3, 0
```

```
20320 DATA 0, 3, 0, 0, 0, 3, 3, 3, 3, 3, 3, 3, 3, 3, 3, 0, 3, 0
20330 DATA 0, 3, 3, 0, 3, 3, 3, 3, 3, 3, 3, 3, 3, 3, 0, 3, 0, 0
20340 DATA 0, 0, 0, 3, 3, 3, 3, 3, 3, 3, 3, 3, 3, 3, 3, 0, 0, 0
20350 DATA 0, 0, 0, 3, 3, 3, 3, 2, 2, 2, 2, 3, 3, 3, 3, 0, 0, 0
20360 DATA 0, 0, 0, 3, 3, 3, 3, 2, 2, 2, 2, 3, 3, 3, 3, 0, 0, 0
20370 DATA 0, 0, 0, 0, 3, 3, 3, 3, 3, 3, 3, 3, 3, 3, 0, 0, 0, 0
20380 DATA 0, 0, 0, 0, 0, 3, 3, 3, 3, 3, 3, 3, 3, 0, 0, 0, 0, 0
```

> **MERGE "9P1**

Run it. If you look carefully, you will notice something annoying (but not unexpected) when the two faces cross. Let's examine this further:

CLS
PUT (20,90), SHAPE%
PUT (30,90), SHAPE2%

Where the two faces overlap, the color is distorted, and **SHAPE%** can be seen through the hair of **SHAPE2%**. This is undesirable; we want **SHAPE2%**'s hair to be black. Changing the **PUT** option won't help. We'll have to use masking.

Masking is the selective erasure of graphics data. As we have seen, if we just **PUT** our shape on the screen, whatever is behind the shape shows through. But if we first clear all dots behind the shape, mask them out, there will be nothing to show through when the shape is drawn.

To create a mask for a shape, we first decide what parts of the background to clear before drawing. For our male face, we want to clear all dots behind the face (Figure 8.14). We create a new dot matrix, with zeros where the screen is to be cleared, and threes elsewhere; convert this dot matrix to a **PUT** array; and **AND** it to the screen before drawing the shape. Let's try it:

```
1250 READ NUMROWSMASK, NUMCOLUMNSMASK : NUMNEWROWS =
     NUMROWSMASK : NUMNEWCOLUMNS = NUMCOLUMNSMASK
1260 ERASE NEWSHAPEMAT%
```

248 Block Graphics

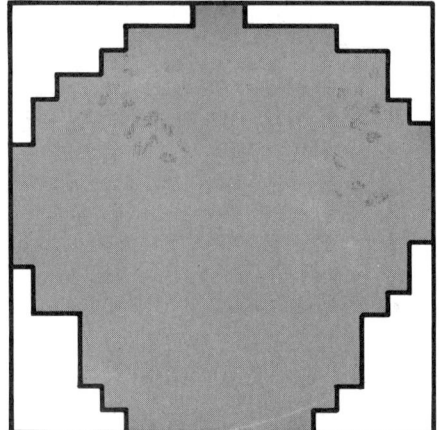

Figure 8.14
The black indicates what part of the dot matrix to clear before drawing. All black dots are coded as zeros, all clear areas as threes.

```
1270 DIM SHAPEMATMASK%(NUMROWSMASK,NUMCOLUMNSMASK),
     NEWSHAPEMAT% (NUMROWSMASK,NUMCOLUMNSMASK)
1280 FOR ROW = 1 TO NUMROWSMASK
1290   FOR COLUMN = 1 TO NUMCOLUMNSMASK
1300     READ SHAPEMATMASK%(ROW,COLUMN)
1310     NEWSHAPEMAT%(ROW,COLUMN) =
         SHAPEMATMASK%(ROW,COLUMN)
1320   NEXT
1330 NEXT
1340 GOSUB 2010       'convert newshapemat% to newshape%
1350 DIM SHAPEMASK%(NEWSIZE)
1360 FOR POSITION = 1 TO NEWSIZE : SHAPEMASK%(POSITION)
     = NEWSHAPE%(POSITION) : NEXT 'copy newshape% to
     shapemask%

6020 PUT (X2,Y2), SHAPEMASK%, AND : PUT (X2,Y2),
     SHAPE2%

20390 '
20391 'mask for male face
20392 '
20400 DATA 18,18
20410 DATA 3, 3, 3, 3, 3, 3, 3, 3, 0, 0, 3, 3, 3, 3, 3,
      3, 3, 3
20420 DATA 3, 3, 3, 3, 3, 0, 0, 0, 0, 0, 0, 0, 0, 0, 3,
      3, 3, 3
20430 DATA 3, 3, 3, 3, 0, 0, 0, 0, 0, 0, 0, 0, 0, 0, 0,
      0, 3, 3
```

```
20440 DATA 3, 3, 0, 0, 0, 0, 0, 0, 0, 0, 0, 0, 0, 0, 0,
      0, 3, 3
20450 DATA 3, 0, 0, 0, 0, 0, 0, 0, 0, 0, 0, 0, 0, 0, 0,
      0, 0, 3
20460 DATA 3, 0, 0, 0, 0, 0, 0, 0, 0, 0, 0, 0, 0, 0, 0,
      0, 0, 0
20470 DATA 0, 0, 0, 0, 0, 0, 0, 0, 0, 0, 0, 0, 0, 0, 0,
      0, 0, 0
20480 DATA 0, 0, 0, 0, 0, 0, 0, 0, 0, 0, 0, 0, 0, 0, 0,
      0, 0, 0
20490 DATA 0, 0, 0, 0, 0, 0, 0, 0, 0, 0, 0, 0, 0, 0, 0,
      0, 0, 0
20500 DATA 0, 0, 0, 0, 0, 0, 0, 0, 0, 0, 0, 0, 0, 0, 0,
      0, 0, 0
20510 DATA 0, 0, 0, 0, 0, 0, 0, 0, 0, 0, 0, 0, 0, 0, 0,
      0, 0, 3
20520 DATA 3, 0, 0, 0, 0, 0, 0, 0, 0, 0, 0, 0, 0, 0, 0,
      0, 0, 3
20530 DATA 3, 0, 0, 0, 0, 0, 0, 0, 0, 0, 0, 0, 0, 0, 0,
      0, 3, 3
20540 DATA 3, 3, 3, 0, 0, 0, 0, 0, 0, 0, 0, 0, 0, 0, 0,
      3, 3, 3
20550 DATA 3, 3, 3, 0, 0, 0, 0, 0, 0, 0, 0, 0, 0, 0, 0,
      3, 3, 3
20560 DATA 3, 3, 3, 0, 0, 0, 0, 0, 0, 0, 0, 0, 0, 0, 0,
      3, 3, 3
20570 DATA 3, 3, 3, 3, 0, 0, 0, 0, 0, 0, 0, 0, 0, 0, 3,
      3, 3, 3
20580 DATA 3, 3, 3, 3, 3, 0, 0, 0, 0, 0, 0, 0, 0, 3, 3,
      3, 3, 3
```

MERGE "9P2

Trying It

Now try it. When the two figures overlap, there will be no distortion. Let's look at masking again. Type:

CLS
PUT (20,90), SHAPE%

Now, we'll mask out part of **SHAPE%**:

PUT (30,90), SHAPEMASK%, AND

A hole the shape of the second figure will be cut out of the first. Now, type:

PUT (30,90), SHAPE2%

The second figure will neatly fall into the hole; there will be no color distortion, and the hair will stay color 0.

8.10: INCREASING ANIMATION SPEED

We can greatly increase the speed of animation, as well as reduce flicker, if we remove the **CLS** line. To do so, we need another way of clearing the screen after each drawing. There are two ways: *XOR clearing* and *zone clearing*.

With *XOR clearing*, we first **XOR** draw all the shapes. Then, just before drawing the new shapes, we **XOR** all the shapes again, to make them disappear. The advantages of this method are that it leaves the background untouched, works for any amount of movement, and is very selective. On the other hand, we must keep the objects' old positions while computing the new.

Zone clearing only works when we know the maximum amount our shapes may move. Suppose this amount is eight dots horizontally. We then add an eight-dot buffer of zeros to the left and right of the shapes (Figure 8.15) and **PSET** draw them. Any object falling within the left or right eight dots will be cleared. The advantages of zone clearing are that it's fast and we don't need to keep track of old objects' positions. But, we must restrict

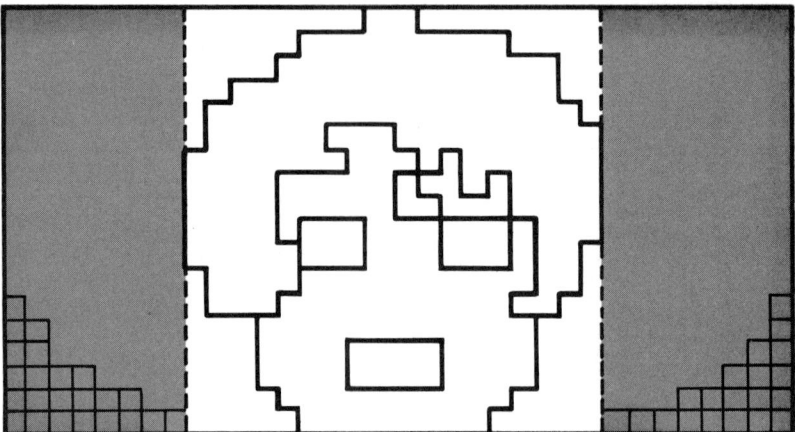

Figure 8.15
Zone clearing. The black indicates an eight dot wide zone of zeros.

the amount we move the shapes, the background is destroyed, and objects cannot be drawn within the clearing zone.

Many versions of Pac-Man use **XOR** clearing, while many versions of Space Invaders use zone clearing.

8.11: BLOCK GRAPHICS FROM ASSEMBLY LANGUAGE

Doing block graphics from Assembly Language is pretty easy. We put the shape data into data tables in the variables segment. When we want to draw a shape we find where the data begins and its size, then move it to the screen.

We'll see how to create the data in a moment. For now, we'll assume it is broken into byte-sized chunks, and that the first two bytes tell the width of the data in bytes and the number of rows of data (minus one).

Plotting the Data

Suppose we want to move three rows of data, four bytes wide, to the screen, placing the first byte in screen location 20H. Then, we move the first four bytes of data to 20H, 21H, 22H, and 23H; we move the second set of four bytes to 2020H, 2021H, 2022H, and 2023H; and we move the last four bytes to 70H, 71H, 72H, and 73H (80 + 20H = 70H).

This is fine if the corner dot falls on the beginning of a screen byte. But what if we want to move the shape to the middle of a byte (for example, to screen coordinate (2,20)). Before plotting, we would have to shift the data in each row, a clumsy, time-consuming process.

Preshifted Data Tables

Instead of shifting the data while plotting, we'll shift the data in advance. In other words, we'll create several tables for each shape; one for every bit on which it could start (Figure 8.16). In medium resolution, we'll need to make four tables; in high resolution, we'll need eight.

As an example, suppose our dot matrix is:

```
3 0 1
1 2 0
```

252 Block Graphics

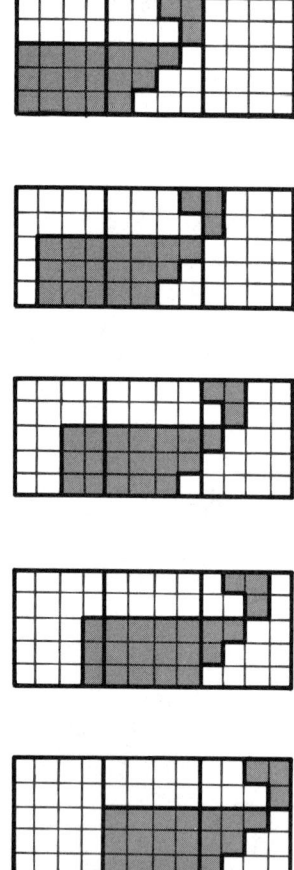

Figure 8.16
We make one table of data for each dot in a byte. The top picture shows data for a whale, to be plotted on dot 0. The next picture is for dot 1, the third for dot 2, and the fourth for dot 3. Note how the whale moves to the right. To move the whale into a new column, we can use the data all over again. The last picture starts one dot to the right of the fourth picture; it uses the same data as the first picture, but starts on a different byte.

For plotting on the first dot in a byte, we use:

11 00 01 00
01 10 00 00

For plotting on the second dot:

00 11 00 01
00 01 10 00

For the third:

00 00 11 00   01 00 00 00
00 00 01 10   00 00 00 00

And for the fourth:

00 00 00 11   00 01 00 00
00 00 00 01   10 00 00 00

Accessing Preshifted Data

To access the preshifted data, we need to make a table telling the starting location of each table of shifted data, for every shape. For example, suppose our preshifted tables are called **shapedat_1**, **shapedat_2**, **shapedat_3**, and **shapedat_4**. The table of starting locations would be:

```
shape_start       dw        offset shapedat_1, offset shapedat_2
                  dw        offset shapedat_3, offset shapedat_4
```

If we had more shapes, we would append the locations of their preshifted tables to the end of the above list.

The Data-Moving Routine

Now that we can find the data, let's look at a routine to move it. We'll assume that the number of the shape to plot is stored in **shape_number**, and that the coordinates to which to move the data are in **x** and **y**.

We begin by finding the starting location of the shape data. We multiply **shape_number** by the number of tables per shape (4 tables for medium resolution, 8 tables for high resolution) and add it to the in-byte position of the dot to which to move the shape. This position is found by **find_start**, a routine derived from **set_dot**.

Then, we find the width and height of the data, which are stored in the first two entries of the table, and move the data. Note how we use **XOR** to switch between even and odd lines, and how we keep track of the beginning column in which to plot the data:

```
;
resolution        db        2         ;3 for high res
shape_number      dw        0
x                 dw        0
```

254 Block Graphics

```
y                       dw      0
;

;
;plot the shape indicated by shape_number
;
plot_shape              proc    near
                        call    find_start      ;returns with AX = dot w/in byte
                        mov     bx,shape_number
                        mov     cl,resolution
                        shl     bx,cl           ;multiply by shape tables per shape
                        add     bx,ax           ;BX = table we want
                        shl     bx,1            ;point to word
                        mov     di,shape_start[bx]      ;DI tells where data starts
                        mov     bl,[di]         ;BL = shape width in bytes
                        inc     di
                        mov     bh,[di]         ;BH = shape height in bytes
                        inc     di
;
p_s_1:                  mov     cl,bl           ;loop through horiz. bytes
                        mov     ch,0
p_s_2:                  mov     al,[di]         ;load data
                        inc     di
                        xor     es:[bp],al      ;xor to screen
                        inc     bp
                        loop    p_s_2           ;loop for one row
                        cmp     bh,0            ;see if last row
                        je      p_s_end         ;if yes, then end
                        mov     al,bl           ;otherwise, find the start of the
                        cbw                     ;next column
                        sub     bp,ax
                        xor     bp,2000h        ;adjust for row change
                        cmp     bp,2000h        ;see if now odd or even row
                        jae     p_s_3           ;jump if now odd row
                        add     bp,80           ;now even, so add 80 to get new row
p_s_3:                  dec     bh              ;for row loop
                        jmp     short p_s_1
;
p_s_end:
                        ret
plot_shape              endp
;

;
;find byte location and dot position of (x,y)
;   return byte location in BP, dot position in AX
;
find_start              proc    near
                        mov     ax,y
                        mov     bx,0
                        shr     ax,1
                        jnc     mult_by_80
                        mov     bx,2000h
mult_by_80:             mov     dx,ax
                        shl     ax,1
                        shl     ax,1
                        add     ax,dx
                        shl     ax,1
                        shl     ax,1
                        shl     ax,1
                        shl     ax,1
```

```
                    add       bx,ax
                    mov       ax,x
                    mov       cl,resolution
                    shr       ax,cl
                    add       bx,ax
                    mov       bp,bx
                    shl       ax,cl
                    xor       ax,x
                    ret
find_start          endp
;
```

11P1.ASM

Creating the Data Tables

We will create the data tables by using a routine very similar to the routine converting dot matrices to **PUT** arrays. Only, we will break our data into byte-sized columns (instead of word-sized columns), and we will save the data in a disk file. Furthermore, we will create tables for the preshifted movements.

Let's look at the program:

```
10 OPTION BASE 1
30 INPUT "shape name";SHAPENAME$
40 OPEN SHAPENAME$ FOR OUTPUT AS #1
200 RESOLUTION = 4
300 GOSUB 1010     'read shape data
500 '
501 'main loop
502 '
510 FOR SHIFT = 1 TO RESOLUTION
520    GOSUB 2010 'make data table
530    GOSUB 3010 'shift right
540 NEXT
550 CLOSE #1
700 END
1000 '
1001 'read shape data
1002 '
1010 READ NUMNEWROWS, NUMNEWCOLUMNS : NUMNEWCOLUMNS =
     NUMNEWCOLUMNS + RESOLUTION
1030 DIM NEWSHAPEMAT%(NUMNEWROWS,NUMNEWCOLUMNS)
1040 FOR ROW = 1 TO NUMNEWROWS
1050    FOR COLUMN = 1 TO NUMNEWCOLUMNS - RESOLUTION + 1
```

256 Block Graphics

```
1060      READ NEWSHAPEMAT%(ROW,COLUMN)
1080    NEXT
1090 NEXT
1900 RETURN
2000 '
2001 'make data table
2004 '
2010 WIDTH. = INT(NUMNEWCOLUMNS/RESOLUTION +.99)
2020 PRINT #1, SHAPENAME$;"_";RIGHT$(STR$(SHIFT),1);
     SPC(18-LEN( SHAPENAME$));"db";SPC(8);WIDTH.;", ";
     NUMNEWROWS - 1
2040 FOR ROW = 1 TO NUMNEWROWS
2050   PRINT #1, SPC(20);"db";SPC(8);
2060   FOR COLUMN = 1 TO NUMNEWCOLUMNS STEP RESOLUTION
2070     IF COLUMN + RESOLUTION > NUMNEWCOLUMNS THEN
         ENDDOT = NUMNEWCOLUMNS - COLUMN + 1 ELSE
         ENDDOT = RESOLUTION
2080     VALUE = 0
2090     FOR DOT = 1 TO ENDDOT
2100       VALUE = VALUE + NEWSHAPEMAT%(ROW,COLUMN +
           DOT - 1) * 2^((RESOLUTION - DOT) * 8/
           RESOLUTION)
2110     NEXT
2120     IF COLUMN+RESOLUTION > NUMNEWCOLUMNS THEN
         PRINT
         #1, VALUE ELSE PRINT #1, VALUE;", ";
2130   NEXT
2140 NEXT
2150 PRINT #1, ";"
2200 RETURN
3000 '
3001 'shift right
3002 '
3010 FOR ROW = 1 TO NUMNEWROWS
3020   FOR COLUMN = NUMNEWCOLUMNS TO 2 STEP -1
3030     NEWSHAPEMAT%(ROW,COLUMN) =
         NEWSHAPEMAT%(ROW,COLUMN - 1)
3040   NEXT
3050   NEWSHAPEMAT%(ROW,1) = 0
3060 NEXT
3100 RETURN

20000 '
20001 'PUT THE SHAPE DATA HERE
20002 '
```

11P2.BAS

Lines **30** and **40** set up the disk file. Lines **510 — 540** shift the table after each conversion. Line **1010 DIM**s **NEWSHAPEMAT%** large enough to be shifted **RESOLUTION** times. Line **2020** stores the width and height of each table; lines **2040 — 2140** break down the data into bytes and save them as a table on disk. Lines **3000 — 3100** shift the dot matrix.

The dot matrix data gets placed at line **20000**.

As an example, let's look at the tables this routine generates for the female face. They have been saved in a file called **SHAPEDAT**:

```
;
shapedat_1          db          7 , 16
                    db          0 , 0 , 21 , 84 , 0 , 0 , 0
                    db          0 , 0 , 85 , 85 , 64 , 0 , 0
                       .
                       .
                       .
                    db          1 , 80 , 0 , 1 , 85 , 64 , 0
;
shapedat_2          db          7 , 16
                    db          0 , 0 , 5 , 85 , 0 , 0 , 0
                    db          0 , 0 , 21 , 85 , 80 , 0 , 0
                       .
                       .
                       .
;
shapedat_4          db          7 , 16
                    db          0 , 0 , 0 , 85 , 80 , 0 , 0
                    db          0 , 0 , 1 , 85 , 85 , 0 , 0
                       .
                       .
                       .
                    db          0 , 85 , 85 , 255 , 213 , 85 , 80
                    db          0 , 21 , 84 , 15 , 21 , 85 , 64
                    db          0 , 5 , 64 , 0 , 5 , 85 , 0
;
```

Animation

We animate figures just as we did in our line graphics programs by placing calls to drawing and translating routines within a main loop:

```
main_loop           proc        near
                    mov         ax,page_2
                    mov         es,ax
                    call        clear_screen
                    mov         shape_number,0
                    call        translate
```

258 Block Graphics

```
                        call        plot_shape
                        call        display_page_2
                        call        evaluate_finished
                        cmp         finished,0
                        jne         main_loop
                        ret
main_loop               endp
;
```

Note that we are using two-page graphics to reduce flicker. Thus, we must define:

```
;
page_2                  segment
                        db          3f40h dup (?)
page_2                  ends
;
```

evaluate_finished and **translate** can be anything. The following move the shape 10 units in the x direction and one unit in the y direction 10 times:

```
;
finished                db          1               ;0 when finished
counter                 db          0

xtranslation            dw          10              ;10 just for testing
ytranslation            dw          1               ;1 just for testing
;

translate               proc        near
                        mov         ax,xtranslation
                        add         x,ax
                        mov         ax,ytranslation
                        add         y,ax
                        ret
translate               endp

evaluate_finished       proc        near
                        inc         counter
                        cmp         counter,10
                        jne         e_f_end
                        mov         finished,0
e_f_end:                ret
evaluate_finished       endp
```

> **11P3.ASM**

clear_screen and **display_page_2** are as used before.
Remember to set the graphics mode before calling **main_loop**.

Multiple Objects, Masking, and Animation Techniques

All techniques discussed in the BASIC section apply to controlling multiple objects, masking and animating in Assembly Language. Using **XOR** or zone clearing will make a very noticeable difference in speed, so much that you will probably have to introduce a delay loop. Sound routines make excellent delay loops. You may like to try writing a video game. Space Invaders is particularly easy.

9

A Graphics Editor

In this chapter we'll explore using the computer as a sketch pad. We'll no longer be interested in creating and animating objects, but only in drawing pictures. We'll make a *graphics editor*—a program to draw and modify pictures. As we add tools to it, we'll learn some new graphics commands and options.

AN OVERVIEW

Our graphics editor will be composed of a series of sketching tools which we will choose and manipulate with the keyboard. For example, one of our tools will be a pencil. We'll be able to pick up the pencil, draw for a little, then put it down. With another tool, we'll be able to spray a pattern over the screen. As a sneak preview of things to come, and for reference, here's a summary of our graphics editor's features:

Normal Function Keys

1 - pencil
3 - lines
5 - rectangles
7 - circles + ellipses
9 - pen

2 - select color
4 - select palette
6 - select background color
8 - clear
10 - help

Alternate Function Keys

1 - paint
3 - spray
5 - cut
7 - copy
9 - move

2 - select paint pattern
4 -
6 -
8 -
10 -

There are three main parts to the graphics editor:

1. A section to interpret commands (including selecting tools);
2. A section to move the tools; and
3. The tool subroutines.

We'll tackle part one in Section 9.1 and part two in Section 9.2. The rest of the chapter, including part of Section 9.2, will be devoted to part three.

9.1: THE FOUNDATION

Let's start by laying down the foundation for our graphics editor. We'll make our program keyboard driven and use the function keys to select drawing tools. As with our animation programs, our editor will center about a main loop that calls subroutines. The main loop will check for and act upon commands. We'll add all our drawing tools as subroutines.

Let's code. As usual, we'll start off by setting up some constants and initializing the graphics screen. The constants in line **140** will be used when checking for command keys:

```
10 OPTION BASE 1
20 RESOLUTION = 4

100 TRUE = -1 : FALSE = 0
110 IF RESOLUTION = 4 THEN MAXXRES = 320 : MAXYRES =
    200 ELSE MAXXRES = 640 : MAXYRES = 200
120 COLOR. = 1
140 ESC = 27 : F1 = 59 : F2 = 60 : F3 = 61 : F4 = 62 :
    F5 = 63 : F6 = 64 : F7 = 65 : F8 = 66 : F9 = 67 :
    F10 = 68

300 '
301 'set graphics mode
302 '
310 IF RESOLUTION = 4 THEN SCREEN 1 ELSE SCREEN 2
320 CLS
330 KEY OFF
```

Now we'll call a subroutine to do final preparations for the main program:

```
400 '
401 'set up
402 '
410 GOSUB 21010        'set up
```

As mentioned, we'll use the function keys to select drawing tools. But BASIC uses these as *soft keys*; when they are pressed, they type out various commands. So first we need to deactivate them. We'll do this in subroutine **21000**:

```
21000 '
21001 'set up
21002 '
21010 FOR KEY. = 1 TO 10 : KEY KEY.,"" : NEXT
      'disable function keys
21600 RETURN
```

Now we're ready for the main loop:

```
500 '
501 'main loop
502 '
510 WHILE NOT FINISHED
520    GOSUB 22010      'get command
600 WEND
700 END
```

Line **520** calls a subroutine to get commands. We'll select drawing tools from this subroutine. Let's look at it:

```
22000 '
22001 'get command
22002 '
22010 COMMAND$ = INKEY$
22020 IF LEN(COMMAND$) = 0 THEN 22600
22030 IF ASC(COMMAND$) = ESC THEN FINISHED = TRUE
22060 IF LEN(COMMAND$) <> 2 THEN 22500 ELSE COMMAND$ =
      RIGHT$(COMMAND$,1) + " "
22500 DUMMY$ = INKEY$ : WHILE LEN(DUMMY$) <> 0 : DUMMY$
      = INKEY$ : WEND           'clear buffer
22600 RETURN
```

> Switch into Chapter 9's directory with:
>
> **CHDIR** "\
> **CHDIR** "CHAPTER9
>
> Load the foundation with:
>
> **LOAD** "1

Line **22010** strobes the keyboard for commands with **INKEY$**. We have already seen how this keeps the program from halting for a command and how it doesn't *echo* typed characters to the screen. If no key has been pressed, then the length of **COMMAND$** will be 0, causing line **22020** to jump to the subroutine's end. If escape has been pressed, then **FINISHED** will be set to true, terminating the main loop. If a function key has been pressed, **COMMAND$** will be two characters long, with a 0 for the first character and the extended character code for the second. Before we examine any two character commands, we'll move the extended character to the first position. This move will allow us to check **COMMAND$**'s value with **ASC**. Line **22060** does this. As we add drawing tool subroutines, we'll check for more commands. Line **22500** clears the buffer.

9.2: FREEHAND SKETCHING—THE PENCIL

Now that our framework is complete, we're ready to add our first drawing tool—the pencil. We'll move the pencil around the screen and leave a trail of dots when we choose.

We'll move the pencil with the arrow keys and indicate its position with a graphics cursor. If we want the simulated pencil to touch the screen, we'll plot points where the cursor lies.

The Graphics Cursor

Let's start by creating a *graphics cursor*. Cursors point to the part of the screen being examined. But the computer doesn't have a cursor for the graphics screen; we'll have to make one ourselves.

A cursor needs two properties: it must clearly indicate what part of the screen is being examined, and it must not destroy any graphics data.

Figure 9.1
We'll use a small arrow for the graphics cursor.

We can satisfy the second requirement by setting up the cursor as a **PUT** array. We'll satisfy the first requirement by using a small arrow for the cursor's shape (Figure 9.1). When we **PUT** an array to a coordinate, the upper left corner of the data gets placed at the coordinate. Therefore, our arrow points to the upper left. We'll convert our cursor to **PUT** array data ourselves (Figure 9.2).

16	WIDTH
4	HEIGHT
55H	
50H	DATA
44H	
41H	

Figure 9.2
PUT array data for the graphics cursor.

Let's load the cursor array from our setup subroutine:

```
21020 DIM CURSOR1%(6) : FOR POSITION = 1 TO 6 : READ
      CURSOR1%(POSITION) : NEXT    'get PUT array for
      cursor1

26000 '
26001 'DATA
26002 '
26003 '
26004 'cursor 1
26005 '
26010 DATA 16, 4, &H55, &H50, &H44, &H41
```

Moving the Cursor

Now let's create a routine to move the cursor. We'll use two variables, **CURSOR1X** and **CURSOR1Y**, to keep track of its position. We'll start the cursor at the center of the screen:

```
130 CURSOR1X = MAXXRES/2 : CURSOR1Y = MAXYRES/2
```

266   A Graphics Editor

We'll use a variable, **CURSOR1SHOW**, to tell if the cursor is currently displayed. Remember that **PUT**ting the cursor twice erases it. **CURSOR1SHOW** will keep us from accidentally erasing the cursor and from leaving cursors on the screen.

We'll start our cursor-moving routine by seeing if the cursor is currently displayed. If it isn't, we'll display it if possible:

```
23000 '
23001 'move cursor
23002 '
23003 '    arrow keys move cursor
23009 '
23010 IF NOT CURSOR1SHOW THEN IF (CURSOR1X >= 0) AND
      (CURSOR1X < (MAXXRES - CURSOR1%(1) * RESOLUTION /
      8)) AND (CURSOR1Y >= 0) AND (CURSOR1Y < MAXYRES -
      CURSOR1%(2)) THEN PUT (CURSOR1X,CURSOR1Y),
      CURSOR1% : CURSOR1SHOW = TRUE
```

Note that **23010** doesn't **PUT** the cursor if part of the array will go off the screen. This prevents **Illegal function call** errors.

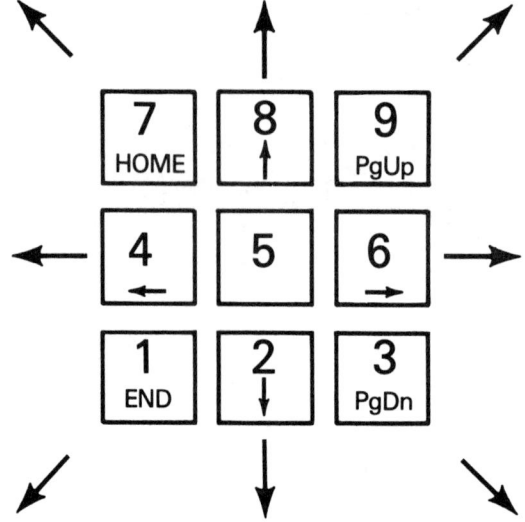

Figure 9.3
We'll move the cursor with the arrow keys.

Now we'll move the cursor with the arrow keys (Figure 9.3). We'll see which, if any, arrow keys have been pressed, and determine by how much to change the x and y coordinates of the cursor's position:

```
23020 IF LEN(COMMAND$) <> 2 THEN 23600
23070 GOSUB 24010        'read movement values
```

```
150 DELTA = 1
160 INS = 82 : CURSLFT = 75 : CURSRT = 77 : CURSDWN =
    80 : CURSUP = 72 : HOME = 71 : END. = 79 : PGUP =
    73 : PGDWN = 81 : DEL = 83

24000 '
24001 'get movement values
24002 '
24003 '     movement according to direction of arrow
      keys
24004 '
24010 IF ASC(COMMAND$) = CURSLFT THEN XCHANGE = -DELTA
      : YCHANGE = 0 : GOTO 24600
24020 IF ASC(COMMAND$) = CURSRT THEN XCHANGE = DELTA :
      YCHANGE = 0 : GOTO 24600
24030 IF ASC(COMMAND$) = CURSUP THEN XCHANGE = 0 :
      YCHANGE = -DELTA = GOTO 24600
24040 IF ASC(COMMAND$) = CURSDWN THEN XCHANGE = 0 :
      YCHANGE = DELTA : GOTO 24600
24050 IF ASC(COMMAND$) = HOME THEN XCHANGE = -DELTA :
      YCHANGE = -DELTA : GOTO 24600
24060 IF ASC(COMMAND$) = END. THEN XCHANGE = -DELTA :
      YCHANGE = DELTA : GOTO 24600
24070 IF ASC(COMMAND$) = PGUP THEN XCHANGE = DELTA :
      YCHANGE = -DELTA : GOTO 24600
24080 IF ASC(COMMAND$) = PGDWN THEN XCHANGE = DELTA :
      YCHANGE = DELTA : GOTO 24600
24090 XCHANGE = 0 : YCHANGE = 0
24600 RETURN
```

Once we call **24000**, we find the new cursor position:

```
23100 NEWCURSOR1X = CURSOR1X + XCHANGE : NEWCURSOR1Y =
      CURSOR1Y + YCHANGE
```

and erase the old cursor:

```
23110 IF CURSOR1SHOW THEN PUT (CURSOR1X,CURSOR1Y),
      CURSOR1% : CURSOR1SHOW = FALSE
```

Then, we update the cursor position, and if possible, plot the new cursor:

```
23120 CURSOR1X = NEWCURSOR1X : CURSOR1Y = NEWCURSOR1Y
23130 IF (CURSOR1X >= 0) AND (CURSOR1X < (MAXXRES -
      CURSOR1%(1) * RESOLUTION / 8)) AND (CURSOR1Y >=
      0) AND (CURSOR1Y < MAXYRES - CURSOR1%(2)) THEN
      PUT (CURSOR1X,CURSOR1Y), CURSOR1% : CURSOR1SHOW =
      TRUE
23600 RETURN
```

Putting It Together For The Pencil

Now that we can control the cursor, let's create our pencil subroutine. We'll base it on the command **PSET**.

PSET plots one point on the graphics screen. Its format is:

PSET (x,y) [,color]

(x,y) tells what point to plot with **color**. The default color is 3 in medium resolution and 1 in high resolution.

Let's try it out. We'll plot a row of dots:

FOR DOT = 1 TO 50 STEP 4 : PSET (DOT,10), 1 : NEXT

To simulate a pencil, we'll set up a Boolean, **PLOT**, to indicate whether or not to **PSET** the dot pointed to by the cursor. We'll toggle **PLOT** with the insert key.

Let's look at the code:

```
1000 '
1001 'pencil
1002 '
1003 '     arrow keys move the pencil
1004 '     insert toggles plot/don't plot
1005 '
1010 GOSUB 23010       'move cursor
1020 IF INSERT THEN PLOT = NOT PLOT
1030 IF NOT PLOT THEN 1600
1040 IF CURSOR1SHOW THEN PUT (CURSOR1X,CURSOR1Y),
     CURSOR1%
1050 PSET (CURSOR1X,CURSOR1Y), COLOR.
1060 IF CURSOR1SHOW THEN PUT (CURSOR1X,CURSOR1Y),
     CURSOR1%
1600 RETURN
```

Note that we erase the cursor before plotting. Thus, when we erase the cursor later (for example, after moving it to a new position) the newly plotted point won't be erased.

We also need to add:

```
23004 '     INSERT goes true if insert pressed
23020 IF LEN(COMMAND$) <> 2 THEN INSERT = FALSE : GOTO
      23600
23030 IF ASC(COMMAND$) = INS THEN INSERT = TRUE ELSE
      INSERT = FALSE
```

We check for the pressing of insert in subroutine **23000** because a letter command could give a one character code with the same ASCII value as insert.

We'll pick up the pencil by hitting F1:

```
540    ON MODE GOSUB 1010
22080 IF ASC(COMMAND$) = F1 THEN MODE = 1
```

> **MERGE** "2 to load all code in this section.

Trying it Out

Hit F1 to pick up the pencil, then move the cursor. Hit insert to start plotting, and hit insert again to stop plotting. Try drawing a circle and a box, and try writing your name.

9.3: CHOOSING THE COLOR

Now let's add a routine to change the color of the dots being plotted. To get the color, we'll read the keyboard until a key has been pressed. We'll use **VAL** to convert this key to a number to which to set the color:

```
2000 '
2001 'change color
2002 '
2003 '     reads one key for color
2005 '
2010 COLOR.$ = INKEY$ : WHILE LEN(COLOR.$) = 0 :
     COLOR.$ = INKEY$ : WEND
2020 COLOR. = VAL(COLOR.$) MOD (16/RESOLUTION)
2600 RETURN
```

Line **2020** prevents **COLOR.** from taking on an illegal value.

We'll call this routine by hitting F2:

```
540 ON MODE GOSUB 1010, 2010
22090 IF ASC(COMMAND$) = F2 THEN MODE = 2
```

We should change color without having to drop and reselect the drawing tool. So, once we change color, we'll return to the previous mode:

```
2004 '     returns to previous mode
```

```
2030 MODE = OLDMODE
22070 OLDMODE = MODE
```

> MERGE "3

OLDMODE gets updated every time **COMMAND$** is two characters long.

Try changing the color: hit F2 and then a number. If you want to erase dots, set the color to zero.

9.4: CHANGING THE PALETTE

To change the palette we'll use a subroutine called by pressing F4. It will read a key from the keyboard, convert it to a number with **VAL**, set the palette with **COLOR**, and return to the previous mode. Because changing the palette is illegal in high resolution, the subroutine will return immediately if called in high resolution:

```
540 ON MODE GOSUB 1010, 2010, 3010

3000 '
3001 'select palette
3002 '
3003 '     reads one key for palette
3004 '     returns to previous mode
3005 '
3010 IF RESOLUTION = 8 THEN 3050
3020 PALETTE$ = INKEY$ : WHILE LEN(PALETTE$) = 0 :
     PALETTE$ = INKEY$ : WEND
3030 PALETTE = VAL(PALETTE$) MOD 2
3040 COLOR ,PALETTE
3050 MODE = OLDMODE
3600 RETURN

22100 IF ASC(COMMAND$) = F4 THEN MODE = 3
```

> MERGE "4

9.5: CHANGING THE BACKGROUND COLOR

If we are in medium resolution, we can also change the background color. The background color is a value between 0 and 32 and also affects the intensity of the foreground color. Changing the background color is similar to changing the foreground color, only we need to read two key strokes:

```
4000 '
4001 'change background color
4002 '
4003 '     reads two digits
4004 '     returns to previous mode
4005 '
4010 IF RESOLUTION = 8 THEN 4600
4020 BKGD$ = INKEY$ : WHILE LEN(BKGD$) = 0 : BKGD$ =
     INKEY$ : WEND
4030 BKGD2$ = INKEY$ : WHILE LEN(BKGD2$) = 0 : BKGD2$ =
     INKEY$ : WEND
4040 BKGDCOLOR = VAL(BKGD$ + BKGD2$) MOD 33
4050 COLOR BKGDCOLOR
4060 MODE = OLDMODE
4600 RETURN
```

We'll set this up as mode 4, called by F6:

```
540 ON MODE GOSUB 1010, 2010, 3010, 4010
22110 IF ASC(COMMAND$) = F6 THEN MODE = 4
```

MERGE "5

9.6: CLEARING THE SCREEN

We'll use F8 to clear the screen:

```
540 ON MODE GOSUB 1010, 2010, 3010, 4010, 5010

22120 IF ASC(COMMAND$) = F8 THEN MODE = 5

5000 '
5001 'clear the screen
5002 '
5010 CLS
5020 CURSOR1SHOW = FALSE
5600 RETURN
```

272   A Graphics Editor

MERGE "6

Note that we have set **CURSOR1SHOW** to false.

9.7: LINE DRAWING

Now we'll add the next major drawing feature—a line-drawing tool. Instead of plotting every point on the line, we'll just specify the line's end points. This will make drawing long and angled lines much easier.

Two cursors are used to specify the end points. The first cursor is moved to the first end point, the second is moved to the second end point, and insert is hit to draw the line.

Manipulating the Cursors

Let's start by adding code to manipulate two cursors. We'll make the second cursor the same shape as the first, but of a different medium-resolution color:

```
21030 DIM CURSOR2%(6) : FOR POSITION = 1 TO 6 : READ
      CURSOR2%(POSITION) : NEXT
26020 '
26021 'cursor 2
26022 '
26030 DATA 16, 4, &HAA, &HA0, &H88, &H82
```

Now we'll modify subroutine **23000** to control two cursors. If **CURCURSOR** is 0, we'll move the first cursor; if it is 1, we'll move the second:

```
23080 IF CURCURSOR = 1 THEN 23200
23140 GOTO 23600
23200 NEWCURSOR2X = CURSOR2X + XCHANGE : NEWCURSOR2Y =
      CURSOR2Y + YCHANGE
23210 IF CURSOR2SHOW THEN PUT (CURSOR2X,CURSOR2Y),
      CURSOR2% : CURSOR2SHOW = FALSE
23220 CURSOR2X = NEWCURSOR2X : CURSOR2Y = NEWCURSOR2Y
23230 IF (CURSOR2X >= 0) AND (CURSOR2X < (MAXXRES -
      CURSOR2%(1) * RESOLUTION / 8)) AND (CURSOR2Y >=
      0) AND (CURSOR2Y < MAXYRES - CURSOR2%(2)) THEN
      PUT (CURSOR2X,CURSOR2Y), CURSOR2% : CURSOR2SHOW =
      TRUE
```

Drawing the Lines

Now, we'll add the routine to draw lines. Controlling two cursors is similar to controlling one, only we need to indicate which cursor to manipulate. We'll use a few closely related approaches throughout this chapter. These variations will give you a brief idea of the possibilities. You may wish to standardize the controlling method later.

For our line-drawing routine, we'll start off moving the first cursor. We'll hit insert to stick it to the screen and bring out the second cursor. The arrow keys will then move the second cursor. We'll hit delete to reposition the first cursor. The second time insert is pressed, we'll draw the line.

To start, check to see if delete has been pressed:

```
23020 IF LEN(COMMAND$) <> 2 THEN INSERT = FALSE :
      DELETE. = FALSE : GOTO 23600
23040 IF ASC(COMMAND$) = DEL THEN DELETE. = TRUE ELSE
      DELETE. = FALSE
```

Now, we're ready for the line-drawing routine:

```
6000 '
6001 'draw lines
6002 '
6003 '     arrow keys move dot cursors
6004'      insert plants first cursor
6005 '     second insert draws line
6006 '     delete returns movement to first cursor
6007 '
6010 GOSUB 23010      'move cursors
6020 IF DELETE. THEN CURCURSOR = 0 : GOTO 6600
6030 IF INSERT THEN IF INSCNT = 0 THEN INSCNT = 1 :
     CURSOR2X = CURSOR1X : CURSOR2Y = CURSOR1Y :
     CURSOR2SHOW = FALSE : CURCURSOR = 1 : GOTO 6600
     ELSE : ELSE GOTO 6600
6100 IF CURSOR1SHOW THEN PUT (CURSOR1X,CURSOR1Y),
     CURSOR1% : CURSOR1SHOW = FALSE
6110 IF CURSOR2SHOW THEN PUT (CURSOR2X,CURSOR2Y),
     CURSOR2% : CURSOR2SHOW = FALSE
6120 INSCNT = 0 : CURCURSOR = 0
6130 LINE (CURSOR1X,CURSOR1Y) - (CURSOR2X,CURSOR2Y),
     COLOR.
6140 CURSOR1X = CURSOR2X : CURSOR1Y = CURSOR2Y
6600 RETURN
```

Line **6010** moves the cursors, and line **6020** returns movement to the first cursor if delete has been pressed. Line **6030** checks if insert has been pressed. If it is the first time insert has been pressed, **CURCURSOR** gets set to 1, and the second cursor's position is initialized to that of the first. If it is the second time insert has been pressed, then the cursors are cleared and a line is drawn. Note that the cursors are cleared so that parts of the line won't be erased when the cursors move.

After drawing, **CURCURSOR** and **INSCNT** are reset, and the first cursor moves to the second cursor's position.

We'll set line drawing as mode 6, called by F3:

```
540 ON MODE GOSUB 1010, 2010, 3010, 4010, 5010, 6010
22130 IF ASC(COMMAND$) = F3 THEN MODE = 6
```

```
MERGE "7P1
```

You may have noticed that the thousands place of the line number indicates the mode of the subroutine. This is helpful in reading the program.

Trying It Out

Hit F3 to get into line-drawing mode. Place the first cursor, move the second, and hit insert. Then, place the first cursor, move the second, hit delete, and reposition the first cursor before drawing.

Next, place the first cursor, position the second, then hit F1, which changes the mode. The second cursor will be left on the screen, and there will be no way to remove it (except by plotting over it in color 0). This is unfortunate, because we can accidentally clog the screen with unused cursors. To get rid of this problem, we'll add the following subroutine to clear cursors and reset parameters:

```
25000 '
25001 'reset parameters to clear screen of junk if mode
      accidentally changed
25002 '   gets rid of any cursors showing, resets
      counters
25003 '
25010 IF CURSOR1SHOW THEN PUT (CURSOR1X,CURSOR1Y),
      CURSOR1% : CURSOR1SHOW = FALSE
25020 IF CURSOR2SHOW THEN PUT (CURSOR2X,CURSOR2Y),
      CURSOR2% : CURSOR2SHOW = FALSE
25030 INSCNT = 0 : CURCURSOR = 0 : INSERT = FALSE :
      DELETE. = FALSE
25600 RETURN
```

We'll call it whenever we switch drawing tools (for example, from pencil to line drawing) or whenever we hit escape to terminate the program:

```
530    IF (OLDMODE <> MODE) AND (MODE <> 2) AND (MODE <>
       3) AND (MODE <> 4) THEN GOSUB 25010      'reset
       parameters
610 GOSUB 25010       'reset parameters
```

We'll also add the following to our clear screen subroutine:

```
5030 CURSOR2SHOW = FALSE
```

Changing DELTA

One annoyance remains: It is very slow to get from one corner of the screen to the other. To move faster, we'll change **DELTA** (used in subroutine **24000**). We'll use the < and > keys to increase and decrease **DELTA** by two (you may want to change the increment). These keys are easy to remember, are unlikely to be used by any other modes, and can be struck easily by the hand hitting the arrow keys. So that we can change **DELTA** from any mode, we'll do the checking in the command section:

```
22040 IF COMMAND$ = "<" THEN DELTA = DELTA - 2
22050 IF COMMAND$ = ">" THEN DELTA = DELTA + 2
```

MERGE "7P2

Run the program again, and adjust **DELTA**.

9.8: DRAWING RECTANGLES

Rectangles are a useful and common shape. The quickest way for us to draw rectangles has been to draw four lines. Now, we'll create a mode just to draw rectangles.

We'll do this by using a special feature of the **LINE** command. In full, the format of **LINE** is:

LINE [(x_1,y_1)] — (x_2,y_2) [,[color] [,B[F]] [,style]]

If we use the **B** (Box) option, then a rectangle will be drawn with corner points (x_1,y_1) and (x_2,y_2). Including **F** fills the rectangle. We will examine **style**, a feature of BASIC 2.0 only, in Section 9.9.

Let's draw a box:

LINE (10,20) — (40,60),1,B

Now we'll draw a set of boxes:

FOR BOX = 1 TO 10 : LINE (150 — 4*BOX, 80 — 4*BOX) — (170 + 4*BOX, 120 + 4*BOX), BOX MOD 4, B : NEXT

Let's try the **BF** option:

LINE (10,20) — (40,60), 2, BF

Note that the box is filled with the color of the box's border. We can use **BF** with color 0 to erase large portions of the screen.

The Rectangle-Drawing Mode

Now let's add a tool to our editor to draw rectangles. We'll position the cursors as for the line-drawing mode, only when insert is pressed, we'll draw a rectangle instead of a line. If * is pressed, we'll fill the rectangle:

```
7000 '
7001 'draw a rectangle with corners of cursor1, cursor2
7002 '
7003 '     movement is the same as for line drawing,
      but if
7004 '     * is used instead of second insert, the
      rectangle is filled
7005 '
7010 GOSUB 23010         'move cursors
7020 IF DELETE. THEN CURCURSOR = 0 : GOTO 7600
7030 IF INSERT THEN IF INSCNT = 0 THEN INSCNT = 1 :
      CURSOR2X = CURSOR1X : CURSOR2Y = CURSOR1Y :
      CURCURSOR = 1 : GOTO 7600 ELSE FILL = FALSE : GOTO
      7100
7040 IF COMMAND$ = "*" THEN IF INSCNT = 1 THEN FILL =
      TRUE ELSE 7600 ELSE 7600
7100 IF CURSOR1SHOW THEN PUT (CURSOR1X,CURSOR1Y),
      CURSOR1% : CURSOR1SHOW = FALSE
7110 IF CURSOR2SHOW THEN PUT (CURSOR2X,CURSOR2Y),
```

```
            CURSOR2% : CURSOR2SHOW = FALSE
7120  INSCNT = 0 : CURCURSOR = 0
7130  IF FILL THEN LINE (CURSOR1X,CURSOR1Y) -
      (CURSOR2X,CURSOR2Y), COLOR., BF ELSE LINE
      (CURSOR1X,CURSOR1Y) - (CURSOR2X, CURSOR2Y),
      COLOR., B
7140  CURSOR1X = CURSOR2X : CURSOR1Y = CURSOR2Y
7600  RETURN
```

We'll start this mode by pressing F5:

```
540 ON MODE GOSUB 1010, 2010, 3010, 4010, 5010, 6010,
    7010
22140 IF ASC(COMMAND$) = F5 THEN MODE = 7
```

MERGE "8

Before continuing, type:

SAVE "GRAPHED
NEW

9.9: LINE'S STYLE OPTION

The last line option, **style**, is available only in BASIC 2.0. It is a 16-bit integer value (4 hex digits). When a line is drawn, the computer looks at the current bit of **style**. If it is set, then the current dot is plotted. If it is 0, the current dot is not plotted. The computer starts by checking the first bit of **style** (the most significant bit) for the first point, the second for the second, and so on. After checking the sixteenth bit, the computer returns to the first.

For example, let's draw a dashed line. We'll set **style** to 11001100 11001100B:

LINE (10,50) — (80,50),1,,&HCCCC

Let's do another:

LINE (10,50) — (80,50),2,,&H3333

A zero bit in **style** causes the background to be untouched.

Now try:

LINE (10,10) — (10,80),1,,&HCCCC

Note how the style pattern appears again, this time vertically.

Complications

Actually, the effect of **style** is more complex than indicated. Depending on the end points, **style** might start at either the first or second end point. For example, try:

CLS LINE (10,80) — (40,80),1,,&H000F

and:

LINE (40,80) — (10,80),2,,&H000F

But now try:

LINE (160,100) — (160,150),1,,&H000F
LINE (160,150) — (160,100),2,,&H000F

The line's angle has an even more interesting effect. Let's try a circle of styled lines:

```
10 CLS
20 FOR ANGLE = 1 TO 360
30     LINE (160,100) - STEP (50 * COS(ANGLE*3.14/180),
       50 * SIN(ANGLE*3.14/180)), 1,, &H2002
40 NEXT
```

    LOAD "9P1

For the bottom half of the circle, every x or y increment advances the bit being examined in **style** (Figure 9.4). But things are more odd for the top half of the circle. It is as if a styled line is rotated, leaving a trail, but with aberrations.

You can use the different way styled lines are drawn to create complex, pretty pictures.

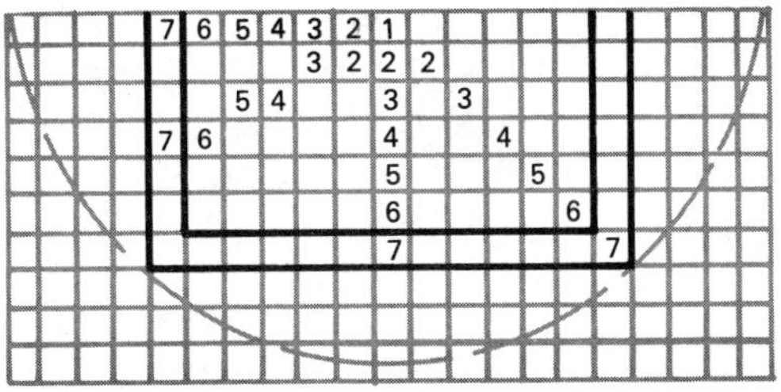

Figure 9.4
For the bottom half of the circle, every increment in the x or y direction advances the bit being examined in style. This figure is drawn with style = &H0040. The dot where the line starts is labeled 1. When the seventh bit of style is reached, a dot is drawn.

Style With Boxes

style can be used with the **B** option, but not with **BF**. Try:

LINE (10,10) — (50,50),2,B,&H9732

Now try:

```
10 CLS
20 FOR BOX = 1 TO 40
30    LINE (140,80) - STEP (BOX,BOX), 1, B, &H233F
40 NEXT
```

> **LOAD "9P2**

Experiment with different patterns. Try drawing a differently styled, differently colored box over the box of line **30**.

9.10: CIRCLES AND ELLIPSES

Now we'll see how to draw circles and ellipses. We'll do this with the **CIRCLE** command. Its format is:

CIRCLE (x,y), radius [,color[,start,end[,axis ratio]]]

CIRCLE draws a circle of radius **radius** with center **(x,y)**. **color** sets the circle's color. **start** and **end** are used to draw incomplete circles. **axis ratio**

sets the ratio of the x to y axis.

With no options, **CIRCLE** draws a complete circle, adjusting for dot width. **radius** gives the horizontal radius. In high resolution, the vertical radius is 5/12 * **radius**; in medium resolution, the vertical radius is 5/6 * **radius**. This makes the circle look correct. Let's try it:

CLS
CIRCLE (30,30), 10

We can specify the color:

CIRCLE (30,30), 10, 2

start and **end** tell from what angle measure to start and end the circle. These angles are in radians, with 0 radians to the right (Figure 3.15).

Let's draw the upper half of a circle:

PI = 3.1415
CIRCLE (60,30), 10, 1, 0, PI

Now the lower half:

CIRCLE (60,30), 10, 2, PI, 0

If **start** or **end** is negative, the absolute value of the angle is used, and a line is drawn to the circle's center. For example, we can draw a wedge with:

CIRCLE (100,30), 10, 1, −.0001, −PI/4

Or a pie chart:

CIRCLE (130,30), 10, 1, −.0001, −PI/2
CIRCLE (130,30), 10, 2, PI/2, −PI
CIRCLE (130,30), 10, 3, PI, 0

axis ratio allows us to change circles into ellipses. It sets the ratio between the x and y axis:

y axis = x axis * axis ratio

If **axis ratio** is less than 1, then **radius** is the x radius. Otherwise, **radius** is the y radius.

For example, to draw an ellipse with an x axis radius of 40 and a y axis radius of 20, try:

CIRCLE (80,80), 40,,,,, .5

Putting Ellipses In Our Program

Now let's add ellipse- (and circle-) drawing capability to our program. We'll use insert to flip from moving the first cursor to moving the second and delete to flip back to moving the first cursor. We'll have three different methods of drawing: if r is hit, we'll draw a circle centered at the first cursor with radius through the second; if d is hit, we'll draw a circle with a diameter between cursor 1 and cursor 2; and if e is hit, we'll draw an ellipse with horizontal axis through cursor 1, and vertical axis through cursor 2 (Figure 9.5).

First reload the graphics editor, with:

LOAD "GRAPHED

Then add:

```
8000 '
8001 'circles and ellipses
8002 '
8003 '     move cursors as for drawing lines
8004 '     if hit r - circle drawn with center =cursor
       1
8005 '                                    radius to
       cursor 2
8006 '     if hit d - circle drawn with diameter
       hitting cursor 1 and cursor 2
8007 '     if hit e - ellipse drawn with vertical axis
       through cursor 2
8008 '                                    horizontal axis
       through cursor 1
8009 '
8010 GOSUB 23010     'move cursors
8020 IF INSERT THEN INSCNT = INSCNT + 1 : IF INSCNT = 1
     THEN CURSOR2X = CURSOR1X : CURSOR2Y = CURSOR1Y :
     CURCURSOR = 1 : GOTO 8600 ELSE CURCURSOR = 1 :
     GOTO 8600
8030 IF DELETE. THEN CURCURSOR = 0 : GOTO 8600
8040 IF INSCNT < 1 THEN 8600
```

282 A Graphics Editor

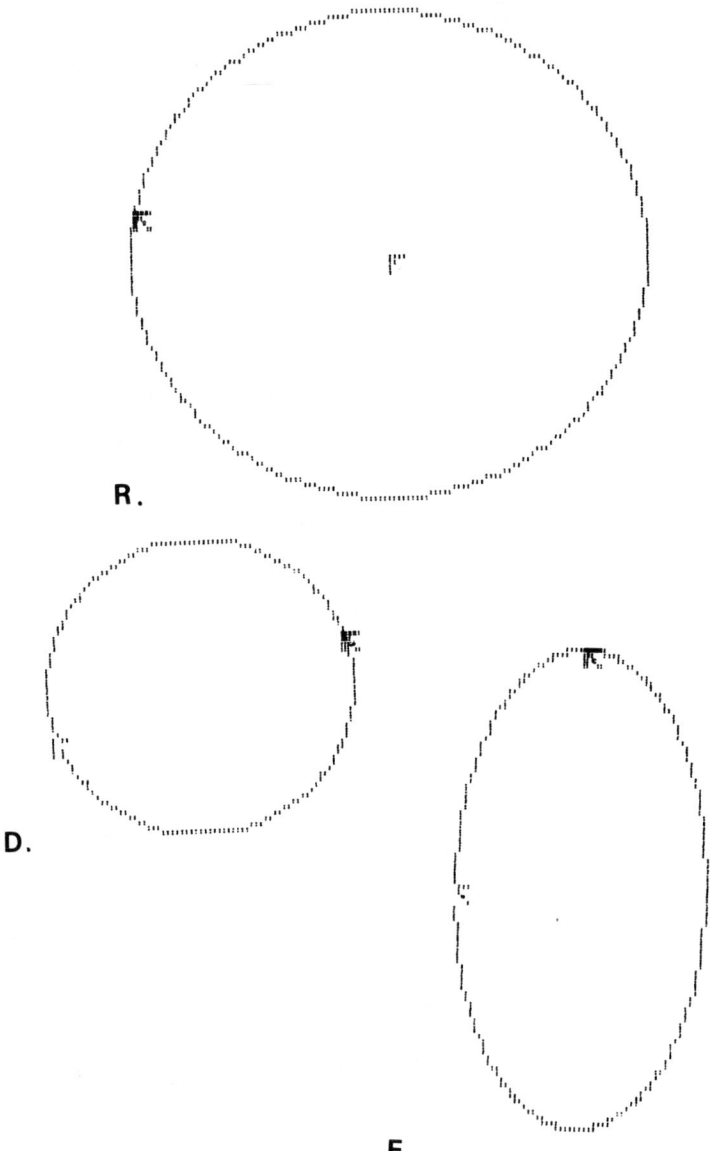

Figure 9.5
r draws a circle with radius through cursors 1 and 2; d draws a circle with diameter through cursors 1 and 2; e draws an ellipse with horizontal axis through cursor 1, vertical axis through cursor 2.

```
8050 IF CURSOR1SHOW THEN PUT (CURSOR1X,CURSOR1Y),
     CURSOR1%
8060 IF CURSOR2SHOW THEN PUT (CURSOR2X,CURSOR2Y),
     CURSOR2%
```

```
8070 IF COMMAND$ = "r" THEN RADIUS = SQR((CURSOR1X -
     CURSOR2X)^2 + (CURSOR1Y - CURSOR2Y)^2) : CIRCLE
     (CURSOR1X,CURSOR1Y), RADIUS, COLOR.
8080 IF COMMAND$ = "d" THEN MIDX = (CURSOR1X +
     CURSOR2X)/2 : MIDY = (CURSOR1Y + CURSOR2Y)/2 :
     RADIUS = SQR((CURSOR1X - MIDX)^2 + (CURSOR1Y -
     MIDY)^2) : CIRCLE (MIDX,MIDY), RADIUS, COLOR.
8090 IF COMMAND$ = "e" THEN AXIS1 = ABS(CURSOR2Y -
     CURSOR1Y) : AXIS2 = ABS(CURSOR2X - CURSOR1X) : IF
     AXIS1/AXIS2 > 1 THEN CIRCLE (CURSOR2X,CURSOR1Y),
     AXIS1, COLOR.,,, AXIS1/AXIS2 ELSE CIRCLE
     (CURSOR2X,CURSOR1Y), AXIS2, COLOR.,,, AXIS1/AXIS2
8100 IF CURSOR1SHOW THEN PUT (CURSOR1X,CURSOR1Y),
     CURSOR1%
8110 IF CURSOR2SHOW THEN PUT (CURSOR2X,CURSOR2Y),
     CURSOR2%
8600 RETURN
```

If insert is pressed, **INSCNT** is increased. The first time insert is pressed, the second cursor is set to the position of the first; all other times, control is simply passed to the second cursor. When delete is pressed, the first cursor is manipulated. Lines **8050** and **8060** clear the cursors in case an ellipse is about to be drawn, **8100** and **8110** replace the cursors.

If r is pressed, line **8070** computes the radius using the Pythagorean distance formula, and draws a circle:

radius $= [(x_1 - x_2)^2 + (y_1 - y_2)^2]^{1/2}$

If d is pressed, then the center of the circle is the midpoint of the line connecting both cursors, and the radius is half the distance between the two cursors:

center $= ((x_1 + x_2)/2, (y_1 + y_2)/2)$
radius $= [(x_1 - x_2)^2 + (y_1 - y_2)^2]^{1/2}/2$

If e is pressed, the center of the ellipse is taken from the x coordinate of the second cursor and the y coordinate of the first. If the ratio between the lengths of the two axes is greater than 1, then **radius** is set to the y radius, otherwise **radius** is set to the x radius:

center $= (x_2, y_1)$
axis ratio $= |y_1 - y_2| / |x_1 - x_2|$
radius $= \max(|x_1 - x_2|, |y_1 - y_2|)$

We'll call circle drawing by hitting F7:

```
540 ON MODE GOSUB 1010, 2010, 3010, 4010, 5010, 6010,
    7010, 8010
22150 IF ASC(COMMAND$) = F7 THEN MODE = 8
```

MERGE "10

Try all three circle-drawing modes. See how to move the cursors to draw several concentric circles. Move ellipses about a central origin to make them look as if they are rotating. Think about using the other **CIRCLE** parameters in the graphics editor.

9.11: PAINTING

Painting—filling of an area with color—is an extremely useful function. In BASIC 1.1 we can only paint areas with solid colors. But in BASIC 2.0 we can fill in areas with patterns, a very powerful capability. (For example, we could paint bricks or paneling on a building.)

Our painting subroutine is based on the BASIC command **PAINT**. Its format is:

PAINT (x,y) [[,paint] [,boundary] [,background]]

(x,y) tells where to begin painting; **paint** is the color or pattern with which to paint; **boundary** indicates the color of the boundary lines of the shape to be filled; and **background**, only valid in BASIC 2.0, is generally useless.

PAINT From BASIC 1.1

In BASIC 1.1, **paint** must be a color number. In high resolution it is either 0 or 1, and in medium resolution it is 0 - 3. Let's try it out in medium resolution:

PAINT (20,20), 1

Because no boundary color was given, the whole screen was filled.
Now try:

PAINT (20,20), 2

The screen will be filled with color 2 instead of color 1. Filling the whole screen isn't particularly useful—**COLOR** would be more efficient. But now let's use **boundary**. First, draw a circle:

CLS
CIRCLE (160,100), 30, 1

We'll fill it with color 2:

PAINT (160,100), 2, 1

Color 2 will fill the circle starting at point (160,100) and extending until a color 1 boundary is met. Let's change the color to color 1:

PAINT (160,100), 1, 1

If we want to change the color again, we'll have to fill until a boundary of color 0.

Now, let's draw another circle:

CIRCLE (160,100), 50, 1

Let's fill the outer circle only with color 3:

PAINT (115,100), 3, 1

As you can see, **PAINT** can fill complex areas. Now, do:

CIRCLE (160,100), 60, 2
PAINT (155,100), 2, 2

Because the outer circle is the only one with color 2 as a boundary, the whole circle is filled.

When filling a shape, we need to make sure that it has no holes. Paint will escape from the smallest of holes, causing unpleasant results. For example, try:

CLS
LINE (10,100) − (50,150), 1, B
PSET (10,112), 0
PAINT (20,120), 2, 1

PAINT in BASIC 2.0

BASIC 2.0 unleashes the power of **PAINT**. We're no longer restricted to simple colors: we can fill areas in with patterns. The patterns are defined as a block of points, up to 1 byte wide and 64 bytes high, to be repeated throughout the area to be filled. So, in high resolution, we can make an 8-by-64-dot black and white pattern; in medium resolution, a 4-by-64-dot four color pattern can be made.

We'll examine creating the repeating patterns in medium resolution. The process is the same, but somewhat easier, in high resolution.

We need to pick a pattern that can be formed by placing a four dot wide pattern next to itself over and over again. Figure 9.6 shows a 4-by-6-dot brick pattern. Note how, when repeated, it will fill an area with bricks.

Developing the pattern is illustrated in Figures 9.7–9.10.

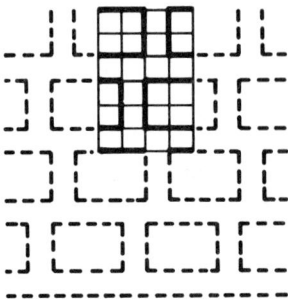

Figure 9.6
A 4 by 6 dot brick pattern. When repeated, it fills an area with bricks.

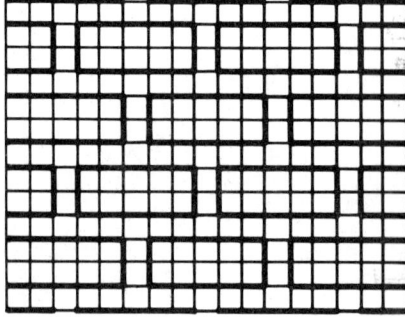

Figure 9.7
Draw the pattern on graph paper.

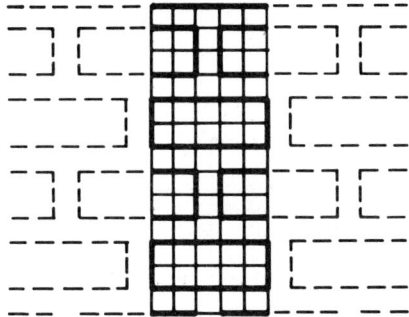

Figure 9.8
Divide it vertically into the smallest pattern which when repeated creates the whole pattern.

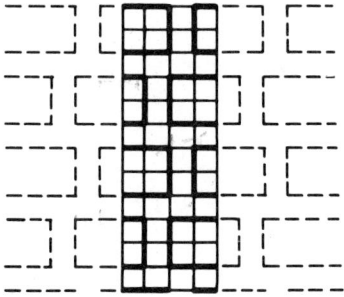

Figure 9.9
Place the pattern into a four dot wide column. Some adjustments may need to be made. For example, bricks can no longer start over the center of the brick below.

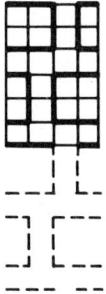

Figure 9.10
Divide the pattern horizontally into the smallest unit which, when repeated, creates the whole pattern.

The pattern needs to be fed to **PAINT** as a string. First, we find the screen data for the pattern (Figure 9.11). We've gone through this process several times before.

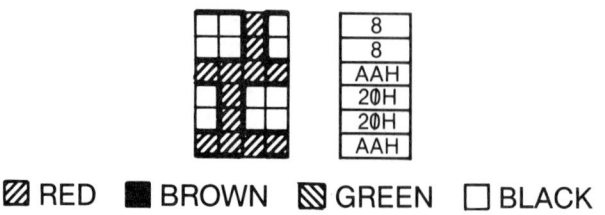

Figure 9.11
Screen data for the brick pattern.

Now, we turn this data into a string using **CHR$**. Our data for the bricks is:

8   8   &HAA   &H20   &H20   &HAA

Therefore, our pattern string is:

BRICK$ = CHR$(8) + CHR$(8) + CHR$(&HAA) + CHR$(&H20) + CHR$(&H20) + CHR$(&HAA)

To paint with bricks, we use **BRICK$** for **paint**:

LINE (30,30) − STEP (30,30), 1, B
PAINT (35,35), BRICK$, 1

You can see how powerful this is. The only drawback is that patterns can only be four dots wide (or eight in high resolution). Also, you cannot use **CHR$(0)** as the pattern string.

The last parameter, **background**, is used to fill an area that has a pattern in it with the boundary color. But, it is so limited that it is ineffective. The *BASIC Manual* gives a sample program using **background**. You may want to try it.

Adding Paint to our Program

Now let's add painting to our program. We'll do it with the BASIC 2.0 **PAINT** capabilities. If you don't have BASIC 2.0, you'll need to change your program accordingly. We'll use the patterns shown in Figure 9.12. You may want to change these or add your own.

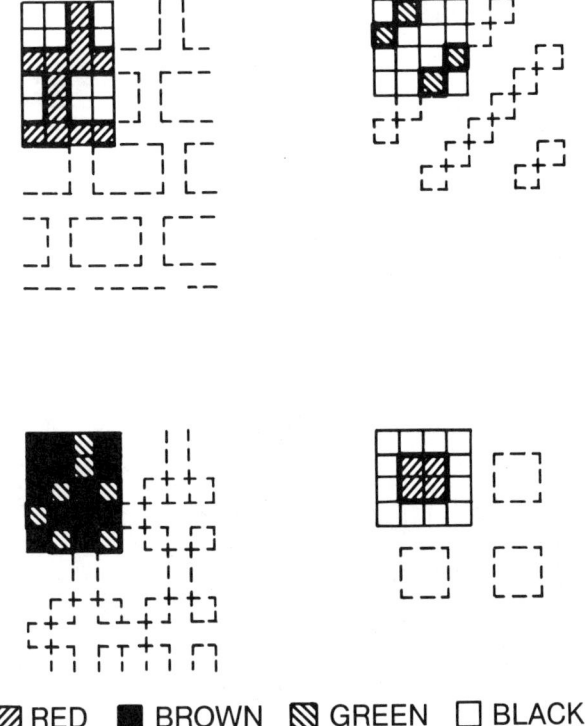

Figure 9.12
Patterns 0 through 3 are the solid colors 0 through 3. Patterns 4 through 7 are shown in the figure. Pattern 8 is the same as pattern 7, but on a color 1 background.

To fill an area, we'll move the cursor into the area, then hit insert and enter the border color. Beforehand, we need to have selected the fill pattern.

We'll start by reading the patterns into a string array:

```
21040 READ NUMPATTERNS
21050 DIM PATTERNS$(NUMPATTERNS)
21060 FOR PATTERN = 1 TO NUMPATTERNS
21070   READ PATTERNLENGTH
21080   FOR POSITION = 1 TO PATTERNLENGTH
21090     READ PAT : PATTERNS$(PATTERN) =
          PATTERNS$(PATTERN) + CHR$(PAT)
21100   NEXT
21110 NEXT
21120 PATTERN = 1
```

```
26040 '
26041 'patterns for DOS 2.0 tiling
26042 '
26043 '       number of patterns
26044 '
26050 DATA 9
26060 '       color 0
26061 '
26070 DATA 1, 0
26080 '
26081 '       color 1
26090 DATA 1, &H55
26100 '
26101 '       color 2
26110 DATA 1, &HAA
26120 '
26121 '       color 3
26130 DATA 1, &HFF
26140 '
26141 '       bricks - color 2
26150 DATA 6, 8, 8, &HAA, &H20, &H20, &HAA
26160 '
26161 '       diagonal stripes - color 1
26170 DATA 4, &H10, &H40, 1, 4
26180 '
26181 '       diamonds - color 1 lines, color 3 bkgd
26190 DATA 5, &HF7, &HF7, &HDD, &H7F, &HDD
26200 '
26201 '       squares - color2 on color 0 bkgd
26210 DATA 4, 0, &H28, &H28, 0
26220 '
26221 '       squares - color2 on color 1 bkgd
26230 DATA 4, &H55, &H69, &H69, &H55
```

Now we'll add a subroutine to select the pattern:

```
9000 '
9001 'select fill pattern
9002 '
9003 '       reads 2 digits
9004 '       returns to previous mode
9005 '
9010 FILL$ = INKEY$ : WHILE LEN(FILL$) = 0 : FILL$ =
     INKEY$ : WEND
9020 FILL2$ = INKEY$ : WHILE LEN(FILL2$) = 0 : FILL2$ =
     INKEY$ : WEND
9030 PATTERN = 1 + VAL(FILL$ + FILL2$) MOD NUMPATTERNS
9040 MODE = OLDMODE
9600 RETURN
```

A Graphics Editor

And a subroutine to paint areas:

```
10000 '
10001 'paint in an area
10002 '
10003 '      move cursor with arrow keys into area to
      fill
10004 '
10010 GOSUB 23010      'move cursors
10020 IF NOT INSERT THEN 10600
10030 IF CURSOR1SHOW THEN PUT (CURSOR1X,CURSOR1Y),
      CURSOR1%
10040 BKGD$ = INKEY$ : WHILE LEN(BKGD$) = 0 : BKGD$ =
      INKEY$ : WEND : BKGD = VAL(BKGD$)
10050 IF PATTERN = 1 THEN PAINT (CURSOR1X,CURSOR1Y), 0,
      BKGD ELSE PAINT (CURSOR1X,CURSOR1Y),
      PATTERNS$(PATTERN), BKGD
10060 IF CURSOR1SHOW THEN PUT (CURSOR1X,CURSOR1Y),
      CURSOR1%
10600 RETURN
```

Note how we need to use an **IF** statement to fill with color 0.

We'll make selecting the pattern mode 9, chosen by alternate-F2, and the painting mode 10, chosen by alternate-F1. We use the alternate-function keys (alt and a function key pressed at the same time) because most of the regular function keys are in use:

```
170 ALTF1 = 104 : ALTF2 = 105 : ALTF3 = 106 : ALTF4 =
    107 : ALTF5 = 108 : ALTF6 = 109 : ALTF7 = 110 :
    ALTF8 = 111 : ALTF9 = 112 : ALTF10 = 113

540 ON MODE GOSUB 1010, 2010, 3010, 4010, 5010, 6010,
    7010, 8010, 9010, 10010

22160 IF ASC(COMMAND$) = ALTF2 THEN MODE = 9
22170 IF ASC(COMMAND$) = ALTF1 THEN MODE = 10
```

MERGE "11

Trying It Out

Paint several areas. Create new fill patterns.

A Graphics Editor

The Mechanics of Patterned Color Fill

You may wonder how the computer can fill a complex area, no matter the size, shape or location, with a complex pattern, regardless of the size and form, without difficulty. The technique is really pretty simple; the pattern is memory mapped over the whole screen. In other words, the same part of the pattern will always appear at a given location. The first byte in every column of the screen gets the first byte of the pattern. The rest of the pattern fills the column, repeating once the last element is used.

The part of the pattern used for a particular dot can be computed as follows:

byte within the pattern = 1 + (y mod patternlen)
dot within the byte = 1 + (x mod resolution)

resolution tells the number of dots per byte. **patternlen** is the length of the pattern. **x** and **y** are the coordinates of the point.

9.12: CALLIGRAPHY PEN

The next tool we'll add to our drawing program is a *calligraphy pen* with a user defined *nib*. This will allow quick filling of areas and calligraphic writing (Figure 9.13).

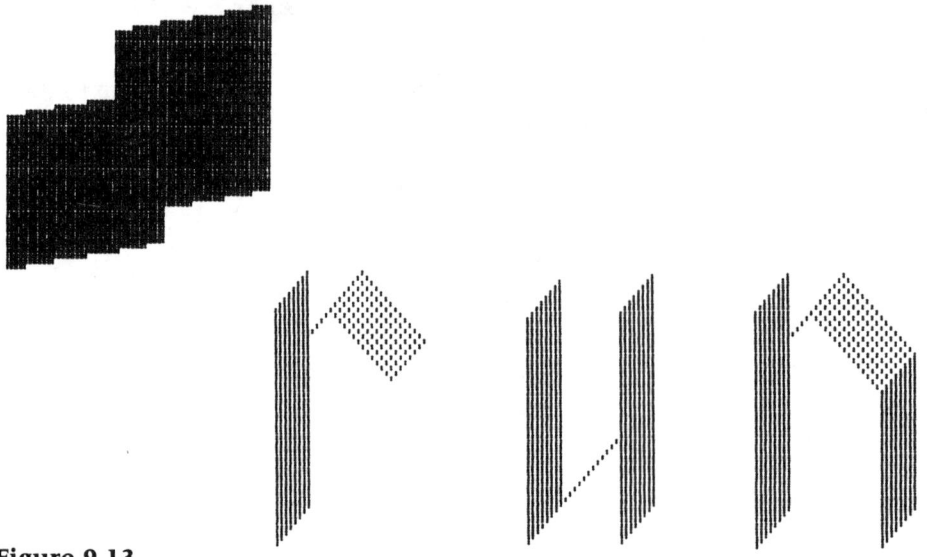

Figure 9.13
The pen.

When we draw with a calligraphic pen, we leave a line the width and angle of the nib wherever we place the pen. We'll simulate this by drawing a line from the cursor, at a user defined distance and angle.

To create the nib, we'll stick cursor 1 on the screen with insert. Then, we'll move cursor 2 until it is the distance and angle from cursor 1 to make the nib, and press insert to save the x and y distance of cursor 2 from cursor 1. We'll then be in drawing mode, and the pen can now be manipulated just as the pencil was. To change the nib, we'll simply press delete and start the process again.

Let's look at the code:

```
11000 '
11001 'pen
11002 '
11003 '     set up angle and length of nib using
        cursors as for drawing
11004 '     lines - drawing mode begins after pressing
        second insert
11005 '     press delete at any time to restart
11006 '     when drawing, move pen around with arrow
        keys
11007 '                 insert toggles draw/don't
        draw
11008 '
11010 GOSUB 23010      'move cursors
11020 IF DELETE. THEN CURCURSOR = 0 : INSCNT = 0 :
      BASEINS = 0 : IF CURSOR2SHOW THEN PUT
      (CURSOR2X,CURSOR2Y), CURSOR2% : CURSOR2SHOW =
      FALSE : GOTO 11600 ELSE GOTO 11600
11030 IF NOT INSERT THEN 11100
11040 INSCNT = BASEINS + (INSCNT + 1) MOD 2
11050 IF INSCNT = 1 THEN CURCURSOR = 1 : CURSOR2X =
      CURSOR1X : CURSOR2Y = CURSOR1Y
11060 IF INSCNT = 0 THEN BASEINS = 2 : CURCURSOR = 0 :
      XSTEP = CURSOR2X - CURSOR1X : YSTEP = CURSOR2Y -
      CURSOR1Y : IF CURSOR2SHOW THEN PUT
      (CURSOR2X,CURSOR2Y), CURSOR2% : CURSOR2SHOW =
      FALSE
11100 IF INSCNT <> 3 THEN 11600
11110 IF CURSOR1SHOW THEN PUT (CURSOR1X,CURSOR1Y),
      CURSOR1%
11120 LINE (CURSOR1X,CURSOR1Y) - STEP (XSTEP,YSTEP),
      COLOR.
11130 IF CURSOR1SHOW THEN PUT (CURSOR1X,CURSOR1Y),
      CURSOR1%
11600 RETURN
```

Note that line **11060** computes **XSTEP** and **YSTEP** once the second insert has been pressed. **BASEINS** is set to 0 during nib defining and to 2 during drawing.

We'll initiate pen drawing by pressing F9:

```
540 ON MODE GOSUB 1010, 2010, 3010, 4010, 5010, 6010,
    7010, 8010, 9010, 10010, 11010
22180 IF ASC(COMMAND$) = F9 THEN MODE = 11
```

We also add the following to the parameter resetting subroutine:

```
25040 BASEINS = 0
```

MERGE "12

9.13: AIR BRUSH

Now we'll see how to add an air brush to our program. We'll spray the fill patterns used by the painting mode onto the screen. The more we go over an area, the more the pattern will appear. We'll also be able to spray one pattern over another (Figure 9.14).

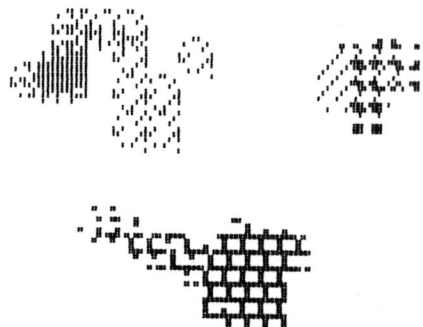

Figure 9.14
We'll spray the paint patterns onto the screen. We can spray lightly or densely, and can spray one pattern over another.

We'll define a spray mask, an **AND** mask that will only allow a few dots of the pattern to the screen at a time, and compute what to **PUT** to the screen to spray the pattern.

Computing what to spray is the most complex part. In order for the pattern to appear, we need to memory map it over the whole screen, as discussed at the end of Section 9.11. Then we need to **AND** it with the spray mask.

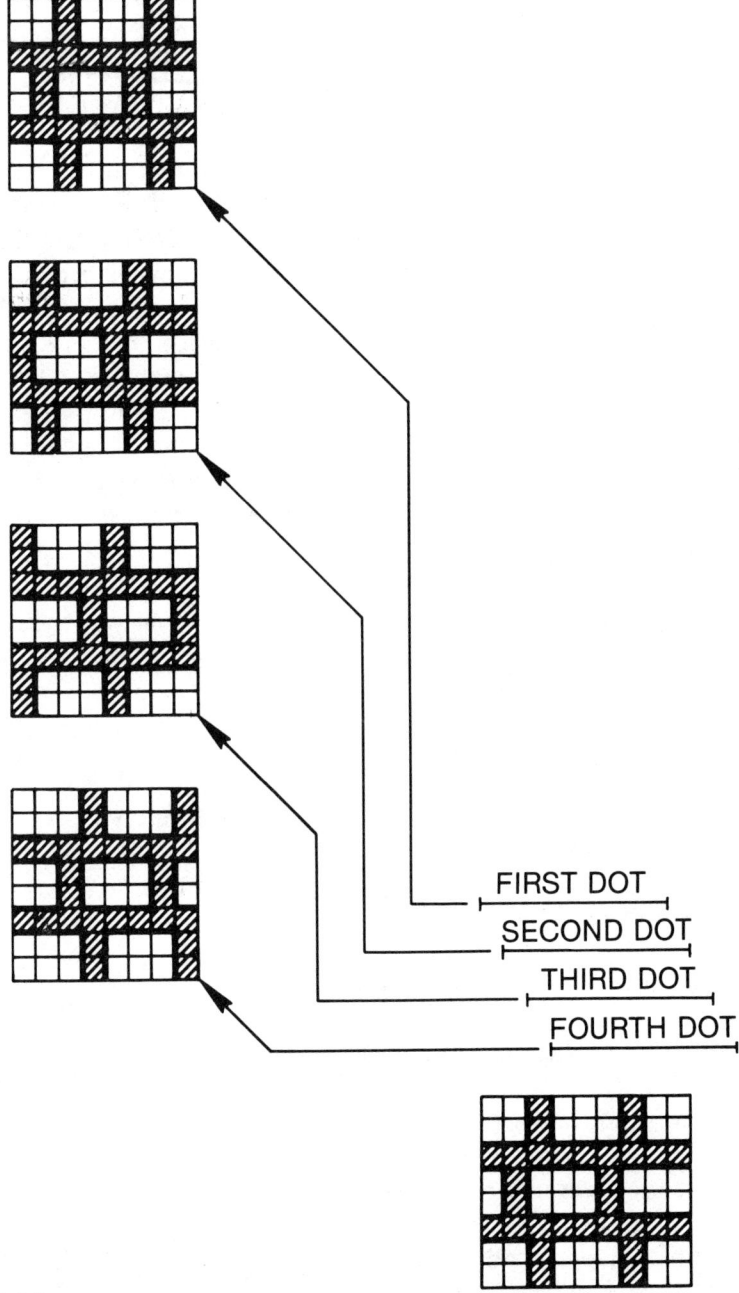

Figure 9.15
We'll need to make a different PUT array for spraying to each dot in a byte.

Determining the Data to PUT

We'll make our spray pattern 8-by-8 dots. For every area we spray, we'll need to figure a **PUT** array to place the paint pattern on the screen. To ensure that the pattern won't be smudged no matter to which x position we **PUT** the spray array, we'll need a different **PUT** array for each dot in the byte (Figure 9.15).

Suppose we are given the pattern byte that belongs in the column we are spraying. We need to shift the dots so that the datum for the dot to which we are spraying (the cursor location) is aligned on the left of the byte. Because the pattern repeats, we can use a trick: we'll circularly rotate the dots in the byte.

Let's look at an example. Suppose we are in medium resolution, and the pattern datum for our byte is 10110111B, and we want to **PUT** an array to the second dot in the byte. First, we'll rotate the datum two dots to the left to get 01110000B. Then, we'll move the bits that were shoved out—1011—to the bottom of the byte and get 01111011B. To make the data eight dots wide, we'll repeat this byte and get a word of data—01111011 01111011B.

Mathematically, we'll manipulate the data as follows. First, we'll compute the number of dots to shift the data to the left:

dots to shift = x mod resolution

If we're in medium resolution, we'll multiply this value by two.
We'll shift the data by multiplying it by $2^{\text{dots to shift}}$:

new data = data ∗ $2^{\text{dots to shift}}$

Then, we'll find the dots that get pushed out:

pushed dots = new data AND FF00H

move them to the low byte:

pushed dots = pushed dots / 256

and **OR** them to the dots not pushed:

new data = (new data AND 00FFH) OR pushed dots

A Graphics Editor 297

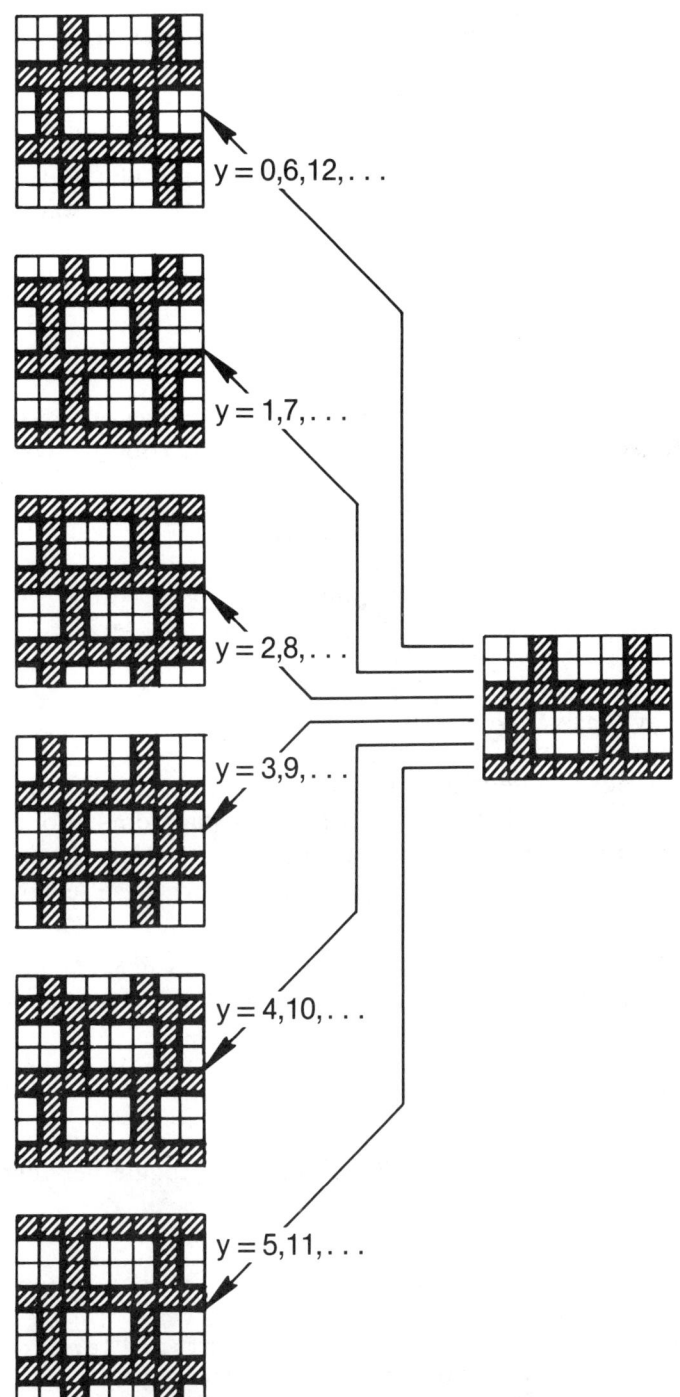

Figure 9.16
The PUT array will start with the $1 + y \bmod \text{pattern len}^{th}$ byte of the spray pattern.

To vertically align the data, we'll start the **PUT** array with the:

1 + (y mod pattern length)th

element of the pattern, then load the next eight elements. If the pattern is less than eight elements long, we'll load from the beginning and repeat (Figure 9.16).

Getting the Spray

Once we have the complete **PUT** array, we need to **AND** it with a spray mask. I use the pattern shown in Figure 9.17. You may want to make your

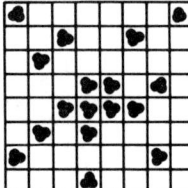

Figure 9.17
The spray mask.

own. We need to develop the **AND** data for both high and medium resolution. In high resolution, simply treat all spray dots as ones, and compute the byte data. In medium resolution, spread the data into a word (2 bytes), and treat all spray dots as two set bits. Convert these sets of data into bytes (Figure 9.18).

We **AND** each byte of the **PUT** array with the spray mask. If the array is for medium resolution, we'll do two **AND**ings for each array element.

The Routine

Let's look at the code. We'll use insert to toggle between spraying and not spraying:

```
12000 '
12001 'air brush
12002 '
12003 '      sprays part of current pattern onto screen
12004 '      move spray with arrow keys
12005 '      insert toggles spray/don't spray
12006 '
12010 GOSUB 23010       'move cursors
```

A Graphics Editor

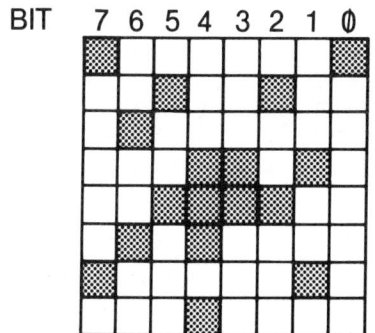

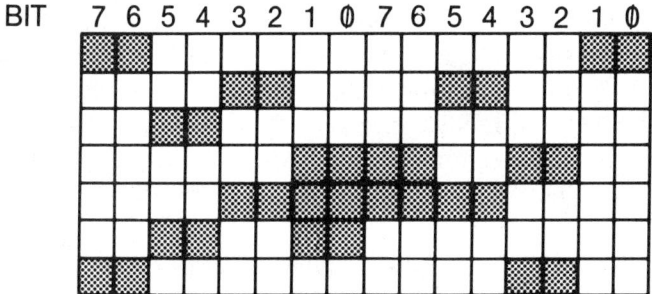

Figure 9.18

```
12020  IF INSERT THEN PLOT = NOT PLOT
12030  IF NOT PLOT THEN 12600
12040  ANDPOS = CURSOR1X MOD RESOLUTION : IF RESOLUTION
       = 4 THEN ANDPOS = ANDPOS * 2
12050  FOR POSITION = 1 TO 8
12060     VALUE = (ASC(MID$(PATTERNS$(PATTERN),1+
          (CURSOR1Y + POSITION) MOD LEN(PATTERNS$
          (PATTERN)),1))) * 2^ANDPOS
12070     PUSHEDVALUE = (VALUE AND &HFF00) / 256
12080     VALUE = (VALUE AND &H00FF) OR PUSHEDVALUE
12090     IF RESOLUTION = 8 THEN VALUE = VALUE AND
          SPRAYHIGH(POSITION) ELSE VALUE = (VALUE AND
          SPRAYMED(2,POSITION)) + (VALUE AND
          SPRAYMED(1,POSITION)) * 256 : IF VALUE > 32767
          THEN VALUE = -(65536! - VALUE)
12100     PATTERN%(2 + POSITION) = VALUE
```

```
12110 NEXT
12120 IF CURSOR1SHOW THEN PUT (CURSOR1X,CURSOR1Y),
      CURSOR1%
12130 IF (CURSOR1X >= 0) AND (CURSOR1X < (MAXXRES -
      PATTERN%(1) * RESOLUTION / 8)) AND (CURSOR1Y >=
      0) AND (CURSOR1Y < MAXYRES - PATTERN%(2)) THEN
      PUT (CURSOR1X,CURSOR1Y), PATTERN%, OR
12140 IF CURSOR1SHOW THEN PUT (CURSOR1X,CURSOR1Y),
      CURSOR1%
12600 RETURN
```

Line **12040** determines how many dots to shift the pattern; **12050** loops through the eight rows of the spray **PUT** array. Line **12060** finds the data for the current element of the spray array. **CURSOR1Y + POSITION** is the y position to which the data will be mapped. Thus, the $1 + (CURSOR1X + POSITION)\ MOD\ LEN(PATTERNS\$(PATTERN))^{th}$ data element is loaded. Remember that **PATTERN** tells the pattern to be drawn, and that the patterns are stored in the string array **PATTERNS$**. Lines **12070** and **12080** rotate this data. Line **12090 AND**s the data with the spray mask. If the data is for medium resolution, 2 bytes of data are **AND**ed with the spray mask bytes for the column, and the resulting word is sign adjusted. Line **12100** saves the data in **PATTERN%**, the spray **PUT** array.

When we start the program, we need to prepare **PATTERN%** and also read in the spray mask data:

```
21130 DIM PATTERN%(10) : PATTERN%(1) = 16 : PATTERN%(2)
      = 8
21140 FOR POSITION = 1 TO 8 : READ SPRAYHIGH(POSITION)
      : NEXT
21150 FOR POSITION = 1 TO 8 : READ SPRAYMED
      (1,POSITION), SPRAYMED(2,POSITION) : NEXT

26240 '
26241 'data for air brush spray pattern
26242 '
26243 '     high res
26250 DATA &H81, &H24, &H40, &H1A, &H3C, &H50, &H82,
      &H10
26260 '
26261 '     medium res
26270 DATA &HC0, 3, &HC, &H30, &H30, 0, 3, &HCC, &HF,
      &HF0, &H33, 0, &HC0, &H0C, 3, 0
```

We'll access spraying with alternate-F3:

```
540 ON MODE GOSUB 1010, 2010, 3010, 4010, 5010, 6010,
    7010, 8010, 9010, 10010, 11010, 12010
```

```
22190 IF ASC(COMMAND$) = ALTF3 THEN MODE = 12
```

> MERGE "13

Trying It Out

Select a pattern with alternate-F2, then get into the air-brush mode. Hit insert once, and watch the spray data appear. Hit insert again, and move over a few dots. Now hit insert again. Experiment with spraying different densities of dots. Then, spray an area very thickly by keeping the spray on and moving over one dot at a time.

Choose a different pattern, and spray over the old pattern. Try filling in some areas. Use different dot textures for shading.

9.14: CUT AND PASTE

Now we'll add a pair of scissors to our set of drawing tools. This is a very powerful editing feature. We'll be able to cut out regions of the graphics screen, and move or copy them around the screen.

We will use **PUT** arrays to move and copy objects. But unlike Chapter 8, we won't create the **PUT** arrays from dot matrices. Instead, we'll use a much quicker process: we'll load the data directly off the screen with **GET**.

GET is the opposite of **PUT**. It moves data from the screen into an array. Its format is:

GET $(x_1, y_1) - (x_2, y_2)$, array name

The array can be of any type. Because we used integer arrays for **PUT** in Chapter 8, we'll use integer arrays here. (For information on using other array types, see the *BASIC Manual*.) Before we **GET** data, we need to **DIM** the array to a size larger than the number of bytes composing the shape:

array dimension = 2 + INT(INT(width * bits per dot / 8 + .9) * height / 2 + .9)

Once we have loaded an array using **GET**, we can use **PUT** just as before. For example, try the following from medium resolution:

LINE (10,10) — (40,40),2,B
CIRCLE (25,25), 5, 1
PAINT (25,25), 3, 1

DIM DRAWING%(2 + INT(INT((40 — 10 + 1)∗2/8 + .9)∗(35 — 10 + 1)/2 + .9))
GET (10,10) — (40,35), DRAWING%

This will load part of the box and painted circle into **DRAWING%**. Now, we'll place this shape elsewhere:

PUT (50,10), DRAWING%

Or:

PUT (50,50), DRAWING%, PRESET

You may wish to experiment further.

The Routine

Now let's add cutting and pasting to our program. We'll have a mode to cut figures, another to copy cut figures, and a third to move cut figures.

Cutting

We'll start by adding the routine to cut figures. The figure will be cut from the box formed by the two cursors (the same box as would be drawn by mode 7). We'll move the first cursor, hit insert, then move the second cursor. Delete will return movement to the first cursor, and ∗ will cut the figure.

Before we cut a figure, we need to do two things: we need to make sure we aren't trying to cut off of the screen, and we need to dimension an array for cutting. Once we cut a figure, we'll keep track of its old location. We'll see why when we discuss moving and copying.

We'll store the cut shape in **CUT%**. To **ERASE** and re**DIM** it later, we need to initialize **CUT%** at the beginning of the program:

```
21150 DIM CUT%(1)
```

Now, we'll add the code for positioning the cutting cursors:

```
13000 '
13001 'cut a figure for pasting or copying
13002 '
13003 '     position cursors to corners of area to cut
13004 '     press * to cut
13005 '
13010 GOSUB 23010      'move cursors
13020 IF INSERT THEN INSCNT = INSCNT + 1 : IF INSCNT =
      1 THEN CURSOR2X = CURSOR1X : CURSOR2Y = CURSOR1Y
      : CURCURSOR = 1 : GOTO 13600 ELSE CURCURSOR = 1 :
      GOTO 13600
13030 IF DELETE. THEN CURCURSOR = 0 : GOTO 13600
13040 IF COMMAND$ <> "*" OR (INSCNT < 1) THEN 13600
```

We'll check if the coordinates of the area to cut are valid, and, if they are, we'll save the coordinates of the upper left corner of the box:

```
13050 IF (CURSOR1X < 0) OR (CURSOR1X > MAXXRES) OR
      (CURSOR1Y < 0) OR (CURSOR1Y > MAXYRES) OR
      (CURSOR2X < 0) OR (CURSOR2X > MAXXRES) OR
      (CURSOR2Y < 0) OR (CURSOR2Y > MAXYRES) THEN 13600
13060 IF CURSOR2X < CURSOR1X THEN OLDCUTX = CURSOR2X
      ELSE OLDCUTX = CURSOR1X
13070 IF CURSOR2Y < CURSOR1Y THEN OLDCUTY = CURSOR2Y
      ELSE OLDCUTY = CURSOR1Y
```

Now, we'll find the dimension of the array, and **DIM** it:

```
13080 CUTLEN = INT(INT((ABS(CURSOR1X - CURSOR2X) +
      1)*8/RESOLUTION + .9) * (ABS(CURSOR1Y - CURSOR2Y)
      + 1)/2 + .9) + 2
13090 ERASE CUT%
13100 DIM CUT%(CUTLEN)
```

We'll erase the cursors, cut the box with **GET**, and then replace the cursors:

```
13110 IF CURSOR1SHOW THEN PUT (CURSOR1X,CURSOR1Y),
      CURSOR1%
13120 IF CURSOR2SHOW THEN PUT (CURSOR2X,CURSOR2Y),
      CURSOR2%

13130 GET (CURSOR1X,CURSOR1Y) - (CURSOR2X,CURSOR2Y),
      CUT%

13140 IF CURSOR1SHOW THEN PUT (CURSOR1X,CURSOR1Y),
      CURSOR1%
13150 IF CURSOR2SHOW THEN PUT (CURSOR2X,CURSOR2Y),
      CURSOR2%
```

304 A Graphics Editor

Finally, we'll set up variables telling where **CUT%** is located and whether it is displayed. These are analogous to **CURSOR1X**, **CURSOR1Y**, and **CURSOR1SHOW**:

```
13160 CURCUTX = OLDCUTX : CURCUTY = OLDCUTY : CUTSHOW =
      TRUE
13600 RETURN
```

Copying

For copying, we'll position the cut shape with the arrow keys, and hit insert to store it. As we move the cursor, we'll **XOR CUT%** across the screen. That way, we can see how the copied shape will appear before we store it on the screen. Let's look at the routine:

```
14000 '
14001 'copy
14002 '
14003 '      copy cut matrix to cursor location. XOR
             until insert pressed
14004 '      then store
14005 '
14010 GOSUB 23010       'move cursors
14020 IF LEN(COMMAND$) <> 2 THEN 14600
14030 IF INSERT THEN 14200
14040 IF (CURCUTX = OLDCUTX) AND (CURCUTY = OLDCUTY)
      THEN 14060
14050 IF CUTSHOW THEN PUT (CURCUTX,CURCUTY), CUT% :
      CUTSHOW = FALSE
14060 IF (CURSOR1X = OLDCUTX) AND (CURSOR1Y = OLDCUTY)
      THEN 14600
14070 IF (CURSOR1X >= 0) AND (CURSOR1X < (MAXXRES -
      CUT%(1) * RESOLUTION / 8)) AND (CURSOR1Y >= 0)
      AND (CURSOR1Y < MAXYRES - CUT%(2)) THEN PUT
      (CURSOR1X,CURSOR1Y),CUT% : CUTSHOW = TRUE
14080 CURCUTX = CURSOR1X : CURCUTY = CURSOR1Y
14090 GOTO 14600

14200 IF NOT((CURSOR1X >= 0) AND (CURSOR1X < (MAXXRES -
      CUT%(1) * RESOLUTION / 8)) AND (CURSOR1Y >= 0)
      AND (CURSOR1Y < MAXYRES - CUT%(2))) THEN 14600
14210 IF CUTSHOW AND (CURCUTX <> OLDCUTX) AND (CURCUTY
      <> OLDCUTY) THEN PUT (CURCUTX,CURCUTY), CUT%
14220 PUT (CURSOR1X,CURSOR1Y), CUT%, PSET : CURSOR1SHOW
      = FALSE : OLDCUTX = CURSOR1X : OLDCUTY = CURSOR1Y
      : CUTSHOW = TRUE
14600 RETURN
```

Lines **14010** to **14030** move the cursor.

If insert hasn't been pressed, we need to erase the shape from its old position, and move it to the current position. But we don't want to erase the original shape. Line **14040** ensures this. Note that line **14050** erases the shape by **XOR**ing it again. Lines **14060** and **14070** draw the shape at its new position. As with line **14040**, we make sure that we don't erase the original shape. Line **14080** updates the cut shape's position.

If insert has been pressed, we need to **PUT** the cut shape at its new location. First, we make sure that it will fit. Then, if the last place **CUT%** appeared wasn't its original location, we erase it with line **14210**. Next we get rid of the cursor, and **PUT** the cut matrix to the screen. This time, we **PSET** it instead of **XOR**ing it.

Moving

Moving the cut shape is just the same as copying it. Only before we draw the shape at its new position, we erase it from its last position. Let's look at the code:

```
15000 '
15001 'move
15002 '
15003 '      same as copy but last drawn cut erased
15004 '
15010 GOSUB 23010       'move cursors
15020 IF LEN(COMMAND$) <> 2 THEN 15600
15030 IF INSERT THEN 15200
15040 IF (CURCUTX = OLDCUTX) AND (CURCUTY = OLDCUTY)
      THEN 15060
15050 IF CUTSHOW THEN PUT (CURCUTX,CURCUTY), CUT% :
      CUTSHOW = FALSE
15060 IF (CURSOR1X = OLDCUTX) AND (CURSOR1Y = OLDCUTY)
      THEN 15600
15070 IF (CURSOR1X >= 0) AND (CURSOR1X < (MAXXRES -
      CUT%(1) * RESOLUTION / 8)) AND (CURSOR1Y >= 0)
      AND (CURSOR1Y < MAXYRES - CUT%(2)) THEN PUT
      (CURSOR1X,CURSOR1Y),CUT% : CUTSHOW = TRUE
15080 CURCUTX = CURSOR1X : CURCUTY = CURSOR1Y
15090 GOTO 15600
15200 PUT (OLDCUTX,OLDCUTY), CUT%
15210 IF NOT((CURSOR1X >= 0) AND (CURSOR1X < (MAXXRES -
      CUT%(1) * RESOLUTION / 8)) AND (CURSOR1Y >= 0)
      AND (CURSOR1Y < MAXYRES - CUT%(2))) THEN 15600
15220 IF CUTSHOW AND (CURCUTX <> OLDCUTX) AND (CURCUTY
      <> OLDCUTY) THEN PUT (CURCUTX,CURCUTY), CUT%
```

```
15230 PUT (CURSOR1X,CURSOR1Y), CUT% , PSET : CURSOR1SHOW
     = FALSE : OLDCUTX = CURSOR1X : OLDCUTY = CURSOR1Y
     : CUTSHOW = TRUE
15600 RETURN
```

Line **15220** erases the shape from its last position. Note that this isn't the shape's original position, but the last place it was copied or moved.

Calling the Routine

We'll call these three subroutines by alternate-F5, alternate-F7, and alternate-F9:

```
540 ON MODE GOSUB 1010, 2010, 3010, 4010, 5010, 6010,
    7010, 8010, 9010, 10010, 11010, 12010, 13010,
    14010, 15010

22200 IF ASC(COMMAND$) = ALTF5 THEN MODE = 13
22210 IF ASC(COMMAND$) = ALTF7 THEN MODE = 14
22220 IF ASC(COMMAND$) = ALTF9 THEN MODE = 15
```

       MERGE "14

Experiment with using the various modes. Draw a shape and cut it. Copy it to various locations. See what happens when you copy it over part of itself. Now try moving the shape. Fill the background with a pattern and move the shape. Also, note how what you see when you position the shape differs from what appears when you store the shape. This difference is because we **XOR** the shape while positioning it, and **PSET** it when storing it. If you want the shape to be **XOR**ed, switch out of the moving or copying mode before pressing insert.

9.15: DISPLAYING A MENU OF AVAILABLE COMMANDS

If you can't remember which keys call which modes or which keys do what for each mode, you may want to have an on-screen help key. Pressing this key should give information on what commands are available or what to type. So as not to destroy the graphics screen, these data need to be **XOR**ed. As an example, we'll set up a key to tell what the normal function keys do. We'll display this menu whenever F10 is pressed.

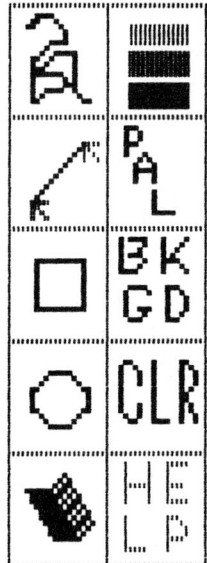

Figure 9.19
A pictorial help menu.

The first thing we do is create the help data. I find a pictorial representation of the keys' functions quickest to understand (Figure 9.19). We need to draw this data on the screen and capture it with the **GET** command. If you are using straight text, you may want to type your messages on the screen, move the cursor out of the way, and use **GET**. Otherwise, use the graphics editor. Draw the help screen, then use the cut mode (alternate-F5) to put the data in a **PUT** array. Exit the program, and directly enter a routine to save the **PUT** array on disk:

**OPEN "O",1,"CUTDATA.BAS" : PRINT #1,"27000 DATA ";
CUTLEN : FOR A = 0 TO CUTLEN STEP 30 : PRINT #1, 27010+A;
" DATA "; : FOR B = 1 TO 30 : PRINT #1, CUT%(A+B);",";:
NEXT : PRINT #1, " " : NEXT**

After this line finishes execution (whether with the error message—**Subscript out of range**—or not) type:

CLOSE #1

The **PUT** array data will now be on disk. You will need to do some editing of the data: the lines need to be renumbered and trailing commas have to be removed.

The Routine

Once we have the help picture data, we need to add a mode to display it from the program. First, we'll read the data into an array. Then, we'll **PUT** the array when F10 is hit. We'll erase the array whenever a new mode is entered. Let's look at the code. To start, we'll read in the **PUT** array for the help menu:

```
21160 READ COMMANDLEN
21170 DIM COMMANDS%(COMMANDLEN)
21180 FOR POSITION = 1 TO COMMANDLEN : READ
      COMMANDS%(POSITION) : NEXT
```

You'll need to merge the file containing the data into the program. Now, we add:

```
16000 '
16001 'display command menu for function keys
16002 '
16010 IF NOT COMMANDSHOW THEN PUT (0,0),COMMANDS% :
      COMMANDSHOW = TRUE
16600 RETURN
```

We'll call the help mode whenever F10 is struck:

```
540 ON MODE GOSUB 1010, 2010, 3010, 4010, 5010, 6010,
    7010, 8010, 9010, 10010, 11010, 12010, 13010,
    14010, 15010, 16010
22230 IF ASC(COMMAND$) = F10 THEN MODE = 16
```

When the mode changes, we'll get rid of the command menu:

```
25050 IF COMMANDSHOW THEN PUT (0,0), COMMANDS% :
      COMMANDSHOW = FALSE
```

To add the code, type:

MERGE "15P1

If you want to load data for the help menu of Figure 9.19, type:

MERGE "15P2

That's all. Try it out. You may want to add a help menu for the alternate function keys as well. You could also display information about each mode as it is entered, or you could type messages, such as "enter the two digit pattern number," when input is required.

9.16: SUGGESTIONS ON ADDITIONAL FEATURES

There are many ways to enhance the graphics editor. You may consider:

1. adding modes for saving and loading pictures from disk. These could interface with an animation package, as discussed in Section 7.2.
2. changing the cursors to icons. Each mode could have a different cursor. For example, free-hand drawing could use a pencil.
3. making the program mouse, joystick, or light pen driven.
4. adding a mode to save the screen in memory. At any time you could reload this screen, undoing any changes. This could be especially useful when you are painting an object that might not have a solid border.
5. using an Assembly Language **XOR** line-drawing routine. Call this routine when moving the cursors for creating rectangles or cutting pictures to let you see the shape's appearance in advance without destroying graphics data. Using such a routine would be the same as discussed in Section 5.4. You would just need to change the **OR** in **set_dot** to an **XOR**.

10

Graphics on the Text Screens

In this chapter we'll see how to do line and block graphics with the text screens. We'll be able to do sixteen color graphics with the color graphics adaptor and 80-by-25 resolution three color graphics with the monochrome adaptor.

All programs in this chapter will be in Assembly Language.

10.1: THE TEXT SCREEN MEMORY MAP

The memory map for the text screens is much simpler than that for the graphics screen. The screen is divided into 25 rows, and either 40 or 80 two-byte-wide columns. In the 40-column text mode there are 40 columns, and each row starts 80 bytes after the last; in the 80-column mode there are 80 columns, and each row starts 160 bytes after the last (Figure 10.1). Each two byte entry tells what character to place on the screen and the background and foreground colors of that character.

The first byte in each column, the *character code*, tells which character to display. It is a number between 0 and 255, corresponding to one of the IBM PC's characters, as diagrammed in Appendix C of the *Technical Reference Manual* and Appendix G of the *BASIC Manual*. Each character fills an 8-by-8-dot section of the text screen. We'll call this 8-by-8 section the *character block*.

The second byte in each column, the *attribute byte*, controls the foreground and background colors of the character block. The high four bits control the background color and the low four control the foreground color (Figure 10.2). If bit 5 of the mode select register (see Section 7.3) is set, then the most significant bit of the attribute byte determines whether the background blinks. If bit 5 isn't set, then the high bit of the attribute byte controls the background's intensity. By clearing bit 5, we'll be able to get all 16 colors (see Figure 1.1) for both the foreground and background.

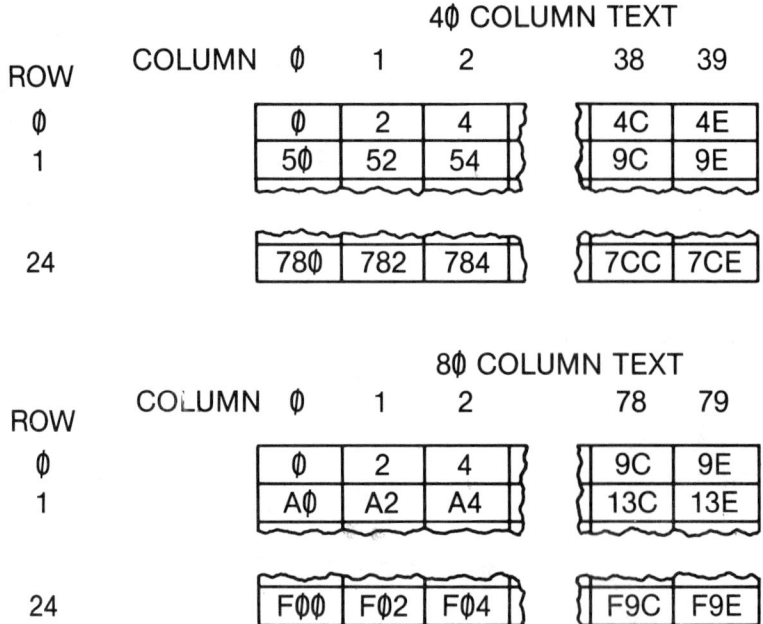

Figure 10.1
The text screen memory map.

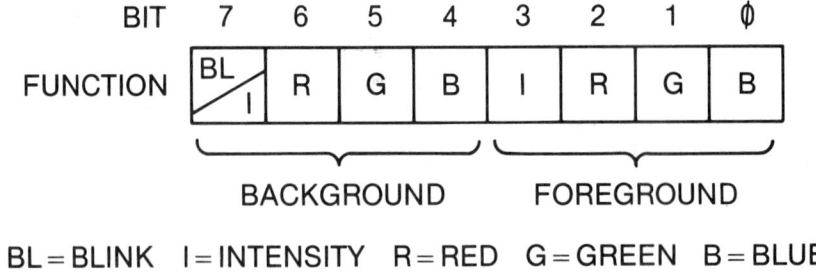

Figure 10.2
The attribute byte.

Drawing With Dots

To best simulate line graphics and to most easily break down block figures, we should draw with characters that look like dots. There are eight such characters: 0H, 2H, DBH, and FFH; DCH and DFH; and DDH and DEH. The first group fills the whole 8-by-8-character block. The second group divides the character block in half horizontally, giving two 8-by-4 dots. Because one dot's color is controlled by the foreground color and the other's color is controlled by the background color, using DCH or DFH doubles the vertical resolution. The third group of characters splits the character block into two 4-by-8 dots, doubling the horizontal resolution (Figure 10.3).

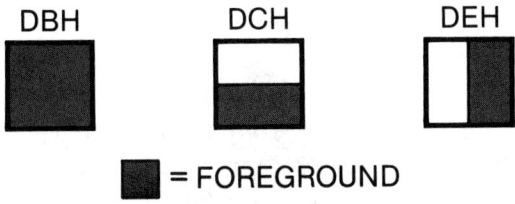

Figure 10.3
Dot-like text characters. The first completely fills the character block, the second splits the character block along a horizontal line, the third splits the character block along a vertical line.

If we want to draw with 8-by-8 dots, we'll use character code DBH. The low four bits of the attribute byte select its color. To double vertical resolution, we'll use DCH. The high four bits of the attribute byte control the top dot's color; the low four bits control the bottom dot's color. To double horizontal resolution, we'll use character code DEH. The high four attribute bits control the left dot's color; the low four control the right's.

10.2: SETTING THE MODE

To set the text mode, we must do three things: call the mode setting interrupt, disable blink, and eliminate the cursor.

As mentioned in Chapter 1, there are two text screens—the 40-column text screen and the 80-column text screen. By using character codes of DBH, DCH, or DEH for dots, we can choose one of six different text modes: 40-by-25, 80-by-25 (40 column), 40-by-50, 80-by-25 (80 column), 160-by-25, and 80-by-50 resolution text graphics. Let's call these modes 0, 1, 2, 4, 5, and 6. Bit 0 of the mode indicates if the horizontal resolution is doubled;

314 Graphics on the Text Screens

bit 1 indicates if the vertical resolution is doubled; and bit 2 indicates if the 80-column screen is used (Figure 10.4). Our mode setting procedure must decide which screen and which character to select, depending upon the text mode selected.

Disabling blink and eliminating the cursor were discussed in Section 7.3.

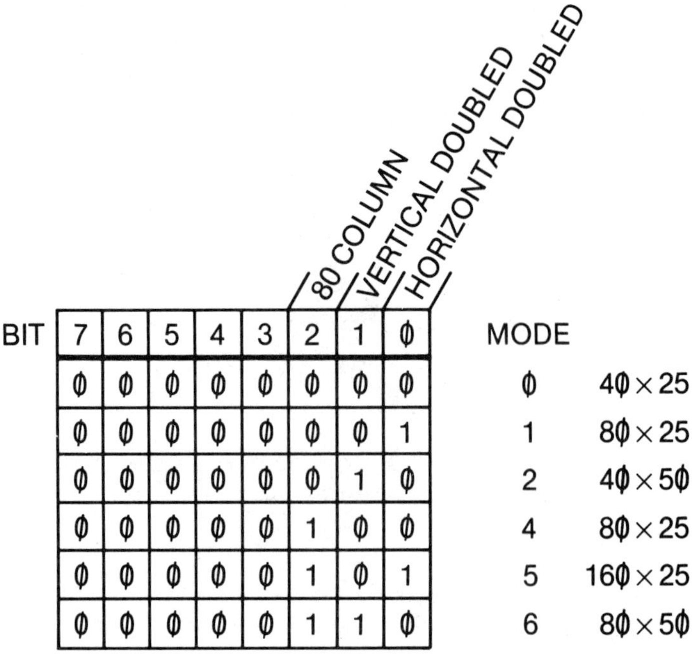

BIT	7	6	5	4	3	2 (HORIZONTAL DOUBLED)	1 (VERTICAL DOUBLED)	0 (80 COLUMN)	MODE	
	0	0	0	0	0	0	0	0	0	40×25
	0	0	0	0	0	0	0	1	1	80×25
	0	0	0	0	0	0	1	0	2	40×50
	0	0	0	0	0	1	0	0	4	80×25
	0	0	0	0	0	1	0	1	5	160×25
	0	0	0	0	0	1	1	0	6	80×50

Figure 10.4
The function of the bits in **text_mode**.

The Routine

Let's look at the routine to set the text mode. **text_mode** indicates which text mode to use. To use the 40-column text screen, we call **interrupt 10H** with:
   AL = 1
   AH = 0
To use the 80-column text screen, we call **interrupt 10H** with:
   AL = 3
   AH = 0

We'll set **character** to either DBH, DCH, or DEH, and set **maxxres** and **maxyres**:

```
;
text_mode       db      4
character       db      ?
maxxres         dw      ?
maxyres         dw      ?
;

;
set_mode        proc    near
                mov     ax,0b800h       ;make ES point to beginning
                mov     es,ax           ;of text screen
                mov     ax,14           ;eliminate the cursor by making
                mov     dx,3d4h         ;the high byte of cursor location
                out     dx,ax           ; = 32
                mov     ax,32
                inc     dx
                out     dx,ax
                mov     maxxres,40      ;set initial maxxres and maxyres
                mov     maxyres,25
;
                test    text_mode,01    ;see if x resolution is doubled
                jnz     x_is_doubled    ;(modes 1 and 5)
                test    text_mode,02    ;see if y resolution is doubled
                jnz     y_is_doubled    ;(modes 2 and 6)
;neither direction doubled (modes 0 and 4)
                mov     character,0dbh
                jmp short s_m_1
x_is_doubled:
                mov     character,0deh
                shl     maxxres,1       ;double maxxres
                jmp short s_m_1
y_is_doubled:
                mov     character,0dch
                shl     maxyres,1       ;double maxyres
s_m_1:
                test    text_mode,4     ;see if 40 or 80 column screen
                jnz     set_80
;40 column text mode
                mov     al,1            ;set 40 column text screen
                mov     ah,0
                int     10h
                mov     dx,3d8H         ;disable blink
                mov     ax,8
                out     dx,ax
                jmp short s_m_end
set_80:
                shl     maxxres,1       ;double maxxres, since 80 columns per
                mov     al,3            ;row. Then, set 80 column text
                mov     ah,0            ;screen
                int     10h
                mov     dx,3d8h         ;disable blink
                mov     ax,9
                out     dx,ax
s_m_end:
                ret
set_mode        endp
;
```

> All of the programs in this chapter appear in the **CHAPT10** directory. This section's program is **2.ASM**.

10.3: CLEARING THE SCREEN

Clearing the screen is easy. We need only fill all the text screen's attribute bytes with zeros. To make line graphics (discussed in Section 10.4) easier, we'll also fill all of the character bytes with **character**:

```
;
clear_screen    proc    near
                mov     cx,1000     ;there are 1000 words on the 40 column
                test    text_mode,4 ;screen
                jz      c_s_1
                shl     cx,1        ;2000 words on the 80 column screen
c_s_1:          mov     al,character
                mov     ah,0
                mov     di,0
                cld
                rep     stosw
                ret
clear_screen    endp
;
```

> **3.ASM**

10.4: LINE GRAPHICS

Adapting our line graphics techniques to text screens is simple. We change **set_mode** and **clear_screen** to those of Sections 10.2 and 10.3 and then change **set_dot** to operate with text.

Once **clear_screen** has filled all character bytes with the character code selected by **set_mode**, we only need to change a character's attribute byte to set a dot. We determine the location of the dot's attribute byte, and whether to set the high or low four attribute bits to the dot's color.

Suppose we want to set screen location **(x,y)** to **color**. Then, if we are in mode 0 or 4, where we don't double x or y resolution:

attribute byte location = y * bytes per row + x + 1
attribute data = color

If we double x resolution (modes 1 and 5), then:

attribute byte location = int(y/2) * bytes per row + x + 1
attribute data = color   if y mod 2 is 0
         = 16 * color   if y mod 2 is 1

If we double y resolution (modes 2 and 6), then:

attribute byte location = int(y/2) * bytes per row + x + 1
attribute data = color   if y mod 2 is 0
         = 16 * color   if y mod 2 is 1

The Routine

Let's look at the new **set_dot**. It assumes that the x and y locations of the coordinate are in **xh** and **yh**:

```
;
x                       dw      ?
y                       dw      ?
xh                      dw      ?
yh                      dw      ?
;

;
;set a dot on the text screen
;
;   assumes x coordinate in xh
;           y coordinate in yh
;           dot's color in color
;
set_dot                 proc    near
                        mov     ax,xh
                        mov     x,ax
                        mov     ax,yh
                        mov     y,ax
                        mov     cl,0         ;initially setting foreground color
                        test    text_mode,1  ;see if x resolution doubled
                        jz      ck_y_doubled
;x doubled
                        shr     x,1          ;divide x coordinate by 2
                        jc      find_row_start  ;see whether to set foreground
                        mov     cl,4         ;or background color to dot color
                        jmp short find_row_start
```

```
ck_y_doubled:
                test        text_mode,2     ;see if y resolution doubled
                jz          find_row_start
                shr         y,1             ;divide y coordinate by 2
                jc          find_row_start  ;see whether to set foreground or
                mov         cl,4            ;background color to dot color
find_row_start:
                mov         ax,y
                shl         ax,1            ;y * 2
                shl         ax,1            ;  * 4
                add         ax,y            ;  * 5
                shl         ax,1            ;  * 10
                shl         ax,1            ;  * 20
                shl         ax,1            ;  * 40
                shl         ax,1            ;  * 80
                test        text_mode,4     ;double again if 80 column screen
                je          find_byte
                shl         ax,1            ;  * 160
find_byte:
                mov         bx,x
                stc                         ;add 1
                rcl         bx,1
                add         bx,ax           ;points to attribute byte
;find data to store
                mov         al,color
                shl         al,cl           ;CL has been set to fore or back ground
;store it
                or          es:[bx],al
;
                ret
set_text_dot    endp
;
```

4.ASM

10.5: BLOCK GRAPHICS

The process for converting block figures to data is the same as for normal graphics, only we can design block figures out of any of the text characters. It is very tricky to double horizontal or vertical resolutions, however, if we don't use the characters we've used for line graphics (Section 10.4).

As with regular graphics, we make a table of data for each block object. The first two bytes tell the width and height of the object. The remaining data tell the attribute and character code for each character in the object. The attribute byte goes first; the character code goes second.

To allow resolution doubling with characters DCH and DEH, we'll write our routine so that it expects two data tables per shape for modes 1, 2, 5, and 6 and one table per shape for modes 0 and 4.

Graphics on the Text Screens   319

Figure 10.5 illustrates creating block data for a figure in doubled horizontal resolution.

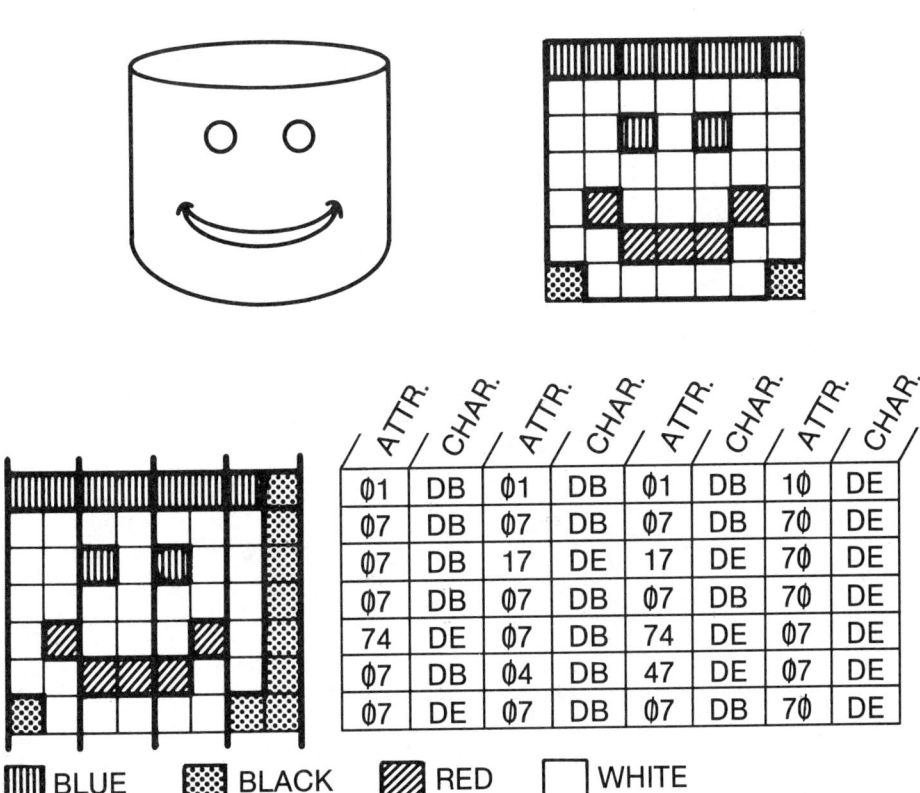

Figure 10.5
Creating text block data for an object: draw the object on graph paper, completely filling in blocks more than half way filled. Break the figure into character wide columns. Determine the character and attribute codes for each character block.

The Routine

Let's look at the routine. It operates just as Section 8.11's **plot_shape**. The only difference is that data for new rows are placed 80 (or 160) bytes after the start of the data in the previous row, and **find_start** is changed:

```
;
shape_number      dw         0
;
```

320   Graphics on the Text Screens

```
;
;PUT OBJECT DATA TABLES HERE
;



;
;
;plot a block object
;
;     the shape is indicated by shape_number
;     (xh,yh) is the location to place the object
;
plot_shape        proc      near
                  call      find_start
                  mov       bx,shape_number
                  test      text_mode,3    ;if not mode 0 or 4, then multiply
                  jz        p_s_a          ;shape_number by 2
                  shl       bx,1
p_s_a:
                  add       bx,ax          ;AX is either 0 or 1 (see find_start)
                  mov       di,shape_start[bx]    ;DI tells where data starts
                  mov       bl,[di]        ;BL = shape width in characters
                  inc       di

                  mov       bh,[di]        ;BH = shape height in characters
                  inc       di
;
p_s_1:            mov       cl,bl          ;loop through horiz. data
                  mov       ch,0
p_s_2:            mov       ax,[di]        ;load data
                  inc       di             ;point to next word of data
                  inc       di
                  xor       es:[bp],ax     ;xor to screen
                  inc       bp             ;point to next character location
                  inc       bp
                  loop      p_s_2          ;draw one row
                  cmp       bh,0           ;see if last row
                  je        p_s_end        ;if yes, then end
                  mov       al,bl
                  cbw
                  shl       ax,1           ;AX = bytes per row
                  sub       bp,ax
                  test      text_mode,4
                  je        p_s_a2
                  add       bp,80          ;if 80 column screen, add 160 to row
p_s_a2:           add       bp,80
                  dec       bh             ;for row loop
                  jmp short p_s_1
;
p_s_end:
                  ret
plot_shape        endp
;


;
;find location of a dot on the text screen
;
;     (xh,yh) gives location
;     returns with BP = location of character code byte
;     AX = 0 if setting foreground color
;        = 1 if setting background color
;
```

```
find_start        proc       near
                  mov        ax,xh
                  mov        x,ax
                  mov        ax,yh
                  mov        y,ax
                  mov        cx,0
                  test       text_mode,2
                  jz         ck_y_doubled
;xdoubled
                  shr        x,1
                  jc         find_row_start
                  mov        cx,1
                  jmp short  find_row_start
ck_y_doubled:
                  test       text_mode,2
                  jz         find_row_start
                  shr        y,1
                  jc         find_row_start
                  mov        cx,1
find_row_start:
                  mov        ax,y
                  shl        ax,1
                  shl        ax,1
                  add        ax,y
                  shl        ax,1
                  shl        ax,1
                  shl        ax,1
                  shl        ax,1
                  test       text_mode,4
                  je         find_byte
                  shl        ax,1
find_byte:
                  mov        bx,x
                  shl        bx,1
                  add        bx,ax
                  mov        bp,bx
                  mov        ax,cx
;
                  ret
find_start        endp
;
```

5.ASM

10.6: MULTIPLE PAGES

Doing multiple page graphics is very simple in text. There are four 80-column text screens and eight 40-column text screens (Figure 10.6). To use more than one page, we need only change **ES** to point to the new screen while clearing and drawing, and then change the 6845's registers 12 and 13 (see Section 7.3) to display the new page.

For example, to draw on the second 80-column text page (the fourth 40-column text page), add:

```
        mov     ax,0b8fah
        mov     es,ax
```

before clearing and drawing. Then, to draw the page, add:

```
        mov     ax,12
        mov     dx,3d4h
        out     dx,ax
        inc     dx
        mov     ax,7
        out     dx,ax
        dec     dx
        mov     ax,13
        out     dx,ax
        inc     dx
        mov     ax,0d0h
        out     dx,ax
```

10.7: NONSTANDARD TEXT MODES

To use nonstandard text modes, discussed in Section 7.3, we need to make a few changes to our text graphics routines.

In **set_mode** we'll need to set **maxyres** appropriately and replace calls to **interrupt 10H** with a nonstandard mode setting routine.

In **clear_screen**, we replace:

```
                mov     cx,1000
                test    text_mode,4
                jz      c_s_1
                shl     cx,1
c_s_1:          mov     al,character
```

with:

```
                mov     ax,maxxres
                mul     maxyres
                test    text_mode,3
                jz      c_s_1
                shr     ax,1
c_s_1:          mov     cx,ax
                mov     al,character
```

When a character is displayed, the character block is filled with the first **n** scan lines of the character data, where:

n = register 9 (of the 6845 registers) **+ 1**

So, we have to change the character used for doubling vertical resolution.

For example, for 200-by-80 resolution graphics, only two scan lines of each character are displayed per character block. So, instead of using character code DCH, we need to use character code F0H. Lines won't be perfect, but they won't look bad.

10.8: TEXT GRAPHICS WITH THE MONOCHROME ADAPTER

All procedures discussed in this chapter apply to text graphics with the monochrome adapter, with a few changes. First, the monochrome board's memory starts at B0000H. So we need to replace references to B800H with B000H. Also, we need to replace references to port 3D8H with 3B8H.

The monochrome board's attribute code operates differently than the color board's (Figure 10.7). Thus, we can't double resolutions, and the monochrome board does not support 40-column graphics. *Do not attempt to use modes 0 — 3. Bit 0 of port 3B8H must always be set.* As a result, the only mode we can use is mode 4. **color** is restricted as well, to 0, 7, and FH.

Sections 10.6 and 10.7 do not apply to the monochrome adapter, because the board has only 4K of memory. The techniques in Sections 10.6 and 10.7 require more memory.

80 COLUMN		40 COLUMN
1	0	1
	1000	2
2	2000	3
	3000	4
3	4000	5
	5000	6
4	6000	7
	7000	8

Figure 10.6
There are four 80 column pages, eight 40 column pages. The memory locations are all in decimal, offset from B8000H.

Appendix A

Math/Computer Terms

This appendix explains math/computer terms used in this book: *array*, *Boolean*, *matrix* and *trigonometric function*.

ARRAY

An array is a variable that can hold more than one value. Perhaps the best way to understand arrays is to look at an example. Suppose we want to store the test scores of three students. We could say:

```
SCORE(1) = 98          'First score
SCORE(2) = 67          'Second score
SCORE(3) = 89          'Third score
```

Here, the array is called **SCORE**. **SCORE(1)** tells the test score of student number one. **SCORE** is the array's *name*. The number within the parentheses is the array's *index*. It tells which entry in the array to examine.

We can use a variable rather than an actual number to index the array:

```
STUDENT = 1
SCORE(STUDENT) = 98
```

will assign the value 98 to **SCORE(1)**. Likewise, we could:

```
FOR STUDENT = 1 TO 3
   PRINT SCORE(STUDENT)
NEXT
```

We can use more than one index for an array. For example, suppose we want to keep the test scores received in two classes by the three students. We could say:

CLASS_SCORES(1,2) = 67   'Class 1, student 2

Or:

FOR CLASS = 1 TO 2
  FOR STUDENT = 1 TO 3
    PRINT CLASS_SCORES(CLASS,STUDENT)
  NEXT

Before we use an array, we need to dimension it. We do this with the **DIM** statement:

DIM arrayname(index1[,index2,....])[,arrayname2(......]

Here, **arrayname** is the name of the array, and **index1** is the largest value that the first index will ever take. Any further indices (**index2**, **index3**, etc.) are defined accordingly.

An array can only be **DIM**med once (in general, that is) in a program. Therefore, it is best to **DIM** at the beginning of programs.

BOOLEAN

A Boolean is a variable that has only two states—true and false. Booleans are used in logical statements. For example:

IF FINISHED THEN PRINT "I'm finished"

will print **I'm finished** only if the Boolean variable **FINISHED** is true.

A variable is considered false if it is equal to 0. Otherwise, it is true. For example:

FINISHED = −1
IF FINISHED THEN PRINT "I'm finished"

will cause **I'm finished** to be printed.

As variables are initialized to zero, all variables used for Booleans are initially false.

MATRICES

Matrices are two-dimensional arrays. They are indexed by their *row* and *column* (Figure A.1). For example, from the figure, **NUMBERS(1,2) = 2**. Mathematically, we write **MATRIX(ROW,COLUMN)** as $\text{matrix}_{\text{row column}}$.

NUMBERS

	COLUMNS		
	1	2	3
ROWS 1	1	2	3
ROWS 2	4	5	6
ROWS 3	7	8	9

Figure A.1
Matrices are composed of rows and columns.

Let's see how to add and multiply matrices. We'll start with addition. We can only add two matrices if they are the same size (that is, if they have the same number of rows and columns). Suppose **A** and **B** meet this condition. If we want to find:

C = A + B

we compute:

C(ROW,COLUMN) = A(ROW,COLUMN) + B(ROW,COLUMN)

for all entries in the matrices. In math terms:

$C_{ij} = A_{ij} + B_{ij}$

Multiplication is more difficult. We can multiply two matrices if the number of columns in the first matrix equals the number of rows in the second. The product will have the number of rows of the first, the number of columns of the second. In other words, suppose **A** has **m** rows and **n** columns, and **B** has **n** rows and **p** columns. Then **C = AB** will have **m** rows and **p** columns. **C(ROW,COLUMN)** is found by taking the sum of **A(ROW,J)** * **B(J,COLUMN)**, where **J** = 1 ... **n** (Figure A.2). Note: **AB <> BA**.

We can also multiply matrices by a scalar (a single number). Let **C** = **kA**, where **k** is a scalar. Then, $C_{ij} = kA_{ij}$.

GRAPHICALLY

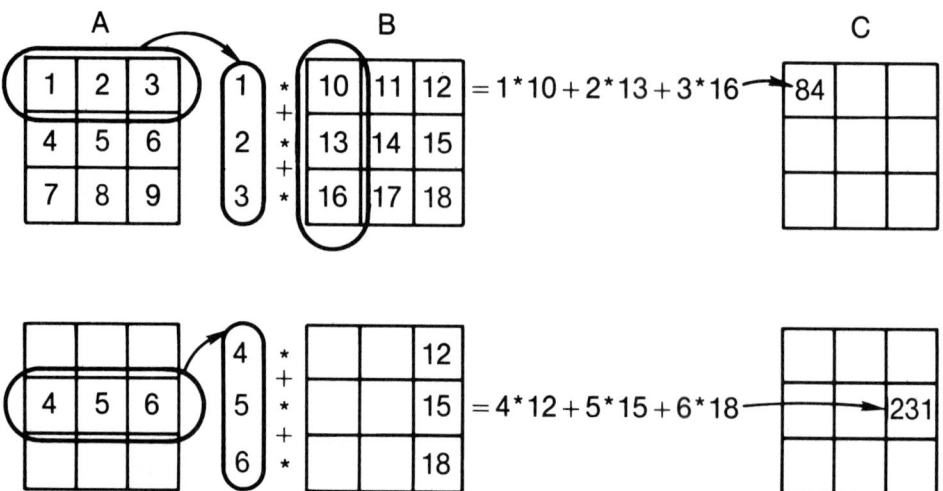

MATHEMATICALLY

$$C_{ij} = \sum_{q=1}^{n} A_{iq} B_{qj}, \text{ WHERE n = NUMBER OF COLUMNS IN A}$$

Figure A.2
Matrix multiplication.

TRIGONOMETRIC FUNCTIONS

The two basic trigonometric functions are *sine* and *cosine* (Figure A.3). Cosine is the same as sine, only it is 90 degrees out of phase. That is, $\cosine(\alpha) = \sine(\alpha + 90 \text{ degrees})$. Cosine is abbreviated cos; sine is abbreviated sin. Trigonometric functions are very useful in figuring out the length of sides of triangles (Figure A.4).

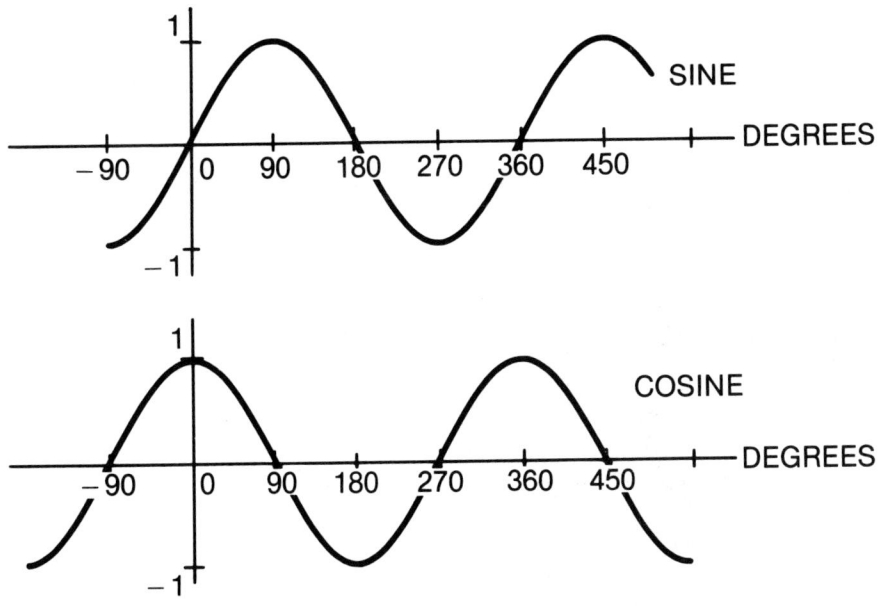

Figure A.3
Sine and cosine.

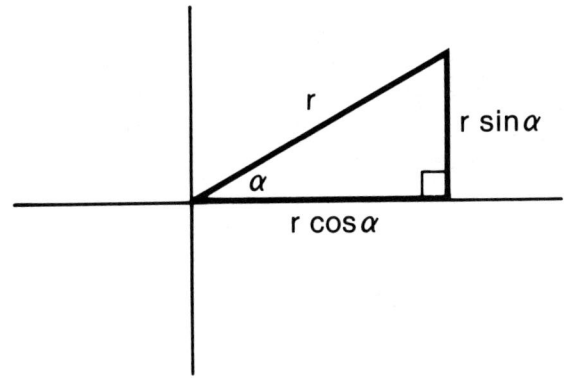

Figure A.4
Trig functions can be used to determine the length of the sides of a triangle.

Appendix B

Using the Optional Diskette

The optional diskette has two sections: extra programs and book programs.

THE EXTRA PROGRAMS

DEMO.EXE—A ready-to-run program demonstrating techniques learned in this book, including: three-dimensional line graphics, true three-dimensional graphics, block graphics, and the graphics editor. Simply type **DEMO**. (Note: make sure the disk is in the default drive. So, if your prompt is **A>**, put the disk in drive A.)

3D.EXE—A complete three-dimensional line graphics package incorporating all of the features discussed in Chapters 4 and 5. Type **3D**.

3D.ASM—Source code for **3D.EXE**.

MATRIX.BAS—A matrix editor containing all of the three-dimensional matrices in this book. Use it to generate your own transformation matrices and to save them as program modules. Includes input, output and math routines. **RUN** it from BASIC.

THE BOOK PROGRAMS

Each chapter has its own subdirectory, containing all programs the chapter uses. The programs are numbered according to the section in which they are discussed. If there are several programs in a section, they are named as **8P1**, **8P2**, etc. You can get into a subdirectory with:

CD directory name

from DOS and:

CHDIR "directory name

from BASIC. Or, refer to a program as **directory name\program name**.
  Remember, the disk only contains the code for each program. You still need to **DELETE**, **LOAD**, and **SAVE** as directed.

CHAPTER 1

2.BAS—The first graphics program

CHAPTER 2

2.BAS—Two-dimensional (2-D) point-line data base
3P1.BAS—Using **LINE**
3P2.BAS—Drawing 2-D figures
3P3.BAS—Adjusting for dot width
4P1.BAS—Translation
4P2.BAS—Animation
4P3.BAS—Fancy translation
5.BAS—Scaling
7.BAS—Color
8P1.BAS through 8P10.BAS—Graphics definition language programs

CHAPTER 3

1.BAS—Three-dimensional (3-D) data
2P1.BAS—Translation
2P2.BAS—Testing z translation
3.BAS—Perspective
4.BAS—Scaling
5.BAS—Rotation
6.BAS—Using matrices
7P1.BAS—Two-cube test data
7P2.BAS—Four-cube test data
7P3.BAS—Total transformation matrix
8.BAS—Keyboard interaction

10.BAS—Reflection
13.BAS—GDL rotation
15P1.BAS—xy clipping
15P2.BAS—z clipping

CHAPTER 4

1P1.ASM—**set_mode**
1P2.ASM—A ready to assemble **set_mode**, including testing code
2P1.ASM—Interrupt driven **set_dot**
2P2.ASM—Calculation driven **set_mode**
3.ASM—**clear_screen**
4.ASM—**draw_line**
5.ASM—**main_loop**
6.ASM—**read_keyboard**
7.ASM—**get_movement_values**
8P1.BAS—Makes trig tables
8P2.ASM—**load_trig_values**
9.ASM—**get_matrix**
10.ASM—**transform_points** and **get_new_coord**
11.ASM—**perspect_to_screen**
12.ASM—**draw_the_lines**
13.ASM—Clipping
14.ASM—**start_it** and new **set_mode**

CHAPTER 5

4P1.BAS—True 3-D
4P2.BAS—True 3-D using **draw_line**
DRWLNBAS.ASM—Source code for **DRWLNBAS.BAS**
DRWLNBAS.BAS—Ready-to-load Machine Language code for **draw_line**; use for 192K machines
DRWLN128.BAS—As above, but for 128K machines
DRWLN64.BAS—As above, but for 64K machines
5P1.ASM—**main_loop**, **ckf1**, **left_right**, and **draw_left_right**
5P2.ASM—Setting low-intensity palette
6.BAS—Printing true 3-D images
7.BAS—Polarized true 3-D

CHAPTER 6

1.BAS—Manipulating multiple objects, method 2
2.ASM—**get_starts** and **get_cur_obj_vals**

CHAPTER 7

1.ASM—**display_page_2**
2P1.ASM—**compact** and **uncompact**
2P2.ASM—Animating with **uncompact**
3P1.BAS—Aligning the screen
3P2.BAS—High-resolution color test

CHAPTER 8

2.BAS—Displaying block graphics
4.BAS—Animation
5.BAS—Multiple objects
7.BAS—Rotating
8.BAS—Scaling
9P1.BAS—The second face
9P2.BAS—The mask
11P1.ASM—**plot_shape** and **find_start**
11P2.BAS—Making shape data tables for Assembly Language
11P3.ASM—**main_loop**, **evaluate_finished**, and **translate**

CHAPTER 9

1.BAS—The foundation
2.BAS—The pencil
3.BAS—Color
4.BAS—Palette
5.PAS—Background color
6.BAS—Clearing the screen
7P1.BAS—Lines
7P2.BAS—Clearing cursors and changing DELTA
8.BAS—Rectangles
9P1.BAS, 9P2.BAS—**style** programs
10.BAS—Circles

11.BAS—Paint
12.BAS—Pen
13.BAS—Air brush
14.BAS—Cut and paste
15P1.BAS—Help menu
15P2.BAS—Help menu data

CHAPT10

2.ASM—set_mode
3.ASM—clear_screen
4.ASM—set_dot
5.ASM—plot_shape and **find_start**
6.ASM—Multiple pages

Any files in the root directory with extension **.CRN** are compacted picture files used for **DEMO.EXE**.

USING THE BOOK PROGRAMS

All BASIC programs are in **LOAD**able or **MERGE**able form, depending upon whether they contain code to add to another program. For example, to load the foundation of the graphics editor, type:

CHDIR "CHAPTER9
LOAD "1

To add the pencil, type:

MERGE "2

The Assembly Language programs contain the variables and procedures. The procedures are offset from the variables. Special instructions on placing code are bordered by asterisks.

DRWLNBAS

DRWLNBS.BAS is for 192K machines. For 128K machines, use **DRWLN128.BAS** and **DEF SEG** to 1F94H instead of 2F94H. For 64K machines, use **DRWLN64.BAS** and add:

1 CLEAR, &HA000

and **DEF SEG** to A00H instead of 2F94H.

TECHNICAL NOTES ON THE EXTRA PROGRAMS

DEMO.EXE starts in 3-D graphics mode, rotating, translating and scaling a cube. It then flips into stereoscopic 3-D mode. Then, it moves block figures, slowing them with a sound routine. Finally, it uses **uncompact** to animate pictures drawn with the graphics editor and compacted with **compact**.

To change the shape drawn by **3D.EXE**, first load it into DEBUG. Find the start of the data segment, by unassembling until you see **MOV DS, xxxx**. Then, change the point and line data. The locations to change, offset from the data segment, are:

number_of_points	283H
xpoints	285H
ypoints	2ADH
zpoints	2D5H
number_of_lines	2FDH
lines	2FFH

Numbers are entered in low-byte, high-byte format.
number_of_points gets twice the number of points;
number_of_lines gets four times the number of lines. There is room for 20 points and 36 lines.

Because of matrix size, the following variables have been changed in **MATRIX.BAS**: VIEWERXCHANGE, VIEWERYCHANGE, and **VIEWERZCHANGE** to **VX**, **VY**, and **VZ**; VIEWERXANGLE, VIEWERYANGLE, and **VIEWERZANGLE** to **VXA**, **VYA**, and **VZA**.

BIBLIOGRAPHY

BASIC Manual, International Business Machine Corporation, 1981.

Disk Operating System Manual, International Business Machine Corporation, 1983.

Hoffmann, Thomas V. "The IBM Color/Graphics Adapter." *PC Tech Journal*, July-August 1983, pp. 26–46, 135–145, 163–166.

Technical Reference Manual, International Business Machine Corporation, 1983.

Tecmar Graphics Master Technical Reference Manual, Tecmar Incorporated, Solon, Ohio, 1984.

Index

6845 registers 216
accommodation 164
alternate display modes *see display mode*
angles 69
animation, block graphics 236
  block graphics in Assembly 257
  increasing block graphics speed 250
  two-dimensional line graphics 37
  using compact and uncompact 208
array 325
aspect ratio 34
Assembly Language routines, testing 126
  interfacing with BASIC 174
attribute byte 311
axis of rotation 68
axis of rotation, principle 71

background color, with color select register 211
binocular parallax 164
blanking the screen 214
blink bit 212
block data, converting dot matrix to preshifted tables 255
  converting dot matrix to PUT array 229
  converting to 223
  plotting in Assembly Language 251
block graphics 223
  on text screen 318
Boolean 326
boundaries, for clipping 107

Cartesian coordinate system, three-dimensional 55
  two-dimensional 10
  with WINDOW 117
center, and scaling 40
  choosing for point-line objects 25
character block 311
character code 311
CIRCLE 279
clearing the screen 136
  block graphics tricks 250
  text graphics 316
clipping 107
  boundaries 107
  in Assembly Language 159
  routine logic 110
  xy 108
  xy with VIEW 119
  z 114
CLS 5
  equivalent in Assembly Language 136
COLOR 3
color fill 292
color select register 211
color-suppression bit 214
colored filtering 169
  from BASIC 170
  in Assembly Language 179
  problems perceiving 171, 179, 203
  using Assembly Language line routine 170
colors 3
  drawing lines with 44
  in GDL 53

Index   339

in high resolution 212
  on composite monitor 215
  table for plotting points 131
compacting graphics screens 204
convergence 164
cursor position 217

data structure, for block data 226
  multiple objects 193
  structured objects 200
  three-dimensional point-line 55
  two-dimensional points and lines 10
delineating curves 17
depth cues, accommodation 164
  binocular parallax 164
  convergence 164
  disparity 164
  linear perspective 164
  overlap 165
  physiological 164
  psychological 164
  shading and shadows 165
DIM 326
disparity 164
display mode, alternate 221
  for text graphics 313
  nonstandard text 322
  setting graphics 124
dot matrix 229
dot width 34
  adjusting in Assembly Language 156
  adjusting with WINDOW 117
  and block graphics 225
  and GDL 48
DRAW 46
  A 102
  B 48
  C 53
  D 48
  E 48
  F 48
  G 48
  H 48
  L 48
  M 46
  N 48
  R 48
  S 52
  TA 102
  U 48
  use of variables 49
  X 51

flicker, preventing 201
focal distance 63
  changing 66
  computing 67
focal plane 63
foreground color, high resolution 212
  intensity 211

GET 301
graphics controller, programming 209
graphics cursor 264
graphics definition language 46
  see also DRAW
graphics editor 261
  air brush 294
  changing background color 270
  changing palette 270
  choosing color 269
  clearing screen 271
  cutting and pasting 301
  displaying menu 306
  drawing circles 279
  drawing lines 272
  drawing rectangles 275
  foundation of 262
  overview of commands 261
  paint 284
  pen 292
  pencil 264

intensity, setting with color select register 211
interfacing Assembly Language and BASIC 174
interpupilary distance 166

keyboard interaction 90
  from Assembly Language 143

LINE 29
  BF options 275
  color option 44
  equivalent in Assembly Language 137
  STEP option 32
  style option 277
line graphics, on text screen 316
linear perspective 62, 164
lines, drawing for true 3-D 170
  drawing from data base in Assembly Language 157
  drawing in Assembly Language 137

mask, block graphics 245
  for air brush spray 298
  table for plotting points 131

matrices 78, 327
  2-D 100
  3-D rotation 80
  3-D scaling 79
  3-D translation 79
  grand total 88
  reflection 98
  shearing 100
  speed of 87
  transformation in Assembly Language 150
memory map, graphics 128
  text screen 311
mode see display mode 120
mode select register 212
monochrome screen, text graphics 323
multiple objects 193
  block graphics 237
  in Assembly Language 197
  manipulating all at once 195
  manipulating one at a time 196
multiple pages, with text screens 321

optional diskette 331
OUT 209

page, graphics 202
PAINT 284
  from BASIC 1.1 284
  from BASIC 2.0 286
palette 4
  with color select register 212
panning 118
perspective 62
  in Assembly Language 156
  rotational change 104
  translational change 103
  true 3-D 166
  variable 103
plotting points 127
  calculating dot position 131
  data to plot 131
  methods 134
  with interrupt 10H 127
point-line data, data base 26
  two-dimensional 13
polarized filtering, for true 3-D 188
preshifted data tables 251
PSET 268
PUT 226
  experimenting with 234
  options 235
PUT array 229
  for air brush 296

rectangles 275
reflection 96
  matrices 98
resolution 1
retrieving graphics screens, normal way 203
rotation 68
  3-D matrices 80
  angles 69
  axis of 68
  block graphics 238
  complications 95
  formulae 75
  in GDL 102
  principal axes 71

saving graphics screen, normal vs. compacted 207
  compacting 204
  normal way 203
scaling, 3-D matrix 79
  block graphics 242
  GDL with S 52
  GDL with variables 49
  three-dimensional 67
  two-dimensional 39
  with VIEW 119
  with WINDOW 118
SCREEN 2
screen coordinate system 31
  converting to in Assembly Language 156
screen position 210
scrolling 218
shearing 99
  matrices 100
slope-intercept form 111
speed, BASIC vs. Assembly 3-D line package 162
  comparison between GDL and non-GDL 52
  comparison between matrix and non-matrix 87
  increasing in block graphics animation 250
  point plotting vs. int 10H 136
  varying translational 42
STEP 32
stereoscopy 165
  determining left and right eye views 166
  see also true 3-D
storing and retrieving objects 199
structured objects 199

text graphics 311
  with monochrome screen 323
translation, 3-D matrix 79
  GDL with variables 49
  relative and absolute 39
  three-dimensional 60
  two-demensional 35
trigonometry 328
  tables in Assembly Language 147
true 3-D, colored filtering 169
  displaying methods 169
  in Assembly Language 179
  polarized filtering 188
  printing images 184
  see also depth cues, stereoscopy
two-page graphics 201
type ahead buffer 92

uncompacting graphics screens 207
using both monitors 216

variable perspective 103
video-enable bit 214
VIEW
  for printing true 3-D images 187
  scaling 118
  windows 119
  xy clipping 118

WINDOW
  adjusting for dot width 117
  converting to Cartesian coordinate system 117
  for printing true 3-D images 187
  panning 118
  scaling 118
  SCREEN option 118
windows, VIEW 118

XOR clearing 250

zone clearing 250

About the Author

Michael I. Hyman is a student in the Electrical Engineering/Computer Science Department at Princeton University. He began working with computers in the seventh grade. His graphics work began in high school and culminated with winning top awards for his 3-D graphics project. It took the top awards at the Westinghouse Science Fair, the National Energy Foundation Fair, the International Science and Engineering Fair, the Junior Sciences and Humanities Symposium, the Navy National Science Fair and the Baltimore Science Fair. Michael has also written for local newspapers and for the computer magazine, *Microkids*. Besides his interest in computers, Michael enjoys the outdoors, music and art.